A Note on the Author

BEN MACINTYRE is a columnist and Associate Editor on *The Times*. He has worked as the newspaper's correspondent in New York, Paris and Washington. He is the author of ten previous books including *Agent Zigzag*, shortlisted for the Costa Biography Award and the Galaxy British Book Award for Biography of the Year 2008, and the *Sunday Times* bestsellers *Double Cross* and *A Spy Among Friends*. His most recent book is *SAS Rogue Heroes*, the first authorised biography of the SAS.

benmacintyre.com

AGENT ZIGZAG

The True Wartime Story of Eddie Chapman:
The Most Notorious Double Agent of World War II

Ben Macintyre

BLOOMSBURY
LONDON · OXFORD · NEW YORK · NEW DELHI · SYDNEY

BLOOMSBURY PAPERBACKS
Bloomsbury Publishing Plc
50 Bedford Square, London, WC1B 3DP, UK
29 Earlsfort Terrace, Dublin 2, Ireland

BLOOMSBURY, BLOOMSBURY PAPERBACKS and the Diana logo
are trademarks of Bloomsbury Publishing Plc

First published in Great Britain 2007
This paperback edition first published in 2016

British Library Cataloguing-in-Publication Data
A catalogue record for this book is available from the British Library.

ISBN: PB: 978-1-4088-8540-6
ePub: 978-1-4088-0684-5

11

Typeset by Hewer Text UK Ltd, Edinburgh
Printed and bound in Great Britain by CPI Group (UK) Ltd, Croydon CR0 4YY

To find out more about our authors and books visit www.bloomsbury.com.
Here you will find extracts, author interviews, details of forthcoming events
and the option to sign up for our newsletters.

CONTENTS

AUTHOR'S NOTE

The true story that follows is based on official papers, letters, diaries, newspaper reports, contemporary accounts and memoirs.

I was first alerted to the existence of the Englishman Eddie Chapman by his obituary in *The Times*. Among the lives of the great and good, here was a character who had achieved a certain greatness, but in ways that were far from conventionally good. The obituary was intriguing as much for what it did not say – and could not know – about Chapman's exploits in the Second World War, since those details remained under seal in MI5's secret archives. At that time, it seemed the full story of Eddie Chapman would never be told.

But then, under a new policy of openness, MI5 began the selective release of hitherto classified information that could not embarrass the living or damage national security. The first 'Zigzag files' were released to the National Archives in 2001. These declassified archives contain more than 1,700 pages of documents relating to Chapman's case: transcripts of interrogations, detailed wireless intercepts, reports, descriptions, diagrams, internal memos, minutes, letters and photographs. The files are extraordinarily detailed, describing not only events and people but also the minutiae of a spy's life, his changing moods and feelings, his hopes, fears and contradictions. Chapman's diligent case officers set out to paint a complete picture of the man, with a meticulous (sometimes hour-by-hour) account of his actions. I am particularly grateful to MI5 for agreeing to my request to declassify additional files relating to the case, and to Howard Davies of the National Archives for helping to facilitate those supplementary releases.

Eddie Chapman's memoirs were published after the war, but the Official Secrets Act prevented him from describing his exploits as a double agent, and his own version of events was often more entertaining than reliable. As his handlers noted, he had no sense of chronology whatsoever. All quotations are cited in the endnotes, but for clarity I have standardised spelling and have selectively used reported speech as direct speech. Chapman's story has also emerged from the memories of the living, people touched, directly or indirectly, by the individuals and events described, and I am grateful to the dozens of interviewees in Britain, France, Germany and Norway – including Betty Chapman – who were willing to talk to me for so many hours, recalling a past now more than half a century old. For obvious reasons, some of those involved in the more clandestine areas of Chapman's life have requested anonymity.

Just weeks before this book was due to go to press, MI5 discovered an entire secret file, overlooked in previous transfers to the public archives, and generously provided me with full access to its contents. That file (which will now become available at the National Archives) gives extraordinary psychological insights into Chapman's character, as seen by his case officers. It is, perhaps, the last missing piece in the Zigzag puzzle.

Zigzag. *n, adj, adv* and *vb*: '. . . a pattern made up of many small corners at an acute angle, tracing a path between two parallel lines; it can be described as both jagged and fairly regular'.

'It is essential to seek out enemy agents who have come to conduct espionage against you and to bribe them to serve you. Give them instructions and care for them. Thus double agents are recruited and used.'

Sun Tzu, *The Art of War*

'War makes thieves and peace hangs them.'

George Herbert

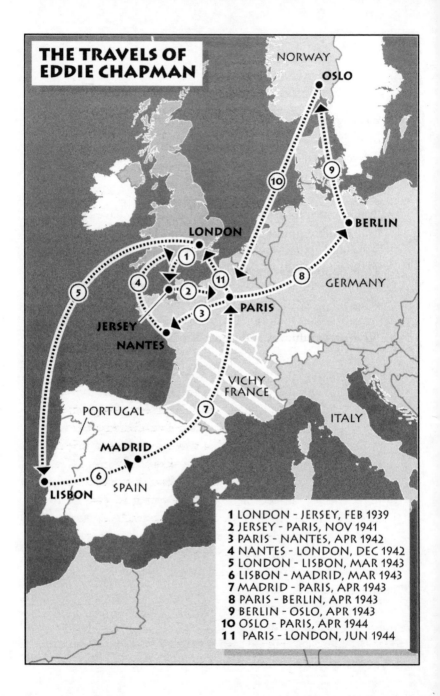

THE TRAVELS OF EDDIE CHAPMAN

NORWAY

OSLO

LONDON

BERLIN

GERMANY

JERSEY

NANTES

PARIS

VICHY
FRANCE

PORTUGAL

MADRID

ITALY

LISBON

SPAIN

1 LONDON – JERSEY, FEB 1939
2 JERSEY – PARIS, NOV 1941
3 PARIS – NANTES, APR 1942
4 NANTES – LONDON, DEC 1942
5 LONDON – LISBON, MAR 1943
6 LISBON – MADRID, MAR 1943
7 MADRID – PARIS, APR 1943
8 PARIS – BERLIN, APR 1943
9 BERLIN – OSLO, APR 1943
10 OSLO – PARIS, APR 1944
11 PARIS – LONDON, JUN 1944

Prologue

2.13 a.m., 16 December 1942
A German spy drops from a black Focke-Wulf reconnaissance plane over Cambridgeshire. His silk parachute opens with a rustle, and for twelve minutes he floats silently down. The stars are out, but the land beneath his feet, swaddled in wartime blackout, is utterly dark. His nose bleeds copiously.

The spy is well equipped. He wears British-issue army landing boots and helmet. In his pocket is a wallet taken from a British soldier killed at Dieppe four months earlier: inside are two identity cards, which are fake, and a letter from his girlfriend Betty, which is genuine. His pack contains matches impregnated with quinine for 'secret writing', a wireless receiver, a military map, £990 in used notes of various denominations, a Colt revolver, an entrenching tool, and some plain-glass spectacles for disguise. Four of his teeth are made from new gold, paid for by Hitler's Third Reich. Beneath his flying overalls he wears a civilian suit that was once of fashionable cut but is now somewhat worn. In the turn-up of the right trouser leg has been sewn a small cellophane package containing a single suicide pill of potassium cyanide.

The name of the spy is Edward Arnold Chapman. The British police also know him as Edward Edwards, Edward Simpson and Arnold Thompson. His German spymasters have given him the codename of 'Fritz' or, affectionately, 'Fritzchen' – Little Fritz.

The British secret services, as yet, have no name for him. That evening the Chief Constable of Cambridgeshire, after an urgent call from a gentleman in Whitehall, has instructed all his officers to be on the lookout for an individual referred to only as 'Agent X'.

Eddie Chapman lands in a freshly ploughed field at 2.25 a.m., and immediately falls face-first into the sodden soil. Dazed, he releases his parachute, then climbs out of his blood-spattered flying suit and buries the bundle. He shoves the revolver into a pocket and digs into the pack for a map and torch. The map has gone. He must have dropped it in the dark. On hands and knees he searches. He curses and sits on the cold earth, in the deep darkness, and wonders where he is, who he is, and whose side he is on.

1

The Hotel de la Plage

Spring came early to the island of Jersey in 1939, and the sun that poured through the dining-room window of the Hotel de la Plage formed a dazzling halo around the man sitting opposite Betty Farmer with his back to the sea, laughing as he tucked into the six-shilling Sunday Roast Special 'with all the trimmings'. Betty, eighteen, a farm girl newly escaped from the Shropshire countryside, knew this man was quite unlike any she had met before.

Beyond that, her knowledge of Eddie Chapman was somewhat limited. She knew that he was twenty-four years old, tall and handsome, with a thin moustache – just like Errol Flynn in *The Charge of the Light Brigade* – and deep hazel eyes. His voice was strong but high-pitched with a hint of a north-eastern accent. He was 'bubbly', full of laughter and mischief. She knew he must be rich because he was 'in the film business' and drove a Bentley. He wore expensive suits, a gold ring and a cashmere overcoat with mink collar. Today he wore a natty yellow spotted tie and a sleeveless pullover. They had met at a club in Kensington Church Street, and although at first she had declined his invitation to dance, she soon relented. Eddie had become her first lover, but then he vanished, saying he had urgent business in Scotland. 'I shall go,' he told her. 'But I shall always come back.'

Good as his word, Eddie had suddenly reappeared at the door of her lodgings, grinning and breathless. 'How would you like to

go to Jersey, then possibly to the south of France?' he asked.
Betty had rushed off to pack.

It was a surprise to discover they would be travelling with
company. In the front seat of the waiting Bentley sat two men:
the driver a huge, ugly brute with a crumpled face; the other
small, thin and dark. The pair did not seem ideal companions for
a romantic holiday. The driver gunned the engine and they set
off at thrilling speed through the London streets, screeching into
Croydon airport, parking behind the hangar, just in time to catch
the Jersey Airways plane.

That evening they had checked into the seafront hotel. Eddie
told the receptionist they were in Jersey to make a film. They had
signed the register as Mr and Mrs Farmer of Torquay. After dinner
they moved on to West Park Pavilion, a nightclub on the pier,
where they danced, played roulette, and drank some more. For
Betty, it had been a day of unprecedented glamour and decadence.

War was coming, everyone said so, but the dining room of the
Hotel de la Plage was a place of pure peace that sunny Sunday.
Beyond the golden beach, the waves flickered among a scatter of
tiny islands, as Eddie and Betty ate trifle off plates with smart blue
crests. Eddie was half way through telling another funny story,
when he froze. A group of men in overcoats and brown hats had
entered the restaurant and one was now in urgent conversation
with the head waiter. Before Betty could speak, Eddie stood up,
bent down to kiss her once, and then jumped through the
window, which was closed. There was a storm of broken glass,
tumbling crockery, screaming women and shouting waiters:
Betty Farmer caught a last glimpse of Eddie Chapman sprinting
off down the beach with two overcoated men in pursuit.

Here are just some of the things Betty did not know about Eddie
Chapman: he was married; another woman was pregnant with
his child; and he was a crook. Not some halfpenny bag-snatcher,
but a dedicated professional criminal, a 'prince of the underworld', in his own estimation.

For Chapman, breaking the law was a vocation. In later years, when some sort of motive for his choice of career seemed to be called for, he claimed that the early death of his mother, in the TB ward of a pauper's hospital, had sent him 'off the rails' and turned him against society. Sometimes he blamed the grinding poverty and unemployment in northern England during the Depression for forcing him into a life of crime. But in truth, crime came naturally to him.

Edward Chapman was born in Burnopfield, a tiny village in the Durham coalfields, on 16 November 1914, a few months into the First World War. His father, a marine engineer and too old to fight, had ended up running The Clippership, a dingy pub in Roker, and drinking a large portion of the stock. For Eddie, the eldest of three children, there was no money, not much love, little in the way of guidance and only a cursory education. He soon developed a talent for misbehaviour, and a distaste of authority. Intelligent but lazy, insolent and easily bored, the young Chapman skipped school often, preferring to scour the beach for lemonade bottles, redeemable at a penny a piece, and then while away afternoons at the cinema in Sunderland: *The Scarlet Pimpernel*, and the Alfred Hitchcock films *Blackmail* and spy drama *The Man Who Knew Too Much*.

At the age of seventeen, after a brief and unsatisfactory stint as an unpaid apprentice at a Sunderland engineering firm, Chapman joined the army, although underage, and enlisted in the Second Battalion of the Coldstream Guards. Early in his training at Caterham he slipped while playing handball and badly gashed his knee: the resulting scar would provide police with a useful distinguishing feature. The bearskin hat and smart red uniform made the girls gawp and giggle, but he found sentry duty outside the Tower of London tedious, and the city beyond beckoned.

Chapman had worn the guardsman's uniform for nine months when he was granted six days' leave. He told the sergeant major that he was going home. Instead, in the company of an older guardsman, he wandered around Soho and the West End, hungrily eyeing the elegant women draped over the arms of men in sharp suits. In a café in Marble Arch he noticed a pretty, dark-haired girl, and she spotted him. They danced at Smokey Joe's in Soho. That night he lost his virginity. She persuaded him to stay another night: he stayed for two months, until they had spent all his pay. Chapman may have forgotten about the army, but the army had not forgotten about him. He was sure the dark-haired girl told the police. Chapman was arrested for going absent without leave, placed in the military prison in Aldershot – the 'glasshouse' – and made to scrub out bedpans for eighty-four days. Release and a dishonourable discharge brought to an end his first prison sentence, and his last regular job. Chapman took a bus to London with £3 in his pocket, a fraying suit and a 'jail-crop haircut', and headed straight for Soho.

Soho in the 1930s was a den of notorious vice, and spectacular fun. This was the crossroads of London society where the rich and feckless met the criminal and reckless, a place of seamy, raucous glamour. Chapman found work as a barman, then as a film extra, earning £3 for 'three days doing crowd work'; he worked as a masseur, a dancer, and eventually as an amateur boxer and wrestler. He was a fine wrestler, physically strong, and lithe as a cat, with a 'wire and whipcord body'. This was a world of pimps and racecourse touts, pickpockets and con artists; late nights at Smokey Joe's and early champagne breakfasts at Quaglino's. 'I mixed with all types of tricky people,' Chapman wrote later. 'Racecourse crooks, thieves, prostitutes, and the flotsam of the night-life of a great city.' For the young Chapman, life in this seething, seedy enclave was thrilling. But it was also expensive. He acquired a taste for cognac and the gaming tables and was soon penniless.

The thievery started in a small way: a forged cheque here, a snatched suitcase there, a little light burglary. His early crimes were unremarkable, the first faltering steps of an apprentice.

In January 1935, he was caught in the back garden of a house in Mayfair, and fined £10. A month later he was found guilty of stealing a cheque and obtaining credit by fraud. This time the court was less lenient, and Chapman was given two months' hard labour in Wormwood Scrubs. A few weeks after his release, he was back inside, this time in Wandsworth Prison on a three-month sentence for trespassing and attempted housebreaking.

Chapman branched out into crimes of a more lurid nature. Early in 1936 he was found guilty of 'behaving in a manner likely to offend the public' in Hyde Park. Exactly how he was likely to have offended the public was not specified, but he was almost certainly discovered in flagrante delicto with a prostitute. He was fined £4 and made to pay a fee of 15 shillings 9d to the doctor who examined him for venereal disease. Two weeks later he was charged with fraud after he tried to evade payment of a hotel bill.

One contemporary remembers a young man 'with good looks, a quick brain, high spirits and something desperate in him which made him attractive to men and dangerous to women'. Desperation may have led him to use the attraction of men for profit, for he once hinted at an early homosexual encounter. Women seemed to find him irresistible. According to one account, he made money by seducing 'women on the fringes of society', blackmailing them with compromising photographs taken by an accomplice and then threatening to show their husbands. It was even said that having 'infected a girl of 18 with VD, he blackmailed her by threatening to tell her parents that she had given it to him'.

Chapman was on a predictable downward spiral of petty crime, prostitution, blackmail and lengthening prison terms – punctuated by episodes of wild extravagance in Soho – when a scientific breakthrough in the criminal world abruptly altered his fortunes.

In the early 1930s British crooks discovered gelignite. At about the same time, during one of his stints inside, Chapman discovered James Wells Hunt – the 'best cracksman in London' – a 'cool, self-possessed, determined character' who had perfected a technique for taking apart safes by drilling a hole in the lock and inserting a 'French letter' stuffed with gelignite and water. Jimmy Hunt and Chapman went into partnership and were soon joined by Antony Latt, alias Darrington, alias 'Darry', a nerveless half-Burmese burglar whose father, he claimed, had been a native judge. A young felon named Hugh Anson was recruited to drive their getaway car.

The newly formed 'Jelly Gang' selected, as its first target, Isobel's, a chic furrier in Harrogate. Hunt and Darry broke in and stole five minks, two fox-fur capes and £200 from the safe. Chapman remained in the car 'shivering with fear and unable to help'. The next was a pawnbroker's in Grimsby. While Anson revved the Bentley outside to cover the sound of the explosions, Chapman and Hunt broke into an empty house next door, cut their way through the wall, and then blew open four safes. The proceeds, sold through a fence in the West End, netted £15,000. This was followed by a break-in at the Swiss Cottage Odeon cinema using an iron bar, a hit on Express Dairies, and a smash-and-grab raid on a shop in Oxford Street. Escaping from the latter scene, Anson drove the stolen getaway car into a lamppost. As the gang fled, a crowd of onlookers gathered around the smoking vehicle; one, who happened to be a small-time thief, made the mistake of putting his hand on the bonnet. When his fingerprints were matched with Scotland Yard records, he was sentenced to four years in prison. The Jelly Gang found this most amusing.

Chapman was no longer a reckless petty pilferer, but a criminal of means, spending money as fast as he could steal it, mixing with the underworld aristocracy, the gambling playboys, roué actors, alcoholic journalists, insomniac writers and dodgy politicians drawn to the demimonde. He became friendly with Noel Coward, Ivor Novello, Marlene Dietrich and the young filmmaker Terence Young (who would go on to direct the first James Bond film). Young was a suave figure who prided himself on his elegant clothes, his knowledge of fine wine and his reputation as a Lothario. Perhaps in imitation of his new friend,

Chapman also began buying suits in Savile Row, and driving a fast car. He kept a table reserved at The Nest in Kingly Street, where he held court, surrounded by bottles and girls. Young remarked: 'He was able to talk on almost any subject. Most of us knew that he was a crook, but nevertheless we liked him for his manner and personality.'

Young found Chapman intriguing: he made no secret of his trade, yet there was an upright side to his character that the filmmaker found curious. 'He is a crook and will always be one,' Young observed to a lawyer friend. 'But he probably has more principles and honesty of character than either of us.' Chapman would steal the money from your pocket, even as he bought you a drink, but he never deserted a friend, nor hurt a soul. In a brutal business, he was a pacifist. 'I don't go along with the use of violence,' he declared many years later. 'I always made more than a good living out of crime without it.'

Chapman – careless, guiltless and Godless – revelled in his underworld notoriety. He pasted press clippings describing his crimes into a scrapbook. He was particularly delighted when it was reported that police suspected American gangs were behind the recent spate of safe-cracking because chewing gum had been found at the crime scenes (the Jelly Gang had merely used chewing gum to stick the gelignite to the safes). By the summer of 1935, they had stolen so much money that Chapman and Darry decided to rent a house in Bridport on the Dorset coast for an extended holiday; but after six weeks they grew bored and 'went back to "work"'. Chapman disguised himself as an inspector from the Metropolitan Water Board, gained access to a house in the Edgware Road, smashed a hole through the wall into the shop next door and extracted the safe. This was carried out of the front door, loaded into the Bentley and taken to Hunt's garage at 39, St Luke's Mews, Notting Hill, where the safe door was blown off.

Mixing with authors and actors, Chapman became conscious of his lack of education. He announced that he intended to become a writer, and began reading widely, plundering English literature in search of knowledge and direction. When asked what he did for a living, Chapman would reply, with a wink, that he was a 'professional dancer'. He danced from club to club, from job to job, from book to book, and from woman to woman. Late in 1935, he announced he was getting married, to Vera Freidberg, an exotic young woman with a Russian mother and a German-Jewish father. From her, Chapman picked up a grounding in the German language. But within a few months he had moved into a boarding house in Shepherd's Bush with another woman, Freda Stevenson, a stage dancer from Southend who was five years his junior. He loved Freda, she was vivacious and sassy; yet when he met Betty Farmer – his 'Shropshire Lass' – in the Nite Lite Club, he loved her too.

The Jelly Gang might mock the dozy coppers studying their abandoned chewing gum for clues, but Scotland Yard was beginning to take a keen interest in the activities of Edward Chapman. A 'gelignite' squad was formed. In 1938, the *Police Gazette* published Chapman's mugshot, along with those of Hunt and Darry, as suspects in a recent spate of cinema safe-breaks. Aware that the police were closing in, early in 1939 the gang loaded several golf bags packed with gelignite into the boot of the Bentley, and headed north. Having checked into an expensive hotel, they broke into the offices of the Edinburgh Co-operative Society, and emptied the safe. As Chapman was climbing out through a skylight, he smashed a pane of glass. A passing policeman heard it, and blew his whistle. The thieves fled over the back wall, and onto a railway line; one of the gang slipped, breaking an ankle, and was left behind. The others met up with car and driver and immediately headed south, but were intercepted by a police car, siren screaming. Chapman fled over a wall, but was caught. The four burglars were thrown into Edinburgh prison, but then, for reasons no-one can explain, Chapman was granted fourteen days bail at £150.

When Case Number Seventeen came before the Edinburgh

High Court, it was found that Chapman and his accomplices had absconded. A general bulletin was issued, photographs were distributed, and every police force in Britain was told to be on the lookout for Eddie Chapman – crook, jailbird, adulterer, blackmailer, safe-cracker, Soho denizen and now among Britain's most wanted men. On 4 February 1939, the gang extracted £476 and 3 shillings from a Co-op store in Bournemouth. Darry had sent a letter to his girlfriend hinting that the gang was heading for Jersey; police intercepted it and a warning went out that the suspects might make for the Channel Islands, and then the Continent: 'Be prepared for trouble as one at least of the men might be armed and all are prepared to put up a fight to resist arrest.'

Which is how Eddie Chapman came to be pounding down a Jersey beach leaving in his wake two plain-clothes policemen, a distraught young woman, and half a sherry trifle.

2

Jersey Gaol

The Evening Post.

Monday, 13 February 1939

STARTLING SCENE AT JERSEY HOTEL

~~~

POLICE SWOOP AT LUNCH HOUR

~~~

Two Guests Handcuffed
Thief Gets Away through Window
Alleged Dangerous Gang of Safe Breakers

A letter sent to a girl in Bournemouth led yesterday to the arrest of two members of a gelignite gang wanted for the 'blowing' of a safe at a co-operative store and the theft of £470. A third man got wind of the impending police swoop on the Hotel de la Plage, Havre-le-Pas, and escaped.

Residents at La Plage Hotel were at lunch when Centenier C. G. Grant of St Helier, and six members of the paid police in civilian clothing entered and, before most of the lunchers knew what had happened, two men had been handcuffed and chase was being given to the third man, alleged to be the leader of the gang. One of them, apparently more alert than the others, made his escape by way of the windows of the dining room overlooking the promenade and got clean away.

The third man, for whom active search still continues, is described as: – Edward Chapman, alias Arnold Edward Chapman, Edward Arnold Chapman, Edward Edwards and Thompson, a professional dancer, slim build, six feet in height, fresh complexion, small moustache, dressed in white shirt, yellow spotted tie, blue sleeveless pullover, grey flannels and brown sandals and no socks. He is believed to be a dangerous character. He may, by now, have obtained a jacket or an overcoat from somewhere as he has money in his possession.

The search for Chapman goes on and all ships are being watched. Anyone who may see this man or who may know anything of his whereabouts is requested to inform the Police Station immediately.

Although the police soon abandoned the chase, Chapman continued running for a mile or so up the beach before doubling back, and then cutting across the island. He found a school, empty on a Sunday, and hid inside. That evening he strolled back into Havre-le-Pas wearing a mackintosh he had found on a peg, the collar turned up. On the edge of town he checked into a tatty boarding house and shaved off his moustache with a soapy penknife. When he came downstairs, the landlady, Mrs Corfield, demanded cash up-front. Chapman gave her what he had in his pocket, and said he would pay the balance in the morning. Without money he was trapped. He would need to steal some more.

In the darkness, Chapman re-emerged and set off towards the West Park Pavilion nightclub, where the gang had spent the previous night. As soon as her lodger was gone, Mrs Corfield put on her bonnet, and headed down to the police station.

Chapman found the Pavilion deserted. He broke in through a window in the gents' lavatory, discovered the office safe, and carried it to the basement. Turning it upside down, he worked off the bottom with a pickaxe and a pair of pincers from the boiler room of the building. Inside lay £15, 13 shillings and 9d in silver, several pounds in coppers, and twelve ten-shilling notes. Chapman returned to the boarding house, his pockets laden, and went to sleep, resolving to steal or bribe his way onto a boat the next morning.

The Evening Post.

Tuesday, 14 February 1939

ALLEGED SAFE BREAKER
BEFORE COURT

~~~

WANTED MAN ARRESTED IN BED
CHARGED WITH BREAKING INTO
WEST PARK PAVILION
ACCUSED APPEALS FOR 'GIRL FRIEND'

~~~

The island-wide search for the man Chapman, who escaped when police raided the Hotel de la Plage, is at an end. Chapman, through information received by the St Helier Police, was found last night in bed in a lodging house in Sand Street, and admitted his identity to police constables. He also admitted breaking into West Park Pavilion last night.

Chapman gave the police no trouble and made a voluntary statement that he had 'done in' the safe.

This morning Chapman appeared before the magistrate, and after being remanded asked if his girlfriend could be allowed to leave the island. 'I have a girlfriend here,' he

been cross-examined by police and watched and I would like to ask if these investigations might cease as she knows nothing of why we are here.'

The Magistrate: 'If she had been wise she would have gone already. We do not want her here. There is nothing against her and she is free to leave the island when she likes.'

The accused was then removed to the cells and his 'girl friend', an attractive blonde with blue eyes and a long said, speaking in a cultured page-boy bob, whose name is tone, 'and she is in a very em- said to be Betty Farmer, also barrassing position. She has left the court.'

Betty had suffered many indignities in the preceding forty-eight hours: being searched by the manageress at the Hotel de la Plage, being grilled by those horrible detectives and then having to move to the smaller, cheaper and far scruffier Royal Yacht Hotel. As Chapman was led from the court in handcuffs, she handed one of his guards a love note to pass to him, written on headed hotel paper. He put it in his pocket, grinned and waved.

Breaking into the West Park Pavilion nightclub had been an act of astonishing foolishness but also, on the face of it, an immense stroke of luck. Darry and Anson had already been shipped back to the mainland to face multiple charges at the Central Criminal Court in London. Chapman, however, had broken the law in Jersey, with its ancient legal code and traditions of self-government, and would now have to face island justice.

On 11 March 1939, Edward Chapman appeared before the Royal Court of Jersey and pleaded guilty to charges of housebreaking and larceny. The Attorney General of Jersey, prosecuting, cited Chapman's extensive criminal record and pointed out that the safe-breaking at the nightclub had been 'done with deliberation and skill which showed considerable experience and showed he was determined to rely on this sort of conduct for a living'. He demanded that this 'dangerous criminal who had failed to accept certain chances that had been given to him' receive the maximum sentence of two years' hard labour. The jury agreed.

Jersey Gaol, Chapman soon discovered, was a 'dreary little cage' where the handful of prisoners stuffed mattresses for eight hours a day and slept on planks raised a few feet off the concrete floor. The prison regime was remarkably lax. The governor, Captain Thomas Charles Foster, a retired soldier, regarded prisoners as an inconvenience in an otherwise pleasant life that revolved around visiting his neighbours, sunbathing and fishing. Foster took a shine to the new inmate when Chapman explained he had been a soldier, and he was soon put to work as the governor's personal batman, weeding the garden and cleaning his house, which backed onto the hospital block.

On the sunny afternoon of 7 July, Captain Foster, Mrs Foster, and their eighteen-year-old son, Andrew, climbed into the family car and headed down the coast to St Brelade to attend the Jersey Scottish Society's annual summer fête, a highlight of the island's social calendar. Chapman was instructed to clean the governor's kitchen in his absence. Chief Warder Briard had taken the day off, leaving Warder Packer to mind the shop. Packer unlocked the front gate to allow the governor's car through. Captain Thomas, resplendent in his kilt, muttered as he motored off that Packer should 'keep an eye on Chapman'.

As the sound of the governor's car faded, Chapman downed his mop, and darted upstairs to the empty bedroom of Andrew

Foster. From the young man's wardrobe Chapman extracted a
grey pinstripe suit, brown shoes, a brown trilby, and two
checked caps made by Leach & Justice of Perth. The suit was
a little tight under the arms, but a reasonable fit. He also found a
suitcase, into which he packed the governor's spectacles, a jar of
sixpences Mrs Foster had been saving, £13 from the governor's
desk drawer, a torch and a poker from the fireplace. Climbing
through a skylight, he scrambled over the roof, dropped into the
hospital compound, scaled a wall topped with glass, and walked
away. Mrs Hamon, who worked in the laundry, noticed a figure
on the roof, but assumed he must be a workman.

An hour later, Warder Packer – who had been busy flirting
with the matron's daughter, Miss Lesbird – casually wandered
into the governor's kitchen to see how Chapman was progressing with his chores. He did not worry unduly to find the house
empty. 'At that moment,' he recalled, 'I still thought Chapman
was playing a joke, and was hiding in the prison.' He searched
the garden and the outhouse; then he summoned the other
warders to help search the prison. Then he panicked. It took a
full two hours to track down Captain Foster at the Scottish
Society fete. The Chief Constable was unearthed in the golf
club, and a posse led by young Andrew Foster was dispatched to
watch the airport. Hotels and boarding houses were scoured,
boats were prevented from leaving harbour, and every policeman and volunteer on the island was mobilised for the greatest
manhunt in island memory.

Walter Picard, resident of Five Mile Road, was one of the few
people on the island unaware that a prisoner had escaped. He had
spent the evening under a hedge with a woman who was not
Mrs Walter Picard. After this encounter, Picard and his girlfriend
were strolling back to his car in the darkness when they were
surprised to see a man in an ill-fitting suit bending over the open
bonnet of the car, apparently attempting to jump-start it.

The man looked startled, but declared: 'Do you know who I
am? I'm a member of the police.' Picard launched himself at the

'car thief'. His girlfriend screamed. A scuffle ensued: Picard was upended and thrown over a wall and Chapman vanished into the night. On the passenger seat of his car, the shaken Picard found a brown trilby, a torch and three sticks of gelignite.

Chapman had passed a most eventful day. Barely a mile from the prison, Mr A.A. Pitcher had obligingly offered him a lift in his car, and driven him to a public telephone box where he had telephoned the airport, only to be told the last plane for the mainland had departed. Pitcher dropped him off at the pier. After a meal at the Milano Café, Chapman had checked into La Pulente Hotel, and ordered a taxi. Telling the Luxicab driver he was 'interested in quarries', Chapman took a tour of the island's mines, and selected his target. That afternoon, when the workers had left L'Etacq Quarry on the western edge of Jersey, Chapman scaled the gate, found the small, reinforced bunker that served as the explosives storehouse, and prised open the door with a crowbar from the quarry tool shed. He emerged with 5lbs of gelignite and 200 detonators. It was while walking down Five Mile Road with his explosive loot that evening that Chapman spotted Walter Picard's parked car and decided to steal it.

Knowing the encounter would be reported immediately, Chapman walked on until he came across an empty bungalow belonging to Frank Le Quesne. He broke in, made himself a cup of tea (using enough tea bags 'for about fifty people', the owner later complained) and fell asleep.

In the meantime, Walter Picard made an edited report to the police, stating that:

> He was driving his car on his way home when he was hailed
> by a young woman, whom he did not recognise, who asked
> him for a lift as far as a bungalow on the Five Mile Road. He
> replied that he would take her as far as his house; he did so
> but she then persuaded him to drive her further on and some
> little distance along the road his lights failed for no apparent

reason. He stopped the car and his passenger then told him
that the bungalow she wished to get to was fairly close and
asked him to walk as far with her. After some demur he
complied with her requests, but only went half way and
then, turning round, saw the lights of his car had come on
again. He approached the car and saw a tall man bending
over the ignition. The stranger turned round and struck him
and then made off.

Even the police found Picard's elaborate story 'strange', and
what Mrs Picard made of it can only be imagined.

Early next morning, a fisherman carrying a large shrimping net
could be seen striding purposefully along Plémont beach. Closer
inspection would have revealed that beneath the fishing overalls
the man was wearing business attire, and beneath that, a striped
bathing suit belonging to Frank Le Quesne. Chapman had
calculated that with holidaymakers enjoying the summer sun,
a bathing suit might be a good disguise. In his pockets he carried
enough explosives to wage a small war.

Later that morning, the divinely named Mrs Gordon Bennet
reported that a man more or less fitting the description of the
escaped prisoner had visited her tearooms on the cliff overlooking the beach. Centenier Percy Laurie, a volunteer policeman, and Police Constable William Golding were sent to
investigate. Both were in plain clothes. Golding decided to
explore the beach, while Laurie searched the caves in the
cliffside. On the sand some holidaymakers were playing football,
observed, from a short distance, by a tall fisherman with a net.
Golding approached the spectator. 'Your name is Chapman,' he
said.

'My name is not Chapman,' said the fisherman, backing off.
'You are making a great mistake.'

'Are you coming quietly?'

'You had better take me,' he replied. As Golding seized his
arm, Chapman shouted that he was being assaulted, and called

on the footballers to come to his aid. Laurie emerged from the caves, and ran to help, several spectators weighed in, and a free-for-all ensued, with the policemen trying to get the handcuffs on Chapman as they, in turn, were attacked by a crowd of semi-naked holidaymakers. The fracas ended when Golding managed to land a punch to Chapman's midriff. 'This appeared to distress him,' said Golding. Chapman's distress also doubtless came from the knowledge that he had eight sticks of gelignite and fifteen detonators in his pockets; a blow in the wrong place would have destroyed him, the policemen, the footballers and most of Plémont beach.

The Evening Post.

Friday, 6 July 1939

PRISONER'S ESCAPE FROM GAOL

~~~

DRAMATIC STORY OF ISLAND-WIDE SEARCH

~~~

ALLEGED ATTACK ON MOTORIST

~~~

GELIGNITE STOLEN FROM QUARRY STORE

~~~

CAPTURED AFTER FIGHT ON BEACH WITH POLICE CONSTABLE

After having been at liberty less than 24 hours, a prisoner who escaped from the public prison was recaptured. Every available police officer in the island had been on duty continuously in an island-wide search.

The missing man was Edward Chapman, possessor of several aliases and a record of previous convictions. He was described as a dangerous man and associate of thieves and dangerous characters and an expert in the use of dynamite.

Chapman was arrested at two o'clock this afternoon after a stand-up fight with a police constable on the sands at Plémont.

When the prison van arrived a large crowd waited to catch a glimpse of Chapman. He appeared perfectly composed and looked around with interest at the people, a smile flitting across his face.

Later, the constable of St Helier expressed his warm appreciation of all ranks of the police who had assisted in the most thrilling man-hunt which has taken place in Jersey for some years.

Captain Foster, the prison governor, was both enraged and humiliated. The prison board castigated him for his 'gross misconduct [in] permitting a prisoner with such deplorable criminal antecedents as Chapman so much unsupervised liberty'. Foster took out his anger on the warders, the prisoners and above all on Chapman, who was brought back to the prison and harangued by the governor, who bitterly accused him of inventing a military past to ingratiate himself: 'You have never been a soldier as you informed me, you are therefore a liar and you deserve a flogging,' he bawled. 'Why did you do it?' Chapman thought for a moment, and gave the only honest reply. 'One, I don't like prison discipline; and two, since I am sure of more imprisonment on completion of my present sentence in England, I thought I would make one job of the lot.'

Back in his cell, Chapman made a bleak calculation. On his release he would be sent back to the mainland and tried on a string of charges, just like Darry and Anson, who were now in Dartmoor. Depending on what Scotland Yard could prove, Chapman reckoned he would be in one prison or another for the next fourteen years.

The Jersey community was close knit and law abiding, and the legal authorities took a dim view of this convict who dared to steal from its prison governor, throw its inhabitants over walls, and provoke pitched battles with its policemen.

On 6 September 1939, Chapman was brought before the Criminal Assizes and sentenced to a further year in prison, to run consecutively with his earlier conviction. The news of his sentencing, somewhat to Chapman's irritation, merited only a single paragraph in the *Evening Post*, for by now the people of Jersey had other concerns. Three days earlier, Britain had declared war on Germany.

3

Island at War

All wars – but this war in particular – tend to be seen in monochrome: good and evil, winner and loser, champion and coward, loyalist and traitor. For most people, the reality of war is not like that, but rather a monotonous grey of discomforts and compromises, with occasional flashes of violent colour. War is too messy to produce easy heroes and villains; there are always brave people on the wrong side, and evil men among the victors, and a mass of perfectly ordinary people struggling to survive and understand in between. Away from the battlefields, war forces individuals to make impossible choices in circumstances they did not create, and could never have expected. Most accommodate, some collaborate, and a very few find an internal compass they never knew they had, pointing to the right path.

News of the war barely penetrated the granite walls of Jersey prison. The prison slop, always repulsive, grew ever nastier with rationing. Some of the warders left to join up, and those that remained provided fragmentary, unreliable information. The Nazi Blitzkrieg, first the invasion of Denmark and Norway in April 1940, then France, Belgium, Luxembourg and the Netherlands, did not touch Chapman; his was a world just 6-feet square. When the Germans entered Paris on 14 June 1940, he was barely midway through his three-year sentence.

Chapman read all 200 books in the prison library, and then reread them. With some aged grammar books, he set about teaching himself French and improving his German. He memorised the poems of Tennyson, and read H.G. Wells's *Outline of History*, a textbook purporting to describe the past but imbued with that writer's philosophy. He was particularly struck by Wells's idea of a 'federal world state' in which all nations would work in harmony: 'Nationalism as a God must follow the tribal gods to limbo. Our true nationality is mankind,' Wells had written. Meanwhile, the evil god of National Socialism marched ever closer.

Chapman read and reread Betty's love-note on the Royal Yacht Hotel letterhead. But soon another letter arrived that temporarily extinguished thoughts of Betty. From an address in Southend-on-Sea, Freda Stevenson, the dancer with whom he had been living in Shepherd's Bush, wrote to inform Chapman that he was now the father of a one-year-old girl, born in Southend Municipal hospital in July 1939, whom she had christened Diane Shayne. She enclosed a photograph of mother and child. Freda explained that she was desperately poor, barely surviving on wartime rations, and asked Chapman to send money. Chapman asked for permission to write to her but Captain Foster refused, out of spite. Freda's unanswered letters became increasingly anguished, then angry. Frustrated at his inability to help Freda or hold his first child, and cut off from the rest of humanity in a sea-bound prison, Chapman sank into bleak depression.

The Evening Post.

Saturday, 29 June 1940

FIERCE AIR RAIDS
ON CHANNEL ISLANDS
HARBOURS BOMBED

HEAVY CASUALTIES IN BOTH ISLANDS

Nine people are known to have been killed and many injured in a bombing and machine gun attack carried out by at

least three German aircraft   struck the pier, causing con-
over Jersey last night.   siderable damage to prop-
   The Harbour was the   erty belonging solely to
chief objective and a bomb   civilians . . .

Chapman was lying on his plank bed when he heard the first
Luftwaffe planes droning overhead. Three days later, the Channel Islands earned the unhappy distinction of becoming the only
part of Britain to be occupied by Germany during the Second
World War. There was no resistance, for the last defending
troops had pulled out. Most of the population opted to remain.
Chapman was not offered a choice. Idly, he wondered whether a
bomb might hit the prison, offering either death or the chance of
escape. The British inhabitants of Jersey were instructed to offer
no resistance and the bailiff, Alexander Moncrieff Coutanche,
who had presided over Chapman's trial, told them to obey
German orders, return home and fly the white flag of surrender.
Hitler had decided Jersey would make an ideal holiday camp,
once Germany had won the war.
   With German occupation, the Jersey prison service was
simply absorbed into the Nazi administration, along with
the police. Sealed away behind stone and iron, the prisoners
were forgotten. The prison food became more meagre than
ever, as the free inhabitants of Jersey competed for the few
resources allowed them by the German invaders. There were
no more letters from Freda. Chapman consoled himself with
the reflection that as long as the Germans controlled Jersey
when he was finally released, they could not send him back to
the waiting manacles.
   The Germans ran their own courts, parallel to the civil
judiciary. In December 1940, a young dishwasher from the
Miramar Hotel, named Anthony Charles Faramus, fell foul of
both. A Jersey islander with a reputation as a tearaway, twenty-
year-old Faramus was sentenced to six months by the Jersey
court for obtaining £9 under false pretenses by claiming an

allowance for a non-existent dependent. The German field court slapped on a further month after Faramus was found to be carrying an anti-German propaganda leaflet.

A furtive, delicate man, with a pencil moustache and darting grey eyes, Faramus was a strange but likeable fellow. He was a hopeless crook, Chapman reflected. He blushed easily, and exuded a 'sort of dispossessed gentleness', though he possessed a sharp, obscene wit. Tall and slender, he looked as if a puff of wind might carry him off. He had worked as a hairdresser in a salon in St Helier, before taking a job at the hotel. Chapman and Faramus became cellmates, and firm friends.

On 15 October 1941, a few weeks short of his twenty-sixth birthday, Chapman was finally released. Gaunt and paper-faced, his weight had fallen to just nine stone. Faramus, released a few months earlier, was waiting for him at the prison gates. Chapman knew nothing of the Nazi invasion of Greece and Yugoslavia, the sinking of the Bismarck or the siege of Leningrad, but the effects of war were visible in the transformation of Jersey. On his last day of freedom, Chapman had wandered a beach thronged with happy, well-fed holidaymakers. Now, it was an island ground down by occupation, exhausted and hungry, beset by all the moral confusion that comes from the choice between resistance, acquiescence or collaboration.

Faramus had rented a small shop on Broad Street in St Helier, and with a few chairs, some old mirrors, scissors and razors, he and Chapman opened what they referred to, rather grandly, as a hairdressing salon. Their clientele mainly comprised German officers, since the Channel Islands – Hitler's stepping stone to Britain – were now a vast, heavily defended barracks, home to the largest infantry regiment in the German army.

Faramus shaved German beards and cut German hair, while Chapman made polite conversation in basic German. One of the few British regulars was a middle-aged former bookmaker from Birmingham by the name of Douglas Stirling. An opportunist of the sort produced by every war, Stirling was a black-marketeer, buying cigarettes, tea and alcohol from the Germans, and then selling these on at a profit to local people. The barber's shop was the ideal front for what soon became a thriving trade that combined illegal profiteering with grooming the enemy.

One morning, setting out on his bicycle from the flat he shared with Faramus above the shop, Chapman momentarily forgot that a new German law required everyone to drive on the right and rode straight into a German motorcycle dispatch rider hurtling around a corner. Neither man was hurt, but the German was furious. Chapman was duly summoned to the police station and interrogated by three officers of the Feldgendarmerie, the German military police. One of these, a small man who spoke good English, eyed Chapman unpleasantly and said: 'Look, we've reason to believe you've got some German arms. Now, where is the German rifle?'

'I haven't got any German rifles,' Chapman replied, bemused.

'Have you any arms?'

'No'

'Now look, we've got our eyes on you, so if you try any trouble, we'll make trouble too. I'm only warning you.'

'Thanks for the warning,' Chapman replied, and left swiftly.

This was no warning; it was a threat. He was fined eighty Reichsmarks for the traffic violation, but more worryingly the interview seemed to suggest he had been singled out as a suspected member of the resistance, or even a saboteur. The run-in with the Feldgendarmerie had unsettled him, and set Chapman thinking of another plan to get him off this island prison. He outlined his idea to Faramus and Douglas Stirling. What if they offered to work as spies for the Nazis? If they were accepted there was surely a chance they might be sent over to mainland Britain, undercover. At the very least it would break the monotony. Stirling was enthusiastic, saying that he would suggest the ruse to his son. Faramus was more cautious, but agreed the plan was worth a shot.

Peering back with many years of hindsight, Chapman

admitted that his motives in 1941 were hazy and confused. He would later claim that the offer to spy for Germany was prompted by the simple and sincere desire to escape and be united with Diane, the child he had never seen: 'If I could work a bluff with the Germans, I could probably be sent over to Britain,' he wrote. But Chapman understood his own nature well enough to know that there was more to his decision than this. 'It all sounds fine talk, now,' he later admitted. 'Perhaps it was phony talk even then, and I don't pretend there were no other motives in the plans I began to turn over in my mind. They did not occur to me, either, in one moment, or in one mood.' He felt a genuine animus towards the British establishment. Like many justly imprisoned criminals, he saw himself as the victim of cruel discrimination. Moreover, he was impressed by the discipline and general politeness of the Germans in their smart uniforms. Nazi propaganda relentlessly insisted that their forces were invincible, and the occupation permanent. Chapman was hungry, he was bored, and he longed for excitement. In his Soho days he had mixed with film stars, and he had long imagined himself as the central character in his own drama. He had played the part of a high-rolling gangster. Now, he recast himself in the glamorous role of spy. There was little thought, if any, given to whether such a course was right or wrong. That would come later.

Chapman and Faramus composed a letter in carefully wrought German, and sent it to the German Command post in St Helier, addressed to General Otto von Stulpnägel, the senior officer in command of the occupation forces in France and the Channel Islands. A few days later Faramus and Chapman were summoned to the office of a German major, where Chapman blithely explained that he and his friend would like to join the German secret service. He listed his crimes, stressed the outstanding warrants he faced in Britain, emphasised his expertise with explosives, and concluded with a spirited anti-British rant. 'His whole theme was revenge,' Faramus wrote later. 'He said he had no time for the English ruling class, and sought only a chance to get even with them.' The major nodded blandly, while a secretary took notes and wrote down the young men's names and addresses. The matter, said the major, would be discussed with 'senior officers'.

After that, nothing seemed to happen. Over the next few days Chapman made a point every time a German came into the shop of reciting a 'tale of loathing for the society that had hounded him, and his hatred for the English and all their works', in the hope that word would filter back to the German authorities. But the days passed, and still no word came from the General von Stulpnägel. Clearly their application had been rejected, or merely ignored, on the longstanding principle that anyone who applies to join an espionage service should be rejected.

Chapman had all but forgotten the plan – and was busy hatching a fresh scheme to open up a nightclub serving black-market alcohol – when, one damp evening in December, he and Faramus were roused from their beds by a furious hammering at the door and the sound of raised German voices. On the doorstep stood two German officers. Chapman's immediate assumption was that the application to spy for Germany had borne fruit. He could not have been more wrong. These were not members of the German intelligence service, but the Gestapo. Chapman and Faramus were not being recruited, but arrested. They were handcuffed, bundled into a Vauxhall waiting in the drizzle, and driven to the dock. The senior officer, a captain, or *Hauptmann*, brusquely informed the pair that they were now prisoners, and if they attempted to escape they would be shot. From the car they were marched onto a small landing barge and manacled to an iron bar bolted to the wheelhouse. The boat engine roared and swung out of the port, heading due south, with the coast of France faintly visible through the drizzle. The Gestapo officers sat in the warmth below decks, while Chapman and Faramus shivered in the biting rain.

The next few hours passed in a miasmic rush of fear and

movement: the port at St Malo in the chill dawn; two hours handcuffed to a bench in the police station where a gendarme slipped them a baguette and some stale cheese; locked inside a compartment on the train to Paris; and finally, arrival at the Gare du Nord, where a military truck and armed escort awaited them. The German guards would not speak and shrugged off every question. Faramus was white with terror, moaning gently, his head in his hands, as they sped with their silent Gestapo escort through the broad boulevards of the occupied French capital. Finally, the truck passed through a broad gateway with iron gates draped in huge ringlets of barbed wire, and into another prison.

Much later, Chapman discovered what had happened. In the weeks before his arrest, several telephone wires on the island had been cut, the latest in a series of small acts of sabotage. The German authorities had consulted the Jersey police, some of whom were now active collaborators. These immediately pointed the finger at Chapman and Faramus, the most notorious of the usual suspects. Chapman reflected ruefully: 'The British police told them that if there was any trouble, I was probably in it.'

For the young criminal this was an entirely new experience: he had been arrested for a crime he had not committed.

4

Romainville

The Fort de Romainville glowers over the eastern suburbs of Paris. A brutal stone giant, by 1941 it had been made into another Nazi vision of hell. Built in the 1830s on a low hill, the hulking bastion was part of the defensive ring constructed around Paris to protect the city from foreign attack, but it also held troops who could be deployed in the event of popular insurrection – a bloated, moated, impregnable monstrosity. For the Nazis, the ancient fort served a similar psychological purpose, as a hostage camp, a place of interrogation, torture and summary execution, and a visible symbol of intimidation, inescapable in every way. Romainville was 'death's waiting room', a prison for civilians – resistance fighters, political prisoners, prominent Jews, communists and intellectuals, suspected spies, political subversives and 'trouble-makers', as well as those who had simply failed to show sufficient deference to the new rulers of France.

This shifting prison population formed an important element in the brutal arithmetic of Nazi occupation: in reprisal for each act of resistance a number of prisoners would be selected from the cells, and shot. An attack on German soldiers at the Rex Cinema in Paris, for example, was calculated to be worth the lives of 116 Romainville hostages. The more serious the incident of defiance, the higher the death toll at the hostage depot. Sometimes, hostages were told which specific act had cost them their lives. Mostly, they were not.

Chapman and Faramus, political prisoners and suspected saboteurs, were stripped, clad in prison overalls, and then taken before the camp commandant, Kapitan Brüchenbach, a stocky little man with thick glasses and eyes 'like two bullet holes in a metal door'. Brüchenbach grunted that he had orders from the Gestapo to detain them until further notice. The fastidious Faramus noted that the man 'stank of drink'.

They were then marched to a barrack building surrounded by a 12-foot barbed-wire fence, and guarded at either end by sentries with searchlights and machine guns. The men were pushed into a room, unheated and lit by a single bulb, containing half a dozen empty bunks, and locked inside. As they lay on rotting straw mattresses, the friends discussed their chances of survival, one with brittle optimism, the other in deepest gloom.

'How would you like to be shot, Eddie?' asked Faramus.

'I don't think I'd mind so terribly as all that,' came the self-deluding reply. 'I've had a pretty good life.'

The next morning, as they filed into the courtyard, Chapman and Faramus learned from the whispers of their fellow prisoners that sixteen people had been executed that morning, in retaliation for the assassination of a German officer in Nantes by members of the resistance. On the door of each cell was a warning: 'Alles Verboten', everything is forbidden. This was no exaggeration. The writing and receiving of letters was not permitted. Red Cross and Quaker parcels were intercepted. The beatings were ferocious, and unexplained. Denied contact with the world outside, the inmates measured time by the movements of the guards and the traffic in the distant Paris streets. Rations were strict and unvarying: a pint of watery vegetable soup, four ounces of black bread and an ounce of rancid margarine or cheese. At first, the two newcomers fished the maggots out of the soup; after a few days they, like everyone else, sucked it all down.

The male and female inmates were allowed to mix in the fort's giant courtyard but sexual relations were strictly forbidden, as one of the guards made clear on their first day with an elaborate, multilingual charade: 'Madame prisonniers. Parler, promenade, ja! Aber NIX, verboten, fig-fig – Nix!' And then, in case of any lingering confusion on the matter, he added: 'NIX. Keine fig-fig!' To Chapman, this sounded like a challenge.

The inmates of Fort Romainville were a peculiar assortment: rich and poor, brave and treacherous, guilty and innocent. Chapman and Faramus were the only Englishmen. There was Paulette, a blonde woman who had been arrested for espionage; Ginette, whose husband had already been executed for spying. Other women were being held as hostages for husbands or fathers who had joined the Free French, or were known to be active in the resistance. There was Kahn, a wealthy German-Jewish banker, along with Michelin – the tyre magnate – two Belgian diamond merchants, and a mysterious individual called Leutsch, a German-speaking Swiss journalist who wore horn-rimmed spectacles and claimed to have worked for British intelligence. Among the French prisoners were the former Minister of Information and a radio journalist named Le François, jailed for refusing to broadcast German propaganda. One woman, a waitress from a café in Montparnasse, was there, she claimed, because she had slapped an SS officer who had fondled her. One old fellow named Weiss, a multilingual eccentric with a pathological fear of water, had been arrested for writing an article discussing how a defeated Germany should be partitioned. Many had simply fallen foul of the invaders. Some claimed to have no idea why they were there.

Every inmate had a different story, yet all guarded their words; some declined to reveal their identities beyond a first name. For the prison was also riddled with informers, stoolpigeons whose task it was to winkle the truth from spies and agitators, and then expose them. Among the inmates, suspicion fell heavily on a Belgian named Bossuet. He claimed to have been born in Cardiff, and could spoke English well, though laced with slang. At first Chapman had warmed to the Belgian, only to be told that Bossuet was a 'professional denouncer', a *mouchard*, who had earned himself the nickname 'Black Diamond'. It was rumoured that his betrayals had sent twenty-two prisoners to their deaths. Most inmates shunned him and some attacked him when the guards were not looking. Eventually Bossuet was removed from the prison. This was seen as proof of Bossuet's guilt, but it was part of the regime of neurosis at Romainville that prisoners arrived and were removed without warning or explanation. A middle-aged man called Dreyfus, a Jewish descendant of the other famous victim of anti-semitism, was briefly held, and then inexplicably released. Immediately it was assumed that he must have turned traitor. 'It wasn't safe to talk to anyone,' Chapman reflected. 'No one knew who was who. No one would talk.'

Yet alongside the corrosive atmosphere of fear and distrust existed an equally powerful urge for intimacy. The ban on sex between prisoners was not just ignored, but violated with abandon. Men and women sought every opportunity: in the washrooms, under the stairs, in the coal store and the darker corners of the courtyard. The barrack rooms had not been designed as cells, and the locks were simple to pick. Elaborate plans were hatched by the inmates to find sexual release. No one ever escaped from Romainville, but here was a way to escape, briefly. Within weeks of arriving in Romainville, Chapman had paired off with the blonde Paulette, who was some ten years his senior, while Faramus had begun a sexual relationship with another female inmate named Lucy. Looking back, both men certainly exaggerated the extent of their 'conquests'. Chapman, more worldly than his partner, seemed to accept the strange merging of sex and fear as the natural order but Faramus, a sexual ingénue, was insistent that these 'were real love affairs, passionate and sincere'. In this closed and treacherous society, where death came without warning or explanation, sexual expression was the only remaining liberty.

While Chapman and Faramus were devising complicated trysts with the female prisoners, their offer to spy for Germany, now long forgotten by them, was slowly progressing through the German military bureaucracy. From Jersey their letter had passed to Berlin, then on to the branch of the German secret service at Hamburg, then back to Jersey again. Chapman was serving two weeks' solitary confinement in the fort dungeons when the letter finally caught up with him, in December 1941. Chapman had been consigned to the *cachots*, the underground cells, after a fight with the hated Bossuet. Prisoners in solitary received one meal of bread and soup every three days. Chapman's cell was lightless, freezing and sodden. In an effort to conserve his body heat, he scraped the gravel from the floor and covered himself with it up to the neck.

Chapman was a week into his sentence in solitary, when he was pulled from the dungeon, escorted under guard to Brüchenbach's office, and locked in a back room. Moments later he was confronted by an SS officer who carefully locked the door behind him. The visitor was tall and spare, with pale blue eyes and hollow cheeks, streaked with broken red veins. He stood looking at Chapman for several moments before he spoke. Then, in perfect English, without a hint of accent, he introduced himself as Oberleutnant Walter Thomas. Without preamble or explanation, he sat down at a desk and began to interrogate Chapman about his past crimes, his experience with explosives, his imprisonment in Jersey, and his proficiency in German. Occasionally he referred to a file. He seemed to know every detail of Chapman's criminal record, not only the crimes for which he had been sentenced, but those for which he was only suspected. The officer spoke with familiarity of Britain, of Chapman's years in Soho, his arrest in Edinburgh and his flight to Jersey; as he spoke, he twined the long fingers of his hands. His expression did not change, but he seemed satisfied by Chapman's answers. Chapman reflected later that his interrogator seemed 'the scholarly, staid' type. After an hour the man indicated that the meeting was over, and Chapman was escorted from the office, not back to the punishment dungeon, but to the barrack room.

'What happened?' Faramus asked, astonished by Chapman's early release from solitary.

Chapman swore him to secrecy and then described his encounter with the SS officer. It must mean, he continued, that their offer to work for Germany had provoked a response at last. 'All right for you,' said Faramus, suddenly fearful. 'They're sure to make use of you. But what about me? What am I worth to them?' Chapman tried to reassure the younger man, but both knew Faramus was right. The Nazis might conceivably find a use for a fit, wily and experienced criminal, with a long record and a convincing reason for hating the British establishment. But what use could the Third Reich find for a slight, twenty-year-old hairdresser whose sole crime had been a failed attempt to acquire £9 by deceit?

Further evidence of the Nazis' interest in Chapman surfaced a few days later, in the form of a military photographer with a Leica camera, who took dozens of pictures of the prisoner, full face and in profile, and then departed.

In early January 1942, Chapman was once more summoned to the Kommandant's office. This time his interrogator could not have been more different to the dead-eyed Oberleutnant Thomas. Arranged across the Kommandant's armchair was a vision of female loveliness: with large brown eyes, long red-painted fingernails, and an expensive black lambswool coat by her side she looked, to Chapman's mind, as if she had just stepped off a film set. Chapman was momentarily stunned by the apparition. Standing alongside her was a man in civilian clothes. Chapman noted his athletic physique and suntanned face; with their elegant apparel and faintly bored expressions, they might have been modelling for a fashion shoot.

The man asked questions in German, which the woman translated into English, with an American accent. There was no attempt to disguise why they had come. Chapman was peppered with questions about what work he thought he could do for the German secret service, and his motives for offering to do so. They demanded to know how much he expected to be paid, and what he would be prepared to do if sent back to Britain undercover. The woman smoked cigarette after cigarette from a long black holder. 'Supposing you didn't feel like coming back to us?' she asked suddenly.

'You'd have to trust me,' Chapman replied.

As the woman picked up her coat to leave, Chapman spotted the label inside: Schiaparelli, the Italian designer. Clearly, he reflected, Nazi spies – if that is what this couple were – could afford the height of fashion.

For a few weeks, normal prison routine resumed, broken only by the ferocious RAF bombardment of the huge Renault factory at Boulogne-Billancourt directly across the Seine from Romainville. The factory was now part of the Nazi munitions machine, making lorries for the German army. On 3 March, the RAF launched 235 low-level bombers at the plant, the largest number of aircraft aimed at a single target during the war. From the barrack windows, Chapman and Faramus saw flares, tracer and flak light up the night, felt the crump of explosive tremble through air, and watched as the city sky turned an evil orange. Chapman could sense his companion's fear. 'They'll probably send you to a civilian internee camp,' he said. 'Or maybe keep you here – if they accept me. Listen Tony, don't worry: leave it to me. Trust me.'

The two Englishmen had been in Romainville for almost four months when Chapman was taken to Brüchenbach's office for what would be the last time. Waiting for him was Oberleutnant Thomas, but this time accompanied by a more senior officer, dressed in the uniform of a cavalry Rittmeister, the equivalent of a captain. At his throat he wore the Iron Cross. Oberleutnant Thomas introduced him as 'Herr Doktor Stephan Graumann'. With an almost courtly gesture, Graumann invited Chapman to be seated, and then began to interrogate him in precise, old-fashioned English, in a soft voice with an upper-class British accent. He asked how Chapman had been treated in Romain-

ville. When the Englishman described his time in the *cachots* on
Brüchenbach's orders, Graumann sneered and remarked that the
Kommandant was 'simply a trained brute'.

Graumann had a lofty, yet benevolent air, and Chapman
found himself warming to the man. He often smiled to himself,
as if enjoying a private joke. He would consider Chapman's
answers carefully, leaning back in his chair, the index finger of
one hand hooked into the side pocket of his uniform, the other
stroking his thinning hair. From time to time he would don
thick-rimmed spectacles and peer at the open file in front of him.
Chapman decided he must be a 'a man of understanding and
tolerance'.

Graumann quizzed Chapman once more about his past: his
catalogue of crimes, his grasp of German and French, the
members of the Jelly Gang and their current whereabouts. Time
after time he returned to the question of whether Chapman was
motivated more by hatred of Britain or by the promise of
financial gain. Chapman responded that both were factors in
his desire to spy for Germany. The interrogation continued for
three hours.

Finally Graumann fixed Chapman with his watery blue eyes
and came to the point. If Chapman would agree to be trained in
sabotage, wireless telegraphy and intelligence work and then
undertake a mission to Britain, he could promise him a substantial financial reward on his return. Chapman agreed on the
spot. He then asked whether Tony Faramus would be coming
too. Graumann's reply was blunt. Faramus was 'no use' to the
German secret service. Graumann picked his words carefully: 'In
times of war we must be careful, and one of you must remain
here.' Though his language was opaque, Graumann's meaning
was obvious: Faramus would remain behind, as a hostage for
Chapman's good behaviour.

As they shook hands, Chapman noticed the fat gold ring with
five black dots on Graumann's little finger, and remarked to
himself on the softness of his hands. These were hands that had

never known manual labour. The voice, the hands, the signet ring: clearly, the man must be some sort of aristocrat. If Chapman could avoid getting into any more trouble, Graumann remarked in the doorway, he would be out of Romainville in two weeks.

Chapman returned to his barrack-cell elated, but also troubled by the veiled 'half-threat' to Faramus. He did not relate the German's words to his cell-mate, but the news that Chapman would soon be leaving alone left the younger man in no doubt that his position was perilous. 'Supposing you slip up,' Faramus pointed out. 'Then I'll be the one to get it in the neck. What if once you have set foot in England, you don't want to come back, Eddie? I don't fancy being shot. Besides, I'm too young to die.'

Chapman tried to reassure him. 'Look here, Tony, let me play this my way. I am gambling with my own life, too, don't forget.' The truth of the remark was undeniable: their fates were now linked. Most Romainville victims never discovered why they had been chosen for death. If Faramus was shot, he would know he had been betrayed by Eddie Chapman. Privately, Faramus reflected that 'agreeing to play Eddie's game might cost me my life'. Could this 'bold bluff' possibly succeed? 'Desperately and fearfully,' Faramus wrote, 'I hoped so, for my sake as well as his.'

On 18 April 1942, Chapman was escorted from his cell. 'Goodbye and good luck,' he said, slapping Faramus on the back and grinning. 'Look me up in London after the war!'

'Goodbye and good luck,' replied the Jerseyman, as brightly as he could.

Chapman was met in the Kommandant's office by Oberleutnant Thomas. The few possessions he had brought from Jersey were returned to him, along with his civilian clothes, while Brüchenbach signed the release papers. Chapman walked out of Romainville gates, and was ushered by Thomas into a waiting car. He was free. But as Thomas observed, as they settled into the back seat and the driver headed west, this was freedom of a very particular sort. 'You are among friends and we are going to help you,' said the German officer, in his clipped, precise English. 'So please do not try anything silly like attempting to escape, because I am armed.' From now on, Thomas added, when in public, Chapman should speak only German.

At Gare Montparnasse, the duo transferred to a reserved first-class compartment on the train for Nantes. In the dining car, Chapman gorged himself. The ascetic-looking Thomas ate little, so Chapman finished his supper for him.

It was evening when the train pulled into Nantes, France's western port where the great Loire flows towards the Atlantic. A burly young man in civilian clothes with an impressively broken nose was waiting on the platform. He introduced himself as 'Leo', picked up Oberleutnant Thomas's suitcase and Chapman's bag of belongings, and led the way to where a large Mercedes awaited them.

Chapman sank into the leather upholstery, as Leo drove the car at high speed through Nante's winding cobbled streets, and then out into open countryside, heading northwest, past neat farms and meadows dotted with Limousin cows. At a roadside village café, a handful of peasants watched expressionless, as the Mercedes sped past. After some seven kilometres, Leo slowed and turned right. They passed what appeared to be a factory and crossed over a railway bridge, before coming to a stop in front of a pair of green iron gates with a high wall on either side. A thick screen of poplar trees shielded from view whatever was behind the wall. Leo hailed the uniformed sentry, who unlocked the gates.

Down a short drive, the car came to rest before a large stone mansion. Chapman was led inside and upstairs to a book-lined study. Here a familiar figure in a three-piece pinstriped suit sat hunched writing over a desk. 'Welcome to the Villa de la Bretonnière,' said Dr Graumann, rising to shake Chapman's hand. 'Come and have a glass of really good brandy.'

5

Villa de la Bretonnière

After Romainville, the Villa de la Bretonnière was paradise. The three-storey building had been built in the 1830s, the same decade as the Paris prison, but it could not have been more of a contrast. It was what the French describe as a *maison de maître*, larger than a mansion, but smaller than a château. It boasted all the hallmarks of a rich man's retreat: oak floors, huge marble fireplaces, crystal chandeliers, and double doors opening onto a large and well-tended garden. The house had belonged to a wealthy Jew, a cinema owner in Nantes, before it was requisitioned and its owner 'relocated'. The building, surrounded by trees and a high wall, suited Nazi intelligence purposes exactly.

That evening, elated by the brandy and Graumann's welcome, Chapman was shown to a room on the top floor. For the first time in four years, the door was not locked behind him. He slept in crisp linen sheets, and woke to the sound of a cock crowing. Chapman thought he had never seen anywhere so beautiful. To the west, the land sloped gently through woodland and fields to the River Erdre. Waterfowl splashed in an ornamental pond, while a litter of Alsatian puppies played on the lawn.

Chapman was escorted to breakfast by Oberleutnant Thomas. In the dining room, Graumann sat at the head of the table, reading a copy of *The Times* and eating a boiled egg. He nodded to Chapman, but did not speak. (The aristocrat, Chapman would

soon learn, did not hold with conversation during breakfast.)
Around the table, half a dozen men were tucking into a feast of
toast, eggs, butter, honey and fresh coffee, all served on the
former owner's best china. Chapman recognised Leo, the
chauffeur with the flattened nose, who grinned back through
broken teeth.

A French maidservant cleared away breakfast, cigarettes were
offered around, and Thomas introduced the other members of
the household. Each man, though Chapman could not know it,
proffered a false name. A ruddy-faced, well-built fellow with a
pearl tie-pin was presented as 'Hermann Wojch'; followed by
'Robert Keller', a slight, blond man in his early twenties,
alongside 'Albert', a balding, middle-aged man with a cheery
countenance. To Chapman's astonishment, the next person to
step forward, wearing plus fours and a gold wristwatch, greeted
him in English with a broad Cockney accent. He gave his name
as 'Franz Schmidt'.

Later, upstairs in the study, Graumann adopted his habitual
posture, with one finger hooked in his waistcoat, and explained
that Chapman was now part of the Abwehr – the German
foreign intelligence gathering and espionage service – and that he
was attached to the Nantes section, 'one of the most important
sabotage training centres of the German Secret Service in
Europe'.

For the next three months, Graumann continued, Chapman
would undergo rigorous training, under his direction: Keller
would be his wireless instructor; Wojch and Schmidt would
teach him sabotage and espionage techniques; Leo would show
him how to jump with a parachute. If he passed certain tests he
would be sent to Britain on a mission and, if successful, he would
be handsomely rewarded. There was no word as to what would
happen if Chapman failed these tests.

Meanwhile, he was free to explore the grounds of La Bretonnière, but Thomas would accompany him at all times. He
should avoid fraternizing with the locals and under no circum-

stances should he bring women back to the house. In the presence of French people he must speak only German, and if any Germans quizzed him, he should explain that he was German by birth but had lived most of his life in America. Officially, he was now part of the Baustelle Kerstang, a military engineering unit repairing roads and buildings in occupied France.

Chapman would need a spyname, Graumann declared, to protect his real identity. What was the name that the English routinely attached to Germans? Fritz? This, he chuckled, would be the codename for the new Abwehr spy number V-6523.

As he struggled to take in the flood of information, Chapman reflected that Dr Graumann, with his pinstriped suit, looked more like a 'respectable business man' than a spymaster. His tone was brisk but benign, and his eyes under heavy lids twinkled. Each time he spoke, his head jerked slightly, back and forth. His voice struck Chapman as being 'surprisingly soft, for a German', but the tone hardened very slightly as the German observed: 'Look, you will see a good many things, but you must realise that with our section things must be kept secret. I'm asking you not to be too nosey.'

For months, the Abwehr had been searching for an Englishman who could be trained as a spy and saboteur and dropped into Britain. The man must be without scruple, adept at concealment, intelligent, ruthless and mercenary. Chapman's arrival at La Bretonnière was not some accident of fate. Rather, he represented the latest, boldest stroke in a war between the secret services of Britain and Germany that had raged, unseen but unceasing, for the previous two years.

Before the outbreak of the Second World War, the Abwehr (literally meaning 'defence') was reputed to be the most efficient intelligence service in Europe. An early appraisal by MI5, the security service controlling counter-espionage in the United Kingdom and throughout the British empire, described the Abwehr as an 'absolutely first-class organisation in training and personnel'. This assessment was overly flattering. One of the most striking aspects of the countries' intelligence services was just how little each side knew about the other. In 1939, SIS, the British Secret Intelligence Service (also known as MI6, and operating in all areas outside British territory) did not know what the German military intelligence service was called, or even who ran it. In a frank self-assessment written after the end of the Second World War, MI5 conceded that 'by the time of the fall of France the organisation of the Security Service as a whole was in a state which can only be described as chaotic . . . attempting to evolve means of detecting German agents without any inside knowledge of the German organisation'.

The Abwehr was equally ill prepared. Hitler had neither expected nor wanted to go to war with Britain, and most Nazi intelligence operations had been directed eastwards. The Abwehr intelligence network in Britain was virtually non-existent. As Britain and Germany squared up for conflict, a strange shadow dance took place between their rival intelligence services: both frantically began building up spy networks, almost from scratch, for immediate deployment against one another. Each credited the other with extreme efficiency and advanced preparations, and both were wrong.

The first serious skirmish took place over a diminutive, dubious and extremely aggravating Welsh electrician called Alfred Owens. A manufacturer of battery accumulators, Owens had made frequent business trips to Germany in the 1930s, bringing back small items of technical and military information which he passed to the Admiralty. In 1936, he was formally enrolled in British intelligence as agent 'Snow' (a partial anagram of Owens). At the same time, however, Owens had secretly made contact with the Abwehr. MI6 intercepted his mail, but when confronted with evidence of his double game, Owens insisted he was working for British interests. MI6 accepted his explanation, for the time being. On instructions from Germany, Owens picked up a wireless transmitter from the left-luggage office at Victoria Station, providing valuable technical information on German radio construction. Then he vanished to Hamburg, and it was assumed he had 'gone bad'.

The day after Britain declared war on Germany, the Welshman resurfaced and telephoned Special Branch to arrange a meeting. At Wandsworth Prison Owens was offered the choice between execution and working as a double agent; once again, he pledged loyalty to Britain. In September 1939, he travelled to Holland, this time accompanied by a retired police inspector, Gwilym Williams, posing as a Welsh nationalist eager to throw off the English yoke. There they met up with Abwehr officer Nikolaus Ritter, and returned to London with valuable information including the keys to various Abwehr radio codes.

The British still had doubts about Agent Snow, and these deepened after an extraordinary series of events in the North Sea. Ritter had asked Owens to recruit another agent for training in Germany, and agreed to send a submarine to pick them up south of Dogger Bank. MI6, obviously eager to plant a double agent within the Abwehr, duly located a reformed conman and thief called Sam McCarthy, who agreed to play the part. As they motored to the rendezvous in a trawler, McCarthy and Owens each became convinced that the other was, in fact, a German spy. Two days before the meeting, McCarthy locked Owens in his cabin and they steamed home. When Owens was searched he was found to be carrying a report describing the operations of the British intelligence services. This was traced to a Piccadilly restaurant manager and sometime MI5 informer called William Rolph. Confronted with the evidence, Rolph admitted he had been recruited by Owens to spy for Germany. As soon as the interrogators had left, he committed suicide by putting his head in a gas oven.

Owens spent the rest of the war in prison, and to this day it is uncertain whether he was a patriot, a traitor, or both. But the Snow case had shown the extraordinary value of running a double agent, and had furnished some vital technical and cryptological clues. The farce in the North Sea demonstrated that the Abwehr was looking to recruit disaffected British citizens, even criminals, as German agents.

Meanwhile, mounting fears of a German invasion prompted a spy scare in Britain of epidemic proportions. The collapse of one European country after another before the Nazi Blitzkrieg could only have one explanation: in each country there must have been a network of German agents behind the lines, aiding the German advance. A similar network, it was assumed, must exist in Britain, plotting to undermine the state. The myth of the German fifth column was born on a most un-British wave of public hysteria, stoked by the press and politicians. 'There is a well-defined class of people prone to spy mania,' wrote Churchill, who was not immune to the mania himself. 'War is the heyday of these worthy folk.'

German spies were spotted everywhere, and nowhere. Police were deluged with reports of strange figures in disguise, lights flashing at night, burning haystacks, and paranoid neighbours hearing strange tapping through the walls. One avid amateur spycatcher reported seeing a man with a 'typically Prussian neck'; Baden-Powell, the original scoutmaster, insisted you could spot a German spy from the way he walked. Anyone and everyone might be a spy. Evelyn Waugh lampooned the frenzy: 'Suspect everyone – the vicar, the village grocer, the farmer whose family have lived here for a hundred years, all the most unlikely people.' The spies were said to be spreading newspaper on the ground to give secret signals to airborne Germans, poisoning chocolate, infiltrating the police, recruiting lunatics from asylums to act in a suicide squad, and sending out murderous agents into the British countryside disguised as women hitchhikers.

Vast energy and resources were devoted to following up the reports, with a complete lack of success. The most grievous outcome of the panic was the internment of 27,000 Germans, Italians and other 'enemy aliens', most of whom were not only innocent, but also strongly opposed to Nazism. The failure to uncover the plotters merely redoubled the conviction that they must be agents of the highest quality. The secret service, wrote an insider, 'was left with the very uncomfortable feeling that there must be agents in this country whom it was unable to discover'.

The simple truth was that, apart from Arthur Owens and his band of imaginary Welsh extremists, the Abwehr had utterly failed to recruit an effective team of spies in Britain before the war. But as Operation Sealion, the plan for the German invasion of Britain, took shape, the German secret service set about rectifying this failure with a vengeance. From late 1940, as the air-duel between the RAF and Luftwaffe intensified, the Abwehr began pouring agents into Britain: they came by rubber dinghy, U-boat, seaplane and parachute; they came disguised as refugees and seamen. Some came armed with the latest wireless transmitters and carefully forged identity documents; others arrived with nothing more than the clothes they stood up in. Between September and November 1940, it is estimated that at least twenty-one Abwehr agents were despatched to Britain, with instructions to report on troop movements, identify and sabotage targets vital to British defence, prepare for the imminent invasion, and then mingle with the retreating British army. A list of prominent Britons to be arrested by the Gestapo was drawn up, and at the Abwehr headquarters in Berlin there was little doubt that Hitler's stormtroopers would soon be marching down Whitehall.

The Abwehr spies were a mixed bag. Some were Nazi ideologues, but most were the human jetsam that tends to float towards the spy world: opportunists, criminals and a handful of fantasists. The vast majority of the 'invasion spies' had one thing in common though: they were amateurs. Many spoke English badly, or not at all. Few had received more than rudimentary training. They were poorly briefed and often ignorant of English life. One was arrested after he tried to pay £10 and six shillings for a train ticket costing 'ten and six'.

The Abwehr would never find out that its entire espionage programme in Britain had been discovered, dismantled and turned against it. Many of its agents, it is true, seemed to vanish without trace, but this was only to be expected. Several had begun sending messages by wireless and secret ink, and a few seemed to be flourishing undercover. That, at least, is what Hitler was told. Yet the more professional and experienced German intelligence officers knew that the calibre of spies being sent to Britain was pitifully low. The little information coming out of Britain was low-grade stuff. No sabotage operation of any note had been carried out.

The Abwehr leadership decided that in order to penetrate Britain's intelligence defences they would need to look beyond the eager amateurs deployed so far. An altogether superior sort of spy was needed: someone handpicked and properly trained by professionals for a specific, highly dangerous mission. This individual should be dedicated, ruthless and, if possible, British. For this purpose, in March 1942, the Nantes section (or *Dienststelle*) of the Abwehr was established as an elite espionage training centre. A *Rittmeister* who was also a rising star within the Abwehr was appointed to run the new spy school, and provided with money, expert trainers, staff, and a spacious mansion just outside the city in the little village of St Joseph. The unit would be answerable to the Abwehr headquarters in Paris, but largely independent.

A young English-speaking Abwehr officer named Walter Praetorius had been appointed to find a renegade Englishman worthy of training as a top-class spy. Praetorius was a committed Nazi in his politics, but a confirmed anglophile in his tastes. His maternal great-grandfather, Henry Thoms [*sic*], had been a Scottish flax merchant who emigrated from Dundee to the Baltic port of Riga, and married a German woman. Praetorius was fiercely proud of his British blood, and liked to remind anyone who would listen that he was a scion of the 'Chiefly line of Clan McThomas'.

The young Praetorius had graduated from Berlin University, and in 1933, aged twenty-two, spent a year at Southampton University improving his English as part of an Anglo-German student-exchange scheme. He intended to become a teacher. In England, Praetorius played the flute, rowed for the university, and began to sport the clothes and airs of an English gentleman. But above all, he danced. The most lasting legacy from his year in Britain was an unlikely but intense passion for English country dancing. He learned the reels and sword dances of his Scottish ancestors, but above all he fell in love with Morris dancing. The English tend to mock Morris dancing, but Praetorius found the dancers with their odd hats and peculiar rituals quite captivating. During the vacation, he cycled around England, photographing folk dances and analysing the dance steps. After months of careful study, he pronounced that Morris dancing was the root of all dancing in the world, and therefore a foundation of world culture (a remarkable theory never proposed by anyone else, before or since).

Praetorius was popular at Southampton, where he was nicknamed 'Rusty' by his contemporaries on account of the reddish tinge to his receding hair, and remembered as a 'kind, gentle type of personality'. But he was also deeply impressionable, one of nature's extremists and liable to fits of excessive and irrational enthusiasm. When he returned to Germany in 1936, his obsession with folk dancing was soon replaced by an even more extreme passion for fascism. According to British police files, his mother was already a 'rabid Nazi', and young Walter embraced the new creed with characteristic fervour and naivety, rising swiftly through the ranks of the Hitler Youth. The 'superiority of the German and Anglo-Saxon races over all others' became an article of faith, and the outbreak of war an opportunity to demonstrate German strength in the ranks of the SS. The death of his only brother, Hans, in Poland in the early days of the war served merely to inflame him further. Rusty, the gentle flautist with the passion for country dancing, had become a committed, unquestioning Nazi.

SS Oberleutnant Praetorius, adopting the spy name 'Walter Thomas' in honour of his Scottish forebears, set to work diligently trawling through paperwork and scouring prisons, refugee centres and POW camps in search of ideal spy material. He travelled to Jersey in search of collaborators, and stayed at the Almadoux Hotel. He interviewed criminals and deserters, British citizens trapped in the occupied territories and even IRA sympathisers, Irishmen who might be recruited to fight against Britain. None would suffice. Then, in late March 1942, Praetorius sent an excited message to the newly appointed chief of the Nantes Abwehr station (or Abwehrstelle), reporting that he had located an English thief in a Paris prison who 'might be trained for sabotage work', and was going to interview him at once.

6

Dr Graumann

Chapman began to explore his new home, with Praetorius (alias 'Thomas') as his guide and guard. Chapman's bedroom, on the top floor of La Bretonnière, was directly above that of Graumann, whose suite occupied most of the first floor. Next door to Chapman slept Keller, whose bedroom was also the radio room. Wojch and Schmidt shared a room, and Praetorius occupied the bedroom next to Graumann. The ground floor consisted of the dining room, an elegant smoking room with wall panels painted in the style of Fragonard, and a large study with desks around the walls and a steel safe in the corner. A pretty gardener's cottage stood alongside the main building, the ground floor of which had been converted into a chemical laboratory for making explosives, with pestles and mortars, scales, and rows of sinister-looking bottles lining the walls.

La Bretonnière had a full contingent of domestic staff: thirty-year-old Odette did the cooking and housekeeping, aided by Jeanette, a teenager. Two gardeners – one a released prisoner – came daily to cut the grass, tend the flower beds, weed the vegetable patch, and feed the chickens, goats and pigs housed in the grounds.

Chapman's training began at once. A Morse set was produced and under the tuition of Keller and Praetorius he was taught to distinguish between a dot and a dash. From there he graduated to the letters with two elements, then three, and finally the entire alphabet in German. He was taught elementary radio shorthand, tricks for memorizing sequences of letters and how to assemble a radio set.

Three days after his arrival, the gardeners were sent home early and Wojch set off a timed explosion in the garden, followed by a demonstration of 'chemical mixing' in the laboratory. The red-faced saboteur handled the volatile compounds with extraordinary dexterity and Chapman, who prided himself on his knowledge of explosives, was impressed: 'He just got hold of the stuff, looked at it, tasted it, and started mixing. I don't think he was a chemist, he'd simply been very well trained.' Every day, Chapman and Wojch would work in the laboratory, making homemade bombs and incendiary devices from simple ingredients such as sugar, oil and potassium chlorate. Chapman was set to work memorizing formulae.

Leo began teaching him how to jump and roll in preparation for his parachute drop. A ladder was erected against the tallest beech tree in the garden, and the height of Chapman's jumps gradually increased, until he could leap from 30 feet without hurting himself. After the years of imprisonment he was in poor physical shape, so Leo devised a strict exercise regime: Chapman would chop wood until his shoulders ached, and every morning Praetorius would accompany him on a four-mile run along the banks of the Erdre. Chapman was deeply affected by 'the beauty of the river near Nantes', reflecting that it was only since leaving prison 'that he had begun to realise how much beauty there was in the world'.

For Chapman these were strangely idyllic days. A bell would summon the men to breakfast at 8.30, and at 10.00 Chapman would practise sending radio messages to the other Abwehr posts in Paris and Bordeaux. The rest of the morning might be taken up with sabotage work, coding exercises, or parachute practice. Lunch was at 12.30, followed by a siesta until 3.00 or 3.30, followed by more training. In the evening they might play bridge, or bowls on the lawn, or walk up the road to the Café des Pêcheurs, a small wood-panelled bar in the village, and watch the sun go down over the river, drinking beer at 3 francs a glass. Sometimes, accompanied by other members of the team, Chapman would drive out into the countryside to purchase black-market food: fresh eggs, bread, hams and wine. The negotiating was done by one of the drivers, a Belgian named Jean, for the French farmers would charge a German more. The food was expensive – a ham could cost as much 2,500 francs – but there seemed to be no shortage of money.

At La Bretonnière, the alcohol flowed copiously. Dr Grau-mann's drinking was particularly spectacular: Chapman calcu-lated that the chief put away at least two bottles of wine a night, followed by glass after glass of brandy. It seemed to have no effect on him whatever. On Saturdays, the household would climb into the unit's four cars, each with French registration and an SS pass, and drive into Nantes, where they would dine at Chez Elle, dance at the Café de Paris, or visit the cabaret, Le Coucou, where black-market champagne cost 300 francs a bottle. Chapman paid for nothing, and was issued with as much 'pocket money' as he desired. On these trips in to town, Chapman spotted 'V-signs', the mark of the French resistance, chalked on walls in public places. Some diligent Nazi had inserted a swastika inside each V, 'thus reversing the propaganda'. A few of the men visited the German-controlled brothel in town – pug-faced Albert was a regular at the establishment, and extolled the charms of *les jolies filles* there with such gusto that the others nicknamed him *Joli Albert*, a most inapt description.

Chapman found Wojch to be particularly good company: 'He liked life, he always had plenty of money, [he was] rather flashy, liked the girls and the drink.' He too was a former boxer and formidably strong. He would challenge the others to a form of wrestling match in which each contestant would clasp his opponent's hand and then try to force him to his knees. Wojch invariably won.

Chapman began to imagine these men as his friends. He never doubted that the names he knew them by were real. He once

heard Thomas referred to as Praetorius, but simply assumed this
must be a nickname.

But for all their bibulous bonhomie, his new companions
were guarded in their words, furtive in their behaviour, and
secretive in their activities outside the walls of the compound.
From time to time Wojch or Schmidt would disappear, for a
week or longer. When they returned, Chapman would discreetly inquire where they had been. The conversation, he
recalled, tended to follow the same pattern:

'Had a good trip?'

'Yes. Not too bad.'

'Where did you go?'

'Oh, out of the country.'

Chapman learned never to demand a direct answer. Once,
when drunk, he asked Wojch whether he had ever been to
America. Wojch's smile was cold: 'What do you want to ask
questions like that for?'

Beneath a veneer of informality, security was tight. All
important documents were held in the office safe. From time
to time Chapman would observe Graumann go into the
garden with a secret document or letter, 'take it out and
light a cigarette [with it] and burn the whole envelope'. At
night, two ferocious Alsatians roamed the grounds, keeping
intruders out and Chapman in. One morning Keller found
Chapman alone in the radio room, and brusquely ordered
him to leave. The door was always locked after that, and
rigged with an electric alarm. When Graumann discovered
that Chapman had taken to swimming in the Erdre in the
early morning, he assembled the staff for a ferocious roasting:
'Good God! Is he going out alone? He has no papers on him.
What if the French police pick him up?'

Later, the chief took Chapman aside, and gently explained:
'Look here, if you are going out swimming, take one of the boys
along with you. If ever you want to go out, they have orders that
you have only to ask, and one of the boys will go with you.'

Inevitably, however, Chapman began to glean snippets of information from his housemates. Leo, Wojch and Schmidt were 'more or less reckless, the lads of the village'. Wojch boasted that he had been an Olympic boxer before the war. He plainly knew London well, and he waxed sentimental over a former girlfriend, an Irish chambermaid in the Hyde Park Hotel. From casual remarks, Chapman picked up that Wojch had been involved in the dynamiting of a Paris hotel before the invasion of France, an attack in which many Allied officers died. Small but telling details emerged about their earlier lives. Thomas wore his English university boating tie at every opportunity, and boasted that he had been the best oarsman at Southampton. Albert revealed that before the war he had been an agent for a German firm in Liberia. Leo had been a boxer and prizefighter.

When Chapman asked Schmidt where he got his Cockney accent from, he explained that before the war he had worked as a waiter in Frascati's, the London restaurant. He had visited several of Chapman's old Soho haunts, including Smokey Joe's and The Nest, and recalled the tea dances at the Regal Theatre near Marble Arch. Slowly it dawned on Chapman that these men must be more than mere instructors; they were experienced, active spies and saboteurs, who had been deployed in France and Britain since before the outbreak of war.

But if some of 'the boys' were coming into sharper focus, their leader concealed his past behind steel shutters of politeness. For wireless practice, Graumann would set Chapman the task of transmitting English nursery rhymes such as 'Mary had a little lamb', and 'This little piggie went to Market'. 'These were things,' Chapman reflected, 'which I thought only an Englishman would know'; but Graumann claimed to have visited England only once. When Chapman remarked to Graumann on his 'terribly English accent', he batted away the implied question, saying he had been taught by a 'very good private tutor'.

One night, over dinner, the conversation turned to dogs. 'I'll show you a photograph of my dog,' said Graumann, rising from

the table. Several minutes later he returned with a torn photograph. The dog was visible, but the face of whoever was holding
it had been torn away.

'Doctor Stephan Graumann' was, in reality, nothing of the
sort. His name was Stephan Albert Heinrich von Gröning. He
was an aristocrat of impeccable breeding, great wealth and
luxurious tastes: indeed, the 'really good brandy' he had poured
down Chapman on his first evening was a fitting leitmotif for his
life.

The Von Grönings had been the first family in the northern
city of Bremen for some eight centuries, amassing a vast fortune
through trading well and marrying better. Over the years the
powerful clan had supplied seventeen members of the Bremen
parliament and one notable eighteenth-century diplomat,
Georg, who studied with Goethe at Leipzig and then served
as ambassador to the court of Napoleon. In recognition of this
achievement, he was awarded the aristocratic title 'von', and the
Von Grönings had been getting steadily richer, and grander, ever
since.

Born in 1898, Stephan had been brought up in circumstances
of extreme privilege. His mother was an American heiress of
German extraction named Helena Graue (hence his *nom d'espion*:
'Graumann'). At home, the Von Grönings spoke English, with
an upper-class accent. Home was a enormous town house in the
main square of Bremen, a self-satisfied statement in stucco and
stone with five storeys, a fabled library, several old master
portraits and an army of servants to wait on young Stephan:
someone polished his shoes, someone cooked his meals, someone else drove him to an exclusive private school in a carriage
with glass windows and the family crest.

Von Gröning's pampered life very nearly came to a premature
end in 1914 when the First World War erupted, and he joined
the army. But not for young Stephan some dowdy and uncomfortable billet in the trenches; he was commissioned as an
Oberleutnant in the legendary White Dragoons, perhaps the

most elite cavalry regiment in the imperial army. Von Gröning took part in one of the last cavalry charges in history, during which most of the regiment was annihilated by British machine-gun fire. He survived, and was awarded the Iron Cross, second class, for bravery. Von Gröning's war was a short one. He contracted pneumonia, then tuberculosis, and was invalided out of the army. His mother sent him to recuperate at Davos, the fashionable health spa in Switzerland, where he met and fell in love with a Welsh woman named Gladys Nott Gillard, who was also tubercular and high-born, but penniless. They married in St Luke's church, Davos, on 19 December 1923.

The Von Grönings rented a large mansion in Davos, called the Villa Baby, and then set off travelling, back to Bremen, to Hamburg, and finally to Bavaria. Along the way Von Gröning acquired a coffee business – Gröning and Schilling – which almost immediately went bust; he began gambling on the stock exchange, and lost a lot more money. Had he not considered it vulgar to count one's wealth, he might have realised that apart from the great house at Bremen and some fine oil paintings, he was heading for bankruptcy.

Charming, brave, intellectually gifted but indolent, at the end of the war Von Gröning found himself at something of a loose end, which is where he remained for the next seventeen years. He had no desire to study. He collected etchings by Rubens and Rembrandt. He travelled a little, drank a lot and took no physical exercise of any kind (he rode a bicycle only once in his life, but declared the experience 'uncomfortable', and never repeated it). After his failed coffee enterprise, Von Gröning would have nothing more to do with business or trade, and fully occupied his time behaving as if he was rich, which he blithely assumed he was. 'He was delightful company, and very clever,' as one member of the family put it, 'but he never actually *did* anything at all.'

Stephan and his wife shared an interest in lap dogs, strong drink, and spending money they did not have; but not much else. They divorced in 1932, on the grounds of Von Gröning's 'illicit association with another woman'. He was required to provide alimony of 250 marks a month, which was paid by his mother. He then agreed to pay Gladys a lump sum of 4,000 marks, but somehow failed to pay that either. Gladys was reduced to teaching English at a school in Hamburg, while her ex-husband would lie on the sofa in the library of the family home for days on end, reading books in German, English and French, and smoking cigars. But they remained friends. Von Gröning did not make enemies easily.

Von Gröning had observed the rise of fascism from a lofty distance. He was a patriotic monarchist and an old-fashioned aristocrat from an earlier age. He had little time for the posturing Brownshirts with their extreme ideas. He regarded anti-semitism as vulgar, and Hitler as an upstart Austrian 'oik' (though at the time he kept that opinion to himself).

The outbreak of the Second World War gave new purpose to Von Gröning's dilettante existence. He rejoined the German cavalry – a very different organisation from the elegant lancers of his youth – and served on the Eastern Front as a staff officer attached to Oberkommando 4 Heeresgruppe Mitte. After a year he applied to join the Abwehr. The secret military intelligence service of the German High Command was something of an ideological anomaly: it contained its share of Nazi fanatics, but alongside them were many men of Von Gröning's stamp – officers of the old school, determined to win the war, but opposed to Nazism. The Abwehr was epitomised by its leader, Admiral Wilhelm Canaris, a spy of great subtlety who ran the Abwehr as a personal fiefdom. Hitler never trusted Canaris, rightly, for the admiral may eventually have put out feelers to Britain, seeking to negotiate an end to the war by removing the Führer.

Espionage appealed to Von Gröning, intellectually and ideo-logically, while his command of languages and knowledge of English and American culture made him a valuable asset in the secret service. The years spent lounging in the library at Bremen had not been entirely wasted: behind the hooded eyes and jovial manner was a practised and cynical student of human nature. His outwardly affable demeanour encouraged others to confide in him, but as a Von Gröning of Bremen, he always maintained his distance. 'He could mix in any company, but he always knew who he was.' He was swiftly spotted as the coming man within the Abwehr, and when Canaris was looking for someone to run his new Nantes spy school, Von Gröning seemed the obvious person to appoint.

Von Gröning liked Chapman. He admired the sheer energy of the man, so different from his own aristocratic languor. And he knew he could turn him into a powerful secret weapon.

The photograph he handed Chapman had once shown Gladys hugging their pet dog, a Sealyham terrier. But before coming downstairs, he had carefully torn Gladys out of the picture. Von Gröning was not going to run the risk, however small, that Chapman might recognise his British ex-wife, and thus obtain a clue to the real identity of 'Dr Graumann'.

Von Gröning bound Chapman ever closer to the team. The psychology was simple, but effective. The Englishman was flattered and spoiled, drawn into an intense atmosphere of secretive camaraderie. Like many brutal men, including Hitler himself, the members of the Nantes Abwehr section could also be sentimental and nostalgic. Von Gröning set up a 'Home corner' – on the bureau in the smoking room, where the men were encouraged to display pictures of their hometowns, and somehow obtained a photograph of Berwick-on-Tweed, the nearest town he could find to Chapman's birthplace of Burnopfield. Birthdays were celebrated with cakes, gifts and torrents of drink. Von Gröning encouraged informality, and allowed the men to daub graffiti on the walls of the unused attics. One drew a caricature of Hitler as a carrot. It was surely Chapman who carefully etched the picture of a blonde woman with a strong resemblance to Betty Farmer.

Von Gröning was privately amused to see the Führer mocked as a vegetable, but he took pains to remind Chapman that he was now part of a victorious German army that had conquered half of Europe and would soon bring Britain and Russia to their knees. Praetorius, as the most committed Nazi in the group, kept up a steady stream of Nazi jingoism.

Inevitably, the combination of healthy living, good food, group bonding and propaganda began to have the desired effect. Chapman felt himself drawn to what he called the 'German spirit', his vanity fed by the belief that this training school, staffed by hard and hard-drinking men, had been established for him alone. Every meal began with the chorus of 'Heil Hitler!', with the Englishman joining in. When Thomas declared that Britain was losing the war, Chapman believed him, though such 'gloating' left him feeling 'sick at heart'.

At the end of a boozy evening, the trainee spy could be found lustily singing *Lili Marlene* with the rest of the crew. *Lili Marlene*, he declared, was his favourite song, expressing 'the hopes of every man who has left his girl behind'.

Chapman's head was being turned by all the attention. But it was not turning nearly so far as Von Gröning imagined.

It is impossible to say when Chapman decided to start spying on his German spymasters. Many years later, he candidly admitted that he did not know quite when, or even why, he began to collect information. Perhaps he was merely taking out an insurance policy against an uncertain future. The instincts of the spy and the thief are not so different: both trade in stolen goods, on similar principles. The value of information depends on the buyer's hunger, but it is a seller's market. Slowly at first, and with great care, Chapman began to build up a stock of secrets that would be of supreme interest to British intelligence.

He noticed the way that Von Gröning assiduously read the personal advertisements in *The Times*, and sometimes the *Manchester Guardian*, occasionally underlining passages and taking notes. He overheard that Wojch had been on a sabotage mission to Spain during one of his unexplained absences, and when the door to the small anteroom off the study was left open, he spotted at least 50 lbs of gelignite in neat stacks. Inside a cupboard in Von Gröning's bedroom he saw racks of German military uniforms 'of every kind in different lockers with all kinds of numbers'. He noted how Von Gröning took the codebooks after radio practice and carefully locked them in the safe. Given the opportunity and some gelignite, Chapman knew he could open that safe.

Chapman would later claim to have manufactured a set of skeleton keys to open and snoop inside various locked drawers around the house. This seems unlikely, given how closely he was monitored, but he certainly eavesdropped on his companions, literally, by boring a small hole under the eaves of his bedroom into Von Gröning's bathroom. (If challenged, he planned to say he was putting down chemicals from the lab, to poison the rats that ran behind the panelling and kept him awake at night.) By pressing his ear to the hole, he could faintly hear the conversation taking place below, though he learned nothing of interest. He began to make notes: of crystal frequencies, code words and the times of radio transmission between Nantes, Paris and Bordeaux. He noted the position of the anti-aircraft gun emplacements in the area, and the German military headquarters at the château on the other side of the river, camouflaged with netting. Although he had been instructed not to, he carefully wrote down the chemical formula of each bomb.

As the training gathered pace, senior officials in the Abwehr began to take an interest in Von Gröning's protégé, and Chapman found himself being inspected and tested, like a prize exhibit at a country fair. In May, Praetorius escorted him to an apartment in the Rue de Luynes in Paris to meet a fat man with a red face, who drank champagne and told English jokes, but who asked a series of penetrating questions. From his demeanour Chapman assumed he must be 'a fairly high bug' in the organisation. Von Gröning would say only that this individual was 'one of our best men'.

Soon afterwards a German in civilian clothes arrived from Angers in a chauffeur-driven car. The stranger was extraordinarily ugly and quite bald, save for a fringe of hair at the back of his head, with discoloured, gold-filled teeth. He wore a thick coat, carried a leather portfolio and smoked cigars continuously. Von Gröning treated him with exaggerated respect. Chapman thought he looked 'like a gigolo'. The bald man grilled Chapman about codes and sabotage. After he had left, Praetorius let slip that the visitor was 'an old Gestapo man', the head of counter-espionage in western France, responsible for catching enemy spies with a team of radio interceptors working around the clock in shifts to pick up 'black senders', clandestine wireless operators sending messages to Britain. The Angers spycatcher had asked that Chapman be transferred to his team for a month, to act as a 'stool pigeon amongst Allied agents in the Germans' hands, and as a general aid in counter-espionage work' – a request Von Gröning had indignantly refused. 'Fritz' was his personal asset, and Von Gröning was not about to relinquish him.

In June 1942, Chapman was taken to Paris for his first real parachute jump. He would start at 900 feet, he was told, and gradually increase to 1,500 feet. After a night at the Grand Hotel and dinner at Poccardi's Italian restaurant on the Left Bank, he was driven to a small airfield near Le Bourget airport, northeast of Paris, where Charles Lindbergh had landed after his transatlantic flight fifteen years earlier. Chapman and his parachute were loaded aboard a Junkers bomber, and minutes later he was floating down over the French countryside. His first jump was a complete success; his second, immediately afterwards, was very nearly his last. The parachute failed to open properly, buckling in a gust of wind when he was 50 feet from the ground. He was swung high into the air, and then smashed down, face first, onto the airfield tarmac. Chapman lost consciousness, one front tooth, one canine, and several molars. A German doctor patched him up and, back in Nantes, Von Gröning sent him to the best local dentist, one Dr Bijet, who set about reconstructing Chapman's battered face. After two weeks of operations, Chapman had a natty new set of gold teeth to replace those he had lost, and the Abwehr had a bill for 9,500 francs. The expense of Chapman's dental work would prompt the first of several heated exchanges between Von Gröning and his Paris superiors.

Chapman's wireless skills steadily improved. Praetorius timed him with a stopwatch, and announced he had attained a speed of seventy-five letters a minute, using a hand cipher (as distinct from one encoded on the Enigma machine) based on the single code word: BUTTERMILK. Without the code word, Praetorius assured him, the code was 'unbreakable'. As he gained in confidence, like most radio operators, Chapman began to develop his own 'fist' – individual characteristics that another wireless operator or receiver could become familiar with. Chapman always ended his transmissions with a 'laughing out' sign: 'HE HU HO HA', or some variation thereof. He called these flourishes 'my little mottoes'.

Soon he graduated from the German transmitter to a radio of British manufacture, apparently seized from a British agent in France. Usually the practice messages were coded from German, but he was also required to transmit in English and French. He sent poems, rhymes, proverbs and sayings. One day he tapped out a message: 'It is very cold here but better than in Russia.' He sent Maurice, the long-suffering chief radio operator in Paris, a message asking him to buy Odette, their housekeeper, a wedding present on his behalf. A little while later he tried out an English joke: 'A man went into a shop and asked the price of the ties displayed. The customer was astonished when he heard the high price and said one could buy a pair of shoes for that price. You would look funny, said the shopkeeper, wearing a pair of shoes round your neck. Fritz.' It was not a good joke, but then the Paris operators seemed to have had no sense of humour at all. 'What silly business is this?' the Paris station responded.

As spring turned to summer, La Bretonnière was a place of quiet contentment, save for the occasional deafening explosion in the back garden. When neighbours complained, they were told that the German engineers were detonating mines found during road construction. In July, Von Gröning reported to Paris that Fritz had passed a series of tests, and was responding well to training. The chief of the Nantes spy school was enjoying himself. Managing La Bretonnière was a little like running an exclusive, intensely private men's club, even if the guests were a trifle uncouth.

Chapman was also happy. 'I had everything I wanted,' he reflected. He also had a new companion. On a black-market expedition in the countryside, Chapman had bought and adopted a young pig, which he christened Bobby. The name was probably a reference to his previous life. The British bobbies (also, less affectionately, referred to as 'pigs') had chased Chapman for years; now Bobby the Pig followed him everywhere. An intelligent and affectionate animal, Bobby lived in the grounds of the house. At Chapman's whistle he would come running, like a well-trained dog, and then lie with his trotters in the air to have his stomach scratched. When Chapman went swimming in the Erdre (Von Gröning had by now relaxed his rules on unaccompanied bathing), Bobby would join him, flopping around in the muddy shallows. Then the Englishman and his faithful pig would walk happily home together through the cowslips and yellow irises.

7

Codebreakers

In the summer of 1942, the analysts of Bletchley Park – the secret code and cipher centre hidden deep in the Buckinghamshire countryside – decoded one of the most bizarre messages of the entire war. It had been sent from the Abwehr station at Nantes to the Abwehr headquarters in Paris, and it read: 'Dear France. Your friend Bobby the Pig grows fatter every day. He is gorging now like a king, roars like a lion and shits like an elephant. Fritz.' (The refined codebreaking ladies of Bletchley did not hold with vulgarity: they substituted the word 'shits' with a series of asterisks.) Britain's wartime cipher experts had penetrated Nazi Germany's most sophisticated codes and read its most secret messages, but this one was, quite simply, incomprehensible.

For several months, Britain's codebreakers and spycatchers had been following the Fritz traffic with avid interest, and mounting anxiety. They knew when this new, highly prized German spy had arrived in Nantes, and when he went to Paris; they knew how many teeth he had knocked out, and what the dentistry had cost; they knew he spoke English, and that he might even be an Englishman. And they knew he was heading for Britain.

The unravelling of Germany's top-secret codes by a peculiar collection of mathematical savants in an English country house was perhaps the most spectacular espionage coup of this, or any other, war. The Radio Security Service began picking up Abwehr signals in August 1940. The wireless set and codes obtained through Arthur Owens, 'Agent Snow', had provided the codebreakers with a valuable head start, and the cryptographers at Bletchley Park ('Station X') were soon reading the Abwehr's principal hand cipher, the old-fashioned manual code. By December another team, under the leadership of the inspirationally eccentric Dillwyn 'Dilly' Knox, had also broken the code used on Abwehr Enigma machines, the portable cypher machine used to encrypt and decrypt secret communications. From that moment until the end of the war, British intelligence continuously intercepted and read the wireless traffic of the German secret service.

One member of the team put the success down to 'brilliant guesswork and a good slice of luck', but it also came through the application of raw intellectual muscle and sheer hard work. The Abwehr's messages had to be intercepted, sent to Bletchley Park, sorted, distributed, the daily machine and message settings worked out, and finally deciphered and despatched to the intelligence services. This extraordinary feat was usually performed by Dilly Knox and his team of large ladies (for some reason he employed only women, and only tall ones) within twenty-four hours. Knox himself frequently went about his work clad in pyjamas and dressing gown; to relax, he would then go for a terrifyingly fast drive in the country lanes around Bletchley. Knox was one of the greatest cryptographers, and the worst drivers, Britain has ever produced. One day he returned from motoring through the countryside and remarked casually: 'It's amazing how people smile, and apologise to you, when you knock them over.'

The successful deciphering of the secret German codes, codenamed Ultra, was the best-kept secret of the war. Its value to the war effort was almost incalculable. Churchill called the intercepts 'My Golden Eggs', and guarded them jealously. The Abwehr never suspected that its messages were being read on a daily basis, and persisted in the mistaken belief that its codes were unbreakable. The wealth of intelligence produced by Ultra decrypts was referred to only as the 'Most Secret Sources'.

For the purposes of counter-espionage, the Most Secret Sources gave early warning of which spies were arriving in Britain, where, and when. As a consequence, most of the 'invasion spies' were picked up the moment they arrived in Britain, and swiftly imprisoned. Several were executed. The Abwehr's attempt to build a wartime spy network in Britain was an unmitigated failure. Crucially, the German intelligence service never realised this, thanks to one soldier, one Oxford academic, and one inspired idea.

At the height of the invasion scare, Major (later Colonel) Tommy Robertson, the MI5 officer who had handled the Snow case, approached his commanding officer, Dick White, and pointed out an obvious truth: a dead enemy spy can do no more harm, but neither can he (or she) do any good. A captured spy, however, could be persuaded to double-cross his German employers in exchange for his life, and then work for his British captors. Snow had already demonstrated the potential value of the controlled double agent, who could persuade the enemy to believe he was active and loyal when he was nothing of the sort. More importantly, over time, the double agent could be used to feed vital disinformation to the enemy. Thanks to the Most Secret Sources, British intelligence could even check whether the ruse was working. Robertson was insistent: instead of putting enemy agents in prison or on the end of a rope, they should be put to work.

Robertson's suggestion was forwarded to Guy Liddell, the subtle-minded, cello-playing director of 'B Division', the branch of MI5 devoted to counter-intelligence. Liddell gave his blessing at once, and, with Cabinet approval, Robertson was duly appointed chief of a new section for catching enemy spies, turning them, and then running them as double agents. The new outfit was given the innocuously invisible name B1A. At the same time, another linked organisation was established, with senior representatives of all the military intelligence services, the Home Forces and Home Defence, to assess the information, true and false, to be sent back via the double agents. The monitoring group was named the 'Twenty Committee', because the two Xs of a double-cross make twenty in Roman numerals. This was precisely the sort of dry classical witticism favoured by the man now appointed chairman of the Twenty Committee: Major (and later Sir) John Cecil Masterman, a distinguished Oxford history don, all-round sportsman, successful thriller-writer and jail-bird.

Masterman and Robertson formed the lynchpins of the double-cross operation, and they ran it with such dazzling success that after the war Masterman could justifiably claim: 'By means of the double-cross agent system *we actively ran and controlled the German espionage system in this country.*' (The italics are his, and deserved.) Theirs was a partnership of equals, and opposites: Robertson was a professional, dealing with the nuts and bolts of running the double agents, while Masterman liaised with the top brass; Robertson was the technician, while Masterman was to become the great theoretician of the double-cross.

Thomas Argyll Robertson was universally known as 'Tar', on account of his initials. Born in Sumatra to colonial parents, Tar had spent much of childhood parked with an aunt in Tunbridge Wells, an experience that was lonely but formative, for it left him with an ability to chat to complete strangers with disarming frankness. He passed through Charterhouse and Sandhurst without, in his own estimation, learning very much, and became, briefly, an officer in the Seaforth Highlanders, and then, even more briefly, a bank clerk. In 1933, at the age of twenty-four, at the invitation of Vernon Kell, the first director general of MI5, he had given up the staid world of banking to become a full-time intelligence officer, initially dealing with political subversion, arms trafficking, and counter-espionage. 'Immensely personable and monstrously good looking', he had the rare knack of being able to talk to anyone, anywhere, about anything. Bishops, admirals, whores, crooks and revolutionaries all found it equally easy to confide in Tar Robertson. Masterman pointed out, a touch acidulously, that 'Tar was in no sense an intellectual'. Tar was no bookworm. Instead he read people. He excelled in a job that 'involved a great deal of conversing with suspect people in pubs . . . meeting, greeting, chatting, charming, chuckling, listening, offering another drink, observing, probing a little, listening some more and ending up with all sorts of confidences the other person never thought he would utter'. He continued to wear the distinctive McKenzie tartan trews of the Seaforth Highlanders, a strangely conspicuous choice of attire for someone running one of the most secret organisations in the world. (The tartan trousers earned him another, more appropriately colourful nickname: 'Passion Pants'.)

John Masterman was cut from very different cloth. It is easiest to imagine him as the antithesis, in every conceivable way, of Eddie Chapman. He was highly intellectual, intensely conventional, and faintly priggish, with a granite sense of moral duty. Masterman was the embodiment of the British Establishment: he belonged to all the right clubs, played tennis at Wimbledon, hockey for England, and cricket whenever possible. Spare and athletic, his face was hard and handsome, as if carved out of marble. He neither smoked nor drank, and lived in a world of High Tables and elevated scholarship, exclusively inhabited by wealthy, privileged, intelligent English men.

A confirmed bachelor, he might have been homosexual, but if so, in a wholly repressed and contented English way. Women were simply invisible to him; in the 384 pages of his autobiography, only one woman is mentioned with affection, and that is his mother, with whom he lived in Eastbourne during the university vacations. In his spare time, he wrote detective thrillers set in an imaginary Oxford college and starring an amateur British sleuth in the Sherlock Holmes mould. These are somewhat dry and unemotional books, more intellectual puzzles than novels, but that was how this clever, desiccated man regarded human nature – as a conundrum to be unpicked by reason. He seems a peculiar creature today, but John Masterman represented English traits that were once considered virtues: *noblessse oblige,* hard work, and unquestioning obedience to the norms of society. By his own account, he was 'almost obsessively anxious to conform to accepted standards', just as Chapman was equally determined to defy them.

Yet Masterman had one thing in common with Chapman: he had spent four years in a prison. By a stroke of terrible ill fortune, as a newly elected fellow of Christ Church in 1914, he was sent on a study course in Germany, and was trapped by the outbreak of the First World War. Masterman was interned in Ruhleben prison with a strange assortment of equally unlucky Britons: sailors, businessmen, academics, jockeys from the Berlin race-course, sportsmen, workmen, tourists and one Nobel Prize winner, Sir James Chadwick, who lectured his fellow prisoners on the mysteries of radioactivity. The young Masterman emerged after four years without visible scars, but weighed down by what he considered to be an inferiority complex. Almost all his friends and contemporaries had perished on the battlefields. 'My predominant feeling was one of shame,' he wrote. 'I had played no part in the greatest struggle in our national history.'

Masterman was already in his fiftieth year when the longed-for opportunity to play his part finally arrived with the offer to work in MI5. He seized it gratefully, and it was Britain's great good fortune that he did, for no man was better suited to the job. If Tar Robertson was the 'real genius' of the double-cross system, as the historian Hugh Trevor-Roper put it, then John Masterman was its moral conscience, meticulously analysing the motivations of men, patiently solving the riddle of the double cross, like a vast and complicated crossword puzzle.

Recruitment to MI5 was through the informal old-boy net-work, and Robertson, with the help of his deputy, a London solicitor named John Marriott, swiftly began putting together a team of gifted amateurs. Section B1A, when finally assembled, included lawyers, academics, an industrialist, a circus owner, at least one artist, an art dealer and a poet. Tar himself was the only professional in the organisation, which started its life in a requisitioned corner of Wormwood Scrubs prison before moving to a large and elegant house at 58, St James's Street, in the heart of London clubland. The team's in-house poet, Cyril Harvey, memorialised the building in camp verse:

> At 58, St James's Street
> The door is open wide
> Yet all who seek to enter here
> Must make their motives crystal clear
> Before they step inside,
> That none may probe with fell intent
> The Secrets of the Government.

Intercepted German spies were first interrogated at a secret military prison, Camp 020. Only then, if suitable for double-agent work, would they be handed over to Tar Robertson and his case officers. If they refused to collaborate, they were either imprisoned, or executed. Sometimes the death threat was overt. Masterman was unsentimental on this score. 'Some had to perish, both to satisfy the public that the security of the country was being maintained, and also to convince the Germans that the others were working properly and were not under control.' All but the most fanatical Nazis agreed to co-operate when faced with this choice, but their motives did not follow any established pattern. Some were merely terrified, desperate to save their skins, but there were also, Masterman found, 'certain persons who have a natural predilection to live in that curious world of espionage and deceit, and who attach themselves with equal facility to one side or the other, so long as their craving for adventure of a rather macabre type is satisfied'.

If the intercepted spy was considered suitable, then the hard work began, starting with a strenuous exercise of the imagination. In Masterman's words, the case officer must penetrate the world of his adopted spy, to 'see with the eyes and hear with the ears of his agent', and create for him a life as close as possible to the one he was pretending to live. If, say, the double agent was claiming to transmit from Aylesbury, then he needed to know what Aylesbury was like and, if possible, to be physically in or very near Aylesbury, since it was suspected that the Germans could pinpoint transmissions, perhaps to within a one-mile radius.

The logistical challenge was immense. Each double agent required a safe house and a staff of at least five people: a case officer, a wireless operator to monitor or transmit his messages, two guards on twelve-hour shifts to ensure he did not run away, and a trusted housekeeper to look after and feed the group. Meanwhile, the case officer had to establish what his agent had been sent to find out, and then reproduce a fake facsimile of it, but without damaging the war effort. An agent who transmitted useless information would be seen as a failure by the Abwehr, and dropped. To maintain German confidence, the double agent must send a mixture of true but essentially harmless information known as 'chickenfeed', extraneous facts, and undetectably false titbits, along with whatever disinformation was agreed upon.

Deciding what could or could not be sent to the enemy was the delicate task of the Twenty Committee. Meanwhile the double agent must be kept busy and happy, because if he turned bad, and somehow managed to inform his German spymasters that he was under British control, then the entire system would be jeopardised. Every double agent, Masterman observed, 'is prone to be vain, moody and introspective, and therefore idleness, which begets brooding, should be of all things most carefully avoided'. Tar Robertson swiftly discovered that, in order to keep these agents sweet, it was sensible to reward them, and not just with their lives. The 'principle of generosity' was thus established, and agents who had brought over cash, as many did, were often allowed to keep a percentage.

The ideal case officer needed to be a combination of guard, friend, psychologist, radio technician, paymaster, entertainments organiser and private nursemaid. It helped if he or she was also a saint, since the individual being cosseted and coaxed in this way was quite likely to be extremely unpleasant, greedy, paranoid, treacherous and, at least initially, an enemy of Britain. Finally, all of the above had to be performed at breakneck speed, because the longer a spy took to make contact with the enemy, the more likely his German spymaster would suspect that he had been captured and turned.

The results show just how brilliantly Tar Robertson chose the men and women 'of high intelligence and clearly defined purpose' who made up his team. Some 480 suspected enemy spies were detained in Britain in the course of the war. Just seventy-seven of these were German. The rest were, in descending order of magnitude, Belgian, French, Norwegian and Dutch, and then just about every conceivable race and nationality, including several who were stateless. After 1940, very few were British. Of the total intercepted, around a quarter were subsequently used as double agents, of whom perhaps forty made a significant contribution. Some of these lasted only a short time before their cases were terminated; a few continued to delude their German handlers until the end of the war. A tiny handful, the very best, were involved in the greatest strategic deception of all, Operation Fortitude, by which the Germans were persuaded to believe that the Allied invasion of France would be concentrated on the Pas de Calais, and not Normandy.

As early as 1942, Tar Robertson's team could be justly proud of its efforts. Scores of spies had been rounded up with the aid of the Most Secret Sources, and many had been recruited as double agents. Yet the B1A team remained in a state of deep anxiety, beset by the possibility that a spy could slip through the mesh, attempt to contact an agent already operating in Britain, discover that he was being controlled, and then blow the entire double-cross network.

Those fears were exacerbated when the body of a man named Englebertus Fukken, alias William Ter Braak, was discovered in

Cambridge. A Dutch agent, Ter Braak had parachuted into Britain in November 1940 but five months later, after running out of money, he had climbed into a public air-raid shelter and shot himself in the head with his German pistol. If Ter Braak could survive undetected in Britain for so long, then other German agents must be at large. Masterman voiced the nagging fear of every wartime spycatcher: 'We were obsessed by the idea that there might be a large body of spies over and above those whom we controlled.'

Moreover, MI5 could not ignore the exceptionally low grade of the spies it had caught. Indeed, the level of ineptitude among the captured spies was such that some in the intelligence service wondered if they were being deliberately planted as decoys: 'Could any intelligence service let alone one run by the super-efficient Germans, be so incompetent?' wondered Ewen Montagu, the naval intelligence officer on the Twenty Committee. Perhaps the Germans were training up a troop of super-spies to follow the dubious duds they had sent over to date. Perhaps an altogether better class of spy was already lurking undetected in Britain, or on the way?

Tar Robertson's spy-hunters therefore pricked up their ears when, early in February 1942, a reference to a hitherto unknown agent, codenamed Fritz, was picked up by British interceptors, decoded by Bletchley Park, and passed to the intelligence services. To judge from the intercepts, the Germans were taking a great deal of trouble over Fritz, who was also referred to as 'C', and sometimes as 'E'. In May, the Paris branch of the Abwehr was instructed to buy a new set of clothes for Fritz. The following week, Nantes demanded a new wireless set from the stocks of captured British equipment. In June, the listeners discovered, some 9,500 francs had been spent on his teeth, damaged during a failed parachute jump – more money than most German spies were allocated for an entire mission.

The Nantes Abwehr began to refer to Fritz as Fritzchen, the diminutive form of the name, suggesting a certain intimacy with this new recruit. From the Most Secret Sources it appeared that Stephan von Gröning, already identified by British intelligence as head of the Nantes Abwehr branch, was particularly taken with Fritz. In June he boasted to Paris that Fritz could 'now prepare sabotage material unaided'. In July he insisted that Fritz was utterly loyal, declaring that 'any connection with the enemy is out of the question'. Paris, more sceptical, replied by wondering if the word 'not' had been accidentally omitted from Von Gröning's message.

Meanwhile, the Radio Security Service reported that Fritz, plainly a novice wireless operator, was practising Morse from the Nantes Abwehr branch, using a variation of the Vigenère code known as Gronsfeld. At first his transmissions had been clumsy, and when he tried to transmit faster he merely succeeded 'in making corrupt characters and in fumbling', but he was improving rapidly. 'When he arrives in this country,' the Radio Security Service reported, 'he will send his messages in English.' After listening to Fritz 'practically every day for several weeks' the interceptor had 'learned to recognise his unmistakable style and to record its peculiarities', the telltale 'fist'. His messages sometimes ended with a cheery '73', shorthand for 'Best regards', or 'FF', meaning 'Is my message decipherable?'; he routinely signed off with the laughing sign, 'HU HU HA HO', then the insulting '99', meaning 'go to hell', or words to that effect. Fritz was turning into a first-rate radio operator, even if his messages were rather peculiar, and sometimes positively offensive.

By late summer, MI5 had assembled a thick dossier on Fritz. But they still did not know his real name, his mission, or the date and time of his planned arrival in Britain. And as for the identity of this shadowy associate nicknamed Bobby the Pig, with the regal appetite and the elephantine toilet habits, that, too, remained a mystery.

8

The Mosquito

One morning, Von Gröning handed Chapman a gun: a shiny American Colt revolver, with a loaded chamber. Chapman had never held a gun before. When he asked why he needed this weapon, Von Gröning replied vaguely that he might want it 'to shoot his way out of any difficulties he might encounter'. Leo taught him how to aim and fire it, using a target erected in the grounds of La Bretonnière, and soon he claimed he could hit a franc coin from 50 feet away.

The revolver was just one sign of Von Gröning's growing trust. The cadaverous Praetorius no longer shadowed his every step, and he was allowed to take walks alone with Bobby, though instructed to remain close to the villa. He was permitted to move out of his top-floor room (having carefully disguised the holes in the wainscoting) and into a bedroom in the gardener's cottage, so that he could practise mixing explosives and incendiary mixtures in the laboratory whenever he desired. The homemade bombs were getting bigger, and more sophisticated. He practised making underwater fuses, and tossing them into the duckpond. There were various tree stumps in the grounds, and Chapman was encouraged to try blowing them up. On one occasion he packed too much dynamite into a large oak stump, which exploded with such force that chunks of burning wood were blasted into the garden of the house next door, narrowly missing a neighbour. Von Gröning was livid. Chapman was not quite the explosives expert he thought he was. While attempting to construct a sulphuric acid fuse, the volatile mixture exploded, burning his hand, singeing off a hank of hair and covering his face with smuts. A French doctor bandaged the hand, and Chapman took to his bed. 'I was suffering more from shock than anything,' he wrote later.

Visitors continued to arrive at La Bretonnière, some to inspect Chapman's progress, others to talk to Von Gröning or to undergo training. One of these was a Frenchman referred to only as 'Pierre', a collaborator with round glasses who, in Chapman's words, 'made all the right Heil Hitler noises'. Pierre belonged to a Breton separatist group, 'Bretagne pour les Bretons', and he was undergoing training as a fifth columnist in case an Allied invasion forced a German withdrawal. On another occasion Chapman was allowed to be present during a meeting with two men, one of whom was introduced as 'Monsieur Ferdinand' and the other, a lad of about eighteen, who appeared quite petrified. These were members of a Gaullist cell, apparently planning to leave France via an established escape route and join the Free French in London. Monsieur Ferdinand, it seemed, was prepared to smuggle Chapman along with them, for the right price. Von Gröning was clearly exploring alternative ways to get Chapman into Britain.

Von Gröning and his protégé grew closer. Chapman's own father had been distant, when he wasn't absent entirely, and he had not seen him now for a decade. Von Gröning, avuncular and apparently kindly, stepped into the role. The affection was not feigned on either part. In the evenings, while Von Gröning soaked up the brandy, Chapman would listen rapt as the older man talked of art, music and literature. They discovered a shared pleasure in the novels of H.G. Wells and the poetry of Tennyson. Very occasionally Von Gröning would stray into politics or military matters. He remained convinced that Germany would win the war, and that any attempt by the Allies to invade France would result in 'a tremendous bloodbath'; but his was the assessment of an experienced soldier, not a statement of ideology. To Chapman's surprise, he praised the tactical skill of the Allied invasion of North Africa, and described the British raid on nearby St Nazaire as 'very cleverly planned and excellently carried out'. In August the Allies launched the disastrous Dieppe raid on France's northern coast, with the loss of 4,000 men killed, wounded, or captured. The German victory was celebrated with a party at La Bretonnière, but Von Gröning also raised a toast to the 'courage and daring' of the Allied commandos.

If Von Gröning's view of the war was nuanced and balanced, then that of his deputy was precisely the opposite. Praetorius and Von Gröning had never warmed to one another. Praetorius regarded his boss as the snobbish remnant of an old world, while the younger man was altogether too enthralled by Hitler for Von Gröning's liberal tastes. The young Nazi insisted the scale of Russian losses meant victory on the Eastern Front was imminent. Stalingrad would fall in 1943, to be followed by a 'full-scale attack on Britain with all main forces from Europe and the Russian Front'. Rommel would conquer all, he insisted, while the prospect of a 'terrific Blitz' on Britain, the land he so admired, sent Praetorius into spasms of delight: 'You can imagine what it would be like with all of our Stukas and all of the men who have been trained and hardened and toughened,' Praetorius exclaimed. 'What could the Americans do?' Chapman was beginning to find him extremely irritating.

One morning in mid-summer, Von Gröning instructed Chapman to pack his bags: he was going to Berlin with 'Thomas' for the next phase of his training. In the early hours of a foggy morning, the train from Paris pulled up in a small railway station on the outskirts of the German capital. A car was waiting for them. Chapman asked where they were heading. Praetorius seemed tense and embarrassed. 'It is rather awkward at the present moment because if anyone realises you are British we should both be shot without any questions being asked.' He then added politely: 'Would you mind not asking any more questions?' They seemed to be passing through densely wooded suburbs, but it was still dark outside and the driver had deliberately dimmed his headlights, so that Chapman could see almost nothing. From the faint shimmer of dawn on the horizon, he judged they were heading north.

After a drive of twenty-five minutes, they passed through a pair of iron gates guarded by three sentries in military uniform, down a long drive lined with flower beds and through a high stone arch, before pulling up in front of a small *Schloss* with a tower, surrounded by trees, a high stone wall and barbed wire fences. At the door stood a man in early middle age, short but athletically built, with a dignified air. His wife, rather taller, hovered anxiously in the background; pictures of their children were arranged in the hall. The little man introduced himself as 'Herr Doktor'. He explained that Chapman was free to wander the castle grounds between lessons, but should on no account try to leave the estate.

Wojch had been a skilled teacher of practical sabotage, but Chapman's new tutor was in a different league. Over the next week Chapman would be given an intensive course in the very latest explosive technology, by a master of the subject. MI5 later identified him as one Dr Ackerman, a professional chemist, and one of the most knowledgeable explosives experts in Germany. Chapman was shown into a laboratory, with rows of cork-stopped glass bottles, test tubes, thermos flasks, measuring scales, pestles and mortars. Patiently, painstakingly, the expert introduced Chapman to an unimagined universe of lethal science, the arcane secrets of explosives, burning mixtures, booby traps and delayed sabotage.

He taught Chapman how to make a time-fuse from a cheap wristwatch, by inserting a small screw with two nuts on it into the celluloid face and then attaching one end of electrical wire connected to a torch battery via the winding mechanism; when the small hand touched the screw, a charge would pass from the battery into a fuse and ignite the explosion. Next he took an alarm clock, and demonstrated how to delay an explosion for up to fourteen hours, by linking the detonator to the winding spring. If no clock or watch was available, he could make a fuse by filling an ink bottle with sulphuric acid, and placing a strip of cardboard between glass and lid; the acid would slowly eat away the cardboard, finally making contact with the fuse screwed into the lid, where the heat of the reaction would detonate the explosive charge.

Next, he took a large lump of coal from the scuttle, and showed Chapman how to drill a hole in it 6-inches deep and pack this with explosives and detonator, disguising the hole with plasticine, boot polish and coal dust. Placed in the coalbunkers of a ship or train, the device would be invisible and inert, until shovelled into the furnace where the heat would ignite the explosion.

Chapman was taught how to dynamite munitions trains and petrol dumps, how to pack an attaché case with explosives and then place pyjamas or a towel on top, to muffle the alarm-clock fuse inside. He learned how to construct a booby trap from a package that exploded when the string around a parcel was cut: inside the string were two strands of wire insulated from one another, so that when cut with scissors an electric circuit was completed, setting off the explosion. Ackerman drew diagrams showing how to connect a series of linked explosives with dynamite wire and detonating fuse, and explained the formula for calculating how much high explosive would be needed to bring down a bridge (*length x breadth x depth x 2 = number of grams of explosive required*). Some of Ackerman's techniques were diabolically cunning: placing a dead butterfly over the wire detonator attached to a railway line would ensure the casual observer would never spot the device, and when the train passed over, the charge would explode, derailing the locomotive.

The little explosives teacher neither smoked nor drank, and paused only for meals. Chapman decided he was a perfectionist:

'He insisted on exact proportions, never hurrying, grinding everything very small and mixing it very carefully.' The ingredients needed to create a bomb could be bought over the counter at British chemists, Ackerman explained: potassium chlorate was a common slug killer, potassium nitrate, a fertiliser, potassium permanganate, a throat gargle; the British used ferric oxide as a floor stain, and ground aluminium as a silver paint powder. The lectures ran on late into the evening. After supper, Ackerman would pull up a chair beside the fire and continue his tutorials, sometimes calling on Praetorius to help translate technical terms.

After five days, the doctor finally seemed satisfied, and Chapman was exhausted. He and Praetorius were picked up by the same driver in the middle of the night, and driven back to the station in darkness.

Back at La Bretonnière, Chapman was warmly greeted by Von Gröning, who announced that he had devised a small test for him. A friend, one Major Meier, was responsible for security in the local factories, including the nearby Battignolle locomotive works. Von Gröning had boasted to Meier that he was training up a sabotage agent, a former burglar who could break into anything; he bet he could even place a dummy bomb in the locomotive factory. Major Meier had accepted the wager. A few nights later, Chapman and Leo hauled themselves over the barbed wire surrounding the factory, slipped passed the slumbering guard and placed a package, addressed to Major Meier, alongside the main office. Von Gröning was delighted; with the money from the wager he threw yet another party in honour of 'Fritz'.

Chapman went back to his mephitic potions in the gardener's cottage. The successful raid on the locomotive works had been enjoyable, but after nearly five months in La Bretonnière, he was growing bored, and frustrated by the enforced chastity. Leaving aside the whores of Nantes, he had barely seen a woman. The others laughed about the lack of female company, joking that they lived 'like bloody monks'.

One evening, Chapman, Albert and Wojch went out on a 'spree' in Nantes, where they picked up some girls in one of the official cars. Unluckily, a Gestapo officer spotted the women climbing into their car and an official complaint was filed. When it reached Von Gröning's desk, he exploded. 'There was a hell of a lot of trouble,' Chapman wrote. Wojch suffered the brunt of Von Gröning's fury: the rotund saboteur with the pearl tie-pin was banished to a unit of the Wachkommando based in distant Rocquencourt near Paris. Chapman never saw him again. In a message to his bosses, Von Gröning noted primly that Fritz, though ideal in every other respect, was apparently prone to what he called 'undesirable emotional activity'.

As always, when bored and sexually stymied, Chapman lapsed into what he called his 'nihilistic' frame of mind. His mood darkened still further when he raised a subject that had been troubling him ever since leaving Romainville, and asked for permission to write to Tony Faramus. Von Gröning refused, but said he would send the young man a food parcel. A little later, Chapman inquired once more: 'Could something be done for him?' Von Gröning told him that this was 'impossible', and changed the subject. Chapman now descended into a dark depression. He would lie on his bed for hours, smoking, and staring at the ceiling. At one point he even asked 'if he could return to the camp at Romainville'. Von Gröning realised that unless he moved fast, and put Chapman to work, he might lose this mercurial young spy prodigy altogether.

On 29 August 1942, Chapman was summoned to Von Gröning's study and presented with a typed sheet of paper. He was told to read it and, if he agreed with the terms, to sign it. The document was a contract, a formally executed agreement to spy on his own country that is surely unique in the annals of legal history. The first section was a list of prohibitions: Chapman must never divulge to anyone the names of his German contacts in Jersey, France or Germany, the places he had been, or the things he had learned. The penalty for violating any of these clauses would be death. Chapman would undertake to spy in the interests of the German High Command, and faithfully perform whatever mission he was set by the Abwehr. As compensation, he would be paid the following sums: while in France he would receive 12,000 francs a month; from the date of his departure, he would be paid 300 Reichsmarks a month, and payment would continue should he be captured; on his return, having completed his mission to the satisfaction of the Abwehr, he would receive the sum of 150,000 Reichsmarks. Chapman estimated this was the equivalent of about £15,000 – in fact, the value was nearer to £250, or around £7,300 at today's prices. The contract was not with the German government, but a personal legal agreement between Chapman and his spymaster: Von Gröning had already signed it, in the name S. Graumann (Doktor).

The final clause was a triumph of German bureaucratic thinking: Chapman would be legally obliged to pay all relevant taxes on these sums in France. The German secret service was about to send Chapman on a mission of treachery in which it was likely he would be killed or executed, and they were worrying about his tax return.

As Chapman was digesting the terms of this extraordinary deal, the German spymaster asked him a question. If Scotland Yard caught him, approximately how many years could Chapman expect to spend in prison? Chapman had considered that question many times himself. He replied that he would probably receive a sentence of between fifteen and twenty years. The older man then turned to Praetorius and observed: 'I don't suppose there would be much danger of him surrendering to the police then.'

Chapman signed the contract, but later found himself pondering that apparently offhand comment. Graumann, a man he had come to admire, had chosen him not because he was special, but because he was a criminal with a past so crooked he would never dare run to the authorities. Chapman had always known that was part of the German calculation, but the remark stung, and it stuck.

Filing away the signed contract, Von Gröning began, for the first time, to outline Chapman's mission: in a few weeks he would be parachuted into Britain with a wireless and enough money to survive for a long period. He would then find a place to hide out and gather a quantity of explosives, with help from his criminal associates if needed. There were many important tasks Chapman could perform in Britain, but his primary target was to sabotage the aircraft factory manufacturing the Mosquito bomber in Hatfield, Hertfordshire.

The De Havilland Mosquito – or *Anopheles de Havillandus* as military wags liked to call it – had proved a lethal nuisance to the Nazis ever since it went into production in 1940. Indeed, its effect on the German High Command was positively malarial. Designed and built at the De Havilland Aircraft Company factory outside London, it was a revolutionary military aircraft. Constructed almost entirely of wood, with a two-man crew and no defensive guns, the little plane could carry 4,000 lbs of bombs to Berlin. With two Rolls-Royce Merlin engines and a top speed of 400 mph it could usually outrun enemy fighters. The Mosquito, nicknamed 'the Wooden Wonder', could be assembled, cheaply, by cabinetmakers and carpenters. It could be used for photo-reconnaissance, night-fighting, U-boat killing, mine-laying and transport, but its main task was target bombing, and being so light and accurate it could destroy a single building with minimal harm to civilians. In the course of the war, Mosquitoes would pick off the Gestapo Headquarters in Oslo, Shell House in Copenhagen, and Amiens Jail.

Reichsmarschall Hermann Göring, Head of the Luftwaffe, was particularly infuriated by the persistent little Mosquito; the mere mention of the plane could send him into a rage. 'It makes me furious when I see the Mosquito,' he once ranted. 'I turn green and yellow with envy. The British, who can afford aluminium better than we can, knock together a beautiful wooden aircraft that every piano factory over there is building, and they give it a speed that they have now increased yet again. What do you make of that? There is nothing the British do not have. They have the geniuses and we have the nincompoops. After the war is over I'm going to buy a British radio set – then at least I'll own *something* that has always worked.'

For reasons therefore both military and political, the Abwehr had been devising a plan to combat the Mosquito for months. If the De Havilland production line could be stopped, by crippling the factory boilers and generator, this could tip the air war in Germany's favour, demonstrate the worth of Von Gröning's new agent, and boost the Abwehr's reputation. It might also mollify the irascible Reichsmarschall.

That afternoon, Von Gröning sent an exultant wireless message to Paris, reporting that he had conducted 'preliminary detailed discussions' with Fritz, and persuaded him to sign a contract. The message was picked up in Britain, where the MI5 officer monitoring the Fritz traffic remarked ominously: 'Things seem at last to be coming to a head.'

9

Under Unseen Eyes

The contract in Chapman's hands may have been legally un-
enforceable, signed with a false name, and frankly absurd, but it
had the desired psychological effect. The prospect of adventure
sent Chapman's spirits soaring once more. The drunken camaraderie of La Bretonnière was pleasant, to be sure, but at the back
of his mind was Freda and the baby in England; also Betty; also
Vera, his ex-wife; and, if none of the aforementioned worked
out, then any number of Soho sirens.

The days accumulated in a succession of tests, trials, details
and delays. The ugly spycatcher from Angers returned, in a
'terrific Chrysler with a wireless', to witness a demonstration of
Chapman's sabotage and shooting skills: he shot a line of wine
glasses from fifteen paces, one after the other, and set off an
acid fuse. The next performance was for a colonel from a
Panzer division, who appeared in a Mercedes: Chapman blew
up a tree stump in a timed explosion using batteries and a
wristwatch. The same evening Von Gröning announced that
he had tickets for the Folies-Bergère, the music hall that was
still playing to full houses in occupied Paris. Chapman was
excited at the prospect of a night out in Paris, although his
pleasure palled somewhat when he overheard Von Gröning
remark on the train that 'the chief wanted to see him'.
Chapman was not being taken to enjoy the spectacle; once
again, he *was* the spectacle.

That evening, as they entered the famous opera house in the 9th Arrondissement, Chapman heard his spymaster whisper to Thomas: 'Let Fritz go first, and *he* will just sit behind.' The show was already underway in a froth of petticoated dancers doing the can-can, when two men in civilian clothes quietly entered and sat directly behind them. One had a moustache and a pronounced limp: 'He kept looking at me the whole time, sort of behind his programme,' Chapman recalled. This individual was most probably Rudolf Bamler, head of Abwehr counter-intelligence and one of the few die-hard Nazis in the organisation. After the show Von Gröning left by taxi, while Praetorius and Thomas walked back to the hotel, pausing to look in the shop windows: 'Each time I looked,' wrote Chapman. 'I saw these two men very carefully studying me.'

Chapman was relieved to get back to the Grand Hotel. As he and Praetorius walked to their rooms, he heard American voices coming from Von Gröning's suite. He turned to his minder: 'Americans?'

'No, it's just two of our fellows having a game,' said Praetorius, quickly. But that evening, by opening a cupboard door and pressing his ear to the folding partition that separated his room from that of Von Gröning, he was sure he could hear his chief talking to two Americans. One of them was saying: 'Well, we would like to see the guy.' Chapman felt certain the 'guy' was him; he recalled that Graumann had remarked that if the De Havilland sabotage was successful, he would be sent on 'a big mission to America'.

La Bretonnière had offered a brief feeling of freedom, but now he had the sensation of being watched and monitored as surely as if he had been back in prison with the warders spying through the slot in the iron door. Everyone, it seemed, was keeping an eye on Chapman: his comrades in Nantes, senior Nazi officials, American spies and even, perhaps, his own countrymen.

One night, in the Café de France in Nantes, Chapman caught sight of a young man regarding him intently from a corner table.

Von Gröning had warned that he was 'in all probability being watched by the British', and had shown him some photographs of suspected agents, none of whom he recognised. Now he was convinced he was being tailed. The fellow was in his twenties, well built, with a side parting, a grey suit and a 'West End' look to him that seemed oddly familiar. Chapman looked away, disconcerted, and when he looked back a moment later, the man had vanished. Chapman did not mention the incident to Von Gröning, but the urge to escape grew stronger: he must get to Britain, before the British got to him.

In September, Chapman was escorted back to Ackerman's *Schloss* in Berlin, arriving once more in the dead of night. 'You have remembered everything,' the little German chemist declared, after he had thoroughly tested his pupil. 'I am highly satisfied with you.' The scientist then launched into a detailed disquisition on exactly how to blow up the De Havilland plant. If the boilers were linked, he should explode the central one using 15 kilograms of dynamite packed into an attaché case and a delay fuse of at least half an hour. The blast should wreck the other two, and three 80-ton boilers, the scientist explained, would mean 240 tons of matter 'exploding in all directions', which should destroy the generator at the same time.

The chemist departed, to be replaced by an older man in civilian clothes, who announced, in English, that he had come to instruct Fritz in the use of 'secret ink'. From a briefcase, he produced a sheet of white paper, and what appeared to be a matchstick with a white head. Chapman was instructed to place the writing paper on a newspaper, and then clean the paper on both sides for ten minutes using a wad of cotton wool wiped 'in a rotary motion'. The paper was placed on a sheet of glass, and Chapman was shown how to sketch a message in block capitals using the matchstick, each word separated by dashes. The stick left no visible mark. Chapman was told he could now write in pencil on both sides of the paper, or in ink on the reverse side from the secret writing, as if it was an ordinary letter. The man then vanished, taking the scribbled sheets. When he returned a few hours later, the paper had been immersed in some sort of chemical solution and the secret message had emerged, 'a faint greeny colour', behind the scrawled pencil. The Professor (as Chapman now christened him) handed over two more matchstick pens, and told him to practise his secret writing twice a week. The letters would be forwarded to him, and he would assess their proficiency.

Chapman returned to Nantes by plane and parachute. After taking off from Le Bourget, a Junkers bomber dropped him in a field near the town airfield. The Nantes unit had been deployed in the area as a reception committee, but Chapman made his own way to the airfield and announced himself to the sentry as 'Fritz'.

Back at la Bretonnière, Von Gröning covered the dining table with hundreds of aerial photographs of potential landing spots – Britain spread out 'like a mosaic'. They agreed that the village of Mundford, north of Thetford in Norfolk, would be ideal, being rural and sparsely populated, but still reasonably near London. He was then shown aerial photographs of the De Havilland factory in Hatfield, pinpointing the precise location of the boiler room.

In preparation for blending in to a country he had not seen for three years, Chapman listened to the BBC at night, and studied the English newspapers along with a London guidebook to refresh his memory of the city streets. Leo was sent to Dieppe to obtain British equipment left over from the raid, while Von Gröning travelled to Berlin in person to collect English paper currency. Chapman was photographed, in a studio in Nantes, to obtain images for his fake identity cards. In it he is leaning forward towards the camera, in matinee idol pose, an oddly intense look on his face. You can almost see the strain of waiting behind his eyes.

The arrangements seemed to gather pace, the final threads weaving together. But then one evening, to Chapman's astonishment, he was taken aside by his German spymaster and asked if he wanted to back out of the mission altogether. 'Look, don't think we're forcing you to go to England, because we have other work if you don't want to go.'

'No,' Chapman replied, momentarily stunned. 'I want to go to England.'

Von Gröning continued: 'If you feel you're not confident that you can do these things, don't go. There's plenty of other work for you here, we can use you on other things.'

Chapman protested that he was ready and able: 'I think I can do what I was set out to do.'

Von Gröning's next suggestion was even more disquieting: would Chapman like Leo to accompany him on this assignment? Chapman had to think fast. With Leo as a minder, his freedom of action would be seriously curtailed, and if the toothless little thug suspected Chapman's motives, he would kill him, on the spot, possibly with his bare hands.

'I don't think that would advisable,' he said quickly. 'Probably one could get through whereas two wouldn't, especially as Leo doesn't speak English.'

Von Gröning dropped the subject, but it had been an unsettling exchange. Was the German warning him, or trying to protect him? He need not have worried; it was another test of his resolve. On 24 September, Von Gröning sent a message to Paris headquarters: 'Fritz is spiritually and physically undoubtedly absolutely fit.'

Like every sprawling bureaucracy, the Abwehr combined nitpicking with inefficiency: first they obtained the wrong type of parachute; then the Luftwaffe seemed unable to locate the correct plane. A bomber was too noisy for a nighttime drop, so inquiries were made for a transport plane from Russia, or the Middle East. The repeated delays frayed everybody's nerves. Finally a Focke-Wulf reconnaissance plane was located, at which point somebody pointed out that several agents had been injured during parachute jumps, so perhaps Fritz should instead be taken to the coast by boat, and then rowed to shore in a rubber dinghy. But what sort of boat?

After much argument, it was agreed to send Fritz by plane. That decision soon became bogged down in a new debate over the drop zone. If Fritz aimed for Thetford, it was argued, the plane might be shot down by night fighters operating around London. The Cambrian Mountains were suggested as an alternative by someone who had plainly never been there. Paris duly instructed Nantes: 'Show Fritz photos of the Cambrian Mountains.' Chapman took one look at these, and dug in his heels. Being dropped over the flatlands of Norfolk was alarming enough, but landing on a frozen Welsh hillside in the middle of winter was a different prospect altogether. Finally, grudgingly, he backed down, and said that if the Abwehr really believed these mountains were 'safer than anywhere else', then so be it. The Welsh hills became the 'new operational objective' and Paris ordered that Fritz be 'made familiar in every detail with conditions in the Cambrian Mountains and means of getting from there to London'. But a few days later the Paris Abwehr chief, exercising every boss's right of irrational self-contradiction, reverted to the original idea, and Mundford was again selected as the target.

Then, in November, just as it seemed all the wrinkles had been ironed out, the entire mission was put on hold. The war lurched into a new phase, Hitler decided to occupy the whole of France, and Chapman was suddenly drafted into the German army.

For several months, the Nazi leadership had been observing the Vichy regime with mounting concern. Since the French collapse in 1940, the collaborationist French government in Vichy, under Henri Philippe Pétain, had been allowed to rule the unoccupied portion of southern France as a puppet-state under Nazi control. But after the Vichy Admiral François Darlan signed an armistice with the Allies in Algeria, Hitler decided to violate the 1940 agreement by invading the zone under Vichy control, in an operation codenamed 'Case Anton'. Every available man would be drafted in to aid the new military occupation, including Eddie Chapman.

The member of the Nantes Abwehr section, now Truppe 3292 of Abwehrkommando 306, were formally attached to an SS division and ordered to head south. The spies donned military clothing: Von Gröning wore the full regalia of a cavalry officer, with double-breasted leather trench coat and forage cap, Praetorius his SS uniform, and the others a variety of military outfits. They looked like the cast of a Gilbert and Sullivan opera. Chapman himself was ordered to dress up in the field green uniform of a lance corporal in the German marines, with a gold-trimmed collar and a yellow swastika armband. He was faintly disappointed that his uniform had no epaulettes, but he was allowed to carry his gun.

On 12 November 1942, Thomas and the others climbed into the Mercedes, while Chapman travelled with Von Gröning in a second car, along with spare tins of petrol, food, and an arsenal of automatic weapons. As they sped south, Chapman passed lines of SS soldiers heading in the same direction and a column of troop-laden trucks that stretched for five miles. French men and women watched from the roadside. To Chapman, some of the bystanders seemed 'shocked, frightened and resentful' but most appeared 'apathetic'. 'There were no scenes or anything,' he noted, 'they just refused to speak and looked very surly as we drove past.' At crossroads and checkpoints, the French gendarmes waved them through and saluted smartly, greeting an occupation they could do nothing to prevent. Several times, the Abwehrkommandos stopped for refreshments, and by the time they reached Limoges, Von Gröning's little war party was, as always, well oiled.

In Limoges, the troop took up billets in a small hotel and linked up with another unit under the command of one Major Reile, a Gestapo officer, who informed them they would be raiding the homes of suspected enemy agents. Armed with pistols and submachine guns, Chapman and the men followed Von Gröning to an apartment building, where they knocked down the door of a flat belonging to one Captaine le Saffre. The suspect had fled, leaving papers strewn everywhere. While the men ransacked the flat, Chapman picked up a handful of papers and stuffed them in his pocket.

At the next house, the troop broke in to find two terrified old ladies cowering under a bed. Von Gröning was dismayed, and even more embarrassed when the women stammered that the man they were looking for had been dead for two years. The German aristocrat had no taste for Gestapo work. By the end of the evening, his troop had raided a dozen houses, most of them empty or occupied by the wrong person, and gathered a grand total of five French suspects, including a seventeen-year-old boy. The terrified Frenchmen, protesting their innocence, were locked in a hotel bedroom without their trousers. Von Gröning later released them all. 'Why should I send them to a concentration camp?' he said. 'They may be guilty, but they may be innocent.' Back at the hotel, Chapman inspected the papers he had gathered from the flat, which appeared to be notes from a diary, 'Rendez-vous with so-and-so at such and such an hour . . .'. He carefully destroyed them.

Truppe 3292's contribution to the occupation had been insignificant: they had netted some 'very small fry' and let them go, looted some booze, and frightened two old women. This still merited a slap-up dinner in celebration. It was Chapman's twenty-eighth birthday. On the way back to Nantes he wondered if his inclusion in the invasion had merely been another part of his training: 'I think it was to see what reaction I would have to the raid.' His reaction was a peculiar one: he had thoroughly enjoyed himself. It was perhaps a sign of his moral confusion, and the effect of living among Nazis for so long, that he would later recall this episode – the midnight raids, the smashing down of doors, the terrified people dragged from their beds, the wearing of his first swastika – as 'a lovely little trip'.

10

The Drop

The invasion of Vichy was Chapman's final test. Having dithered for so long, the Abwehr now swung into action with bewildering speed: Von Gröning announced that Chapman would be leaving for Britain within days. He reported that Fritz seemed 'visibly relieved' by the news. Paris had sent a questionnaire, a detailed list of the intelligence he might usefully supply from Britain, and together they rehearsed the details of his imminent mission.

He would be dropped over Mundford at around two in the morning. Simultaneously, a bombing raid would be carried out 'some place further inland' to draw off any night fighters. On landing he should dig a hole in an inconspicuous spot, and bury his parachute, overalls, helmet, jumping boots, leggings and entrenching tool. Every item would be British-made. Wearing his civilian clothes (they discussed obtaining a British army uniform, but rejected the idea) he should hide out somewhere until dawn and then, using a compass and map, make his way the thirty or so miles to Norwich and take a train to London. Once there, he should make contact with his old accomplice, the notorious Jimmy Hunt, and send his first transmission three days after landing, between 9.45 and 10.15 a.m.. Paris, Nantes and Bordeaux would all be listening out for his signal. Von Gröning here remarked that 'British red tape' would probably mean that if he were captured, it would take some time before British intelligence got around to using him for deception purposes. If there was a long delay, said Von Gröning, he would suspect the worst.

Most importantly his first message, and all subsequent messages, should be preceded by five Fs. This was his 'control sign', the agreed signal that he was operating of his own free will. If the message did not start FFFFF, Von Gröning would realise he had been caught and was transmitting under duress. Naturally, if someone was pretending to be Chapman, they would not know the agreed 'control sign', and Von Gröning would again conclude that he had been captured. Likewise, if a message was preceded by PPPPP, that would be an emergency warning that he was being watched by the security services or tailed by the police.

Thereafter, Chapman would be expected to transmit every morning between 9.45 and 10.15, on an all-mains transmitter of British manufacture taken from a captured British agent, which could be operated inside a room without an external aerial. He should transmit at a set frequency, and take five radio crystals in case of difficulties. All messages should be in English, using the same cipher system but a new code word: CONSTANTINOPLE.* If, for any reason, he could not use his transmitter, he was to insert the following advertisement in the personal column of *The Times*: 'Young couple require small country cottage near Elstree or Watford with modern conveniences.' He would then send messages, using the secret ink, to a safe house in neutral Portugal, addressed to:

Francisco Lopez Da Fonseca
Rua Sao Mamede 50-51
Lisbon

These would be picked up by a German agent in Lisbon, and forwarded to Von Gröning.

* See Appendix 1

The sabotage of the De Havilland aircraft factory (codenamed 'Walter', a reference to Praetorius/Thomas) was Chapman's primary mission, but not his sole objective. He should also gather and send information on US troop movements, particularly convoys, and note destination labels attached to railway freight cars, divisional signs, evidence of shipbuilding and any other military intelligence he could glean. He should also send weather reports to aid bombing raids, specifically describing cloud height, temperature, wind direction and strength, and visibility. To some extent, Chapman could use his own initiative. If the De Havilland premises proved impregnable, he might attack the aircraft propeller factory at Weybridge in Surrey, or sugar and rubber refineries, or merely do 'nuisance work' by leaving bombs in attaché cases in tube station luggage lockers. Von Gröning was reassuring: 'Take your time. Think of things very quietly. It doesn't matter if you don't succeed. Don't run any unnecessary risks. If you can come back we have something else for you to acquit, some other valuable task.' He could, if he wished, recruit more members of the Jelly Gang as accomplices.

In order to pay his criminal contacts, obtain the necessary explosives, and live generally, Chapman would be given £1,000 in used notes (worth approximately £33,000 today). That should be 'enough to be going on with', said Von Gröning, adding that more cash, if needed, could be provided through agents already in Britain. Von Gröning refused to identify these individuals, saying that contact would be arranged by radio. 'Of course our agents are there. We have them, we have the connections, but we have to be very, very careful not to take any risks.' Chapman wondered if Wojch had already been sent ahead to wait for him, help him, or, quite possibly, to spy on him.

Von Gröning continued his briefing. The day before Chapman was ready to carry out the sabotage he should send a message stating: 'Walter is ready to go,' and the time of the planned explosion. Reconnaissance planes would then monitor the effectiveness of the attack.

If Chapman was unlucky enough to fall into the hands of the British secret services, said Von Gröning, he should 'give as little information as possible, offer his services, and ask to be sent back to France'. Then he should immediately contact the Abwehr, which would employ him as a triple agent, after staging 'a number of small acts of sabotage' to convince the British of his bona fides.

Chapman's mission would last three months, after which he was to make his way back to France, in any one of three ways: a U-boat could be sent to pick him up off the English or Scottish coast, at a location to be arranged by wireless; alternatively, he could travel to the Republic of Ireland, where there were 'various people who would assist him to return'. The third and, Von Gröning stressed, the best escape route, would be to go to neutral Portugal. Once in Lisbon, he could make his way to the safe house on Rua Sao Mamede, introduce himself as Fritz to Senhor Fonseca, and give the password: 'Joli Albert'. Chapman's safe passage would then be arranged through the German consulate. Once back in France, he would receive his money, and a hero's welcome.

Von Gröning painted a tantalising picture of the financial and other rewards Chapman could expect from a grateful Third Reich. After making a report in Berlin, he would be sent on an extended 'holiday', with visits to all the major cities in Germany. He might be asked to carry out an important mission in the US, but he could be posted wherever he wished, and perhaps even receive his own Abwehr command. Chapman had once remarked that he would like to attend one of the great Berlin rallies where Hitler addressed the rapt crowds. Von Gröning promised that this could be arranged. Indeed, he would do more: he would get Chapman a good seat 'in the first or second row' even if it meant dressing him in the uniform of a high official. Von Gröning had never shown much enthusiasm for Hitler himself, but seemed only too happy to smuggle Chapman into a Nazi rally and place his spy as close as possible to the Führer.

Chapman judged this a good moment to raise, once again, the subject of Faramus in Romainville. Von Gröning was soothing. 'Don't you worry,' he said, 'we're going to send Faramus a parcel. I haven't had news from him myself but I'm going to look up the question and see what's happening about him – he'll be well looked after.'

If Chapman was reassured, he should not have been, for poor Faramus had by now been swallowed up by the Holocaust. No longer a hostage for Chapman's good behaviour, he was now but a mote in the toils of a murderous bureaucracy. Chapman believed that he still held his friend's life in his hands; in fact, even if he had failed or defected, no one would have remembered to kill Tony Faramus. He had been selected for death already. At the moment Chapman was packing his bags in Nantes, Faramus was being transported by cattle car to the Nazi concentration camp at Buchenwald.

Faramus had been summoned from his cell in Romainville without explanation, taken to a transit camp at Compiègne, and then loaded onto a cattle train with 120 other prisoners, in a truck intended for eight animals. Death came slowly, by suffocation, dysentery, thirst. After a few days, 'it was hard to tell the living from the dead, so small had become the margin between them'. The living stood shoulder to shoulder with the dead, for there was no room to fall. Five days after leaving Compiège, the death train drew up at Buchenwald, near Weimar. Of the 120 people packed into the truck, sixty-five were still alive, and those barely. Among the survivors was little Tony Faramus, who pondered, as he was led away to slavery: 'It was hard to believe that such carnage was the work of man.'

On 12 December 1942, Von Gröning threw a farewell party at la Bretonnière. A goose was killed and roasted, and toast after toast was drunk to the success of Chapman, Fritz, Little Fritz. Everyone sang *Lili Marlene*. Von Gröning, who had drunk to excess even by his own extreme standards, was in an ebullient mood: 'If you do this for us, you will have nothing more to worry about. Your whole future will be made when you come back. Don't you worry, it will be quite alright. I'll have another bottle of champagne with you.'

Praetorius ushered Chapman to one side. He seemed uncomfortable, fidgeting and twitching even more than usual, and whispered: 'I have rather an embarrassing thing to do, but for every agent we do it, but it is only matter of form and I hope you won't be insulted.'

'What is it?'

Praetorius explained that before heading to Britain, Chapman must be thoroughly searched, for any labels, receipts, tickets or other items from France or Germany that might indicate he was a spy from occupied territory. Chapman could not be allowed to leave with 'anything which could possibly be recognised as coming from us'.

'You don't mind?' Praetorius asked.

'Of course not.'

So far from objecting, Chapman was grateful for the inadvertent warning from 'Thomas'. When everyone else had staggered drunkenly to bed, Chapman took all the notes he had made, the radio frequencies, formulae, codes and names, and burned every scrap.

In the morning, a doctor arrived to give Chapman a full medical examination, and then, with Praetorius and Von Gröning standing over him, he packed his British canvas rucksack with everything that a German spy might possibly need in enemy territory, and much that he might not:

1 entrenching tool
1 wireless
1 Colt revolver, loaded, with spare chamber
2 handkerchiefs
12 detonators, carefully packed in sawdust in case he hit the ground hard
chocolate

grape jelly
1 hat
1 razor
1 compass
1 matchbox, with 'matches' for secret writing
1 pair spectacles (clear glass)
2 clean shirts
1 British army map
1 ID card in the name of George Clarke of Hammersmith
1 ID card in the name of Morgan O'Bryan of Dublin,
electrical engineer.

Every item was either of British manufacture, or made to appear
so. Even his wallet was filled with everyday items, taken from the
dead at Dieppe: two deck-chair tickets, one Torquay golf club
ticket, one YMCA hostel receipt, and family photographs, all of
people Chapman had never met. Here, too, was Betty's love
note on Royal Yacht Hotel headed paper, now badly creased
and frayed – the only authentic item among the frauds.

With a peculiar expression, Von Gröning now handed Chapman a single brown pill, wrapped in a tiny cellophane package,
explaining that Chapman could swallow it 'if there was any
trouble'. The word 'trouble' did not need defining. Both men
knew what happened to captured German spies; what might be
done to a spy who was also British did not require elaboration.

Chapman bade farewell to the men of the unit, to Bobby the
Pig, and to La Bretonnière, the only 'home', as he put it, he had
known in ten years. He had found 'genuine comradeship' here,
albeit with some remarkably nasty people. Before leaving, he
handed Praetorius 500 francs, and told him to buy a drink for the
boys.

That night Chapman, Von Gröning and Praetorius stayed at
the Hôtel des Ambassadeurs in Paris. In the morning, Prateorius
searched him as promised, and then handed over a canvas bag
sealed with oilskin containing £990 in used notes of varying

denominations. Had Chapman looked inside the moneybag, he
might have spotted that the wads of money were held together
by bands stamped 'Reichsbank, Berlin', with 'England' written
on them in pencil. In an unbelievable act of thoughtlessness, the
Abwehr had given Chapman a cash package that immediately
identified him as a German spy. Having checked every inch of
his clothing for clues, Praetorius had handed Chapman a death
sentence in used notes.

Waiting at Le Bourget airfield was a Luftwaffe colonel whom
Chapman recognised from his parachute practice. The colonel
seemed to know all about Chapman's mission, for he discussed
with him the merits of the Mosquito bomber, and the importance
of halting its production. 'You have beautiful planes,' he added.

The colonel introduced a pilot, a tall, blond young man
wearing an Iron Cross and struck Chapman as 'extremely shy',
who then led Chapman across the tarmac towards a sleek black
plane, 25-feet long with twin engines and machine guns mounted
on each side. This, the pilot explained with pride, was a Focke-
Wulf of the latest design, adapted for parachuting. A square
section had been cut from the floor of the fuselage, and replaced
by a wooden panel, wedged tight with packing material. Pulling a
release handle caused the trap door to drop away. Chapman
would be taken across the Channel by a three-man crew: the
young pilot, Leutnant Fritz Schlichting, Überleutnant Karl
Ischinger, the navigator and commander, and an *Unteroffizier* as
wireless operator and gunner. They would be communicating by
an intercom 'of the larynx type'. Chapman noticed that the pilot
appeared to be deliberately standing in front of the control panel,
as if to prevent his passenger from inspecting it.

At the hut, Chapman slipped his flying overalls on top of his
civilian clothes, the old suit that he had taken to Jersey all those
years ago. As he buttoned up the flying suit, strapped on his
kneepads and laced up his landing boots, Chapman noticed that
his hands were shaking.

There was a delay as they waited for a weather report from

Britain. Chapman smoked cigarette after cigarette. To make conversation, Chapman asked what the chances were of being shot down by flak or night fighters. The young pilot laughed, and said they could 'evade attack' using a device to deflect sound: from the ground the plane would appear to be at least one kilometre behind its actual position. Chapman realised that none of the crew was wearing a parachute, and felt a tiny surge of reassurance.

Shortly after 11 p.m. the pilot beckoned Chapman towards the plane. Von Gröning and the Luftwaffe colonel walked alongside as he clomped over the tarmac. It was slow going, encumbered by the knee pads and landing boots, the parachute and bulky kitbag strapped to his back. Chapman shook hands with the friend whose real name he did not know, who declared that the moment he received the first message from Fritz he would break out the champagne at La Bretonnière. 'We shall be waiting, the Colonel and I,' said Von Gröning. 'We shall definitely be waiting.'

Chapman squeezed through the cockpit hatch, and the pilot instructed him to kneel over the floor hole, facing the rear of the plane. The gunner was already seated at the rear. The navigator scrambled in behind.

At 11.25 the Focke-Wulf soared upwards from Le Bourget into the darkness. The sole illumination inside the cockpit was a tiny hand torch held by the wireless operator. As the plane banked, Chapman caught glimpses of many small lights in the distance. They climbed higher. He thought he could smell sea air. Suddenly the cockpit was freezing, despite the meagre warmth from a heater. The wireless man indicated that Chapman should strap on his oxygen mask. From time to time the navigator would write something on a small piece of paper, and hand it over his head to the pilot. If Chapman lay face down, the pack squeezed the breath out of him. On his knees, he was unable to straighten his back or turn around. Chapman felt cramp creeping up his body. Something warm and tickling ran over his chin. He had failed to strap the mask tightly enough;

blood was seeping from his nose. As they crossed over the English coast north of Skegness, he saw searchlights slicing the sky. The plane seemed to spiral down, the engines in a fighting scream, and then rose again. Passing over the Cambridgeshire fens, the Focke-Wulf performed a strange figure-of-eight dance in the sky. Chapman fastened his helmet and tied his parachute cord to a bolt overhead. The crew seemed unperturbed: 'Far from being nervous or apprehensive, they laughed and joked,' as if on a joy ride.

Chapman felt the pilot tap him on the back. He tore off the oxygen mask, got to his knees, and yanked the release handle. The trap door vanished beneath him, and he jolted downwards, but instead of falling through air, he was suspended, head down, on the underside of the plane, the air rushing past him, tearing his breath away. His outsized pack had caught on the sides of the hatch. He dangled, helpless, for what seemed like an age, but was in truth no more than ten seconds. Then he felt a blow in the small of his back – the boot of the wireless operator – and he was somersaulting down. A loud crack, a jolt, and the parachute obediently fluttered open above him. Suddenly it was utterly quiet. The blood dripped off his chin. In the far distance, he saw searchlights jousting in the dark. Below he heard the wail of a siren, signalling the all-clear. For a strange moment he wondered if that might be France down there, and not England. Could this be another of Von Gröning's tests? For twelve minutes, he drifted down through the still, windless night, towards a spot in the darkness below, which was at least twenty miles from where he was supposed to be.

11

Martha's Exciting Night

At 1.48 on the morning of 16 December, Sergeant Joseph Vail of the Littleport Police heard what he thought must be two separate planes, or one with two very powerful engines, over the west side of the town. An alert was immediately relayed to every police station in the area: 'Keep a close watch in area Wisbech – Downham Market – Ely as a plane has been spotted circling in the neighbourhood having come south from the Lincolnshire coast. Suggest it might be Nightcap, although not in expected area.' Another telephone call was made to a number in Whitehall, then another to the home of Major Tar Robertson, who got up, and put on his tartan trousers. At this point, Eddie Chapman's feet had not yet touched the ground.

Operation Nightcap was the codename for MI5's 'Fritz-trap'. As early as October a message had been intercepted revealing that Fritz would 'very soon be going on his holiday', and a warning had been sent to security service liaison officers in three different areas of the country to expect the arrival of an enemy agent:

Agent X is probably under 30 and about six feet tall. He may use the name Chapman. He speaks English, French and German. He is a trained wireless operator. It is possible that Agent X may be supplied with means of committing suicide e.g. poison tablets. On arrest he should therefore be immediately searched, detained pending inquiries and sent up to London under escort.

For months, British radio interceptors had monitored every dot and dash of the Fritz traffic, until they imagined they knew the man intimately. From the Most Secret Sources, the counter-espionage team had obtained a broad idea of Fritz's mission, although not of the plan to target the De Havilland Mosquito factory. The traffic suggested that there were three possible drop-zones: Mundford, North Norfolk, and the Cambrian Mountains, with the last-named regarded as the most probable. Robertson had even discovered Fritz's real surname, although this initially proved more of a red herring since MI5 had spent several fruitless days investigating the entirely innocent Robert William Chapman, a soldier who had been reported missing in the Western Desert and who might, it was surmised, have been recruited by the Abwehr while a prisoner of war.

The spycatchers of B1A knew the details of Fritz's dentistry, the names on his fake ID cards, and even the approximate length of his hair after the Most Secret Sources reported: 'It may be of intelligence interest that Fritzchen said in clear at 1300 GMT today that he "could not keep his schedule this morning as he was having a hair cut".' They knew that his password was 'Joli Albert', the colour of his boots, and the poisonous contents of his turn-ups.

But MI5 also knew that the chance of catching Fritz, even with the information from the Most Secret Sources, was slim.

There had been much debate within B-Division, the counter-espionage branch of MI5, about the best way to ensnare him. A full police dragnet, with roadblocks and house-to-house searches, was rejected on the grounds that it offered 'too many possibilities of leakage and subsequent press notices'. If an enemy agent was alerted to the hunt, the Germans might realise that their messages were being read, and the Most Secret Sources must be protected at all costs. Another option was to prepare a 'flying column' of Field Security Police – or FSPs – the military police attached to the security service, which could be mobilised to the drop-zone at short notice. This, too, was rejected, since it might 'cause problems with local police and offer only a small chance of success'.

Finally, it was decided to set up a combination of traps, and hope that at least one was sprung. As soon as the Most Secret Sources received an indication that Fritz was on his way, Operation Nightcap would be mobilised, Dick White would be called at his private telephone number in London, and regional liaison officers and Fighter Command would be placed on alert. An intelligence officer stationed at Fighter Command would track incoming planes, and if an enemy aircraft was spotted that seemed to be heading for one of the three target areas, he would alert the night-duty officer at MI5, who would then contact the chief constable in the area with instructions to scour the countryside, but discreetly. If the plane was shot down, the parachutist would bail out and could then be picked up. If, however, the spy managed to land undetected, the police should 'comb out' boarding houses and hotels. Participants in Nightcap were told sternly: 'Whatever you do you should emphasise to all your collaborators the vital necessity of keeping the search as quiet as possible . . . the public must *not* be told that a parachute agent is being looked for.' If the police were asked why they were whacking every bush and looking up every tree, they should 'pretend to be looking for a deserter'.

Despite the elaborate preparations, MI5 was well aware that its net was full of holes. This was clearly a well-trained agent, a 'fully fledged saboteur . . . capable of operating his W/T set perfectly'. Being English, Fritz was equipped with the finest camouflage a spy could have, and he was about to be dropped in any one of three remote, sparsely-populated areas, each up to twelve miles in diameter: he had money, a gun and, to judge from the Most Secret Sources, plenty of gumption. MI5 was realistic: 'We quite realise that our plans do not offer more than a 40% chance of finding our man if he keeps his head and plays his part well.'

Fighter Command did pick up the Focke-Wulf, and six fighters from Number 12 Fighter Group were sent in pursuit. One of these got within range but then 'the instruments of the plane packed up for no understandable reason'. The German plane got away, and only Sergeant Vail's vigilance ensured that Operation Nightcap happened at all. Because Chapman had struggled for vital moments to extricate himself from a plane flying at 350 miles per hour, he had landed well outside the expected drop-zone. In the end, the person who ensured the capture of Agent X was Eddie Chapman.

Martha Convine could not sleep. She had been woken by a plane, droning loudly overhead, and lay wondering whether it was German. She was getting drowsy, when the all-clear siren had woken her up again. Her husband George, foreman of Apes Hall Farm, Ely, was snoring steadily of course, because George could sleep through the Battle of Britain, and recently had. Martha was finally dropping off, when she heard a loud banging on the door.

Martha shook George awake, put on her dressing gown, and peered out of the window into the darkness. 'Who is it?' A man's voice replied: 'A British airman, had an accident.'

It was 3.30 in the morning. For the last hour, Chapman had been stumbling around the wet celery fields in the darkness, dazed and still traumatised from being dangled out of an aircraft at terrifying speed. He had almost hit an empty barn on the way down, and he seemed to have lost his map. Finally he had found the eighteenth-century stone farmhouse, and shone his torch through the window in the door. On the hall table lay an English telephone book – a relief since it meant, of course, that the glutinous mud that had been steadily caking his boots for the last hour was British, and not French.

While George sleepily lit the lamp, Mrs Convine went

downstairs and opened the door. The figure on the doorstep might have emerged from a swamp. Martha 'noticed he had blood on his face'. He was also wearing a lounge suit. You can't be too careful in wartime, so Martha asked him where his plane was. He gestured vaguely at the surrounding countryside: 'Across the fields,' he said, mumbling that he had come down by parachute.

'I thought I heard a "Jerry",' said Martha.

'Yes,' the man said, nonsensically. 'That would be a cover plane for ours.'

Indeed, he really did not start making sense until he was sitting by the range in the kitchen with a cup of tea in his hand. He had asked to use the telephone and George, who was a special constable and knew the number by heart, dialled the police station at Ely for him. The man spoke very quietly into the mouthpiece, but Martha distinctly heard him say that he had 'just arrived from France', which was thrilling.

By the time Sergeants Vail and Hutchings arrived in the police car with two constables it was 4.30, the parachutist had drunk three cups of tea and eaten four slices of toast, and was evidently feeling much better, even cheery.

Convine led the policemen to the living room, where the man was chatting with Martha. Vail reported that: 'He shook hands with us and appeared agitated, but pleased to see us.' He then reached into his pocket and pulled out a pistol, saying: 'I expect the first thing you want is this.' He unloaded the gun and handed it to Vail, along with another loaded magazine.

When Vail asked where he had arrived from, the man replied: 'France, I want to get in touch with the British Intelligence Service. It is a case for them. I'm afraid I can't tell you much.'

An oblong parcel, sewn in sacking, lay on one of the living-room chairs. The man explained that it contained his 'radio transmitter, chocolate and shirts'. When Vail asked if he had any money, he stripped off his shirt to reveal 'a small package strapped to his back between his shoulder blades', which he removed and handed over. Inside, the astonished officer glimpsed wads of bank notes. He also produced his wallet, with an identity card for 'George Clarke'.

'Is that your real name?' asked Vail. The man just 'shook his head and smiled.'

While the constables went to find his parachute, the man became 'extremely talkative', boasting about the senior German officers he knew and declaring, apropos of nothing at all, that the only way to invade Europe was from Africa via Italy. Vail wondered if he might be 'dazed' from his descent. The man smelled slightly of celery.

The exotic visitor and his police escort departed in the police car. George said he was going back to bed, as there was work to do tomorrow. But Martha sat in the kitchen as dawn came up, thinking about the strange events of the last few hours. Later that morning, while doing the dusting, she found a British army reconnaissance map down the back of the sofa, which must have fallen out of the man's pocket. When she spread it out on the kitchen table, she saw that Mundford was circled in red crayon. The man had been 'very polite', Martha Convine thought, and underneath all that mud and blood he was probably rather handsome. She could not wait to tell her neighbour, but knew she could not. Sergeant Vail had said they must not breathe a word of what had happened to anyone, which was also thrilling.

At police divisional headquarters Chapman was stripped, body-searched, issued with a new set of clothing and brought before the Deputy Chief Constable, who shook his hand in a friendly manner. Chapman was wary: he did not like being inside a police station and he was not in the habit of telling the truth to policemen. His answers were cagey.

'Name?'

'George Clarke will do, for now.'

'Trade or profession?'

'Well, put me down as independent.'

The Chief Constable picked up the canvas bag containing the

radio. 'That should not be opened except by the Intelligence Service,' Chapman snapped.

The brown pill had been found in his turn-up. Did he have any more?: 'They had better have a look.'

Chapman gave a most selective account of his story, starting in Jersey and ending with the 'very terrifying experience' of being suspended upside down from a German plane.

Why had had he gone to the Channel Islands? 'For a holiday.'

Why was he imprisoned in Romainville? 'For political reasons.'

Then he clammed up. 'I have had a rough passage,' he said. 'I need to speak to the British secret services, when I will have a very interesting story to tell.'

The secret services were just as keen to hear Fritz's story. Two men in civilian clothes arrived in a Black Maria. Papers were signed, and Chapman was driven through the morning traffic to London and the Royal Patriotic School in Wandsworth, where he was formally detained under article 1A of the 'Arrival from Enemy Territory Order'. Then he was loaded back into the car. He did not know, and hardly cared, where he was going. The excitement, fear and exhaustion of the previous twenty-four hours had drained him. He barely noticed the sandbagged doorways of the city at war. After half an hour, they turned through a gate in a high wooden fence, topped by double rolls of barbed wire, and drew up in front of large and ugly Victorian mansion.

Two men in gym shoes led Chapman to a room in the basement, with a bench and two blankets, and locked him inside. A man with a monocle opened the door, peered hawkishly at him, said nothing, and then went away. He was stripped again, and ordered to put on flannel prison trousers and a coat, with a 6-inch white diamond shape sewn on the back. A doctor appeared, and ordered him to open his mouth. The medic spent several minutes probing and tapping at his teeth, particularly the new dental work. Then he tested Chapman's heart, listened to his lungs, and declared him to be in the peak of condition, though 'mentally and physically spent'. A man with a camera arrived and took photographs from the front and in profile.

Chapman fought to keep his head up. With a supreme effort he stared into the lens. The face in the picture is drained by fatigue and stress. There is caked mud in the tangled hair, and a trace of dried blood in the moustache. But there is something else in the face. Behind the drooping eyelids and stubble lies the very faint trace of a smile.

12

Camp 020

Lieutenant Colonel Robin 'Tin Eye' Stephens, the commander of Camp O20, Britain's secret interrogation centre for captured enemy spies, had a very specialised skill: he broke people. He crushed them, psychologically, into very small pieces and then, if he thought it worthwhile, he would put them back together again. He considered this to be an art, and not one that could be learned. 'A breaker is born and not made,' he said. 'There must be certain inherent qualities: an implacable hatred of the enemy, a certain aggressive approach, a disinclination to believe, and above all a relentless determination to break down the spy, however hopeless the odds, however many the difficulties, however long the process may take.' In photographs, Stephens might be the caricature Gestapo interrogator, with the glinting monocle and '*vays* of making you talk'. He certainly did have ways of making people talk, but they were not the brutal, obvious ways of the Gestapo. Behind the tin eye was an instinctive and inspired amateur psychologist.

Born in Egypt in 1900, Stephens had joined the Gurkhas, the legendarily tough Nepalese troops, before moving to the security service in 1939. He spoke Urdu, Arabic, Somali, Amharic, French, German and Italian. This multilingualism should not be taken to indicate that Stephens was broadminded about other races and nations. He was ragingly xenophobic, and given to making remarks such as: 'Italy is a country populated by undersized, posturing folk.' He disliked 'weeping and romantic fat

Belgians', 'shifty Polish Jews' and 'unintelligent' Icelanders. He also detested homosexuals. Above all, he hated Germans.

In 1940 the government set up a permanent centre for the interrogation and imprisonment of suspected spies, subversives and enemy aliens in Latchmere House, a large and gloomy Victorian house near Ham Common in West London. Latchmere House had been a military hospital in the First World War, specialising in the treatment of shell-shocked soldiers. In Stephens's words, it had 'lunatic cells ready made for a prison'. Secluded, forbidding and surrounded by multiple barbed wire fences, the interrogation centre was codenamed Camp 020. Colonel Stephens, extrovert and short-tempered, terrified his underlings almost as much as the prisoners. He never removed his monocle (he was said to sleep in it) and though everyone called him 'Tin Eye' as a consequence, very few dared do so to his face. But there was another side to this bristling martinet. He was a superb judge of character and situation; he never lost his temper with a prisoner, and he condemned the use of violence or torture as barbaric and counter-productive. Anyone who resorted to the third degree was immediately banned from Camp 020.

Away from the interrogation cells, Tin Eye could be charming and very funny. He was a frustrated writer, as can be seen from his reports, which have a delightful literary flourish; some of his more extreme statements of prejudice were simply intended to shock or amuse. He thought of himself as a master of the interrogative arts. Some of his colleagues thought he was quite mad. What few disputed was that he was outstanding at his job: establishing the guilt of the enemy spy, breaking down his resistance, extracting vital information, scaring him witless, winning his trust and then, finally, turning him over to Tar Robertson for use as a double agent. No one could turn a spy like Tin Eye.

At 9.30 on the morning of 17 December, Eddie Chapman found himself in Interrogation Room 3 of Camp 020, facing this strange, angry-looking man with the uniform of a Gurkha and the eye of a basilisk. Stephens was flanked by two other officers, Captains Short and Goodacre. The three officers made a grim and forbidding tribunal. That was part of Tin Eye's technique. 'No chivalry. No gossip. No cigarettes . . . a spy in war should be at the point of a bayonet. It is a question of atmosphere. The room is like a court and he is made to stand up and answer questions as before a judge.'

The room was bugged. In another part of Camp 020, a stenographer recorded every word. 'Your name is Chapman, is it?' barked Tin Eye.

'Yes, Sir.'

'I am not saying this in any sense of a threat, but you are here in a British Secret Service prison at the present time and it's our job in wartime to see that we get your whole story from you. Do you see?'

The threat didn't need to be made. Chapman told him everything, in a great tumbling torrent of confession. He told Stephens about his dismissal from the Coldstream Guards, his criminal past, his time in Jersey prison, the months in Romainville, his recruitment, his training in Nantes and Berlin, and the parachute drop. He told him about the codes he knew, the sabotage techniques he had learned, the secret writing, the passwords, codewords and wireless frequencies. He told him about Graumann and Thomas, Wojch and Schmidt, and the ugly man from Angers with the gold teeth. He explained how he had gathered information, and then destroyed it at the last moment.

When Chapman began to describe his decision to take up full-time crime, the interrogation veered close to farce.

'Well, then it gets rather difficult, Sir. I started running around with a mob of gangsters.'

'What do you mean?'

'I can't say exactly how I drifted in.'

'What made you turn over to these curious people?'

'It's rather difficult to say.'

When he described his mission to blow up the machine room of the De Havilland aircraft factory, Stephens interrupted.

'Pretty hazardous undertaking, isn't it?'

'Yes.'

'You were rather a favourite. Did they trust you?'

'Yes.'

'They said they thought rather highly of you, that you could get in anywhere and do virtually anything?'

'Yes, I could.'

Stephens turned the discussion to the contents of Chapman's kitbag. He pointed out that the cash had come wrapped in bands that immediately identified it as German, and 'would have cost him his neck' when they were spotted.

'The man who was supposed to search you, proceeds to identify your currency with a German label?' asked Stephens, incredulously.

'That's the fault of Thomas,' said Chapman, equally astonished. 'In the excitement he probably forgot to take it off.'

Stephens made a note. The process of distancing Chapman from his German handlers, by undermining his faith in their efficiency, had begun. So when Chapman recalled the conversation with Von Gröning, in which the older man had laughingly said that Chapman would never dare betray them because the British police would lock him up, Stephens again interjected. 'That was plain, unvarnished blackmail,' he said, in mock outrage, and was delighted when Chapman, 'with some bitterness, said he felt that all along'.

After two hours of interrogation, Stephens left Chapman in the company of Captain Short, a rotund, owlish figure, as cheery as his boss was menacing. Today this technique would be called 'good cop-bad cop'; in his secret guide to interrogation techniques, Stephens called it: 'blow hot-blow cold'.

'They treated you pretty well, didn't they?' said Short, in a sympathetic tone.

'Yes, I had a very good time there.'

'Particularly after having been in prison in Jersey and the other concentration camp.'

'How long have I to remain in this one? I mean, I've taken quite a lot of risks getting information which I thought would be of value, and [it is] valuable I think.'

Stephens had Chapman exactly where he wanted him. The spy seemed keen to tell all, with apparent honesty. He wanted to tell more. He wanted to please his captors. And he wanted to get out of prison.

In his office, Stephens took a telephone call from the policeman who had accompanied Chapman back to London: 'I don't know what this man may tell you, Sir. He came with a German parachute, but I recognised him at once – he was in my platoon some years ago.' By an odd coincidence, the two men had been in the Coldstream Guards together, and the policeman now related how Chapman had gone AWOL and was then cashiered. The information tallied precisely with the story Chapman had told: so far, then, he was telling the truth.

The interrogators began to turn up the heat. Chapman was allowed a break, and some food, but then they were back, probing, deliberately misrepresenting what he had already said, worrying away at any fissures in his story to find out if he was lying, or holding something back. In Stephens's mind, 'No spy, however astute, is proof against relentless interrogation.' The MI5 officers worked in shifts, late into the night. 'Physically and mentally it will wear down the strongest constitution in the end,' Stephens predicted.

The information continued to pour out of Chapman: in the course of forty-eight hours he gave more than fifty descriptions of separate individuals, from Graumann the spymaster to Odette the cook. Chapman described things of vital importance and utter triviality; he described the flak emplacements at Nantes, the location of the Paris Abwehr headquarters, his part in the occupation of Vichy France, and the price of black-market butter. He described the Breton nationalists, the treacherous Gaullists and the sundry other dodgy characters that had passed through Nantes. He told them some things they knew, such as the wireless codes they had already broken, which allowed them to test Chapman's truthfulness; but he also told them much that was new, and priceless, creating an astonishingly detailed picture of German espionage methods. He seemed not only eager to impart information, but offered suggestions as to how it might be used. Surely, said Chapman, by acting on this intelligence, Britain could break the Abwehr code and intercept messages between the various units.

The interrogators offered a vague response, but inside they rejoiced, for Chapman's suggestion showed that the Most Secret Sources were still intact: 'It is quite clear from his remarks that he has not the slightest idea that we have been breaking the messages which have passed between these stations during the last few months,' wrote the interrogators. It swiftly became apparent that Chapman would not have to be cajoled into acting as a double agent for Britain, but was itching to get to work. One motive for his willingness became clear when he described what had happened to Tony Faramus.

'He is a hostage for my good behaviour,' explained Chapman.

'For your good behaviour in France, or here?'

'Here. The idea was to use him as a kind of lever to make me do my work here.' If Chapman could convince his German masters that he was doing their bidding, then, he explained, his friend's life might yet be saved. Stephens made another note.

While Chapman's memory was scoured for valuable information, his luggage was simultaneously being searched for clues. The matches for secret writing and the evil-looking brown pill were sent for scientific analysis; the bank notes were individually examined, their serial numbers noted, to try to establish where they had come from; the fake identity cards were subjected to ultra-violet light scanning by HM Stationery Office, their precise chemical composition and typography analysed and compared to the genuine article; the wireless was sent to the Special Operations Executive (responsible for sabotage and espionage behind enemy lines) to find out if it had come from a British agent operating in France, and if so, which one. Chapman was quizzed about every item in his wallet. He explained that only one was really his own: 'That was a private letter written by a girlfriend to me – a girlfriend of mine before the war – I brought that back with me.'

Chapman's every statement was compared to the evidence in the Most Secret Sources, to try to catch him in a lie. When Chapman's chronology was erroneous, as it frequently was, they would go over the times and dates again and again, until satisfied that any errors were 'natural inexactitudes', not deliberate distortions. Scotland Yard was asked to provide details of his criminal record, to check out his extravagant claims of villainy; when the record arrived, it was found that many of the crimes Chapman had admitted to were not on it.

Stephens later claimed that Chapman had also 'confessed to an experiment in sodomy' during his Soho years. It is hard to know what to make of this: there is no trace of this confession in the interrogation transcripts. Tin Eye, moreover, was an extreme homophobe, who prided himself on his ability to identify and expose experimental sodomites. Chapman may have had a homosexual affair earlier in his youth but it is certain that he had been heterosexual, to an almost pathological degree, for many years. By way of recommendation, Stephens noted approvingly: 'Today there is no trace of sodomy and gone is any predilection for living on women on the fringes of society.'

With the evidence Chapman was providing, British intelligence was swiftly building up a picture of the entire Abwehr system in France. The German secret service had been so certain of its unbreakable code that the personnel at the various units often used their own names in wireless correspondence. That information was now merged with Chapman's descriptions, allowing them to identify the different players in the organisation. Chapman would have been astonished.

British intelligence had long ago established that the head and deputy head of the Nantes Abwehr section were Rittmeister Stephan von Gröning and Oberleutnant Walter Praetorius. But the man Chapman knew as 'Wojch' was really Feldwebel Horst Barton, while 'Schmidt' was Franz Stoetzner, both suspected saboteurs who had come to England before the war to work as waiters sponsored by an association of British restaurateurs and hoteliers. 'Leo' was a known German criminal named Leo Kreusch, and 'Albert' a former travelling salesman named Albert Schael. The Gestapo officer from Angers who had tried to recruit Chapman was probably Dernbach, 'one the principal counter-espionage agents in France'. Piece by piece, they began to put faces to names: even the pilot of the Focke-Wulf and the beautiful translator at Romainville were identified. Tar Robertson was impressed at the way Chapman had been kept in the dark over the identities of his German comrades: 'On no occasion has anyone's real name become apparent to him,' he wrote. When one of the interrogators casually dropped the name 'Von Gröning' into the conversation, Chapman's failure to react proved he had never heard it before.

Establishing a complete picture of Chapman's life in France would take time, but time was already running out. The day after his arrival at Camp 020, Chapman scribbled a message for Colonel Stephens, pointing out that 'today was the supposed start of my transmission' and recalling Von Gröning's observation about British red tape.

'It is important that we have a connection with the "Boche"

at earliest possible moment,' he wrote, perhaps deliberately deploying the sort of language favoured by Stephens. 'Dr Graumann especially stressed the point. He may suspect we may be arranging something. He probably thinks it would take much longer for me to commence, if I was arranging anything with yourselves.'

The same day, the Radio Security Service began to pick up the German reply station in Paris. Every three minutes, starting at 9.45 a.m., Maurice sent out a message, calling for Fritz to respond. MI5 now faced a quandary. If contact was delayed, Von Gröning would suspect something had gone wrong; but if they responded without being absolutely certain that Chapman was playing straight, then the results could be catastrophic. It was decided to wait a day or two, in order to get Chapman, and his motives, 'in sharper focus'.

By evening, Chapman had still received no response from Stephens. He had been interrogated now for forty-eight hours with only brief intermissions; he was tired and anxious. Unless contact was made soon the consequences could be dire. He was also torn: between the affection he still felt for Von Gröning and the urgent need to betray him; by the desire to save his own skin, and that of Tony Faramus; between self interest and some greater good, as yet undefined; between loyalty to his friends, and duty to his country. He wrote another, much longer letter to Stephens. It is an extraordinary document, a combination of self-pity, self-examination and self-assertion, reflecting the internal agony of the spy. It is the statement of a man groping his way through moral darkness towards the light:

Mon Commandant,
One does not expect gratitude from one's own country – but allow
me to draw your attention to a few facts. For thirteen months now I
have been under German rule. During this time even when
undergoing detention I was treated with strict fairness and friendli-

ness. I made many friends – people who I respect and who I think came to like me – unfortunately for them and for me.

I set out from the first day to try to mass together a series of facts, places, dates etc. concerning the German organization, which I think would be a task fairly formidable even for one of your trained experts. From the start I was very much handicapped, my knowledge of German was slight, my French even less – two languages most essential for this work. I studied French until I mastered it, even learning the slang. I read it now as fluently as English. Then, sir, for nine months I listened to every conversation I could hear. I opened many drawers containing documents 'gehein' [secret] written on all of them. I bored very small holes from the bathroom to the room of Dr Graumann, a man very much my friend.

Don't think I'm asking for any friendship now, it's a little late – on the other hand this strange thing patriotism. I laugh a little cynically when I think of it sometimes. I have fought the fight and my country won (why I can't explain). I wish like hell there had been no war – I begin to wish I had never started this affair. To spy and cheat on one's friends it's not nice it's dirty. However, I started this affair and I will finish it. Don't think I ask anything for this, I don't. It seems very strange to be working for two different governments – one offers me the chance of money, success and a career. The other offers me a prison cell.

There is not a great deal of time left to arrange things.

Yours sincerely,

Eddie

While Chapman was penning this heartfelt note, Stephens was gathering together his four interrogators for a conference on what to do with this remarkable and potentially very valuable crook. As Stephens pointed out, Chapman had accepted that he was in a strange position, wanted by the British police but offering – pleading – to work for British intelligence. 'If Chapman is to be believed, he offered to work for the Germans as a means of escape [and] on landing he immediately put himself at the disposal of the British authorities to work against the Germans.' The preliminary psychological profile indicated that Chapman's motives, despite his personal affection for Graumann, were 'hatred for the Hun coupled with a sense of adventure. There is no woman in the case and no bargain for rehabilitation. He is possessed of courage and nerve.'

But there was plainly a problem. If Chapman was allowed his liberty, he would surely be picked up by the police. He had even remarked on it to Stephens: 'As I figure it out, with my brilliant past, I am due for a stretch of something like fourteen years.' Worse, he might link up with his criminal gang again. But if he was kept under guard in Camp 020, Stephens predicted, 'he will go sour and might attempt a break'. The only way to operate him safely would be to place him at half-liberty, under surveillance but not in prison, 'under control in a quiet, country place'.

'My opinion,' Stephens declared, 'is that Chapman should be used for XX [Double Cross] purposes . . . and then sent back to France to join a party of saboteurs already in training to be sent to America for a really big job.'

The interrogation team unanimously agreed. There was a risk in sending Chapman back into France. He might be exposed by the Germans, or he might confess all to them; he might even change sides again. But the potential benefits of having a spy at the heart of the German secret service outweighed the dangers. That evening Camp 020 sent a message to the Double Cross team in St James's Street: 'In our opinion, Chapman should be used to the fullest extent . . . he genuinely means to work for the British against the Germans. By his courage and resourcefulness he is ideally fitted to be an agent.'

Tar Robertson had been following every twist of the developing case and agreed to send one of his case officers to take a look at Chapman the next day. Before Chapman could be inducted into the XX fold, he would need a codename. By convention, the names of agents should be plucked from thin air, mere handles that did not connect in any way with their real identities. But the convention was constantly flouted. 'Snow' of course was a partial anagram of Owens; another double agent was called 'Tate' because Robertson thought he looked like the comedian Harry Tate; it was said that Dusko Popov, a rather louche Yugoslavian agent, had been named 'Tricycle' because of his taste for three-in-a-bed sex. The name selected for Edward Chapman could not have been more apt.

On the evening of 18 December, Tar sent a message to all B1A personnel: 'We have chosen the name of Zigzag for Fritzchen.'

13

35, Crespigny Road

The man despatched by Tar Robertson to handle Zigzag was Captain Ronnie Reed, a young, unobtrusive radio expert, and an inspired choice. A thin-faced man with a spindly moustache, spectacles and a pipe, he looked like an archetypal, middle-ranking army officer. Indeed, he looked so much like an archetypal, middle-ranking army officer that when Tar Robertson needed a photograph to put on a fake identity card for Operation Mincemeat – in which a dead body, dressed in army uniform and carrying misleading information, was deliberately washed up on the coast of Spain – he chose a picture of Ronnie Reed. Reed looked just like everybody else, and nobody at all.

Reed's father, a waiter at the Trocadero restaurant, had died in the Battle of the Somme in 1916, and his mother brought him up in a tenement in King's Cross. From the Saint Pancras Church of England School, he had won a scholarship to the Regent's Park Polytechnic School, where he studied engineering and developed a passion for radios. He could build a wireless from scratch and with his schoolfriend Charlie Chilton (who went on to become a celebrated radio presenter and producer) he would broadcast to the world from his bedroom with a homemade transmitter: Ronnie would sing a warbling rendition of Bing Crosby's *Dancing in the Dark* while Charlie strummed the guitar.

The outbreak of war found Reed working as a BBC radio engineer by day, and flying through the ether by night with the call-sign G2RX. One night, Reed and his mother had taken cover during an air raid, when a police car drew up. Reed was summoned from the shelter and driven, through the falling bombs, to Wormwood Scrubs. A man was standing at the prison gate. 'Ah, Mr Reed, we've been waiting for you. Come in,' he said. He was led through dimly lit corridors to a cell on the first floor.

Inside the cell, flanked by two guards, was a man in flying uniform, his face covered in blood.

'This man is a parachutist,' said an officer with red tabs on his uniform, who had entered the cell behind Reed. 'He's supposed to transmit tonight back to Germany. We want you to go out into a field in Cambridge, and transmit, and make sure he sends the message we have prepared.'

That night, Reed and the parachutist, Gösta Caroli, soon to become double agent 'Summer', sat in a pigsty in a Cambridgeshire field and sent a Morse code message to Hamburg: : 'I'm going underground for a few days, while I sort out some accommodation, and I've arrived safely.'

So began Reed's career in the secret service.

Shy, gentle and reserved, Reed was easy to overlook, but he was the 'humble genius' of wartime wireless work, perfectly tuned to the arcane mysteries of the radio. He also had the knack of identifying the 'fist' of another operator, and then of being able to imitate it precisely – he was probably the best Morse-code mimic in Britain. Reed's skills made him indispensable to Robertson's team, and soon he was monitoring all double agent radio traffic. One of his tasks was to stand over agents as they transmitted back to the Abwehr, to ensure they were not inserting coded messages. If an agent was unwilling or unable to transmit then Reed would send the message himself, complete with the agent's telltale 'fingerprint'. But Ronnie Reed was more than just an accomplished radio ham; under Robertson's guidance, he was developing into a first-rate intelligence officer, incisive, sympathetic, and virtually invisible.

In Chapman's cell, Reed shook hands with his new charge for the first time. The young officer had planned to take an instant dislike to this unrepentant criminal with the 'lurid past'. But like most people, and against his will, he found himself charmed.

Reed frankly explained that if Chapman was to work for MI5 he would need to live a hermit-like existence. Any contact with the police, the Bohemians of Soho or the criminal fraternity would be forbidden. Instead, Reed explained, 'he would have to work for us under strict supervision in almost complete isolation from other members of the community'. Chapman laughed and said that after all the recent excitement a quiet life would be most welcome. Reed said he would return the following day to make the first transmission to Germany, and left Chapman to draft a message, using the Constantinople code and the FFFFF control sign. Reed would then check it, and sit beside him as he transmitted it.

As changeable as ever, Chapman seems to have been buoyed by his conversation with Reed, for he now sent another letter to Stephens. Gone was the peevish, introverted tone. Now he was positively chatty:

Mon Commandant,
Merci pour votre bonté. As we have little time to get to know each other – let me start and give you a little explanation. At the present moment my story is very difficult to tell. My mind is such a frenzied mass of names, formulas, descriptions, places, times, explosions, radio telegraphy and parachute jumping, small but important conversations, intrigue playing against intrigue. On top of this you must try and imagine a brain – weakened by three years of imprisonment and many months in the punishment cell . . . sometimes in trying to put facts together I really thought I was going mad . . . these things are not untrue, they have all passed – but dates, names, times, are all jumbled in my head higgledy-piggledy, like some giant jigsaw puzzle . . . To conclude Mon Commandant. Be a little patient with me if my places and dates and times don't

*coincide . . . I'm afraid that whole thing has rather passed like a
dream: it's for you to try and make it a realisation.*

Eddie

Tin Eye Stephens was accustomed to intimidating new arrivals
at Camp 020. He was not used to being addressed in this
facetious tone or told what to do, let alone by an oikish young
burglar in prison garb. But instead of exploding, as he might have
done, Stephens just chuckled, and tucked the note in the Zigzag
file.

The next morning, Chapman was picked up by Reed and two
burly Field Security Policemen in a Blue Maria, and driven 150
yards from the front gate of Latchmere House to the Equestrian
Club, a small concert hall within the grounds used as a club-
house, with a 25-foot flagpole that Reed thought would serve as
an aerial. The place was deserted. While the FSPs stood guard,
Reed set up Chapman's wireless.

At 10.02 a.m., under Reed's vigilant gaze, Chapman tried to
contact his Abwehr controllers. At 10.06 the reply station
responded that it was receiving him 'rather weakly' and with
interference, but gave the go-ahead. Agent Zigzag then tapped
out his first message as a double agent: 'FFFFF HAVE
ARRIVED. AM WELL WITH FRIENDS. OK.' He added
his usual laughing coda: 'HI HU HA.'

In the afternoon, the Most Secret Sources reported that the
Abwehr stations in France had confirmed that this message was
'definitely Fritz' because they 'recognised his style of sending and
especially the method he adopts for signing off his messages'. The
deception was up and running.

The following morning, Reed and Chapman found it
impossible to renew the contact with Paris. It appeared that
the transmissions were being picked up in Nantes, but not at
the main receiving station in the capital. A second message was
sent 'blind': 'FFFFF GET MORRIS [*sic*] BRING YOUR SET

NEARER COAST. MUST HAVE BETTER RECEPTION.
F. OK'

By late December they received the first direct message from
Von Gröning: 'THANKS FOR MESSAGE. WISH GOOD
RESULTS. OK.'

So far the double-cross seemed to be working, although it
would be two weeks before the problems of reception and
transmission could be ironed out. The radio traffic was codenamed ZINC, and filed alphabetically alongside Zigzag.

Chapman seemed more than co-operative, Reed reported,
and was still producing a steady stream of valuable intelligence:
'Zigzag's powers of observation are extremely good and he is
being quite truthful in whatever he tells us.' (Reading that
assessment, John Masterman noted that he was sceptical that
such a man even understood the concept of complete honesty.)

Special Branch set about tracing the rest of the Jelly Gang.
Jimmy Hunt, it transpired, had been convicted of warehouse
breaking and larceny in 1938; Darry was still in Dartmoor, on a
seven-year stretch; the others were all either deserters, doing
time, or dead. This was ideal. There was no chance of accidental
contact, and with the members of the gang safely out of the way
they could be brought into the story with no danger that they
might turn up unannounced. Chapman had been instructed to
contact his old chums, and perhaps bring one back. Hunt seemed
the ideal candidate. As Masterman pointed out, 'the Germans
had not a photograph of Hunt, but only a general description,
[so] it would be possible to impersonate him by someone with a
Cockney accent'. Hunt the safebreaker would play a central role
in the coming drama, without once leaving his prison cell.

Gradually it was starting to dawn on Chapman's handlers that
they had obtained a double agent of potentially huge value.
When Camp 020 mistakenly passed the identity of Zigzag to
another branch of the intelligence service, there was a loud
squeal of protest from Masterman, the master of the double-
cross, at this 'gratuitous' sharing of information. B1A was jealous

of its new treasure, and while Tar was happy to pass on his intelligence findings, he was not about to share Zigzag with anyone.

The forensic investigations confirmed how highly the Germans prized Agent Fritz. The quality of his equipment was declared to be first class. The cash he had brought was genuine British currency, not the forged stuff that the Abwehr had often palmed off on lesser agents. The match heads were impregnated with quinine, which the boffins in the science department described as 'a very good means of secret writing'. The brown pill was potassium cyanide, instantaneously lethal. The wireless was traced to a British SOE agent. Only in the matter of the forged ID cards did the Abwehr seem to have cut corners. The Stationery Office dismissed them as amateur forgeries and liable to be spotted as such by any observant policeman. 'It does seem rather extraordinary that the Germans should not take a little more trouble in constructing their documents,' Tar complained, as if miffed that the Germans were not trying hard enough. One unsolved mystery was how the Focke-Wulf had managed to escape the pursuing RAF fighters: the Air Ministry could only conclude that 'something queer was taking place in connection with the plane and the radio beams associated with it'.

Camp 020 was no place to run a double agent. If Zigzag was to be effective, he must be kept happy, and that would require creature comforts at least comparable to those of La Bretonnière. Chapman had been pampered by the Germans: 'They pandered to his vanity, granted him liberty and treated him with respect.' MI5 must now try to find a red carpet, or the nearest equivalent, and roll it out for Zigzag.

Corporal Paul Backwell and Lance Corporal Allan Tooth were, by common agreement, the two best Field Security Policemen in British intelligence. Both had been policemen before the war, and would enjoy successful careers in the intelligence corps after it. They were bright, well educated and good-natured; they were also large and, when they wanted to be, extremely intimidating. Tar Robertson summoned Backwell and Tooth to his office and told them to take a car to Camp 020, where they would pick up one 'Edward Simpson', 'a dangerous criminal who is wanted by police and who has been released in order to carry out an operation of an extremely hazardous character'. They should accompany this man to a safe house in north London where they would live with him until further notice. Robertson was in deadly earnest: 'The success of this operation depends upon the utmost degree of secrecy.' A photographic pass would be issued in the name Simpson, indicating that he was performing 'special duties for the War Office', which could be produced if they were ever challenged by officials.

'There is no reason to doubt Simpson's loyalty to this country and you are not therefore to regard yourselves as his guards,' Robertson continued. 'You should look upon yourselves rather as chaperones, whose duty it is to prevent him getting into trouble with the police and with his old criminal associates, to act as a screen between him and the outside world.' 'Simpson' should never be left alone, day or night. He should not communicate with anyone, use the telephone or send letters. If he attempted to escape, Tooth and Backwell should not hesitate to 'place him under restraint' and then contact either Reed or Masterman. Both policemen would be issued with firearms.

At the same time, they should provide him with companionship. 'This regime is bound to be irksome,' said Tar, 'and you must therefore do your best to make his life as agreeable as is possible in the circumstances.' They could take him to the local pub of an evening: each officer would receive £5 as a beer float, and Simpson would also be provided with cash in order to be able to 'stand his round'. Having gained his confidence, the policemen should note down anything he said of importance, and encourage him to talk about his past. In short, they should guard him, befriend him, and then spy on him. If Backwell and Tooth thought it strange that they were being expected to keep a known crook out of the hands of the police, they were much too discreet to say so.

Days before Christmas, Backwell and Tooth, in plain clothes, arrived at Camp 020, collected Chapman's personal property, and escorted him from his cell. Chapman, without preamble, asked Backwell if he might borrow a pound, as he wanted to give a tip to the sergeant 'who had looked after him so well'. (Only Chapman would swan out of Camp 020 as if checking out of a smart hotel.) They drove north. In the car, Chapman's chaperones introduced themselves as 'Allan' and 'Paul' and explained they would now be his 'permanent companions, friends who were protecting him from police and his previous criminal associates'. Chapman said little as they drove. 'Conversation was strained,' Backwell reported.

No one paid any attention to the three men who climbed out of the car and walked up the garden path of 35, Crespigny Road – a nondescript detached house, on a quiet street, in the unremarkable north London borough of Hendon. A few of the neighbours were 'digging for victory' in their front gardens, but none looked up. It would have taken a neighbour of exceptional inquisitiveness to spot that Number 35 never took down its blackout curtains (many people did not bother), or that the locks had been changed, or that a man with a thin moustache had arrived that very morning to erect an aerial on the back roof.

Inside Number 35, Backwell locked the door, and the three housemates began, in his words, to 'settle in'. Reed had set up the radio room on the upper floor; Chapman's bedroom was next door, while the two FSPs shared the third bedroom. The housekeeper, Mrs West, would not be arriving for a few days, so the policemen divided up the chores: Tooth would do the shopping and Backwell the cooking. When Chapman was out of earshot, they divvied up their other task: 'Allan and I agreed to concentrate on different aspects of Eddie. Allan studied his character, likes and dislikes, while I kept to the factual side and noted everything of interest that he said in conversation.'

Chapman was anxious. He complained of sleeping badly, and showed no inclination to leave the house. Like a couple of burly mother hens, Tooth and Backwell set about 'making Eddie feel at home'. Backwell asked Chapman what reading material he enjoyed, and was astonished to discover his love of serious literature. 'His taste was unusual for anyone who had lived his kind of life,' thought Backwell, who bought him some German novels, the works of Alfred Tennyson, and the plays of Pierre Corneille, in French.

Gradually, Chapman seemed to relax. His days were filled with further interrogations, sending wireless messages under Reed's supervision, and making plans. In the evenings, he read, smoked, listened to the radio and chatted with his amiable guards. Privately, Backwell and Tooth compared notes on their ward. They were struck that German propaganda seemed to have had an 'enormous' effect on him; at first he dismissed BBC reports of Allied advances, claiming that he knew Germany was winning the war, that Russia was exhausted. The Allies, he insisted, would never succeed in invading France. Backwell decided to mount his own propaganda campaign, by exposing him to such patriotic literature as *I, James Blunt*, H.V. Morton's novel imagining a Britain under Nazi rule. 'Gradually we made him realise that German propaganda, however convincing it had been, was far from the truth.'

After a few days of communal living, Backwell and Tooth reported that Chapman now appeared 'quite happy', and 'a mine of information'. Their companion seemed to know all about sabotage, and 'often speaks of various methods of destroying pylons, bridges, petrol tanks, etc'. Often he insisted on conversing in French. The policemen agreed they were living with a most peculiar fellow. One moment he was reading classical literature in the original French and quoting Tennyson, and the next he would be discussing the best way to blow up a train.

One night, as they were relaxing after dinner, Chapman wondered aloud 'what it was that made him leave Germany

to come over here'. He continued musing in the same vein: 'In
Germany he could have lived well, both now and after the war.
He was not forced to come.' The two policemen pondered the
same question. His politics seemed to be based on a close reading
of H.G. Wells: 'He has no sympathy with nationalism and in the
post-war reconstruction he would like to see a world federation.'
Tooth decided that, in his heart, Chapman was a patriot: 'He is
proud to be British and wants us to win the war.' On the other
hand, he was apparently impelled by some internal recklessness.
'It seems that he is a man to whom the presence of danger is
essential,' Tooth wrote. 'I feel that it is for this reason that he
would be undertaking his return to France, for he is virtually a
man without a country.'

Some days later, Chapman let slip that he had a private plan of
his own, but then he changed the subject, remarking: 'It is such a
wild scheme it would not be thought feasible.' Tooth duly
reported Chapman's remarks to Reed and Robertson, adding: 'I
can only glean that the success of these plans depends entirely on
Dr Graumann keeping a promise that he should visit Berlin,
when I gather something of great importance was to take place.'

Chapman showed no remorse for his past, and regaled his new
companions with extravagant tales of his own villainy, such as
the time he broke into the Grimsby pawnbrokers and the raid on
Express Dairies. The information was duly added to MI5's
growing list of Chapman's undetected crimes. 'I think we should
keep these new adventures entirely to ourselves, but have it on
record,' wrote Reed.

The interrogators, spycatchers and double-crossers of MI5
(Reed excepted) were usually upper class and the products of
English public schools. Most had never encountered a man like
Chapman before, and their first instinct was to despise this
uncouth fellow with his flamboyant manner. Yet in almost
every case they came first to like, and then to respect him,
though never entirely without misgivings.

As Christmas approached, espionage experts all over London

Eddie Chapman, 16 December 1942.
Photographed at Camp 020, MI5's secret wartime interrogation centre, in
the hours following Chapman's landing by parachute in Cambridgeshire.

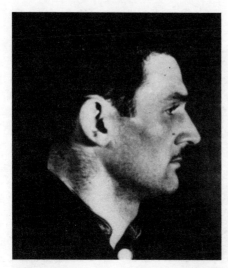

Chapman at Camp 020, muddy-faced after landing in a damp celery field.

Chapman eating Christmas dinner, 1942, at the MI5 safe house, 35, Crespigny Road. The photograph was taken by Allan Tooth, his police minder.

While the previous photograph shows Chapman grinning merrily, another reveals the spy looking more morose – a reflection, perhaps, of his violent mood swings.

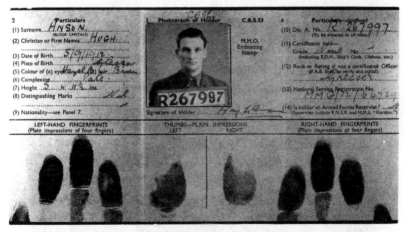

An Irish identity pass for Chapman created by Nazi forgers, one of two fake ID cards he carried with him in 1942. The photograph, taken in a studio in Nantes, shows Chapman in typical matinée-idol pose.

The merchant seaman's pass forged for Chapman by MI5 in the name of 'Hugh Anson', a former member of his criminal gang.

Jersey under Occupation: a British police sergeant takes orders from a Nazi officer.

Norway under Occupation: Vidkun Quisling, collaborator-in-chief and Nazi puppet, inspects the 'Viking Regiment' composed of Norwegian Nazi volunteers.

The entrance to Fort de Romainville, the nineteenth-century Paris fortress which was transformed into a Nazi concentration camp.

Faramus (*right*), aged about twenty-three, in the Mauthausen-Gusen death camp.

Anthony Charles Faramus playing a POW in the 1955 film *The Colditz Story*.

The Mosquito bomber under construction at the De Havilland aircraft factory in Hatfield, Hertfordshire.

A Mosquito – the 'Wooden Wonder' – being prepared for a bombing run over Germany.

The De Havilland aircraft factory, with Mosquitoes on the airfield behind.
The two men leaning against the wall may be Allan Tooth and Paul Backwell,
Chapman's MI5 minders.

The faked sabotage of the De Havilland plant: tarpaulins have been draped over
the buildings, painted to simulate damage from an explosion, while debris has been
spread around the area.

The *City of Lancaster*, the 3,000 ton merchant vessel, commanded by Captain Reginald Kearon, which carried Chapman to Lisbon.

The coal bomb constructed by Nazi engineers in Lisbon which Chapman agreed to take on board the *City of Lancaster*.

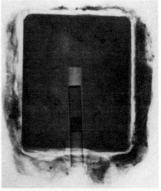

An X-ray of the coal bomb showing a block of explosive with cylindrical fuse, encased in moulded plastic and painted to resemble a lump of Welsh coal.

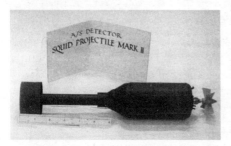

The doctored photograph sent to Lisbon in 1944 for the Operation Squid deception. The ruler is eighteen inches long but appears to be only six inches, thus making the depth charge appear to be one-third of its real size.

wondered what to do about Eddie Chapman, and what made him tick.

When he was not thinking up new ways to deceive and double-cross Nazi Germany, John Masterman, historian and athlete, liked to think about cricket. Sometimes he thought about espionage and cricket at the same time. 'Running a team of double agents,' he reflected, 'is very much like running a club cricket side. Older players lose their form and are gradually replaced by newcomers. It is not always easy to pick the best players to put into the field. Some of the players required a good deal of net practice before they were really fit to play in a match.' In Chapman he seemed to have discovered a batsman of astonishing natural ability, who needed no additional training and who might well knock up a fantastic innings. If, that is, he did not stalk off the pitch, and then reappear to open the bowling for the other side.

Masterman entertained these thoughts as he lay on the floor of the barber's shop in the Reform Club on Pall Mall. At the start of the war he had resided in the United University Club; then when a bomb blew the roof off, he had moved in to the Oxford and Cambridge. Not long after that, the barber at the Reform Club had died and his salon had closed; Masterman was invited to make his digs there instead, an offer he readily accepted since the club was only a few minutes walk from B1A headquarters. And so now he spent his nights on the floor where the hair clippings of 'great and clubbable' men had fallen ever since 1841.

Sleeping on a thin mattress on the hard tiles was not easy. The cook at the Reform did his best with the rations, but the food was seldom anything but grim. The electricity shut down with monotonous irregularity. Baths were doled out in strict rotation, and were always cold. But Masterman loved living at the Reform: 'I had, with my memories of my uselessness in the First War, a kind of unconscious wish for trials and discomfort.' He watched his fellow men at war (the women were, as ever, invisible to him) and reflected on their stoicism. One night the

Carlton Club was hit by a bomb. The members of the surrounding clubs, in pyjamas and slippers, formed long lines to save the library from the flames, passing books from hand to hand and discussing the merits of each as they passed. Such people, thought Masterman, 'made defeat seem impossible'. This strange warrior monk would spend the rest of his war in this masculine world of institutional food, hard floors and cold baths. And now, with a new, intensely fit, first-class batsman to send to the crease, John Masterman was as happy as he had ever been in his life.

On the other side of London, in Latchmere House, the commandant of Camp 020 was also thinking about Agent Zigzag. Tin Eye Stephens regarded most enemy spies as 'the rabble of the universe, their treachery not matched by their courage'. But Chapman was different − the 'most fascinating case' to date. Unlike every other captured agent, he had not displayed even a flicker of fear. He seemed to crave excitement, and very little else. 'What manner of man is the spy?' Stephens pondered. 'Is he patriotic, brave? Is he of the underworld, a subject of blackmail? Is he just a mercenary? Spies who work for money alone are few, but they are dangerous.' For a crook, he observed, Chapman was strangely uninterested in money. He seemed genuinely patriotic, but not in the Hun-bashing, jingoistic way that Stephens epitomised. What Chapman seemed to want was another breathless episode in the unfolding drama of his own life. If MI5 could stage-manage the next act with enough flair, Tin Eye reflected, then Zigzag might be their biggest star yet.

On Christmas Eve, Maurice, the German wireless operator in Paris, sent a message to Agent Fritz: 'PLEASE COME AT NINE FORTY FIVE AND FIVE PM QRQ.' (The sign 'qrq' was ham shorthand for 'send more quickly'.) The Germans were still apparently having difficulty picking up Chapman's transmissions. Ronnie Reed had fiddled with Chapman's radio and could find no fault, but he was not too alarmed. The patchy link would buy them some more time.

Far more worrying was something that Chapman had said. Soon after arriving in Crespigny Road, he asked Reed to find Freda Stevenson, his former lover and the mother of his child. Chapman had only vaguely alluded to Freda before. Now he explained that he had never held his own daughter, now three-years old, that he was still in love with Freda, and that he wanted to see them both, urgently. Reed said he would try to find her.

Freda was an unknown quantity. Allowing Chapman to contact her might lift his spirits, Reed reflected, but it would complicate the case. If Chapman was serious about his feelings for a woman he had not seen for years and a child he had never met, would that affect his willingness to return to France? Perhaps Freda had remarried; perhaps she had given the child up for adoption. Reed concluded: 'We should know the exact situation concerning them before Zigzag visited them, rather than run his neck into what might be an extremely awkward situation.' But as the days passed, Chapman's requests to see Freda and Diane grew more urgent. Reed stalled, and every time he did so, Chapman's face would fall, and he would shuffle off to his room. Backwell and Tooth treated him like a particularly fractious and unpredictable teenager. 'Eddie had moods,' wrote Backwell. 'If things did not go as he planned, he would go upstairs to bed and stay there for hours on end and refuse to eat. He never got annoyed with Allan and me on these occasions. But we left him alone when he felt like this.'

Chapman's deteriorating temperament cast a pall over the Christmas celebrations at 35, Crespigny Road. Backwell roasted a chicken with sausages. Tooth took some photographs around the Formica-topped kitchen table: the series offers a strange reflection of Chapman's volatile mood swings: in one snap he is drinking beer and grinning at the camera, in the next he appears sunk in misery.

Another reason for Chapman's frustration was the continuing difficulty in communicating with his German spymasters. His wireless could pick up messages sent from France, but he was unable to make direct contact and had to send his replies 'blind'. Soon after Christmas, Reed announced that he had solved the problem. Chapman had casually remarked that during his time in La Bretonnière he had noticed a loose switch on the wireless, which he had fixed by soldering it with a hot poker. This, noted Reed primly, is 'a method not calculated to provide a really satisfactory electrical connection'. He took the machine home, mended the switch himself, and returned the next morning saying he was sure it would now work.

Chapman had written and encoded a simple message overnight. Reed checked it over, approved it, and switched on the wireless. At 9.45, a connection was made with the Paris receiving station. Everything was working perfectly. But in their haste and excitement to see if the repair had worked, they made a mistake. It was the first error of the entire case, but it was also the very worst mistake they could have made. At 9.47 on 27 December, Chapman tapped out the following message: 'CALL AT 1000 IF PARIS UNABLE RECEIVE ME. OK FRITZ. HU HA HU HO.' The acknowledgement came back that the message had been clearly received. Reed and Chapman were jubilant.

Ten minutes later, they were sitting over a cup of tea in the kitchen when Chapman suddenly turned pale, and stammered: 'My God, I believe I forgot the Fs.'

14

What a Way Out

The wrath of Tar Robertson was terrifying to behold. Tin Eye Stephens was so angry so much of the time that his underlings had become used to it; but Tar practically never lost his temper. 'He was non-judgemental,' said one friend. 'He saw the best in everyone.' On the morning of 28 December, when Reed stutteringly informed his boss that he had just sent a message on the Zinc traffic without the agreed 'all OK' sign, Robertson did not see the best in Reed. He saw red.

By omitting the five Fs from the start of the message Chapman and Reed had accidentally indicated to Von Gröning that Fritz was being controlled by British intelligence. Not only had this probably scuppered one of the most promising double agents of the war, there was a risk it could tip off the Abwehr to the fact that other supposedly loyal agents were being similarly controlled. The entire Double Cross system might be in danger.

Reed was crippled with embarrassment and contrition. For a wireless operator of his experience, this was a mistake so elementary as to be almost unforgivable. Part of Reed's job was to watch for so-called 'control signs' which an agent might surreptitiously insert into his traffic to alert a German handler that he was working under duress. Sometimes these tip-offs were minuscule: omitting a word of greeting, the addition (or omission) of an X or a full stop. But Chapman's agreed sign, to indicate that he was still a free agent, was obvious and unmistakable; MI5 knew what it was; it had been used in each of Zigzag's messages to date.

Young Reed fired off a volley of painful excuses. 'From the fact that both Zigzag and I completely forgot about them [the five Fs], it can be seen that they are a very easy thing to omit,' he grovelled. He pointed out that Chapman would 'undoubtedly have done the same thing if he had been operating as a free agent', which was hardly the point. He also claimed that since 'Zigzag has already sent two messages including the five Fs, I personally do not feel that this omission is as bad as it would have been had it occurred earlier during his traffic'. This was the flailing shame of a man desperately trying to mollify his incandescent boss.

The same evening, at the second agreed receiving window of 5.00 p.m., Chapman and Reed sent another message, this time making no mistake. 'FFFFF SORRY DRUNK OVER XMAS FORGOT FFFFF. HAPPY XMAS. F.'

'They may forget about the inclusion of the five F's themselves,' wrote Reed, with a confidence he did not feel. For the next twenty-four hours MI5 anxiously scanned the Most Secret Sources, expecting to see a flurry of transmissions indicating that Von Gröning now knew that his agent had been caught and was transmitting under British control. Finally, the interceptors picked up a laconic message: 'Message of 14 letters from Fritzchen deciphered. It was found that this did not begin with 5 enciphered F's.' Von Gröning had believed the second message. A stupid mistake on one side had been cancelled out by an equally foolish error on the other, and poor, frazzled Reed could breathe again. Much later, he would claim the mistake was merely 'annoying'. At the time it was mortifying.

Chapman was relieved, but increasingly restless. A life of domesticity locked up in a suburban house with two ex-policemen was not quite how he had envisaged the role of a spy. He began to agitate for a decision about what would be done with him. He drew up a note, under the heading: 'Work I could possibly do in France', and gave it to Reed:

> Preparations should now be put in running order for my return. I have been given to understand that my liberty is to be given to me on my return to France – It has been suggested by Dr Graumann I should make a tour of Germany. But of course I think I can also stay in Paris. There are many points which could be attacked and I can give fairly good schemes for attacking them . . . I can supply detonators and a small quantity of dynamite and details of places to be attacked. If I were given two or three good men and allowed to train them myself, allowed to fix things up for them in France, allowed a free hand in my own methods, I am sure I can accomplish good work. On the other hand if we only want information then again I must be trained more thoroughly in German as my knowledge is not enough and also in different army and navy specialities. This is rather a long job and if the people who are preparing the things for my departure will come and see me and take down my ideas I am sure good results will be obtained.

Laurie Marshall, Reed's deputy, was duly dispatched to Crespigny Road to hear Chapman's ideas, which ranged from the simple and effective to the dramatic and bizarre. If he was returned to Nantes, Chapman explained, he could conceal coded information in the 'silly joking messages' he sent in his radio transmissions; more ambitiously, if the British sent out a sabotage team, he could try to supply them with explosives and detonators from the stock in Graumann's office in La Bretonnière. 'The men must be very resolute and prepared to lose their lives,' Chapman insisted. Among the possible targets would be Gestapo offices, Abwehr HQs and SS officers. Chapman had noticed that senior Abwehr officers often sent one another cases of cognac as gifts; it would be comparatively easy to make a booby trap from one of these, and pack it with 'sufficient explosive to destroy a whole building'. Marshall found Chapman's enthusiasm 'a little sinister', but reported that the discussion had provided 'an excellent indication of the way Zigzag's mind is working'.

There was no sign, as yet, that the Abwehr suspected anything was amiss, but to sustain Von Gröning's faith in his agent some sort of demonstration of Chapman's skills would soon be required. 'We should do all that we can to arrange a speedy and spectacular explosion of some kind at the De Havilland works,' wrote Masterman. This staged act of sabotage should then be widely reported in the press, and certainly in *The Times* – Von Gröning's British newspaper of choice.

It was an article of faith among the Double Cross team that a double agent should, as far as possible, live the life the Germans believed he was living, and do the things he claimed to be doing. Masterman called this 'the principle of verisimilitude, the imperative necessity of making the agent actually experience all that he professes to have done'. It is far easier, under interrogation, to tell part of the truth than to sustain a latticework of pure lies. If Chapman was going to pretend to have blown up the De Havilland factory, then he must go and case the joint, precisely as he would if he were genuinely bent on sabotage.

Chapman and Backwell made the 10-mile journey to Hatfield by bus, and got off at the stop just beyond the factory. Chapman carefully surveyed the target as they walked slowly around the perimeter fence. Near the main entrance, as arranged, Backwell stopped and stood with his back to the plant, while Chapman looked over his shoulder and described, while pretending to chat with his friend, everything in sight: the gate appeared to be manned by a single police guard, and inside the compound Chapman thought he could see three possible powerhouses. In the field he counted twenty-five aircraft, Chapman's first sight of the sleek wooden Mosquitoes. Even to the eyes of an amateur they were beautiful little planes, which 'also conveyed an air of warlike viciousness'. A little further along, the fence ran behind the garden of The Comet public house. Next door to the pub was a small café. The morning shift was just arriving, and the guard plainly knew all the factory workers by sight, for he nodded to each as they passed, entering the names on a list.

Chapman and Backwell repaired to the café for a cup of tea. In the corner of the tearoom sat a man in uniform, a lance corporal, who stared at them but said nothing. Could he be an Abwehr spy, sent to see if Fritz was performing his mission? Or was he just a vigilant serviceman on leave, wondering why two men were chatting in undertones next to an important military factory in the middle of a war? Would he give the alarm and have them arrested? Backwell rejected the thought: 'He seemed more nervous than suspicious.' Perhaps the corporal was just late back from leave.

That night, with the agreement of the factory owner, who had been brought into the plot by MI5, Backwell and Chapman returned and inspected the area more thoroughly. Four large transformers were housed inside a walled yard. Nearby was a building beside an empty swimming pool. In their reconnaissance photographs the Germans had incorrectly identified this as a subsidiary powerhouse, when it contained only an old boiler and pump for the disused swimming pool. At night, the main entrance was still guarded, but a smaller gate, alongside the pub, was simply left locked. Chapman explained that, if he was really trying to cripple the factory, he would climb over this small gate in the middle of the night, clipping the barbed wire on top and using the pub as cover. He would then plant two suitcases, each filled with 30 lbs of explosives: one under the main bank of transformers, and the other in the supposed subsidiary powerhouse. Each of these would be primed with a wristwatch fuse on a one-hour delay. If such an attack were mounted in reality, it 'would completely ruin the output of the whole factory'. Of course, not even a super-spy would be able to lug 60 lbs of explosive and two suitcases over a barbed-wire gate on his own:

for this fictional feat of sabotage, Chapman would need an equally imaginary accomplice. Jimmy Hunt would be the ideal man for the job, and since he was still firmly incarcerated, he was in no position to object.

On New Year's Eve, Chapman sent a message to Von Gröning: 'FFFFF WENT DOWN AND SAW WALTER. IT IS VERY DIFFICULT JOB. IT CAN BE DONE. I HAVE CLOTHES TICKETS ETC.'

The inside of the De Havilland plant was only one picture Chapman would have to be able to paint with confidence on his return to France. If he was to convince Von Gröning that he had reestablished contact with his Soho criminal friends, then he would have to go to Soho; if he was going to claim that he had landed near Ely and then taken the morning train to London, he would have to be able to describe what the place looked like in daylight. His German spymaster had asked for additional information such as troop movements and defensive measures, and if he was going to maintain his credibility he would have to start delivering – or at least appearing to deliver – what they wanted. Clearly, he could not do this cooped up in Hendon. He would need to go and do some snooping; John Masterman and the censors on the Twenty Committee could then decide what could be safely sent to Von Gröning.

MI5 sensed that the Abwehr was becoming impatient. Fritz had been in Britain for three weeks when a message arrived demanding: 'PLEASE SEND SPECIFIC INFO ON MAIN GOVERNMENT AND WAR OFFICES.' A few days later another message landed: 'PLEASE GIVE NAME PLACE AND SHORT DESCRIPTION OF YOUR ARRIVAL.'

Chapman swiftly replied: 'FFFFF LANDED TWO MILES NORTH OF ELY AND BURIED GEAR. TOOK TRAIN NEXT DAY WITH TRANSMITTER TO LONDON AND LATER CONTACTED FRIENDS. ALL OK. FRITZ.' But Von Gröning had plainly had enough of cheery but vague reassurances. He wanted some particulars. So Backwell and Tooth now instituted a series of day trips for their housemate. They took him back to Ely, to the spot where he had landed, and traced his notional walk to Wisbech railway station, where they ate fish and chips. They visited the spots that a German spy might visit: they walked around the Hendon aerodrome, the London railway termini, and the parts of the City of London that had suffered recent bomb damage. They began to drop in more often at the Hendon Way pub, where the three men became 'well known and accepted'. No one asked them questions; there was something about the two older men, sitting in front of their beer in the corner of the snug that did not invite familiarity.

They went clothes shopping in the West End, keeping a lookout for military transport vehicles, American army signs, bomb damage, government offices and criminals who might recognise Chapman. 'Eddie soon began to regain his confidence,' Backwell reported; 'In spite of this he never tried to lose either Allan or myself, and seemed nervous if we were away from him for a short time.' Such trips were vital background for Chapman's cover story, but more than that they 'helped to keep his mind occupied'. As Backwell and Tooth were discovering, Chapman's mind, when left unoccupied, tended to turn to dark thoughts, dwelling on Freda and his daughter, and his own sexual frustration.

Chapman seemed 'terribly restless'. He remarked that he did not know how to translate the technical German words used in bomb-making, so a German teacher, Mrs Barton, was sent to Crespigny Road to provide personal tuition. John Masterman, like a don with a demanding student, suggested he be given the four-volume Muret Saunders German dictionary, to study in bed. More books and magazines were provided, but Chapman could not sit still for more than a few minutes. One night he confessed to Tooth that he had 'feelings of nihilism – when he feels his life is empty and nothing really matters'. Reed was becoming increasingly alarmed by Chapman's depressive outbursts, his fidgety impatience and repeated references to sex. 'His inherent boisterousness and vitality soon turned to the path of the inevitable feminine relaxation . . . Many attempts were made to sublimate these emotions and direct his energy into more profitable channels.'

Reed, Tar Robertson and John Masterman held a planning meeting and agreed that Chapman's restlessness made it 'quite impossible to run him as a long term double agent in this country', for he was temperamentally unsuited to the 'cloistered life'. A broad strategy was laid out: the sabotage of the De Havilland factory would be faked, as elaborately, loudly and convincingly as possible; Chapman would claim credit with his German spymasters, and then return to occupied France, probably via Lisbon; he should not take back accomplices, or contact other Allied agents in France, but carry out intelligence and perhaps sabotage work on behalf of Britain, to be specified at a later date.

That evening, Reed visited Crespigny Road to explain the decisions that had been made. Chapman was sitting in a chair looking 'very pale'. Tooth explained in an undertone that he had been listening to the radio, when Chapman had walked in and heard a 'reference to secret inks and troop movements'. The news referred to some entirely unconnected event, but for a ghastly moment Chapman – as ever assuming a central role in any drama – had thought the report must be about himself, and was still in shock

Reed initiated a general conversation about the future. He pointed out that if the simulated attack on the De Havilland plant worked out as hoped, then the Germans would be delighted and might want to keep him in Britain. Would Chapman be prepared to stay, and perhaps carry out other, faked acts of sabotage?

Chapman shook his head. 'I have another, more personal matter to conduct on my return, in Berlin.'

'Any individual enterprise, on your part, no matter how

commendable, would probably be less satisfactory than our recommendations,' said Reed.

Chapman was tart: 'Since you don't know my plans, how can you judge?'

'I think you should tell us exactly what you propose to do.'

'I will not do that. You would think it absurd and impossible. As I am the sole judge of whether I can pull it off, it is best if I keep it to myself.'

Chapman was stubborn, but with 'a great amount of patience and sympathy', Reed pressed him, again and again, to say what was on his mind. Finally, Chapman relented, and took a deep breath.

'Dr Graumann has always kept his promises to me, and I believe he will keep the promises he made about what will happen when I return. He believes I am pro-Nazi. I always said "Heil Hitler!" in the presence of groups of people and expressed admiration for Hitler as a man and for the Nazi philosophy. Whenever Hitler was speaking on the radio, I always listened with rapt attention, and I told Dr Graumann how much I would like to be present at a Nazi rally where Hitler spoke.' Graumann had promised to obtain Chapman a seat near the podium, 'in the first or second row' . . . even if it meant dressing him in the uniform of a high official.

'I believe Dr Graumann will keep his promise.' Chapman paused. 'Then I will assassinate Hitler.'

Reed sat in stunned silence, but Chapman was still talking. 'I am not sure yet exactly how I will do it, but with my knowledge of explosives and incendiary material it should be possible.'

Reed recovered his composure sufficiently to protest that it would be extremely difficult to get close enough to the Führer to throw a bomb. 'Whether or not you succeeded, you would be liquidated immediately.'

Chapman grinned. 'Ah, but what a way out.'

Reed did not try to dissuade him. Late into the evening they discussed the possibilities. Chapman explained that he could never lead a normal life in Britain, given his past; nor could he remain in occupied France forever. Here was an opportunity to give meaning to his life, albeit by forfeiting it.

Writing up his report that night, Reed tried to divine what drove this latest, extraordinary twist in the Zigzag affair. In part, the offer to assassinate Hitler seemed to spring from the suicidal nihilism that sometimes weighed on Chapman. But he was also hungry for fame, seeking 'the big way out'. Reed remembered how Chapman had once hoarded newspaper clippings of his crimes: 'He can think of no better way of leaving this life than to have his name prominently featured throughout the world's press, and to be immortalised in history books for all time – this would crown his final gesture.' There was something desperate about this self-appointed mission; a crooked man's offer to assassinate a truly evil one. Yet there was also something else, a strange spark of heroism, a sense of moral obligation in a person whose only duty, hitherto, had been to himself. Reed was moved. 'I believe he has a considerable amount of loyalty towards Great Britain.'

15

Freda and Diane

Where was Freda? Chapman's inquiries were persistent. What had been a request was now a demand. He was petulant, and becoming confrontational. One night he confided to Backwell that the care of Freda and Diane was the only thing that now mattered to him. He must make amends. The policeman reported: 'He wants to provide for the [child] in whom, he has said, his one interest lies.' He even spoke of taking custody of Diane, if Freda was in difficulty, but conceded that this was 'impossible' in the current circumstances. He asked Tooth, in the event of his death, to give Diane the complete works of H.G. Wells on her sixteenth birthday. But at the same time he wondered if it would be better for his daughter never to 'know of his existence, [since] he would only handicap her and cause her pain and trouble'.

'Personal matters occupy a great deal of his attention,' Backwell reported. If killing Hitler was one self-appointed mission for Chapman, then caring for Freda and Diane was the other.

One night, he lost his temper and scribbled a furious note to Tar Robertson: 'My sources of information have practically run dry. I can be of no further service here, and for many, many personal reasons I don't wish to stay here one day longer.' Backwell passed on the letter, with an accompanying note: 'He feels his present position is intolerable, being in the country again, and yet unable to see old acquaintances and do as he

pleases . . . E is essentially a man of action who cannot by nature
follow a stereotypical form of living.' Backwell was convinced
that only a meeting with his former lover and their daughter
would put Chapman back into a reasonable frame of mind. 'The
question of Freda always seems to be at the back of his mind,' he
wrote. 'The arrangement of a meeting with Freda would almost
completely solve his problems.'

Reed was doubtful. There was no telling how Freda might
react to a reunion. The security risk was too great, since 'if she
bore any malice and realised Zigzag was back in the country she
would probably go to the police and cause an embarrassing
situation'. Even if a reunion went well, Freda would somehow
have to be incorporated into Chapman's cover story, possibly
putting her and the child at risk. He told Chapman that the
police were still trying to trace Freda while the 'authorities'
considered his request. Chapman reacted badly. He became even
more 'truculent and moody', and took to his bed. Reed was now
alarmed. Chapman plainly believed MI5 had already found
Freda, but was deliberately keeping them apart. And he was
right.

Police had tracked down Freda Elsie Louise Stevenson almost
immediately, because for some years Freda had been trying to
find Eddie Chapman 'in connection with an application for a
maintenance allowance'. She was now living with her daughter
in a boarding house at 17 Cossington Road, Westcliffe-on-Sea,
Essex.

Freda's life had grown steadily bleaker in the years since
Chapman left her at the age of nineteen. She had been living
in the flat in Shepherd's Bush when he vanished in 1939, a few
weeks before she discovered she was pregnant with Diane. She
had tried to find Eddie, first through a parade of Soho barmen,
then by asking around his criminal associates, and finally by
going to the police. This was how she learned that he was in
Jersey, in prison. She sent letters, and photographs. There was
never any reply. Then came the invasion, and there was no

longer any point in writing. A rumour went around the London underworld that Chapman had been shot by the Germans while trying to escape from Jersey.

Freda moved on. She had trained as a dancer, but when war started there was less and less dancing to be done. She moved to Southend, to be near her mother. A pale, frail creature, with large brown eyes and a small, down-turned mouth, she was trusting and gentle by nature; but also astonishingly resilient, and a ferociously protective mother. Her father, a bus driver, had died before she was born, so she, too, had been raised fatherless. She did not ask, or expect, much from life, and with what little life gave her, she made do. In August 1941, she had met and married a much older man called Keith Butchart, the manager of a balloon works. The marriage foundered almost immediately. One night, when Butchart was out drinking, Freda gathered up little Diane, burned her new husband's suit in the fire, and moved out.

She was living in a boarding house, and working part time as a firewoman, when the two officers from Special Branch arrived. In the front parlour, they asked her lots of questions about Eddie Chapman. When they went away, Freda hugged Diane, and felt a small glimmering of hope.

Back at Crespigny Road, Tooth and Backwell found that their role had expanded to include the care and maintenance of Chapman's libido. Not only did they have to cook, clean and find entertainment for their ward, they were now expected to help him find women of easy virtue. The two policemen accepted this new duty with cheerful resignation. Up to now MI5 had sought to steer Chapman away from what Reed had delicately termed 'feminine relaxation'. Now they were instructed that if Chapman wanted to relax, he should be encouraged to do so.

On 15 January, after dinner at the Landsdowne pub, Chapman and Backwell went to a part of New Bond Street known to be a red-light area. After a hurried negotiation in a doorway,

Chapman picked up a prostitute, who took him to a flat above a shop. 'Luckily there was a pub just opposite,' reported Backwell, 'and he promised to meet me there in about half an hour. He was as good as his word.' A few days later, the crook and the policemen went out 'relaxing' together. In Lyons Corner House, they met two girls, Doris and Helen, and invited them out to dinner. The men agreed beforehand that if anyone asked what Chapman did they would say he was a member of the armed forces 'just back from abroad' – a cover story that would also explain why he was so unfamiliar with life in wartime Britain. He had last lived in London in 1939, and it took weeks before he adapted to a world of coupons and rationing, blackouts and bomb shelters.

The visit to New Bond Street, perhaps inevitably, afforded only temporary relief. Soon Chapman was more depressed than ever. His minders came up with more elaborate diversions. One night, with Chapman wrapped up in coat, hat and scarf, they took him to see the stirring wartime film epic *In Which We Serve,* starring Noel Coward, Chapman's old acquaintance from his earlier life. Chapman was warned to be alert, and if he saw anyone he knew to make himself scarce and then meet his minders at a pre-arranged place. For a while the system worked well, and several times Chapman was able to spot former associates before they saw him. 'There was one amazing thing about Eddie,' Backwell reported. 'When it came to faces and descriptions he was superb. Often in London he would single out faces that he had seen before in a quite different place.'

But Chapman's own features were also distinctive. One evening, at the entrance to Prince's restaurant in the West End, Chapman came face to face with a 'cat-burglar' in a brown, double-breasted suit, whom he had known before the war. Flushed and 'slightly drunk', the man thrust out a hand and said: 'Hullo, stranger, fancy seeing you.' Tooth prepared to intervene, but Chapman 'looked hard at the man, said a formal "Hullo", and continued down the stairs.' The man followed, apologising for his mistake but still insisting that Chapman was the 'split [*sic*] image of someone he knew'. Chapman now broke into French – 'some jocular remark about having a twin' – and left the astonished man in the doorway. Backwell believed the bluff had worked: 'The man apologised and left, somewhat bewildered but, I think, fairly sure he had made a mistake.' Chapman claimed he had forgotten the man's name; none of his minders believed him. 'I suppose it is natural for Zigzag not to reveal the identity of this cat-burglar out of a sense of loyalty to his previous criminal associates,' reflected Reed. 'After all, it is really not our concern.'

The incident merely served to reinforce Chapman's frustration with his semi-captivity, in which he could observe the London he knew, but never be a part of it. He demanded to see Winston, his younger brother who he believed to be in the army, but was told (falsely) that 'so far our inquiries indicated that his brother was in India'. One night he contemplated climbing out the window at Crespigny Road and heading to the West End, but a flash of conscience stopped him, the realisation that 'it was not in the interests of his work or of his companions'. Yet he hankered for his old friends, and asked Reed to find Betty Farmer. Reed was not certain whether this was for amorous purposes, or to apologise for having abandoned her so spectacularly in a Jersey hotel dining room three years earlier. As always, Chapman's motives were hard to read: here was a man who kept every option open, who seemed congenitally incapable of taking a bet without hedging it. The last trace of Betty Farmer was her tearful statement to the Jersey police back in 1939. She had vanished. Reed thought this was just as well. Chapman's emotional life was already complicated enough.

It was decided to arrange a meeting with one of the very few people of Chapman's acquaintance who could be trusted: Terence Young, the film-maker, who was now an intelligence officer attached to the Field Security Section, Guards Armoured Division, in the Home Forces. In the intervening years, Young had become something of a celebrity as an up-and-coming film director and there were moves afoot to take him out of uniform to make propaganda films. Churchill was said to have taken a 'personal interest' in the project. Young was approached by Marshall of B1A, and asked, over tea at Claridge's, whether he would meet Chapman, in conditions of strict secrecy, to 'talk to him about some of his old friends' and 'build up his morale'. Young was delighted to agree, saying he had often wondered what had happened to his wicked old friend. 'He said that Zigzag was a crook and would always be one,' Marshall reported, 'but an extraordinary fellow.'

Young went on to describe the glamorous, roué world Chapman had inhabited before the war, the people he knew from 'the film, theatrical, literary, and semi-political and diplomatic worlds', and his popularity, 'especially among women'. Could Chapman be trusted with intelligence work, Marshall inquired? Young was adamant: 'One could give him the most difficult of missions knowing that he would carry it out and that he would never betray the official who sent him, but that it was highly probable that he would, incidentally, rob the official who sent him out . . . He would then carry out his [mission] and return to the official whom he had robbed to report.' In short, he could be relied on to do whatever was asked of him, while being utterly untrustworthy in almost every other respect.

Chapman and Young were reunited over a late dinner in a discreet corner booth at the Savoy, with Marshall as chaperone. They seemed 'delighted to see each other and conversation was very animated', Marshall reported. As the drink flowed, however, the discussion turned to the war, and Young expressed the view that an Allied victory was 'inevitable'. Chapman shot back that this was 'smug and complacent', before launching into a paean about 'Hitler's idealism and the strength and efficiency of the German soldier'. Despite the re-education efforts of Tooth and Backwell, the effects of living among Nazis for so long still lingered. On the way home to Crespigny Road, Marshall warned Chapman of the 'folly of expressing such views, no matter how true they might be'.

Chapman's faith in German military efficiency was being undermined in another way: the Abwehr was still having technical difficulty with its wireless receivers. The Most Secret Sources revealed that a new radio station, codenamed 'Horst' and manned by a full-time operator identified as Leutnant Vogy, had been set up specifically to receive Fritz's messages at St Jean de Luz. But on 14 January, Maurice sent a message saying Chapman should continue to send his messages 'blind', because the new aerial had blown down. This new proof of ineptitude offered an opportunity to put the Germans on the defensive. The next message from Fritz to Von Gröning was, in Chapman's words, 'a stinker': 'FFFFF DISGUSTED AND WORRIED BY LACK OF RECEPTION. THIS IS A HOPELESS BUNGLE. HAVE BEEN PROMISED FULL SUPPORT AND MUST HAVE IT. WORK GOING SPLENDIDLY. HAVE FULL LIST OF ALL YOU WANT. YOU MUST DO SOME-THING TO CLEAR UP THE TROUBLE. F.'

For the next few days, Abwehr radio traffic was studied to gauge the effects of this broadside. There was nothing. Plainly, the radio operator had simply decided to suppress the irate message in order, in Reed's words, 'not to reap the wrath' of Von Gröning. Not for the first time (or last) the smaller cogs in a large machine took a unilateral decision to prevent the boss from finding out about their own incompetence. A few days later, Maurice sent a meek message saying that the aerial had been fixed and 'new arrangements have been made'. From that moment on, transmission and reception worked perfectly.

Backwell took Chapman shopping, for bombs. If Chapman was going to convince the Germans he had wrecked the De Havilland factory with explosives, then he must test whether it was possible, in reality, to obtain the necessary ingredients. It was astonishingly easy. At Timothy Whites they bought potassium chlorate in the shape of weed killer. At Boots in Harrow they picked up potassium permanganate and nitrate of saltpeter; J.W. Quibell in the Finchley Road was happy to sell Chapman sulphur powder, moth crystals and aluminium powder in the form of silver paint; flour and sugar could be bought, for a price, at any grocer. Britain might be in the grip of rationing, but buying the materials for a homemade bomb was a piece of cake. (In fact, obtaining the ingredients for a decent cake would have been rather harder.) Chapman's shopping list was never queried: when he mistakenly asked for 'Kalium' (the German for potassium), a pharmacist's assistant merely thought he was being asked for calcium. Back at Crespigny Road, Chapman experimented 'on a small scale' with mixing various explosives. This time he did not practise blowing anything up: unlike the neighbours at La Bretonnière, the good people of Hendon would certainly not have tolerated lumps of burning tree-stump whizzing around their back gardens. 'This kept Eddie busy,' wrote Backwell, but 'he was terribly restless, and could not concentrate for long on any one thing.'

Perhaps Chapman should have been content, making bombs, brushing up his German, meeting old friends, sending sharp little notes to his German masters and gathering together the strands of a cover story, but he was miserable. His longing to see Freda and the child had become an obsession. He talked of little else. Reed realised that a problem was about to ignite a crisis: 'In this frame of mind he might easily have gone bad on us when he returned, and revealed to the enemy his association with us. Even if this did not happen he would probably have been unwilling to carry out any of our instructions and would have acted entirely on impulse and his own fancies.'

Marshall, Reed's deputy, was sent to Crespigny Road to have a heart-to-heart with Chapman over a bottle of whisky. Marshall was a sympathetic character, and an excellent listener. As they drank and talked, Chapman began to open up as never before. He spoke entirely in French, which 'tends to break down his natural reserve and to lead him to express his innermost

thoughts', Marshall noted. Chapman talked of his harsh childhood, his resentment at his lack of education, his impatience and
his desire to make amends for the past, and of his desire to find a
rationale for living, or dying.

They talked until 3.00 in the morning. Marshall's nine-page
account of this 'serious and intimate' conversation is one of the
most revealing documents in the Zigzag files: a complete
character study of a man wrestling with differing elements in
his own nature.

'He is endeavouring, perhaps for the first time, to understand
himself and the meaning of life,' wrote Marshall. 'During the last
three years he has discovered thought, H.G. Wells, literature,
altruistic motives and beauty. Although he does not regret his
past life he feels he has no place in society and it would be better
if he dies – but not needlessly. He wishes to make retribution for
the bad things he has done. He cannot be satisfied that he has
done something of value unless he actually performs some
concrete action himself.'

He confessed that he was torn between patriotism and
egotism, and 'fighting against himself'. Hitherto, he had always
'acted for himself and had done what he wanted to do'; but he
had changed. 'Now he had realised that he must consider other
people and he was finding it very difficult.' At one stage
Chapman turned to his companion with a pained expression
and asked: 'Do you consider that personal life is more important
than one's country or ideals?'

Marshall replied that he did not.

The next question was still more profound: 'What do you
think is the purpose of life?'

This time Marshall had his answer: 'I said that I believed that
man was climbing to some high destiny, that he had struggled
from his ape-like existence to his present state of civilisation, that
he was gradually climbing and that it was the duty of every one
of us to help man onwards in his ascent.'

Realising how high-minded this must sound, Marshall added

quickly: 'This does not necessarily mean we have to be "goody-goody". War is a bestiality.'

Chapman pondered Marshall's words, and remarked that this credo was similar to that of H.G. Wells and, insofar as he had one, his own philosophy. They spoke of socialism and capitalism, patriotism and duty. 'It rather seemed,' thought Marshall, 'as if he had come on these things for the first time, and thought them great discoveries, as indeed they are.'

Now it was Marshall's turn to ask a question: 'What personal part do you propose to play in helping man in his struggle?'

Chapman's reply was bleak: 'My life is of little value and it would be better for me to die – not to throw my life away needlessly, but to do something by which I could make retribution [*sic*] for the wrongs I have committed.'

Marshall shot back that this was 'the coward's way out. If you cause yourself to die now, that is an admission of defeat. You are now a thinking man. Man must progress, and you must play your part in making that progress possible. It is for you to decide whether a British victory would help mankind in his upwards progress, or whether it would be better if Nazi principles prevail.'

Chapman replied that he had already made his mind up on that score: 'England cannot be allowed to lose the war.'

Marshall reflected that Chapman 'has seen too much brutality and horror, the cowed French population [and] the brutality of the Gestapo,' to be able to stand aside. Marshall made his way home from Crespigny Road in the freezing London dawn, convinced that Chapman would now 'play his part'.

Reed was fascinated by Marshall's report of his evening with Chapman, describing it as 'a most valuable character study'. It revealed a man anxious to do his duty, but also determined to find some sort of resolution to his inner turmoil. Finding Chapman's 'higher destiny' in the war against Hitler would not be possible until he had made peace closer to home. It was time to unleash Operation Freda.

On 26 January 1943, Freda and Diane were driven up to London, and lodged at the Brent Bridge Hotel. The reunion took place that night. Backwell and Tooth, such gentle jailers, provided flowers, a bottle of champagne and babysitting services. While Freda Stevenson and Eddie Chapman got reacquainted in an upstairs room, the policemen played with three-year-old Diane in the hotel lobby. Eddie had been coached to tell Freda that he had escaped from Jersey, and that in return the police had dropped all charges. 'He would now join the army and be posted overseas.' She accepted the explanation without question. The following day, Freda and Diane moved into Crespigny Road, to become, in Backwell's words, 'part of the household' now comprising one crook and double agent, one dancer-turned-firewoman, one energetic toddler and two long-suffering policemen.

Freda had re-entered Chapman's life as abruptly and completely as he had left hers, almost four years earlier. In this bizarre parody of domesticity, Chapman no longer demanded trips to the West End or meetings with his former cronies, but seemed 'quite content to limit himself to our own circle'. Of an evening the young couple would walk, arm in arm, to the Hendon Way, while one policeman followed at a discreet distance, and the other looked after Diane and did the chores.

Of course, the twin tasks of running an expanded household while operating an untested double agent did present logistical challenges. Freda had moved into Chapman's bedroom. The challenge was, therefore, 'to get Freda up, dressed and downstairs before 9.45 am, as the tapping of the key could be heard in the bathroom or on the stairs'. There was the additional difficulty that Mrs West, the cleaner, came in during the mornings, but had to be prevented from operating her vacuum cleaner when Chapman was transmitting.

One evening, at around 7.00, Chapman announced that he and Freda were retiring to bed. 'Eddie, we're on the air at 9 o'clock,' whispered Reed as the couple left. 'Don't forget.'

At 8.00, Reed tiptoed up the stairs and knocked gently on the door. 'You've got an hour, Eddie.' There was no reply.

At 8.45, Reed banged on the door. 'You've only got fifteen minutes, Eddie.'

Chapman poked his head around the door. 'Oh no, not just fifteen minutes,' he said, and vanished inside again.

Reed was wondering whether he would have to go in and insist on *coitus interruptus* himself when, with minutes to spare, a tousled Freda finally emerged.

Freda responded to the subterfuge with an impressive lack of curiosity. Her lover was seldom out of sight of one, and usually two, burly men, who monitored his every move. More men, usually in civilian clothes but including one with striking tartan trousers, came and went at odd times of day, and Freda was often told to take a long walk with the toddler. Sometimes Eddie could be heard practising German nouns. There were some very odd-looking chemicals in the kitchen cupboard. 'Freda must have got very used to the strange happenings,' Backwell reflected. 'But she never asked any questions.' When she and Chapman had lived together in Sterndale Road, there had been strange comings and goings and peculiar men whose presence and business was never explained, so it may have seemed just like old times. 'Although she knew very little of what was going on, she accepted things without question and became quite accustomed to the three of us always being together,' wrote Tooth.

The transformation in Chapman's mood was immediate. 'Since he has seen Freda and the child, E has been in very good spirits and says that his whole outlook towards the future has changed. He now has a "raison d'être". He has lost interest in other women and in going to the West End, and says he is quite prepared to remain in this neighbourhood, working on his cover story and preparations for his return to France.' In place of the gloomy grouch of before, the new Chapman seemed positively ebullient. He doted on his daughter, a bubbly child whose vitality and noise filled the house. Chapman's black nihilism gave way to an equally extreme optimism, and exaggerated self-confidence. He even began to discuss what he might do when the war ended, something he had never done before. He talked of moving to Poland with Freda, and setting up a cabaret, or simply returning to crime since he doubted 'his capacity to live a law-abiding life'. But he also wondered whether there might be a place for him in the secret services, as this 'would fulfil his need for excitement'.

Tooth privately doubted very much whether MI5 would welcome Chapman as a permanent addition to its ranks, but noted that at least the young man was feeling positive: 'Previously, he had no faith in the existence of a future for him, and had little desire for it.' Having achieved one mission – reuniting with Freda and his child – Chapman was now eager to complete the next, the fake sabotage of the De Havilland factory.

'What a man!' wrote Ronnie Reed, on learning that Operation Freda had succeeded beyond all expectations. 'It is extraordinary how obvious a course of action seems after it has been taken. The introduction of a specific woman into the case overcame nearly all difficulty and re-orientated the whole picture of his emotional problems and his attitude to life.' By an odd coincidence, it was discovered that Chapman's divorce from Vera Freiberg had been made absolute during his time in prison. He promptly proposed to Freda, who sensibly suggested that they might wait until after he had returned from active service.

There was more than mere altruism in MI5's pleasure at the turn of events: an Eddie Chapman with a fiancée and child in Britain was far less likely to defect to Germany. Given his previous record, Chapman's marriage proposal today might well be forgotten tomorrow, but as Reed noted sagely 'this resolution provides a strong incentive for him to return to Allied Territory'. Chapman's British spymasters were, on the whole, honourable and upright men, but they knew a useful lever when they saw one. Just as the Germans held Faramus as a hostage for

Chapman's loyalty, so MI5 could now be expected to look after Freda, just so long as Chapman behaved himself. Of course, the matter was never expressed in such bald terms. There was no need to be so vulgar.

As for Freda, perhaps she genuinely never realised her pivotal role in the unfolding drama, nor imagined that the polite gentleman visitors who treated her so courteously had an ulterior motive; maybe she never asked any questions because she really never suspected a thing. But then again, Freda was a born survivor, and if she did understand the part she was playing, she was far too canny to say so.

16

Abracadabra

Persuading the Germans that the De Havilland aircraft factory had been wrecked, without causing any real damage, would require some powerful magic. So a magician was summoned. Enter, Jasper Maskelyne: professional conjuror, star of the West End, and Britain's most flamboyant secret weapon. Maskelyne came from a long line of magicians, alchemists and astronomers (his grandfather had been a celebrated stage conjurer in Victorian Britain) and by the 1930s he was already well known as a master-illusionist, specialising in sleight of hand and exposing the fraudulent claims of spiritualists. He was also a skilled inventor (one of his most lasting gifts to humanity is the coin-operated toilet door. When you 'spend a penny', you owe it to Jasper Maskelyne). He looked as a conjurer ought, with lacquered centre-parting, film-star moustache, top hat and magic wand. He was very clever, and insufferably vain.

When he first offered to contribute his magical skills to the war effort he was dismissed as a showman (which he was) and put to work entertaining the troops. But eventually General Archibald Wavell, the imaginative commander of British forces in North Africa, realised that Maskelyne's talents might be applied to the battlefield. Maskelyne was sent to the Western Desert, where he assembled 'The Magic Gang', possibly the most eccentric military unit ever formed, whose members included an analytical chemist, a cartoonist, a criminal, a stage-designer, a picture restorer, a carpenter and a lone professional soldier to fill out the military paperwork. The gang set about bamboozling the enemy. They built fake submarines and Spitfires, disguised tanks as trucks, and successfully hid part of the Suez Canal using a system of revolving mirrors and searchlights that created a blinding vortex in the sky nine miles wide.

For his greatest trick, Maskelyne helped to win the Battle of El Alamein by creating an entire array of 'tricks, swindles and devices' to convince Erwin Rommel that the British counter-attack was coming from the south, rather than the north. In 1942, the Magic Gang built over two thousand dummy tanks and constructed a bogus water pipeline to water this phony army. The half-built pipeline was easily spotted from the air, and the slow progress of its construction seems to have convinced the Germans that no attack was possible before November. Rommel went home on leave, and the attack started on 23 October. After the victory, Churchill praised the 'marvellous system of camouflage' that had helped to make it possible.

This, then, was the ideal person to help make the De Havilland factory disappear in a puff of smoke. According to Charles Fraser-Smith, a supplier of military gadgets to the secret services who would later be immortalised as 'Q' in the James Bond novels, Maskelyne was called in to make it 'look, from the air, as if the place had been blown to Kingdom Come'. In consultation with Tar Robertson and Colonel Sir John Turner, head of the Air Ministry camouflage section, a plan for faking the sabotage of the factory began to take shape.

At first the planners contemplated laying asbestos sheets across the roof, and then simply starting a large fire which would surely be spotted by German reconnaissance. Masterman vetoed this idea, pointing out that the flames would make a very tempting target for the Luftwaffe, with the 'danger that the Germans may try to bomb the factory while the fire is burning'. Instead, it was decided to erect a veil of camouflage so convincing that it would seem, from the ground as well as from the air, as if a very large bomb had exploded inside the factory power plant.

The camouflage technicians constructed four replicas of sub-transformers out of wood and papier-mâché, painted a metallic grey. Two of these would be rolled over, as if blown sideways by the force of the blast. Meanwhile the real transformers would be covered with netting and corrugated iron sheets painted to look, from high above, like a 'vast hole' in the ground. On the night of the deception, the large green wooden gates to the transformer building would be replaced by a pair of mangled and broken green gates. The walls of the smaller building would be draped with tarpaulins, painted to look like the half-demolished remnants of a brick wall, while the other walls would be covered in soot, as if blackened from an explosion. Rubble and debris would be spread around the compound to a radius of 100 feet. Colonel Turner assured Tar that the reconnaissance pilots, as well as any German agent sent to inspect the damage, would be utterly fooled.

Chapman tapped out a message to Von Gröning: 'FFFFF WALTER READY TO GO. BEGIN PREPARATIONS FOR MY RETURN. F'

Military meteorologists studied the weather forecast and the passage of the moon, and decreed that the attack would be best staged on the night of 29/30 January, when there should be little cloud cover (allowing the Germans to see what had been done) but long hours of darkness. That night, the moon would not rise until 2.30 in the morning, giving the conjurers at least three hours of darkness in which to perform.

Building a convincing stage-set was only one half of the production. To convince the Germans, the press reviews would have to be fixed as well, and for that only one newspaper would suffice: *The Times* – 'The Thunderer', the organ of the British establishment. Chapman had arranged to send Stephan von Gröning messages through *The Times*; MI5 would now employ the same direct method of communication to feed him a lie.

The editor of *The Times* was Robert Barrington-Ward, a pillar of press probity who shared the same alma mater as John Masterman. Even so, Masterman warned that getting Barrington-Ward to play ball might be 'extremely difficult'. Masterman briefly laid the situation before him, emphasised the importance of the deception, and then asked if the newspaper would agree to 'publish a small paragraph on the Saturday morning following the incident'. Barrington-Ward refused, politely, regretfully and adamantly, observing that 'though he would like to help, the suggestion that he should insert what was in fact a bogus notice in *The Times* cut across his whole policy. Not only the reputation but the public utility of *The Times* depended entirely on the principle that it should never insert any items of news which it did not believe to be true.' Masterman remonstrated. The single paragraph deception was such 'a small thing in itself'. But Barrington-Ward did not budge: 'The answer is respectfully no'.

The editor of *The Times* was technically right: when an independent newspaper, even in wartime, deliberately publishes falsehoods, it ceases to be either independent, or a newspaper. Barrington-Ward also dissuaded Masterman from trying to 'plant' the false story in the press via the Ministry of Information, since this would either involve lying to the newspapers or, worse, letting journalists in on the ruse, a strategy certain to end in disaster since most hacks are, by nature, incapable of keeping a secret. Instead, Barrington-Ward advised Masterman to make a 'private approach' to others of his profession who might adhere to less firm ethical principles: the *Daily Telegraph*, perhaps, or the *Daily Express*. Masterman was not used to being lectured on ethics. Somewhat embarrassed, the two men shook hands and agreed they would both regard the negotiation as 'not having taken place'.

Arthur Christiansen, editor of the *Express*, was either less fastidious, or more patriotic, or both. He, too, pointed out that the hoax 'meant him deliberately publishing something in the paper which he knew was not true', but he was happy to oblige. Indeed, he relished the idea of pulling the wool over German eyes but pointed out that under wartime censorship rules he was not supposed to publish anything likely to encourage the enemy. Reporting the destruction of a vital aircraft factory was firmly in the category of unprintable news and if he did so, 'the censors, as soon as they saw the paragraph, would be shouting down his 'phone'. They struck a compromise: Christiansen would publish the fake report, but only in his earliest edition, which was sent to Lisbon, from whence it would be distributed, via the German consulate, to Germany and the occupied territories. If the Germans ever discovered that the notice had appeared only in the first edition they would simply conclude the censor had spotted it and forced the editor to cut it out of later editions. Masterman drafted a one-paragraph account of a news event that had not happened, and never would. Christiansen, chuckling, translated it into journalese.

Chapman sent a message alerting Von Gröning to the planned date of the sabotage: 'FFFFF ARRANGEMENTS FOR WAL-TER ARE NOW COMPLETE. OBJECTIVES ARE SUB-STATIONS'.

The last elements of the elaborate deception were slotted into place. Fighter Command was instructed to watch out for reconnaissance planes over the Hatfield area, but on no account to attack them. If any factory employees asked about the painted tarpaulins, the factory owner would say that this was part of a test 'to see if high altitude photography can pick up minor damage'. If the press turned up they should be told that 'something had occurred, but very small and not worthwhile reporting'. That should get the rumour-mill grinding.

As darkness fell, a team of camouflage experts from the Royal Engineers, including a number of stage designers who had worked at the Old Vic, slipped into the De Havilland aircraft factory and set about perpetrating the fraud. It seems likely that

Maskelyne led the team, though he may simply have watched from the wings. That was typical of the man: now you saw him, and now you didn't. This was prestidigitation on an industrial scale, yet in a few hours the camouflage team was finished, and Ronnie Reed watched them disappear into the 'inky blackness'. Shortly before midnight the people of Hatfield were woken by a loud explosion.

Dawn broke on a panorama of devastation. The site of the bogus blast was 'surrounded by chaos', in Reed's words. Brick, rubble, bent iron, lumps of concrete and splintered wood were spread around the substation courtyard. From the side, the smaller building appeared to have been struck with a giant mallet, while the dummy transformers lay smashed among the debris, like the guts of some vast disembowelled animal. Even the boiler-room operator was convinced, for he arrived at the factory office 'in a state of great excitement', shouting that the building had been struck by a bomb. A screen was swiftly erected, as if to keep out prying eyes.

Tar Robertson surveyed the conjurer's handiwork, and professed himself delighted. 'The whole picture was very convincing,' wrote Reed. 'Aerial photography from any height above 2,000 feet would show considerable devastation without creating any suspicion.' The weather conditions were not ideal, with thick cloud cover, but if 'the other side paid a visit' they would witness a 'scene of destruction', a con trick painted on canvas. This, wrote Fraser-Smith, was 'Maskelyne's masterpiece'.

Chapman dispatched a triumphant wireless message: 'FFFFF WALTER BLOWN IN TWO PLACES.' That night, an exultant Stephan von Gröning ordered 'champagne all round' at La Bretonnière. A reply duly arrived: 'CONGRATULATIONS ON GOOD RESULT OF WALTER. PLEASE SEND INFO ON NEWSPAPER REPORTS. WILL DO ALL WE CAN ARRANGE YOUR RETURN. STATE PROPOSITIONS.'

DAILY EXPRESS

Monday, 1 February 1943
First edition

FACTORY EXPLOSION

Investigations are being made into the cause of an explosion at a factory on the outskirts of London. It is understood that the damage was slight and there was no loss of life.

The very terseness of the newspaper report was designed to imply there was more to the story. The first edition was printed at 5.00 a.m., and copies were dispatched, as usual, to Lisbon.

By a pleasing coincidence, the day after the bombing, Hermann Göring, who had boasted that no enemy aircraft could fly unscathed over Berlin, was due to address a military parade in the German capital. Before he had begun speaking, Mosquitoes from 105 Squadron droned overhead, and began pounding the city, disrupting the procession and enraging the head of the Luftwaffe. The same afternoon, Mosquitoes from 139 Squadron inflicted similar indignity on a parade being addressed by Dr Goebbels. Once more the Mosquito had demonstrated its worth. With what satisfaction the German High Command must have received the news that the Mosquito factory was now in ruins, thanks to a German sabotage agent.

The tone of Von Gröning's congratulatory message to Agent Fritz suggested that the Abwehr was in no hurry to bring him back, given the excellent results achieved so far. MI5, however, wanted to return Chapman to France as soon as possible, before the police found out that they were sheltering a known criminal. As Tar remarked: 'The Security Service is, as matters stand, compounding two felonies at least, and a great many more which it believes to have been committed.' Chapman, buoyed with new-found confidence, was just as keen to get to work, as a spy, a saboteur or an assassin.

Chapman's offer to kill Hitler was rejected, without fanfare or explanation. MI5's files are suspiciously silent on the subject. Although the proposition must have been debated at the highest levels, in the declassified documents there remains no trace of this. The official report on the Zigzag case describes in detail Chapman's proposal to blow up the Führer, but the passage immediately following – which presumably records the response to the offer – has been blanked out by MI5's internal censor.* Perhaps the veto came from Churchill himself. In May 1942, British-trained Czech partisans had killed Reinhard Heydrich, Hitler's potential successor and the head of Reich security, but the hideous wave of reprisals that followed had persuaded the British Cabinet to rule out further assassination attempts. Perhaps Chapman was too loose a cannon to be fired at such a moving target. It is equally possible that Chapman, now he had discovered love and fatherhood, was no longer so keen 'to depart in a blaze of glory'.

Reed believed Von Gröning's promise to send Chapman to a Nazi rally had been 'vague'. On the contrary, it had been most specific. Despite his own reservations about Hitler, Von Gröning had responded enthusiastically to the idea of placing Chapman in close proximity to the Führer, even if that meant disguising him as a German officer. This raises another, intriguing possibility. Von Gröning, like many members of the Abwehr, was fundamentally opposed to the Nazi regime. Some Abwehr officers had been plotting to bring down Hitler since 1938, and the July plot to assassinate the Führer the following year would lead to the abolition of the Abwehr and the execution of Canaris himself. Had Von Gröning seen in Chapman a potential tool for assassinating Hitler? Did the German aristocrat himself cherish an ambition 'to be immortalised in history books for all time'?

* See National Archives, File KV2/459. Document 254 B, paragraph 50.

Had he divined that his prize spy, for all his apparent commitment, might have an ulterior motive for wanting to get alongside the Nazi leader? Were Chapman and Von Gröning secretly working together to this end? The answers will probably never be known, because British intelligence quietly quashed the idea. John Masterman seldom made, and almost never admitted, a mistake. Yet after the war he still wondered if a grave error had been made when MI5 'declined to encourage' Chapman's proposal to kill Hitler: 'Perhaps we missed an opportunity, for Zigzag was an enterprising and practical criminal.'

Within MI5, debate still raged over what to make of Chapman. Reed, Masterman and Robertson were certain that he was 'frank and straightforward', though mercurial. 'His sincerity can hardly be doubted,' insisted Reed. The Cockney scholarship boy from the tenements of King's Cross understood Chapman's harsh background, and could speak his language. Others were unconvinced. Captain Shanks, one of Reed's brother case officers, decided Chapman was a fraud, 'a man whose stock-in-trade is the attractive, suave and agreeable manner, a superficial elegance . . . He gives the impression of the rolling stone who has gathered no moss, but acquired a certain amount of polish.' Shanks thought it 'possible' that Chapman's character contained 'a spark of decency', but he was doubtful. Here was a profiteer and a pirate who had agreed to work for the Germans out of pure self-interest, and was now offering his services to Britain with the same base motives. 'Chapman is no fool, he may have decided to run with the hare and hunt with the hounds. It is difficult to accept that a man who has all his life been an enemy of society should be actuated by any patriotic sentiments.' Shanks conceded that 'whether a patriot or opportunist, Chapman has undoubtedly done this country a service', but he could not conceal his distaste.

Such observations were partly true, but they also reflected the gulf between the predominantly upper-class and well-educated doyens of the secret services, and the working-class, unschooled crook with whom they were now in league. It had not escaped the notice of the more snobbish case officers that Chapman tried to cover up his North Eastern accent with 'a refined manner of speaking', but that he struggled to sound educated. 'His natural and instinctive speech is at times ungrammatical,' noted one interrogator. 'But I think it is to be admired that a man of his background and character should have acquired even the rudimentary culture which he has.'

In no instance was the social gulf wider than between Eddie Chapman and Victor, Lord Rothschild – peer, millionaire, scientist, and the head of B1C, MI5's explosives and sabotage section.

Lord Rothschild was the product of Eton, Cambridge, Clubland and the topmost drawer of British society. He had an inherited title, everything money could buy, and an IQ of 184. Malcolm Muggeridge, the journalist and writer who worked in intelligence during the war, found him unbearable, suffused with 'the bogus certainties of science, and the equally bogus respect, accorded and expected, on account of his wealth and famous name'. But he was also oddly shy, and entirely fearless, with a boyish love of explosions. As head of B1C (with a staff of exactly two secretaries) Rothschild's role was anti-sabotage: to identify parts of Britain's war effort vulnerable to attack, and to defeat German sabotage plots. One of his tasks was to ensure that Winston Churchill's cigars were not booby-trapped. Another, far less amusing, was to dismantle German bombs: explosives concealed in coat hangers, bombs disguised as horse droppings, Thermos flasks packed with TNT. This he did with astonishing coolness in a private laboratory paid for out of his own capacious pocket. 'When one takes a fuse to pieces,' he wrote, 'there is no time to be frightened.' Most people were happy to take Lord Rothschild's word for this.

As a trained German sabotage agent, Chapman obviously needed to be dismantled and examined by Lord Rothschild as carefully as any bomb. They met twice, talked for hours, and got on famously: the crook and the peer, two men with nothing in common save a shared interest in loud bangs. They discussed booby traps and incendiary devices, coal bombs, train bombs and the various ways to scuttle a ship. Chapman explained German techniques for making fuses out of wristwatches, ink bottles, and electric bulb filaments. He showed Lord Rothschild how to conceal a rail bomb with a butterfly, how to hide dynamite in blocks of marzipan, and how to make a detonator from a patented stomach medicine called Urotropin.

Rothschild absorbed it all with astonishment and admiration: 'I think it's terrific what you've kept in your mind. It's a hell of a sweat committing things to memory.'

'I've had quite a lot of experience of setting these things,' Chapman replied.

'Of course you knew a certain amount about this business before, didn't you?'

'I've had quite a little experience getting into places.'

'Are you an expert on electrical matters?'

'Not an expert, but I did start my hectic career as an electrical engineer.'

'The trouble about you is that you're too good at this sort of thing . . . I mean the average chap who presumably the Germans would get hold of wouldn't be so skilled with his fingers as you are.'

And thus they burbled on, delighting in one another's expertise, a highly trained scientist and an equally well-trained burglar.

'How do you open a safe then?' asked Rothschild.

'Well, you stick the dynamite in the keyhole and you don't damage the safe, only sometimes you put a little too much in and blow the safe door up, but other times you're lucky and the safe just comes open.'

Thus the scion of a great banking dynasty learned how to rob a bank.

When the conversation turned to the faked sabotage of the De Havilland factory, Rothschild grew wistful. 'I'd like to have done it with you,' His Lordship sighed. 'It would have been fun, wouldn't it?'

When they had finished with the past, they turned to the future.

'What are you going to do when you go back?' Rothschild asked.

'Well, I'm rather waiting for suggestions. I mean if I can be of any help, I want to do everything I can to assist.'

Rothschild had a suggestion: he would like to get his hands on some German bombs, detonators, and other gizmos: 'I think they ought to provide us with a little equipment.'

'Well, what would you like?'

'Some of their gadgets. If you do ever think of paying us a visit again, we'd rather like to have some German equipment instead of our own, you know. It's more interesting in some ways, isn't it?'

When Ronnie Reed appeared, in the middle of a discussion about how to make a bomb out of a piece of coal, Rothschild turned to him with all the enthusiasm of a child: 'We were just saying that we two would rather like to do a little show together – blow something up.'

Finally, with reluctance, Lord Rothschild wound up an interrogation that reads like a chat between two old friends with a shared hobby: 'We've been gassing away for a hell of a long time,' he said happily.

Chapman rose and shook hands with the chubby, beaming peer he knew as 'Mr Fisher'. 'Well, many thanks, goodbye,' said His Lordship. 'And good luck in case I don't see you again before you go off on one of your trips.' He might have been sending Chapman off on a jolly holiday, instead of a mission into the heart of Nazi Germany.

The Greater the Adventure

Major Tar Robertson came in person to congratulate Chapman on the success of the fake sabotage operation. They sat in the front room of 35, Crespigny Road, while Backwell and Tooth busied themselves in the kitchen, and Freda took Diane for a walk, again.

'I consider you to be a very brave man,' Tar declared. 'Especially in view of the fact that you are prepared to go back to France and carry on working for us.' Of the many spies that had passed through Camp 020, only a 'few, a very few', could be considered genuinely stout-hearted. Chapman, he said, was the bravest so far.

Tar then set out the broad lines of his mission. Once Chapman had learned his cover story, he would be returning to occupied France as a long-term counter-intelligence agent with the principal aim of acquiring information about the Abwehr. He should accept any mission offered to him by the Germans, and then contact Allied intelligence as opportunities arose. Chapman would not be provided with a wireless, since this could too easily lead to his exposure, and nor would he be put in contact with British agents operating in France, being 'far too valuable to risk by any such link-ups'. Arrangements would be made to enable him to pass on messages, but he should not attempt to communicate, unless he had information of the highest urgency, until contact was safely re-established.

'I am not at all keen for you to take any action in France
which might get you into trouble with the German authorities,
and I am most anxious for you not to undertake any wild
sabotage enterprises,' Robertson declared. Killing Hitler was not
on the agenda.

Before Tar could continue, Chapman raised a question that
had been troubling him since his conversation with Lord
Rothschild. If he returned with an accomplice – Leo, say,
or Wojch – 'people for whom he had a certain liking', then
presumably he would be expected to hand them over to the
police on arrival, 'knowing that in doing so these people would
be sentenced to death'. He was not sure he could do that. He
had never betrayed an accomplice yet. Tar responded that
although this was a matter for the law, he was 'pretty certain
that we would take every possible step to see that his wishes
were granted'. Chapman would not have to deliver his friends
to the hangman.

Tar resumed: 'We are preparing a cover story as near to the
truth as possible so that if you are cross-examined in detail by the
Germans, you need only tell them the truth.' The chief of
Double Cross had studied German interrogation techniques, he
knew the dangers Chapman would be facing, and he had even
drawn up a checklist of ways to withstand the pressure: 'Always
speak slowly, this enables hesitation to be covered when necessary; create the impression of being vague; do not appear to be
observant; give the impression of being bewildered, frightened
or stupid; feign drunkenness or tiredness long before they
actually occur.' Chapman might well face physical torture, drugs,
or anaesthetic, Tar warned, but German interrogators generally
preferred to get results by 'procuring *mental* breakdown . . . by
making the witness uncertain, uncomfortable, ridiculous or
embarrassed, by stripping him naked or dressing him in women's
underwear, making him stand facing the wall, making him sit on
a three-legged chair so that it is a constant effort to keep his
balance'. Chapman would probably face two interrogators: 'one

with a brutal manner, the other suave'. Above all, he should stick to his cover story, and never tell an unnecessary lie.

For all his expert advice, Robertson also knew that if Chapman fell into the hands of the Gestapo, and they chose to disbelieve him, they would break him. And then they would kill him.

The first task was to get Chapman back behind enemy lines, but the Abwehr seemed in no hurry to remove him. Despite Chapman's request to be picked up, the Most Secret Sources revealed that the matter was not even being discussed across the Channel. In response to the request for 'propositions', Chapman sent a message: 'FFFFF PICK UP BY SUBMARINE OR SPEEDBOAT. WILL FIND SUITABLE POINT ON COAST. TRYING TO GET SHIPS PAPERS. SEE BACK PAGE EXPRESS FEB 1.'

The response, a few days later, was blunt: 'IMPOSSIBLE PICK YOU UP BY SUBMARINE'. Instead, it said, Chapman must return by the 'NORMAL' way, in other words by ship to Lisbon. This had always been Von Gröning's preferred route, but there was nothing normal about booking a passage to neutral Portugal in the middle of a war. 'The suggestion was absurd,' said Reed, 'for Zigzag, being in the possession only of a poor identity card, aged 28 and having no business whatsoever, could not possibly go as a passenger.' The Germans probably knew this, and the suggestion was merely a ruse to keep him profitably in place. It was clear, said Reed, that 'any attempt to return to occupied territory would have to be made by Zigzag alone'. To Chapman's way of thinking, the refusal to send a U-boat was evidence that his German bosses were 'not over-anxious to pay him the £15,000 they had promised'.

Masterman believed there was a chance the Germans might eventually send a submarine but was 'not prepared to offer any odds', and trying to keep Chapman out of trouble while awaiting that distant possibility was an 'unenviable and practically impossible task'. Chapman must make his own way to Lisbon, with the help of MI5. Reed asked an MI5 agent in

Liverpool to find out how a man might be shipped, under a false identity, as a crewman aboard a British merchant vessel sailing to Portugal. The agent reported that such a scheme was feasible, 'provided the man could look and behave like a seaman'.

While Reed began planning Zigzag's departure, Chapman made his own preparations. A handwritten note duly arrived on Tar's desk under the heading, '<u>Points I would like to have done</u>'. It was his last will and testament. 'The Germans have given me a contract for £15,000' he wrote,

> this contract is at present in Berlin. I am to be given the money on my return to France. If anything happens to me I want the things which I have arranged for my daughter Dianne [*sic*] Chapman to be carried on – for this I appoint two of my friends – Allan and Laurie [Tooth and Marshall] to see what I want doing is carried out. Freda Stevenson is to divide the money equally between herself and daughter. If it is not possible for me to get the money out of the country, then I hope that when the Allies enter Germany they will make the Germans pay up 'Quoi meme'. This I have explained to Ronny [Reed]. In return I offer to do my best and obey any instructions given to me.

Some £350 had already been made over to Chapman from the money he had brought from France: from this, he asked that Freda be paid a regular weekly stipend of £5. When the money ran out, he hoped that MI5 would continue to pay the money until he was 'in a position to repay and continue the payments'. If he came by additional cash in France, he would try to channel the money back to Freda via a watchmaker he knew in Nantes who made regular trips to neutral Switzerland, whence money could be transferred to Britain.

'Zigzag is fully convinced that the Germans will pay him,' wrote Laurie Marshall. 'He does not ask the British authorities to pay any money to him or to his descendants.'

This was all most confusing for the more literal-minded members of MI5. Here was a grasping thief who seemed to have no interest in money for himself. Backwell had also noted that while Chapman was keen 'to get as much money as he can from the Germans, he does not seem very interested in the financial side of the undertaking'. He was scrupulous in paying his share of expenses, and once remarked wryly that with the cash he had brought over, he was 'paying for his stay' at Crespigny Road.

Under Masterman's 'principle of generosity', double agents should be compensated. But how much? Laurie Marshall, an accountant in peacetime, now began totting up Chapman's net worth as a spy. First, there was 'the risk to his life which he will incur on our behalf: he will do his utmost not to betray us [but] if his betrayal of the Germans is discovered he will pay with his life'. An additional factor was the value of the information he might obtain in the future: 'If Zigzag successfully reinstates himself with the Germans, he will be in a unique position to give us full information on the activities of the German SS in France, as soon as we are able to catch up with him.' Yet there was also an entry on the other side of the ledger: 'We cannot be absolutely certain that Zigzag, once returned to his friends in Nantes, will maintain 100% loyalty to us, nor can it be sure that he will fully carry out the mission given to him – he may carry out some individual task of his own. It is not considered that he will fail us, but we cannot have complete certainty.'

The equation was therefore: Chapman's life plus the value of his intelligence, minus the possibility that he might turn traitor, fail, or head off on some wild freelance mission. The accountant carefully added it all up and advised that: 'Substantial payment be made now to Zigzag [and] a further substantial payment should be promised after the successful completion of his mission or our obtaining information that although he had worked loyally for us, his mission had been unsuccessful owing to his being suspected by the Germans.' The money should be added to the cash already paid over, and if Chapman failed to return the total would automatically be paid to Freda and her daughter. In the meantime, a savings account would be opened, and the money invested in a 3 per cent war loan. That way the man being sought by British police and employed by two rival secret services would not only be profiting from the war, but investing in it. The money would be held in the London Co-Operative Society. Chapman had always favoured Co-Ops, though more for what he might take out of them than for what he could put into them.

So far, Zigzag's double-cross had gone without a hitch and that, to Reed's cautious mind, was a cause for concern: 'It was almost too good to be true and much more reasonable that arrangements should go a little wrong.' Chapman agreed: everything was 'going rather too smoothly'. Von Gröning would surely appreciate him even more if matters appeared to go slightly awry. Jimmy Hunt, or his fictional doppelgänger, would be the fall guy.

Chapman had already informed the Germans that he had recruited Hunt as an accomplice, and that he owed him £15,000 for his notional part in the De Havilland factory sabotage. Since it had been decided that Chapman would be returning alone, the fictional Hunt now needed to be disposed of, preferably in such a way as to put the wind up the Germans.

On the morning of 9 February, midway through sending a message to France, Chapman and Reed deliberately broke off the transmission with 'PPPPP', the agreed danger signal. Once again, the Germans failed to spot the warning. Reed was incensed: 'After making such careful arrangements for Zigzag to indicate that the police were on his track, they had failed him in practice.' The stakes would have to be raised.

The following day another message was sent: 'FFFFF DANGEROUS TO CONTINUE TRANSMITTING. THINGS GETTING AWKWARD. ESSENTIAL COME BACK WITH JIMMY. HAVE IMPORTANT DOCUMENTS. SHIPS PAPERS HARD TO OBTAIN.'

The story Chapman would tell the Germans was this: Jimmy Hunt had seen the German message refusing to send a submarine and, suspecting that he might not be paid, had begun to make trouble, demanding that he accompany Chapman back to France; the PPPPP signal had been sent, he would explain, because Jimmy had spotted a police car, which they suspected might be intercepting radio transmissions.

Once again, the German reply was complacent, ignoring the 'awkwardness' Chapman had referred to and requesting more information on the bombing of the factory. Chapman sent a terse message saying that the substations at the factory had been 'completely destroyed' by placing '60 lbs of gelignite under the transformers'. This was followed by another message saying he had 'seen a chance to return to Lisbon and asking if preparations had been made to receive him'. To this, there was no reply. Clearly, the Germans must be made to sit up and pay more attention.

On 12 February, the *Evening Standard* carried a news item under the headline 'Gelignite Inquiries' on the front page: 'A man was questioned at Shepherd's Bush police station last night in connection with the possession of gelignite.' The *News Chronicle* carried a similar story, reporting that '185 names have been taken during a club raid in Hammersmith'. Both stories were, of course, fake, placed in the newspapers with the connivance of their editors.

Chapman now sent his last wireless message: 'FFFFF JIMMY ARRESTED. SEE EVENING STANDARD FEBRUARY 12TH FRONT PAGE. CLOSING TRANSMITTER AT ONCE. WILL TRY AND GET TO LISBON. FRITZ'. In an internal memo, Reed ordered: 'No further transmissions are to be made on Zigzag's transmitter.' The fictional Jimmy Hunt had served his purpose, and could now be liquidated. The ZINC traffic was ended.

Chapman's last, panicky message seemed to have the desired effect. The Most Secret Sources picked up a worried transmis-

sion from Von Gröning, ordering radio operators in Paris and
Bordeaux to continue scanning the airwaves for any word from
his agent; to do anything else, he said, would be 'absolutely
inexcusable'.

In a single blow, MI5 had convinced the Germans that a prize
agent was now in mortal danger, Hunt had been removed from
the picture, and a little more time had been bought in which to
prepare Chapman's return trip to the Abwehr.

For a month, Chapman had been allowed, in Reed's words,
'to live as man and wife with Freda and his illegitimate child'.
Now the time had come to break up the strange domestic
arrangements at Crespigny Road. Backwell and Tooth were
almost as sorry to see Freda and Diane leave as Chapman himself.
Theirs had been a strange, homely world, a cocoon from the
grim realities of the war. Tar Robertson arranged for Eddie and
Freda to spend their last night together, not in Crespigny Road,
but in the grander surroundings of a bedroom in the St James
headquarters. There is an oddly touching exchange in the
transcript of one of Lord Rothschild's interviews with Chapman.
The two men were in the middle of a complicated discussion
about detonators, when Ronnie Reed interrupted:

'Victor, do you mind if Eddie just has a word with Freda on
the telephone?'

'No, rather not, of course not.'

When Chapman had left the room, Reed explained to
Rothschild: 'As it's her last night in London we thought it
would be advisable for her to spend her last night here. He's just
getting her to bring some clothes.'

'Beautiful,' said Lord Victor.

It *was* rather beautiful.

'Freda returned home,' wrote Backwell in his diary, 'and we
settled down to some concentrated grilling.'

Chapman's life would depend on his ability to tell his cover
story 'unhesitatingly'. Hour after hour, day after day, Chapman
was coached on every detail of the tale he must tell the Germans,

from the instant he landed to the moment of Hunt's 'arrest'. After a week of this, a Field Security Policeman named Hale was brought in to play the part of a German interrogator: he aggressively pummelled Chapman with questions: where had he lived, who had he seen, how had he obtained explosives, and what had he discovered? Hale repeatedly tried to trip him up with strange questions such as: 'What shoes was Jimmy Hunt wearing?' He tried to bluff him, accusing him of being a British spy, and alarming him by claiming that there had been a German observer at the factory on the night of the explosion whom they would shortly produce. Chapman was 'not shaken in any way'. When Hale demanded to know what had happened to the members of the Jelly Gang, Chapman did not miss a beat: 'Poor Freddy Sampson, he was taken as a deserter by the RAF; Tommy Lay is still serving four years in Wandsworth and Darry is doing seven years in Dartmoor. I am not sure what George Sherrard is up to, but he is living in Kilburn and probably mixed up in some monkey business.' As for Hunt, Chapman would say he had been released on bail after his arrest on explosives charges.

Reed, who monitored the trial interrogation, was pleased at the way Chapman had withstood the bullying tactics. He was a natural liar: 'We can rely upon his ingenuity to fill in small details and incidents of an amusing character which always give an added basis for believing that a man's story is true . . . Zigzag is not easily rattled during an interrogation and unless the enemy have some knowledge of his having worked for the British Intelligence during his stay in this country (something which is highly unlikely) I do not believe he will experience any real difficulty in persuading them that he has carried out his mission to their satisfaction.'

Part of that mission had been to collect military and other information. If Chapman was to convince his German bosses of his bona fides, he must not only tell a convincing story, but also bring back some goodies. Chapman drew up a list of all the things he had seen that the Abwehr might be remotely interested in; from this, Reed removed anything that might be useful to the enemy; then they added some additional information, interesting but essentially harmless; and finally some believable fictions, that would set the Abwehr guessing. The resulting mixture – chickenfeed garnished with grains of truth – was approved by the Twenty Committee, and then written out on fourteen sheets of plain writing paper with the secret ink matchsticks. Chapman sketched out a series of army divisional signs, some accurate, some imaginary: 'Blue starfish with curling tentacles on yellow background', 'blue hands and white clouds over top of shield', and so on; he revealed that Llandudno was home to the Inland Revenue office (a building even MI5 officers might be happy to see bombed), and that the Ministry of Agriculture had a branch at Africa House, Kingsway; he sketched a map of the military aerodrome at Hendon, and described the defences around Green Park and Hyde Park in central London: 'AA guns camouflaged and concreted. Few lorries or troops. Piquet guards, ATS, some huts. Four masts, possibly radio, near trees, approx 24 rockets stand and iron and stone ammunition shelters, empty.' Reed calculated there was information here of sufficient interest to persuade the Abwehr that Chapman was in earnest, and in sufficient quantity to show he was keen.

Among themselves, the officers of MI5 discussed what additional information Chapman might reveal to the Germans if he was exposed as a double agent or, worse, turned traitor. Chapman had always been driven in and out of Camp 020 and other sensitive military installations at night. Stephens thought he might have 'picked up the names of officers or warders', but nothing of any great value. Robertson was also sanguine: 'There is no information in Zigzag's possession which we should in the least mind him imparting to the Germans should he be disposed to go bad on us,' he wrote, adding quickly: 'we do not in fact consider that he would go bad.'

There was one secret, above all others, that Chapman must never know. 'It is imperative that no hint should be given to him about Most Secret Sources,' wrote Reed. Chapman had no inkling that the Abwehr codes had been broken. But in some ways, his information had been *too* good: he had provided clues that he believed would help Britain to break those codes – which indeed they would have done, had the codes not be broken already. If he was forced to reveal what he had told MI5, then the Abwehr might conclude that its codes were now vulnerable and change them, providing Bletchley with a new headache. Chapman must be made to believe the Abwehr codes were still invulnerable, by painting a 'gloomy picture . . . regarding the capabilities of our interception organisation to pick up and decode radio messages'. Reed told Chapman that MI5 could gather German wireless transmissions, but found it difficult to trace enemy agents transmitting in Britain, and almost impossible to crack German codes without 'a vast number of intercepts'. Even with the information Chapman had provided, Reed said sadly, 'the successful solving of any cipher must take a very long time'. This was all untrue, but Chapman replied that Reed's assessment confirmed what he had been told by Von Gröning 'that the code in use by their radio stations was a most difficult one and practically impossible to break'. If he was exposed, Chapman could be relied on to confirm the Abwehr's belief that its wireless transmissions were secure. Ultra was safe in Zigzag's hands: the deception agent was effectively deceived.

Having recited his cover story until he was bored stiff, Chapman was set to work memorising a questionnaire listing all the information he might usefully acquire when back in occupied territory. This, too, had to be carefully vetted. MI5 interrogators had gathered much useful information from the questionnaires of captured German spies, since these often revealed gaps in Abwehr knowledge and areas of particular concern. Tar Robertson was insistent: Chapman must only be given 'instructions which, if he were captured and forced to reveal them to the other side, would not convey information to the enemy'. Chapman's questionnaire was astonishingly broad, covering just about every aspect of the Abwehr organisation including its codes, personnel, buildings, relations with the Gestapo, favourite hotels, and plans in the event of an Allied invasion. SOE wanted to know about counter-espionage techniques, most notably the wireless interception station run by Dernbach – the bald spycatcher of Angers. Rothschild asked if Chapman would be kind enough to dig up information on sabotage targets in the UK, chemicals used by saboteurs, and camouflage techniques.

Chapman agreed to all the requests, even the impossible ones, for he was in the highest of spirits. The prospect of peril seemed to work on him like a drug, with Backwell noting that: 'In spite of the fact that he has quieted down in many ways, it seems that he is a man to whom the presence of danger is essential.' Robertson agreed, reflecting that this 'deep-seated liking for adventure, movement and activity is more likely to be the cause, than the effect, of his criminal career'.

The mission was to be open-ended, in time as well as content, for as Rothschild observed: 'You may see lots of openings, which at the moment are a closed book.' He might bring back a team of saboteurs, or go to America, or volunteer to train a team of German fifth columnists to remain in France in the wake of an Allied invasion and German retreat: 'Obviously if he were to gain control of such an organisation the value to the Allied cause would be immense,' wrote Reed. Chapman should use his own initiative: 'It all depends on the opportunities that you see presented to you when you go back,' Rothschild told him. MI6, as the service operating outside British territory, might have had a claim to Chapman's services, but MI5 was already running Agent Zigzag, and intended to continue doing so.

For reasons both practical and personal, the B1A team was confident that Chapman would not turn traitor, not least because of the rekindled emotional bond with Freda, and their daughter. Soon after they parted, Freda sent Chapman a passionate letter, which MI5 intercepted and copied, before passing it on. 'You will see that the incentive for him to return to this country is quite strong,' Reed remarked, as he showed the letter to his boss. Then there was the money: he might be about to be rewarded with a small fortune by the Germans, but his first priority was providing for his family in Britain, and that would depend on remaining loyal. But most important was the character of Chapman himself. Robertson believed him to be 'genuinely inspired with patriotism', and though he might be a criminal, the potential intelligence windfall from having a spy at the heart of the German secret service was an opportunity too good to squander on the basis of mere morality. Tar concluded that given 'the excellent personal relations which Zigzag appears to enjoy with various officers, it would be of the greatest possible value to get him back into those circles with the added prestige of having successfully completed a mission on their behalf'. Reed was emphatic: 'He will be greeted as a hero.'

As the hour of departure loomed, the case officer reported that Chapman was as ready as an agent could be. 'Zigzag is confident that he can put over his story and his morale is extremely good . . . While his interrogation in Berlin may be arduous, after the first few days he should have no difficulty in continuing the old life he used to lead before coming here.'

If, 'by some unhappy chance', his collaboration with the British was uncovered, he could probably survive by playing triple agent. But to do that, he would have to explain why he had included the FFFFF message, the sign that he was acting freely, *from the outset*. In Tar's words, 'it is very important to have an alternative cover story for a final emergency, which satisfactorily explains the deliberate untruth of the primary cover story'. Reed came up with an ingenious solution.

If Chapman was exposed, he should say that MI5 'had detained Freda as a hostage and had forced him to return to France' by threatening to 'shoot this woman'. As proof that he had tried to warn Von Gröning he was under control, he could point to the message, sent after Christmas, in which he had omitted the FFFFF signal. He could claim that the British had then spotted the omission, and forced him to include it thereafter. In this way, a mistake might just be turned to Chapman's advantage. Reed admitted that this explanation was a long shot, to be deployed as 'a very last resort', but if Chapman found himself backed into a corner, it 'might possibly enable him to escape with his life'.

The safe house on Crespigny Road, Chapman's unextraordinary home for three extraordinary months, was packed up. His wireless set was stacked away in a cupboard – he planned to tell Von Gröning he had buried it – along with the fake ID cards, the cash, and the poison pill. He solemnly shook hands with Paul Backwell, before climbing into the waiting Black Maria with Reed and Tooth, who would accompany him to Liverpool for the next stage. Tar had told him: 'Except in special circumstances we do not expect to hear from you, if at all, for a considerable time.' What Tar did not say, and both men knew, was that there was a strong likelihood, once he left British shores, that they would never hear from Zigzag again.

It fell to Colonel Stephens to write the final report that sent Chapman on his way, and he rose to the occasion magnificently, pulling out all the literary stops. Tin Eye wrote with professional pride and frank admiration, in prose of the deepest purple:

> The story of many a spy is commonplace and drab. It would not pass muster in fiction. The subject is a failure in life. The motive is sordid. Fear is present. Patriotism is absent. Silence is not the equipment of a brave man, rather it is the reaction to a dread of consequence. High adventure just means nothing at all.
>
> The story of Chapman is different. In fiction it would be rejected as improbable. The subject is a crook, but as a crook he is by no means a failure. His career in crime has been progressive, from Army desertion to indecency, from

women to blackmail, from robbery to the blowing of safes. Latterly his rewards have been large, and no doubt he despises himself for his petty beginnings. The man, essentially vain, has grown in stature and, in his own estimation, is something of a prince of the underworld. He has no scruples and will stop at nothing. He makes no bargain with society and money is a means to an end. Of fear, he knows nothing, and he certainly has a deep-rooted hatred of the Hun. In a word, adventure to Chapman is the breath of life. Given adventure, he has the courage to achieve the unbelievable. His very recklessness is his standby. Today he is a German parachute spy; tomorrow he will undertake a desperate hazard as an active double agent, the stake for which is his life. Without adventure, he would rebel; in the ultimate he will have recourse again to crime in search of the unusual. The risk is considerable, but so long as there is a chance of success I think the risk should be taken.

For Chapman, only one thing is certain, the greater the adventure, the greater is the chance of success.

Stowaway Spy

Captain Reginald Sanderson Kearon, master of the merchant ship the MV *City of Lancaster*, had spent his war being shot at by German torpedoes. He had taken command of the MV *Assyrian* in 1940, only to have it sunk under him by a U-boat. Then he took the helm of the MV *Belgravian*, until that was also torpedoed. On both occasions he had been the last man to leave his sinking ships.

Kearon was one of thousands of unsung heroes of the Merchant Navy who continued to ply the oceans throughout the war transporting vital supplies. The merchant ships travelled in convoys, often under-gunned and ill-defended. This was not like other forms of warfare: it was dirty, often boring, and enormously dangerous. The enemy was usually invisible.

The 3,000-ton *City of Lancaster* had been built by Palmers of Jarrow in 1924 as a coal ship; now she carried food, building supplies, munitions, and anything else needed to sustain the war effort, wherever the Empire required it. Her thirty-man crew were mostly Liverpudlian Irishmen, hard men who worked their hearts out at sea and drank themselves incapable on shore. The *Lancaster* was as battle-scarred as her captain. She had evacuated 2,500 people from St Nazaire in 1940, and seen the ship alongside her bombed and sunk with all hands. She had been stalked by German U-boats and attacked by Heinkel bombers, and she had fought back with her 10- and 12-pounders, two anti-aircraft guns and a pair of machine guns, fore and aft. No one pretended it was a fair fight.

A big, bluff Irishman born in Arklow on the coast of County Wicklow in 1905, Kearon looked like Neptune in uniform. His hair had gone grey but the edges of his wide beard were still rust-red, as if corroded by salt spray. A strong mixture of sea water, rum and rage ran in his veins, making him entirely fearless, beloved and feared by his crew in equal measure, and apparently unsinkable. Having spent three years as a floating target, and had two ships sunk under him, this sea dog was longing to bite back.

The *City of Lancaster*, bound for Freetown in Sierra Leone via Lisbon, was at Liverpool docks taking on a cargo of pipes, mail and parcels for POWs, when Captain Kearon was summoned to the shipping office on the quay. Waiting for him was a thin, slight man in civilian clothes with an inadequate moustache. He introduced himself as Major Ronald Reed (he had been promoted). Politely, but authoritatively, the little man explained that he worked for British intelligence. Captain Kearon, he said, would soon be taking on a new crew member, one Hugh Anson, as an assistant steward. This man was a double agent, performing a vital secret mission for the British government, and Kearon would be responsible for his wellbeing on board. In Lisbon he would jump ship. The desertion would leave the *City of Lancaster* short-handed, Reed said, but this was unavoidable. Kearon should report the incident as normal, just as he would for any other crew member. The crew should be told that Anson was a former criminal who had served five years in prison in Lewes, but who had been released early, with the help of the Prisoner's Aid Society, on condition that he join either the Merchant Navy or the armed forces. His cover – as 'a man who had a bad record but who it was thought had turned over a new leaf' – would help explain his lack of nautical experience, and when he vanished in Lisbon, it would simply be assumed that he had turned over an old leaf.

Reed was grave: 'From now on this man's life is in your hands.

It is absolutely essential that no word of his mission should become known to the crew.' Finally he produced a large bulky envelope, tied with string, sealed with a blue seal and stamped 'OHMS', On His Majesty's Service. The package should be locked in the ship's safe, and then handed to 'Anson' on arrival in Lisbon. Inside was Chapman's Colt revolver with a spare loaded chamber, fifty £1 notes, and a ration book and clothing book made out in the name of Hugh Anson. There were also press clippings, describing an explosion at a factory in north London.

Back in his hotel room, Reed wrote that Captain Kearon 'impressed me as being discreet'. Reginald Kearon, in truth, was thrilled to have a British spy on board his ship.

Chapman and Tooth had checked in to the Washington Hotel. Reed was staying at the rather more comfortable Adelphi. Even in the secret world, the officer class had privileges and it was safer that the three conspirators not be seen together, just in case anyone was watching.

Hugh Anson was the name of the petty criminal who had been the driver of the Jelly Gang's getaway car. In his cover story, Chapman would explain to the Germans that he had paid Anson £100 for all his identity cards, and had then substituted his own photograph for that of Anson, who agreed to 'lie low' for two months before reporting the missing documents. Chapman would claim that he had obtained his seaman's papers by bribing one Frani Daniels, a criminal contact at the shipping office. The real arrangements for shipping out Chapman had proved far more intricate. The MI5 counterfeiters had put together a 'complete set of forged civilian papers', including a National Service registration form, a National Health Insurance card and an unemployment book. But obtaining the correct seaman's papers was proving a 'vast and complicated' business. Finally, with the help of a local MI5 operative named Hobbes, Reed decided to steal a selection card from the catering department of the Merchant Navy. Hobbes walked into the Liverpool shipping office pretending to be inspecting the fire precautions, and walked out with the necessary papers – which Reed then fraudulently filled out over a beer in the corner of the Flying Dutchman pub next door. 'This course, though morally incorrect, was practically suitable,' Reed reported.

That evening was spent going over arrangements for communicating with Britain when and if Chapman gained access to a German radio. Reed decided that the best way to send messages was by means of a simple code embedded in Chapman's 'ham chat', the little flourishes he had always added to his messages, notably his 'laughing out' signs.

The message QLF is a jocular sign meaning 'please send with your left foot', and 99 means something a little more insulting. If Chapman sent 'QLF', it would indicate that his German spymasters were 'completely satisfied'; if he sent '99', it would mean they were 'suspicious'. More complex messages could be sent using the various combinations of the laughing sign:

HU HU HU: no information to impart
HA HA HA: Nantes Abwehr unit is closing down
HI HA HU: I am going to Berlin
HA HU HI: I am going to Paris
HU HI HA: I am going to Angers
HE HE HE: I am going to America
HE HE HE HA: A group of Americans have gone to the USA and are operating there

'The "laughing out" sign occurred throughout Zigzag's traffic [and] it is not thought that any question will be raised by the enemy,' wrote Reed.

If he gained unsupervised access to a wireless, he should send messages in the usual way but encoded on the word DELIGHT-FUL. Chapman had been invited by the Germans to invent a code word for his first mission, and had come up with CONSTANTINOPLE. If, in the future, he was asked by the Germans to think up another code word, it was agreed that he would select POLITENESS. Unbeknownst to Chapman, Bletchley Park could already read any message he sent, but having the codeword beforehand would make the lives of the codebreakers even simpler. 'We shall not have the bother of having to attempt to solve his messages but will be able to do so immediately,' wrote Reed.

Von Gröning had always passed on his copies of *The Times* to Chapman. When a message from Zigzag had been safely received, Reed would post a message in the personal columns of the newspaper, on either the Tuesday or Thursday after receipt, stating: 'Mrs West thanks the anonymous donor of the gift of £11'. The second digit of the number would describe the number of the message received. So if MI5 had picked up six messages, Mrs West would thank her unknown benefactor for £46. With luck, the fictional Mrs West (a small tribute to the housekeeper at Crespigny Road) should end up a wealthy woman.

Finally, Reed and Chapman laid an 'elephant trap'. Chapman was instructed to tell his Abwehr masters that, before leaving Britain, he had made arrangements 'that if any other members of the German secret service require assistance', they could contact the safecracker Jimmy Hunt at the telephone number: Gerrard 4850. When the telephone was answered, the caller should say: 'It is Lew Leibich speaking, and I would like to speak to Jimmy.' The number would be directly linked to a telephone on Ronnie Reed's desk at B1A, who would arrange an appropriate reception committee.

With a map of Lisbon, Reed and Chapman located the German safe house on the Rua Mamede, and the German consulate. Reed also made Chapman memorise a Lisbon telephone number, to be called in case of emergency. Ralph Jarvis, the MI6 representative in Lisbon, had already been alerted that an important agent was en route. The Radio Security Service and Bletchley Park were instructed to keep a watch for any reference to Fritz in the Most Secret Sources.

At the end of the evening, Chapman announced that he wished to write a farewell letter to Freda. Reed suggested he send it via Laurie Marshall, who would forward it. The letter was copied and duly sent on to Freda. The letter of adieu remains classified, but the covering letter to Marshall reads: 'Goodbye for the present, I shall soon be back with you at 35 – thank you for your kindness to me – please give or forward this letter to Freda.' This was not the tone of a man in fear for his life.

The following day, Chapman presented himself at the Board of Trade office. The clerk accepted the forged paperwork without demur, merely remarking that the shipping company had sent another assistant steward to the *City of Lancaster* and clearly 'did not know what they were doing'. Chapman was told to report to the ship, and prepare to sail the following day. They returned to the hotel, where Tooth packed Chapman's belongings, including two new white steward's uniforms and fourteen sheets of what, to the naked eye, appeared to be plain, white writing paper, and searched his clothing for anything that might betray him, just as Praetorius had done so many months before. Chapman then set off for the docks, Reed reported, 'in the approved style with kitbag over his shoulder'.

Tooth and Reed followed 'at a very respectable distance'. Possibly the distance was too respectable, for 'somehow or other, after trudging for a number of miles around the docks, Zigzag disappeared'. One moment he had been walking ahead, doing a very reasonable impression of a jolly jack tar, and the next he had vanished. Reed wondered if Chapman had suddenly had second thoughts and absconded. With rising anxiety they searched the docks but could find neither Chapman nor, infuriatingly, the *City of Lancaster*. Finally, they gave up, and began walking dejectedly back to the hotel. They had told Chapman to meet them at the Adelphi, but 'some sort of feminine intuition' told Reed that his spy might just have returned to his own, less classy hotel: 'Sure enough Zigzag was in the bar, with a prostitute.'

They decided not to interrupt him, but tiptoed away, leaving him to finish his negotiations. From the Adelphi, they called the bar of the Washington and got Chapman on the line, who cheerfully reported that he had found the boat, left his kit on board, and been instructed to return the next morning at 8.00 a.m. 'He did not wish to dine with us as he was "busy",' Reed reported, delicately. They agreed to rendezvous in Reed's room at the Adelphi at 9.00 p.m.

Reed and Tooth dined at the hotel, and just before the appointed hour climbed the stairs to Reed's suite. On opening the door, they found Chapman inside: 'Zigzag had, in some way, managed to obtain entry and was reclining on the bed awaiting dinner which he had ordered on my telephone, together with a number of bottles of beer.' In the space of a few hours Chapman had confirmed all the qualities that made him a great crook, a superb spy, and a most fickle man: he had written a love letter to the mother of his child, vanished, slept with a prostitute, broken into a locked room, and helped himself to room service at someone else's expense. He had also, it emerged, stolen Reed's gold-plated scissors and nail file, 'which he had coveted for a time'. This was all as Young had once predicted: Chapman would do his duty, while merrily picking your pocket.

Reed could not bring himself to be angry. Indeed, the incident deepened his affection for this strange young man he had known for all of eight weeks. 'Zigzag is himself a most absorbing person. Reckless and impetuous, moody and senti-mental, he becomes on acquaintance an extraordinarily likeable character. It is difficult for anyone who has been associated with him for any continuous period to describe him in an unbiased and dispassionate way. It was difficult to credit that the man had a despicable past. His crimes of burglary and fraud, his association with "moral degenerates", and his description as a "dangerous criminal" by Scotland Yard is difficult to reconcile with more recent behaviour.'

Chapman's past *was* despicable; his recent actions had been almost heroic (with lapses); but his future remained quite unknowable. At the docks, Chapman waved, and headed up the gangplank of the *City of Lancaster*, leaving Reed to reflect: 'The case of Zigzag has not yet ended. Indeed, time may well prove that it has only just begun.'

19

Joli Albert

On 15 March 1943, the *City of Lancaster* steamed out of the Mersey to join the convoy assembling in the Irish Sea, forty-three merchant vessels in all, escorted by three destroyers and four more lightly armed corvettes. The ships formed into lines, with the escorts on either side, ahead and astern, like sheepdogs, moving the flock forward, wary for predators. Hugh Anson, the new assistant steward, was told to find a berth with the gunners and then report to the Captain's cabin. As the convoy sailed south, Chapman and Kearon held a hushed and hurried consultation. The Captain, 'fearing prying fingers', offered to safeguard any of his passenger's secret spy equipment, and was rather disappointed to be handed some ordinary sheets of writing paper. He locked them away in the safe, being careful not to get his fingerprints on them. Kearon explained that he would treat Chapman like any member of the crew, but in the course of the passage he would expect him to behave in an unruly fashion, since this would confirm his cover story as a 'bad lad' and help explain his disappearance when they reached Lisbon.

If they reached Lisbon. That afternoon, a lone German bomber streaked out of the sky and released its payload, narrowly missing a 5,000-ton cargo boat carrying explosives and ammunition. High above, the Focke-Wulf reconnaissance planes circled. 'Nervous expectancy showed on every face', and Chapman noticed that the crew slept fully clothed. Not that he had time to notice much, as Snellgrove, the chief steward, put him to work scrubbing out, serving meals, and generally doing the dogsbody work expected of a rookie. Chapman complained, loudly. Snellgrove noted that 'Anson was seasick most of the time and quite useless at his job'.

That night, as the convoy headed into the Atlantic, Chapman was woken from a queasy sleep by the ship's alarm. On deck, still fumbling with his lifebelt, he was sent staggering by a huge explosion, followed by another. Two merchant ships and a tanker were burning furiously, and by the light of the flames Chapman could make out the dark shapes of the other ships. A torpedo had struck the ammunition ship. Captain Kearon shut down the engines, and starbursts lit up the sky. The U-boats, it seemed, had slunk away again. The windows of the ship's bridge had been blown out, and glass lay around the deck. There was no further attack that night, but Chapman could not sleep.

The next morning Captain Kearon told him that seven ships were missing from the convoy, three of which had been sunk by collisions during the night, or from damage incurred by the exploding munitions ship. Chapman reflected that this was just the sort of information he might usefully pass on to the Germans in Lisbon, since it would confirm what they already knew, but demonstrate keenness on his part. For the same reason Chapman began making daily notes of the ship's position and course. Since German reconnaissance planes were already tracking the ships, 'no harm would be done by giving the position of the convoy to the enemy'. The Captain agreed, and offered to let Chapman see the ship's log-book in order to chart their exact position. With his remaining secret ink, Chapman carefully wrote down the information on a sheet of writing paper.

Captain Kearon was relishing his new role as spy's assistant. But the rest of the crew did not know quite what to make of the new steward. Word of Anson's prison record spread quickly, and it was agreed he was clearly 'a high-class burglar'. He seemed to have plenty of money, a gold monogrammed cigarette case and he wore an expensive wristwatch. Anson's nickname in Soho, he confided, was 'Stripey', on account of the time he had spent in striped prison garb. But for a crook, he was surprisingly polite and cultured; he read books in French 'for pleasure'. 'Several members of the crew were impressed by his good education,' Kearon later reported. 'The gunlayer summed up the general opinion that he was man of good family gone wrong.' One evening, Chapman astonished the ship's company by announcing that he would compose a poem, there and then. With a pencil and an envelope he set to work, and then declaimed the result. The eight-line poem, which survives in MI5's archives, was plainly intended to be autobiographical, the story of Stripey, who lives hard, survives on his own cunning, and has multiple girlfriends. It ends:

Happy go lucky, come what may
Three cheers for Stripey, hip hip Hooray.

As poetry goes, this little spasm of doggerel may not have been up to much, but to the ears of Chapman's messmates it was Shakespeare, further evidence that they were in the presence of a genuine gentleman robber. Anson was certainly bolshy enough to be a poet, for he grumbled unceasingly. The Captain duly noted down his poor attitude in the ship's log: 'He said he did not like sea life as no one did their share of work, he said he did most of the work. This is definitely untrue, as I, master, have observed.'

On the 18th the *City of Lancaster* steamed into the Tagus, and tied up at Santos Quay. Portugal was still neutral, though its dictator was inclining to the Nazis, and Lisbon was a boiling cauldron of espionage, awash with refugees, smugglers, spies, hustlers, arms dealers, wheeler-dealers, middlemen, deserters, profiteers and prostitutes. It was Chapman's kind of town. John Masterman described Lisbon in his post-war novel, *The Case of the Four Friends*, as a 'sort of international clearing ground, a busy ant heap of spies and agents, where political and military secrets and information – true and false, but mainly false – were bought and sold and where men's brains were pitted against each other'. The Allied and Axis powers maintained safe houses, dead drops, fleets of informants and small armies of competing spies, as well as official consulates and embassies, all under the thin veneer of neutrality. The Abwehr even ran its own bars and brothels, for the express purpose of extracting information from sex-starved and drunken British sailors.

The crew of the *City of Lancaster* assembled on deck for a lecture about avoiding strong drink and loose women while on shore. The bosun, Valsamas, distinctly overheard Anson whisper: 'Pay no attention. That's just a lot of bullshit.'

On land, the assistant steward joined four of his crewmates at the British Seamen's Institute in Rua da Moeda, where all proceeded to get loudly drunk, in the traditional manner. Anson declared that he would pay, but after an hour of steady drinking at MI5's expense, the new assistant steward told one of the gunners he had 'business to attend to' in town with an old acquaintance.

'If I find this friend I am well away,' he confided.

When Gunner Humphries pressed him about the identity of his friend, Chapman merely winked and remarked mysteriously: 'No names, no packdrill.' He agreed to meet them later at George's, a brothel-bar on the dockside.

A few days earlier, Bletchley Park had decoded an Abwehr message to another double agent, codenamed 'Father', indicating that the safe house at 50, Rua Sao Mamede had been 'brûlé', or burned. MI5 had no way of warning Agent Zigzag that his contact address had metaphorically gone up in smoke.

Chapman's taxi dropped him at a large, dirty building, deep in the working-class district of the city. The door was answered by a young girl, who fetched her mother. '*Joli Albert*,' said Chapman brightly, and then in halting Portuguese: 'My name is Fritz. May I see Senhor Fonseca?' This declaration was met with 'blank

faces'. He tried again in German, English and French. Finally he
wrote the name 'Fonseca' on a piece of paper. This provoked a
flicker of recognition, and from the ensuing mime he understood that Senhor Fonseca was not in. He wrote down the word
'telephone'. After some more gesticulating, the girl led him to a
nearby café, dialed a number, and handed the receiver to
Chapman. A man's voice answered. '*Joli Albert*' said Chapman.
The password was no more effective, but at least the man spoke a
form of French. He agreed to meet Chapman at the café next
door. With deep misgivings, Chapman waited, smoking heavily
and drinking foul Portuguese brandy. Finally a slim young man
in his late twenties appeared, with a much older man, who spoke
German. Once more Chapman gave his password, and explained
that he needed to see a senior Abwehr officer. Their alarmed
expressions indicated how badly the plan had gone awry. Clearly
they 'did not know anything about the matter', and with every
word he uttered, Chapman was putting himself in greater peril.
He apologised for his mistake and told the two men to 'forget
the whole business'. Then he ran.

Back at George's Bar, the party was in full swing. Chapman
slipped into throng of sailors and tarts, his return almost unnoticed, and was soon in conversation with an English-speaking
Portuguese barmaid called Anita. She was twenty-six, thin, with
a dark complexion, wavy black hair and deep brown eyes; she
was also a prostitute and a paid MI6 informant. She would later
tell British intelligence that the man everyone knew as Anson
had confided that his real name was Reed. Ronnie would have
been scandalised.

Chapman spent the night with Anita in a small hotel near the
harbour, wondering if the Germans had given up on him,
whether he was heading into a trap, and whether his career
as a double agent was already over.

Early next morning, Chapman entered the smart lobby of the
German Legation on Rua do Pau de Bandeira, and told the
sleepy man at the front desk that his name was Fritz, he was a

German agent, and he would like to see the senior Abwehr officer. The man yawned, and told him to come back in two hours. When he returned, the receptionist was markedly more alert, even attentive. An official of some sort appeared, and told Chapman to go to a house in the nearby Rua Bueno Aires. Outside the address he had been given, a Fiat car was waiting with the engine running and two civilians in the front seat. Chapman was told to sit in the back and was driven in silence to yet another address, a flat at 25, Rua Borges Carniero. There he was escorted upstairs, where the two men politely invited him to explain his business: Chapman told the story he knew by heart, for the first of what would be many recitations. The taller of the two, clearly senior, nodded and occasionally asked questions, while the other, a small, fat man, took notes. When Chapman had finished, the tall man thanked him politely, told him to remain on board his ship, but to kindly return to this address the following day.

That evening Captain Kearon could be heard roasting Steward Anson for spending a night ashore without permission, and warning him bluntly about the perils of venereal disease. When Anson told the Captain to 'mind his own business', Kearon exploded and told him 'any future offence must entail prosecution at home'. The crew agreed: Anson was on very thin ice.

Though Captain Kearon put on a grand show of fury, the master of the *City of Lancaster* was deeply relieved to see Chapman return. When they were alone, Chapman described how he had spent two days being ferried and shunted from place to place, and added that if and when he came to make a report to MI5, he could tell them the Abwehr is a bureaucratic nightmare. Kearon would later state: 'He instructed me to report that the organisation worked just the same as it does in London. He said Ronnie would be pleased to hear that!' Kearon made a suggestion: when Chapman was ready to leave the ship, he should start a fight. This would allow the Captain to punish him, and provide the obvious rationale that Anson had jumped ship to avoid another prison sentence in Britain.

When Chapman returned the next day to Rua Borges Carniero, he was ushered into the presence of an elegant young man in horn-rimmed spectacles, who introduced himself as 'Baumann' in excellent English, and 'apologised for the inconvenience' of the previous day and Germany's failure to welcome him with due fanfare. The man offered Chapman a cigar and a glass of brandy, and invited him to tell his story once more. The identity of Chapman's suave interrogator is uncertain: MI5 would later identify Baumann, alias Blaum, alias Bodo, as an officer who had served as chief of the Abwehr sabotage section in Lisbon since 1942. But it is equally possible that Baumann was Major Kremer von Auenrode, alias Ludovico von Kartsthoff, the head of the Lisbon Abwehr station. Chapman himself believed that Baumann was 'connected with Johnny', the German codename for agent Snow. Owens's German controller had been a Major Nikolaus Ritter, alias Doktor Rantzau. Whoever he was, Baumann seemed to know a great deal about Chapman's time in France, his mission and its results.

Chapman handed over the sheets of paper with secret writing, and then made Baumann an offer he had been mulling over since setting sail for Lisbon. During his sabotage training in Berlin, Chapman explained, he had learned how to construct a coal bomb by drilling a cavity into a large lump of coal, and then packing it with high explosive. Placed in the bunkers of a ship, the device would remain unnoticed until shovelled into the furnace, whereupon it would explode, sinking the vessel.

If Baumann would provide him with such a bomb, said Chapman, he would hide it among the coal on the *City of Lancaster*, then jump ship as planned, and send the boat, her captain and crew to the bottom of the Atlantic Ocean.

Tar Robertson was unflappable. But when the latest batch of wireless intercepts arrived from the Most Secret Sources on the morning of 21 January, he almost took flight. Agent Zigzag had been in Lisbon two days, and already he seemed to be contemplating an act of gross treachery by offering to sink the ship that had taken him there.

In a top-secret message, the Abwehr station in Lisbon had informed Admiral Wilhelm Canaris that Agent Fritz was in a position to sabotage a British merchant vessel with a coal bomb, and requested authorisation to proceed. The operation required permission from the Abwehr chief himself, since it 'contravened the established policy of the Abwehr not to undertake sabotage in or from Portugal'. To make matters worse, the same message described the precise route to Lisbon taken by the *City of Lancaster*, and how many ships had been sunk in the attack on the convoy: this information could only come from Chapman. At the very least he had 'told the Germans more about his convoy than he should have done'. At worst, it was further evidence of treachery.

Robertson convened a crisis meeting, and drew up a series of aims, in order of priority. First, to protect the ship and its crew; second, to preserve the Ultra secret and the Most Secret Sources; and finally, 'not to interrupt Zigzag's mission unless he was, or it seemed probable that he was, double-crossing us'.

Reed could not believe that Chapman would turn traitor so swiftly. Had he been forced or instructed to carry out the sabotage, or was it his own idea? 'Whatever view we took of Zigzag's character and patriotism we could not run the risk of taking it for granted that he would not, in fact, commit the sabotage,' he wrote. While the meeting was still in progress, Berlin sent a message approving the sabotage of the *City of Lancaster*.

MI6 had also read the cables, and offered to use its own people in Lisbon to neutralise Zigzag. Robertson told them to wait. The *City of Lancaster* was not due to leave port for a few days, and since Chapman was planning to jump ship just before she set sail, there was probably still time to intercept him, and the coal bomb.

Major Reed, wrote Tar, was 'acquainted with the relevant facts and considerations'. Moreover, 'the master and Zigzag both know Mr Reed and it is therefore easier for him to approach them with less chance of arousing German suspicion'. Reed must fly to Lisbon at once, where he should find Chapman and interrogate him immediately. Unless Chapman volunteered information about the sabotage plot, freely and without prompting, he should be arrested at gunpoint and 'brought back in irons'. Chapman might be surprised to see Reed pop up in Lisbon, but there was no reason he should deduce that the Abwehr's messages had been intercepted: 'It would be quite natural for us to send Mr Reed out to ascertain if he had contacted the Germans and what they had said.'

Little Ronnie Reed, the radio ham who had joined up because he liked to play with wirelesses, was about to find himself a leading player in a rapidly unfolding drama that might require him to bring a known criminal back to justice at the point of a gun.

While Reed was scrambling to catch the next passenger flight to Lisbon, Chapman went back to Rua Borges Carniero to pick up the bombs. A few days earlier he had handed Baumann a sample lump of coal from the ship's bunkers. Welsh coal has a distinctive grain and colour, and the German forgers had achieved remarkable results. Baumann now presented him with two irregular black lumps about 6-inches square – in shape, weight and texture indistinguishable from real Welsh coal. Rather than drill out an existing piece of coal, as the Doctor had done, in order to pack in more explosive Baumann's engineers had taken a canister of explosive with a fuse attached, and moulded a plastic covering around it, which had been painted and covered in coal dust. The only clue to the lethal contents was 'a small aperture, the diameter of a pencil, in one face'.

Chapman was impressed: the bombs, he declared, 'could not possibly be detected'. He told Baumann he would plant them in the bunkers that night, and jump ship the following morning. Baumann confirmed that all the necessary paperwork was ready to get him out of the country, including a new passport with a photograph taken in Lisbon two days earlier.

That evening, Chapman walked up the gangplank of the *City of Lancaster*, somewhat gingerly, with two large coal bombs in a rucksack strapped to his back. He did not know that Ronnie Reed was hurtling towards Portugal as fast as wartime air travel could carry him; nor did he know that Captain Jarvis of MI6 had posted an agent to watch the ship, and was standing by for orders to seize and, if necessary, kill him.

But Chapman was not going anywhere near the furnace, and he had no intention of blowing up the ship. He was simply using his initiative, as instructed. His friend and fellow bomb-enthusiast, that courtly and well-bred 'Mr Fisher', had asked him to obtain some German sabotage 'toys', and that was precisely what he intended to do. Mr Fisher, he reflected, would be thrilled to get his hands on the two beauties in his backpack.

Once on board, Chapman carefully stashed the rucksack in his locker. He then approached a large gunner by the name of Dermot O'Connor, who was dozing on his bunk, and punched him hard on the nose. The brawny Irishman had been identified by Chapman as the crewmember most likely to be goaded into a brawl without asking awkward questions. This conjecture was proven entirely accurate.

O'Connor erupted from his berth like a surfacing killer whale, and the two men set about thumping one another with enthusiasm, noise and any weaponry that came to hand. There are two versions of how the fight ended: according to Chapman's self-flattering account, he finished off O'Connor by whacking him on the head with a half-empty bottle of whisky; according to Captain Kearon (and every other witness), O'Connor neatly felled Chapman by head-butting him in the eye. Chapman was carried off to the sick bay, bleeding profusely and shouting that the Irishman had violated 'the Queensberry rules'. When they had been patched up, both men were fined half-a-day's pay by Captain Kearon, who loudly told Chapman that he was now in serious trouble.

A farcical staged scene followed:

Captain Kearon: 'Have you met a better man at last?'

Anson: 'After fighting him fairly and beating him by the Marquis of Queensberry rules he head-butted me in the face. The people on this ship are hooligans.'

Kearon: 'Are you the only decent one on board then?'

Anson: 'Yes.'

At dawn the next day, Assistant Steward Anson, the left side of his face cut and badly bruised, was detailed to take Captain Kearon his early morning tea. Chapman knocked on the door of the Captain's cabin and slipped inside, carrying a tea tray in one hand, and a rucksack with two large bombs in the other. Chapman had earlier explained to Kearon that he was 'trying to get a special bomb on board for transport to home', and he now thrust the coal bombs into the Captain's hands, explaining that 'he had put to them the proposition that he should sabotage the *City of Lancaster* and the enemy had agreed'. Kearon was no shrinking violet, but even he quailed at being handed 10 lbs of high explosive in his bed by a man with a face that seemed to have gone through a meat grinder. He announced that he would weigh anchor immediately and head home. Chapman insisted that the bombs were safe unless heated, and that any change of plan would only attract German suspicion. The Captain was eventually 'persuaded to carry on his usual route and act as though nothing had happened'. Now wide awake, Kearon opened the safe, extracted Chapman's package, pushed the two evil-looking bombs inside, and shut the door, quickly. Chapman stuffed the papers and money in his rucksack and handed the revolver back to the Captain, 'as a present'. In return, the Captain gave Anson the address of his sister-in-law, Doris, who lived in Oporto, just in case he had any trouble. They shook hands, and Chapman slipped away into the dawn.

Captain Kearon's cameo role in British military espionage was over. The British spy had acted his part superbly, the Captain reflected. 'He lived up to his reputation as a jail-bird very realistically.' This was not, perhaps, entirely surprising.

That afternoon the Most Secret Sources picked up a message from the Lisbon Abwehr station confirming that Fritz had completed his mission. The news was relayed by Captain Ralph Jarvis of MI6 to Ronnie Reed of MI5 when he arrived at Lisbon airport at 5.30 p.m. on Tuesday, 23 January, travelling under the name Johnson, an official with the Ministry of War Transport. Reed's heart sank. If Chapman had planted the bomb he was a traitor guilty of attempted murder, and the tons of coal in the ship's bunkers would somehow have to be sorted through, piece by piece. Jarvis explained that Captain Kearon had been interviewed by his agents at the shipping office and 'denied emphatically that Hugh Anson had any connection whatsoever with British intelligence'. Reed replied that the Captain probably thought he was protecting a British agent, and obeying orders to 'tell absolutely no one about the connection'.

Captain Kearon and Ronnie Reed met, alone, at the Royal British Club in Lisbon. The MI5 case officer could tell immediately from the Captain's buoyant and conspiratorial expression that his fears were unfounded. Kearon explained that Chapman had 'behaved magnificently', that the 'plot' to sabotage the ship had been a ruse to obtain the bombs, and that two lumps of exploding coal were now sitting in the safe of his ship, which he would be only too happy to pass on as soon as possible. Anson had specifically told him that 'the coal was High Explosive and was to be given to Ronnie', and had suggested that MI5 should stage some sort of fake explosion on board, 'in order to send up his prestige' with the Germans.

Kearon also described how he and Chapman had agreed that the ship's course and the attack on the convoy could be reported to the Germans without endangering British shipping, and how

Chapman had valiantly allowed himself to be flattened by a large Irish gunner for the sake of his cover story. When the waiter was not looking, he passed over the names and addresses in Lisbon Chapman had left with him, and a revolver.

Reed sent a jubilant telegram to Tar Robertson: 'Convinced Z playing straight with us.'

The relief was shared in London. Not only had Chapman demonstrated his loyalty, but British intelligence now had two intact bombs of a type they had never seen before. 'This is typical of the risks that Chapman has been prepared to undertake on our behalf,' wrote Tin Eye Stephens. He had offered to carry out a sabotage mission knowing that when the *City of Lancaster* did not sink at sea, he would inevitably be suspected of double-dealing, 'with possibly fatal results to himself'. Yet he had been prepared to take the chance. 'He thought that the value to the British of getting examples of the devices used by the Germans justified the risk to himself.'

Slightly less thrilled by the outcome was MI6. Relations between the sister services were often strained, and the men of external espionage did not appreciate the men of internal security encroaching on their patch. MI6 flatly refused to contemplate staging a fake sabotage of the *City of Lancaster* in Lisbon, pointing out that this would be 'politically complicated'.

Jarvis of MI6, in civilian life a merchant banker, put the wind up poor Ronnie Reed by pointing out that the coal bombs might be activated by a delay fuse rather than heat, and could explode at any moment. Reed did not share Lord Rothschild's insouciant approach to high explosive. He thought better of packing the bombs in his luggage: 'It would be most unfortunate if an explosion were to take place in the plane on my return journey home, both for the plane, the political consequences, and myself . . .'.

Rothschild instructed that the bombs should be photo-graphed, x-rayed, placed in a heavy iron box padded with cork, and then sent to Gibraltar on the next British vessel, addressed to

'Mr Fisher' c/o ANI, Whitehall. In Gibraltar, the package would be picked up from Captain Kearon by an MI5 agent who would say: 'I come from Ronnie'. Rothschild was insistent on one point: the bombs should be sent 'if possible intact and not sawn in half'. Only someone like Rothschild could imagine that anyone else would *want* to saw up a lump of coal packed with high explosive.

Damp Squib

No one paid much attention to the Norwegian sailor with the livid black eye who boarded the afternoon flight from Lisbon to Madrid, and sat quietly at the end of the aeroplane. He carried a Norwegian passport in the name of Olaf Christiansson, describing him as a seaman, born in Oslo. There was a party of Norwegians on board, but their quiet compatriot did not engage them in conversation. Indeed, he could not, because he did not speak a single word of Norwegian.

At Madrid airport, a stocky little man with rosy cheeks emerged from the waiting crowd. 'Are you Fritz?' he whispered. 'Yes,' said Chapman, '*Joli Albert*'. At the Hotel Florida, Chapman dined on roast pork, drank a bottle of sticky Spanish wine, and slept for twelve hours. The next five days passed in a blur. Chapman lost count of the nameless German visitors who came and went, asking the same questions, or very slightly different questions. Sometimes the interrogations took place in his hotel room, or in the lounge, or nearby cafés. The rosy-cheeked German gave him 3,000 pesetas and told him he might want to stock up on clothes, tea and coffee and 'other articles difficult to obtain in Occupied Europe'. So he was going back to France. Through the Madrid streets, Chapman was followed, discreetly, by a smiling little shadow.

The man who had first interviewed him in Lisbon, later identified by MI5 as Abwehr officer Konrad Weisner, reappeared at the Hotel Florida and announced he would be accompanying Chapman to Paris. In a private sleeper compartment, Chapman lay awake as the stations rumbled by in the darkness: San Sebastian, Irun, Hendaye, Bordeaux. At dawn on 28 March, the train pulled into the Gare d'Orsay: waiting on the platform was Albert Schael, Chapman's moon-faced drinking companion from Nantes, the original *Joli Albert* and the first familiar face he had seen. They embraced like old friends, and as they drove to the Abwehr apartment on the Rue Luynes, Chapman asked where Doctor Graumann was. Albert, speaking in an undertone so the driver could not hear, hissed that he had been sent to the Eastern Front 'in disgrace'.

The cause of Von Gröning's banishment is unclear. Chapman later learned that his spymaster had quarrelled with the head of the Paris Branch on an issue of 'policy', and Von Gröning's prodigious intake of alcohol had then been used as an excuse for removing him. Von Gröning later claimed that he had wanted to send a U-boat to pick up Chapman but had been overruled, sparking a furious disagreement. It is equally possible that, like other members of the Abwehr, Von Gröning's loyalty to Hitler had come under suspicion. Whatever the cause, Von Gröning had been stripped of his post in Nantes, and ordered to rejoin his old unit, the Heeresgruppe Mitte, in Russia.

Chapman considered Dr Graumann an 'old friend', but more than that, he was a protector and patron. If anyone could shield Chapman from the Gestapo, it was Dr Graumann. His disappearance was a serious blow. The interrogations continued: the Luftwaffe colonel who had seen him off at Le Bourget airport and the pilot, Leutnant Schlichting, quizzed him about his jump and landing. They were followed by an army officer, unnamed and unfriendly, and then a civilian, who rattled off a series of 'about 50' technical questions about British military installations and weapons, none of which Chapman could answer. Whenever Chapman inquired after Dr Graumann he would receive 'vague replies' to the effect that he was 'somewhere on the Eastern Front'. Finally,

Chapman screwed up his courage to announce that he wanted to see Dr Graumann immediately and that he 'would not give his story or work for anyone else'. The request, and accompanying fit of pique, was ignored, or so it seemed.

The general tenor of the questions was affable, but persistent. Chapman was allowed to 'amuse himself' in the evenings, but always accompanied by Albert and at least one other minder. But his request for an 'advance' on the money owed him was flatly rejected. After an angry protest, he was given 10,000 francs to spend, which was later increased, with evident reluctance, to 20,000. This was not the hero's reception and untold riches he had been hoping for. The disagreement left Chapman feeling distinctly uncomfortable.

Chapman memorised the faces of his interrogators, and the few names he could glean. But most of his mental energy was devoted to telling and retelling the story, half truth, half fiction, that had been seared into his memory over the days and weeks in Crespigny Road. The story never altered, and Chapman never faltered, though he was careful to offer only vague timings and dates, mindful of Tar Robertson's warning: 'Timing is the essential factor to conceal, the cover story must not be too precise.' He knew the story so well that, at times, he believed it himself. We know the story, because a verbatim transcript survives:

I landed at about 2.30, in a ploughed field. I was at first stunned by my descent, but on recovering my sense I buried my parachute under some bushes by a small stream running along the edge of the field. I undid the package which had been strapped to my shoulders, taking with me the transmitter and putting the detonators in my pockets. I could see a small barn not far away and, after approaching this cautiously, I realised that it was deserted and entering through a window I climbed up into the loft and slept until daybreak. I was not aware of the time I awoke, because my watch had stopped. It had apparently been broken by my descent. I left this barn and walked along a small road and on to the main road, travelling in a southerly direction, until I saw a signpost which said Wisbech. A study of my map showed me I must be somewhere near Littleport, and when I arrived in the village I saw the name on the railway station. Inspection of the times of trains to London showed that one was leaving at 10.15. I caught this and arrived at Liverpool Street at about a quarter to one. I entered the buffet there, had a drink and bought some cigarettes and, after staying for a few minutes, went to a telephone booth in the station and called Jimmy Hunt at the Hammersmith Working Men's Club. Whoever answered the phone said that Jimmy would be in at about 6 o'clock, so I took the underground train to the West End and went to the New Gallery Cinema, where I saw 'In Which We Serve'. I thought it best not to walk about the West End in daylight so soon after arriving.

I stayed at the cinema until blackout time and then phoned Jimmy again at the Club. He was very surprised to hear my voice, but arranged to meet me at the underground station at Hyde Park. When he arrived we went into a nearby public house and I told Jimmy that I had managed to escape from Jersey and that I had so many things to talk over I thought it would be better if we could go somewhere quieter. I was especially anxious that the police should not know that I was back in the country, so Jimmy said that we had better go to one of his cover addresses in Sackville Street where he was living with a girl. I told him I did not want anyone else to see me, so he phoned her and told her to go out for a time as he had a business friend calling on him. She was used to disappearing when Jimmy had 'shady' business to transact so this did not appear unusual.

On arrival at the flat in Sackville Street I explained the whole thing to Jimmy. I told him that when I was imprisoned in

Jersey I had decided to work for German Intelligence; that
they had treated me extremely well and had promised me a
considerable amount of money if I would carry out a mission
in Britain. I had brought £1,000 with me and had been
promised £15,000 if I succeeded in sabotaging De Havillands. It was an invaluable opportunity for Jimmy to obtain
quite a lot of money and the protection of the German
government to get him out of the country. I showed him the
radio transmitter I had brought with me and said that I
required some place where I could work this. Jimmy told me
that the police had been after him quite a lot lately and that
he had been considering renting a house in Hendon. Meanwhile, however, it would be advisable for me to stay at the
flat in Sackville Street and keep pretty quiet.

I went along to the house in Hendon on Saturday and I
transmitted from there for the first time on Sunday morning.

I explained to Jimmy how necessary it was for me to start
straight away and obtain the materials for my sabotage at De
Havillands. We agreed it would be unwise for me to go out
very much, in case the police were on my track, but Jimmy
said that there remained some gelignite at St Luke's Mews
which we had used on jobs before the war.

I went to De Havillands with Jimmy one day round about
the new year, and we surveyed the whole factory from the
road nearby. We saw that there were three places which we
thought should be our primary objectives. We decided to
hold a reconnaissance at night time and entered by an
unguarded gate, which had only a small amount of barbed
wire attached to it. Near the boiler house, we came across six
huge power transformers in a yard. By climbing over a wall,
it was possible to gain access, and we realised that an
explosive charge under one, or perhaps two of the trans-

formers would completely ruin the output of the whole factory. We looked around and found another subsidiary power house near a building which was by the swimming pool; it was bounded by a high fence and contained two more transformers which obviously handled considerable power. We decided it would be necessary to place about 30 lbs of explosive under each transformer, and thought it would be possible to fit this into two suitcases.

On the night arranged we went up there at about 7 o'clock and parked the car behind a garage in the front of the factory. We had some coffee at a place nearby and then crept through the gardens of a house at the back of the 'Comet' and slipped through the barbed wire at the unguarded gate. Jimmy made for the transformers near the swimming pool and I tackled the one near the power house. We left one hour's delay on each of our explosive mixtures, and stopped our car on the bypass about two miles away from De Havillands. Fifty-five minutes after, we heard two immense explosions, about 30 seconds apart. As soon as this occurred we came straight back to London.

The day after we had arranged for the sabotage, I had arranged to meet a girl at The Hendon Way called Wendy Hammond, who worked at a subsidiary of De Havillands. She told me that there had been an awful mess and that people at the factory were trying to hush it up and say that nothing had occurred. It was clear that there had been considerable damage, and some people were injured, but no one wanted to admit it.

Jimmy was often with me in the bedroom when I transmitted and he took a great deal of interest in the radio messages which we received. He was especially interested to know whether there was any chance of receiving his

£15,000 and when you sent the message to say that it was impossible to pick me up by submarine he became somewhat truculent and thought that the chances of receiving the money were extremely remote. He said that he would come back with me to Lisbon and see that he was paid. Unfortunately, as you know, he was arrested on suspicion of possessing gelignite, and later the Hammersmith Club was raided to see if he had any other confederates. He was released by the police after he had been detained for about a week, but I did not have very much contact with him after that. Owing to the arrest of Jimmy it was not possible for him to come with me, and it would have been very much more difficult to obtain two sets of documents to get out of the country, so of course I had to come alone.

Sticking to the broad lines of the cover story was easy enough; the challenge was to remain alert while seeming relaxed, to maintain consistency, to anticipate the thrust of the interrogation and stay one question ahead. What was it Robertson had said? Speak slowly, be vague, never tell an unnecessary lie. The rules were all very well in the living room at Crespigny Road, but under the relentless probing of expert Abwehr interrogators Chapman could feel his grip slipping, as the truth and lies merged. The donnish Masterman had warned him: 'The life of a secret agent is dangerous enough, but the life of the double agent is infinitely more precarious. If anyone balances on a swinging tightrope it is he, and a single slip can send him crashing to destruction.' No one could balance forever, with so many hands tugging at the rope.

After ten gruelling days in Paris, Chapman was told he would be travelling to Berlin. The journey would take him to the heart of Nazism, but something also led him to suspect it 'would bring him nearer to Graumann'. That suspicion was confirmed when Albert took him aside, and suggested that whatever might happen in Berlin, he should 'reserve the more interesting details of his experiences in England for the time when he might meet Graumann'. The ingratiating Albert asked Chapman to put in a good word for him with Dr Graumann.

The train to Berlin was packed with soldiers, but a first-class compartment had been reserved for Chapman and his new minder, an officer he knew as 'Wolf'. When an army major insisted on taking a seat in the reserved carriage, Wolf summoned the train police and the furious man was ejected, shouting that he would report the offence to Himmler himself.

From Berlin station, he was whisked to a small hotel, La Petite Stephanie, off the Kurfürstendamm. The grilling continued. Chapman was getting tired. The anxiety was fraying his confidence. He slipped. An interviewer, apparently from Abwehr headquarters, casually asked him to describe how he had constructed the suitcase bomb used in the De Havilland sabotage. Chapman explained again how torch batteries attached to a detonator had been strapped to the right side of the suitcase using adhesive tape. The man pounced: in earlier interviews, in Paris and Madrid, Chapman had described how he had attached batteries to the *left* side. Chapman forced himself to think quickly but answer slowly, as Tar had instructed: 'I had two suitcases – one set of batteries was fixed to the right side, and one to the left.' A sweaty moment passed.

The next day, a tall, slim naval officer appeared at La Petite Stephanie, introduced himself as Müller, and presented Chapman with a brand new German passport made out in the name 'Fritz Graumann'; place of birth: New York; father's name: Stephan Graumann. It was the strongest hint yet that his old spymaster was back in the game. Müller told Chapman to pack and be ready to leave in an hour: they were going to Norway.

Back in Bletchley, the codebreakers charted Zigzag's meandering route as he criss-crossed Europe from south to north: they passed on Chapman's new passport names, Norwegian and German, and noted that the supposed sabotage of the

City of Lancaster had 'certainly raised his stock' with his German bosses.

There was only one hitch: the bombs had not gone off, and though the Germans did not appear to suspect Chapman, they were becoming impatient. 'The Germans have shown the greatest interest in the *City of Lancaster* and are naturally anxious to discover if the act of sabotage actually took place,' Masterman warned. Anita, the prostitute from George's Bar, reported that Jack, an indigent black beachcomber who lived under a nearby bridge, had been approached by two Germans who offered him 2,000 escudos for information about sailors from the British ship. The Abwehr had broken all the rules to smuggle the bombs aboard the *City of Lancaster*, but the ship was still intact: Canaris wanted results. Ewen Montagu, the naval representative on the Twenty Committee, issued a warning: 'There must either be an explosion or Zigzag is blown.'

Some sort of incident would have to be staged on board the ship: Operation Damp Squib was born.

Victor, Lord Rothschild was a little disappointed to be told he could not blow up a 'perfectly good merchant ship', but settled for 'as big a bang as possible, together with a lot of smoke'. The prospect of even a moderate explosion aboard the *City of Lancaster* sent his blue blood racing: 'A good decent bang would be a good idea. I do not know how much of a bang one can make without doing damage. I suppose it depends where the bang takes place.'

Together Rothschild and Reed cooked up an elaborate scenario. When the ship docked in Britain, Reed would go aboard, disguised as a customs officer, accompanied by another agent in similar disguise carrying an explosive device in an attaché case. This agent, 'who will previously have been to MI5 head office for tuition in working the bomb', would pretend to search for contraband, plant the bomb in the bunker, light the fuse, and then get out of the way, quick. When he heard the explosion, the agent would 'fall down and pretend he has hurt his arm, which will be bandaged by the master'. He would then explain that 'he was poking the coal in the bunker when there was a hissing noise, followed by an explosion which blew him over'. The crew would then be interrogated and sailors' gossip would do the rest. 'The story of the sabotage will get back to the enemy through some members of the crew,' Reed predicted.

The operation required a special bomb that would make plenty of noise and smoke without killing the MI5 agent who set it off, igniting the coal, or sinking the ship. Rothschild turned to his friend and fellow explosives-enthusiast, Lieutenant Colonel Leslie Wood of the War Office Experimental Station, who duly produced a device guaranteed to make a 'sharp explosion, accompanied by a puff of reddish smoke, approximately three minutes after ignition'. Wood sent a parcel to Rothschild by courier: 'Herewith your three toys: one for you to try yourself, not in the house! The other two for your friend to play with.'

Operation Damp Squib was a very silly plan. It was complicated, risky and involved far too much play-acting ('binding up a notional injury is fortuitously introducing unnecessary "business" of a dangerous kind', warned Masterman). Damp Squib was vetoed, much to Rothschild's annoyance, and he vented his frustration by blowing up all three toys himself.

Instead the bomb would have to be 'discovered' when the ship reached Glasgow; this would be followed by a full interrogation of everyone on board: 'When the *City of Lancaster* next touches at Lisbon, German sub agents will certainly try to get in touch with members of the crew and will get the impression (probably in most cases from some intoxicated seaman) that something curious had happened on the voyage because there was a formidable inquiry when the ship returned to the UK. This is all that is necessary in order to build up Zigzag.'

Sure enough, when the ship put in at Rothesay docks on 25 April, a small army of Field Security Police clambered aboard and began rummaging through the coal bunkers, tossing the coal over the side, piece by piece. The gawping crew noticed that 'as each piece of coal was thrown into the dock they all ducked'. Finally, after some five hours, an officer, 'who was very dirty and smothered in coal dust', was seen emerging from the bunkers, triumphantly 'holding in his hand an object which looked like a lump of coal'. Every member of the crew was then interrogated, with particular emphasis on the voyage to Lisbon and the disappearance of Assistant Steward Hugh Anson.

Auto-suggestion worked its magic: sailors who had noticed nothing out of the ordinary about their former shipmate, now declared that they had suspected Anson was a German spy from the moment he came on board. They recalled his gold cigarette case, his wads of cash and 'swanking' manner, his general incompetence at sea, his good manners, and his apparent education 'beyond his station'. Under interrogation all sorts of sinister details emerged: the way he had boasted of his crimes, bought drinks for everyone, and then slipped away from George's Bar. Why, he even wrote poetry and read books in French. One of the crew produced Chapman's poem as conclusive proof of the man's fiendish brilliance. 'The standard of the poetry does not come up to the flattering adulation of the crew,' one of the interrogators remarked dryly, but to the men of the *Lancaster*, the accumulated evidence pointed to one conclusion: Anson was a multilingual, highly educated Nazi spy who had tried to murder them all with an 'infernal machine' hidden in the bunkers.

As 'a spur to rumour-spreading', the crew was solemnly sworn to secrecy. The gossip raged through Glasgow docks like a brushfire, to Reed's delight: 'Approximately 50 people now regard Zigzag as an enemy agent and know about this bomb business, and it will grow in the telling, which is precisely the result [we] wish to have.' The rumour was passed to other seamen, and from there, through countless bars, to different ships, other ports, and from thence across the seas. It even reached the ears of the owner of the *City of Lancaster*, who was livid: 'He has no objection to helping put agents on board, but he thinks it is going a bit far when they leave explosives around on the ship.'

From the lowest bars of Europe, the story of how a top German spy had tried to sabotage a British ship, reached German High Command, the FBI, and the highest levels of the British government. A copy of the Zigzag file was sent to Duff Cooper, the former Minister of Information who now supervised covert operations as Chancellor of the Duchy of Lancaster, who in turn showed it to Winston Churchill. Cooper reported that he had 'discussed Zigzag at some length with the prime minister who is showing considerable interest in the case'. MI5 was instructed to give the case the highest priority and to inform Churchill immediately 'if and when contact is reestablished with Zigzag'.

J. Edgar Hoover, the FBI chief, was also watching Zigzag's trail. Through John A. Cimperman, the FBI liaison officer based at the American embassy in London, Reed and Rothschild channelled 'comprehensive memoranda' on the Chapman case to the American government. 'I promised Mr Hoover that I would let him have appreciations of the sabotage aspects in return for their co-operative attitude,' wrote Rothschild. Chapman was fast becoming a secret star worldwide: in Washington and Whitehall, in Berlin and Paris, his exploits, real and unreal, were discussed, admired and wondered at.

It was at this moment that Zigzag-Fritz, the most secret spy in the Most Secret Sources, vanished from the wireless traffic, abruptly and completely.

The Ice Front

Stephan von Gröning never spoke of the horrors he witnessed during his second stint on the Eastern Front, but he was 'deeply affected' by the experience. He recalled one episode only: being sent to reopen a church that had been closed by the Communists, in some small town that the Germans had overrun. He remembered how the village people entered the building and fell to their knees. Von Gröning was not a religious man, but he had been moved by the expression of profound piety in the midst of a pitiless war. In the last few months he had aged by several years. His hair was now grey, the face more sallow and drooping. His hands shook until stilled by the first drink of the morning. Much of his dissipated hauteur had dissolved in the freezing winds of Russia. At the age of forty-five, Von Gröning had begun to look like an old man.

But the erect figure in the military greatcoat waiting behind the barrier at Oslo airport was still instantly recognisable. 'Thank God you are back,' said Von Gröning. 'He appeared really moved.' As for Chapman, he was genuinely delighted to see 'the old man', his affection undimmed by the months he had spent betraying him, and his intention to continue doing so. Von Gröning introduced the chubby, balding figure in naval uniform beside him as Kapitan Johnny Holst – his real name, for once. The man grinned cheerily, and welcomed Chapman to Norway in execrable English.

As they drove into the city, Von Gröning explained that Chapman would soon be free to 'enjoy a well-earned holiday', but before that, he must be interrogated one last time, and a full, definitive report had to be sent to Berlin.

Von Gröning had arrived only a few days earlier and taken up residence in a smart 'bachelor flat' at 8, Grønnegate near the presidential palace, where he now opened a bottle of Norwegian aquavit to celebrate Chapman's safe arrival. The party began. An attractive young woman named Molli was the first guest to arrive, then a tough and shrewd-looking German called Peter Hiller and finally Max, a Pole with long hair and flashy jewellery. Chapman remembered little of his first night in Oslo, but he recalled that the guests seemed 'pleased to see him and were very enthusiastic about his success in England' and none more so than Von Gröning. When Chapman asked for news of the rest of the Nantes team, the German was vague. Walter Thomas, he said, was currently in Berlin, and would shortly be travelling to Oslo to resume his duties as Chapman's 'companion'. Inwardly, Chapman groaned: the young Nazi with the passion for English country dancing was such grim and earnest company. The 'hard-drinking Holst', currently dissolving into the sofa to the strains of a German drinking song, seemed a far more jovial chum. Soon afterwards, a fight broke out between Holst and Hiller over Molli's charms, and Chapman passed out.

The interrogation started the next morning, despite the seismic hangovers of both interviewer and interviewee. Von Gröning was a masterful inquisitor. For a start, he knew his subject intimately and the best ways to feed Chapman's vanity, ignite his anger and prick his pride. Behind the heavy lids he seemed half-asleep at times, but then he would dart a question under Chapman's guard that would leave him scrambling. The interrogation continued for two weeks with every word re-corded and transcribed by Molli Stirl, the woman at the party who was secretary of the Oslo Abwehr station. Von Gröning was unrelenting and meticulous, but there was something different about the way he questioned Chapman, something far removed from the harsh grilling in Spain, France and Berlin. Von Gröning wanted Chapman to get it right: when he made an error, of chronology or fact, he would gently lead him back, iron out the inconsistency, and then move on again. Von Gröning was on Chapman's side; he was willing him to succeed, for Chapman's sake, but also for his own.

Chapman sensed the shift in their relationship. In Nantes, he had been dependant on Von Gröning's goodwill, eager for his praise, flattered by his attention. The roles had not quite been reversed, but equalised. Chapman needed Von Gröning to believe him, and Von Gröning needed Chapman to succeed, forging a strange, unspoken complicity. At times, the older man seemed almost 'pathetically grateful' to Chapman, without whom he might still be wading through the slush and blood of the Eastern Front. Von Gröning was 'proud of his protégé', but he was also reliant on him, and that, Chapman reflected, was his 'best security'. Von Gröning's status had plummeted when Chapman disappeared; his return had raised Von Gröning's stock in the Abwehr once more. Chapman was more than just another spy: he was a career investment, the 'man who had "made" him in the German Secret Service', and they both knew it.

The mutual dependence of spy and spymaster was not peculiar to Chapman and Von Gröning; it was the central defining flaw of the German secret service. The Abwehr's decentralised structure allowed individual officers to control their own networks of spies. Wilhelm Canaris sat in judgment over all, but the separate branches, and even individual officers within the same branch, operated with a degree of independence, and in competition. In the British secret services case officers shared responsibility since a spymaster whose self-interest was bound up with the success of his own agent could never see that agent clearly. 'Absolute personal integrity and the exclusion of all personal considerations is the first and fundamental condition of success,' insisted Masterman. In the Abwehr, by contrast, each spymaster was ambitious for his own spy to the point where he might suppress his own suspicions and insist on the loyalty or efficiency of an agent despite evidence to the contrary. Even when a spy was useless, or worse, the spymaster would be unwilling to admit the failure, on the assumption, logical but fatal, that it was 'better for selfish reasons to have corrupt or disloyal agents than to have no agents at all'.

Did Von Gröning see Chapman clearly through those watery blue eyes? Several times Chapman noticed his 'watchful' expression and wondered if his yarn had been unravelled by this man who knew him better than any other. As one associate put it: 'Stephan made up his own opinion, he was secretive, and he did not tell people what he was thinking unless they asked.' If Von Gröning suspected he was being lied to, that the entire tale of sabotage, heroism and escape was a monstrous fabrication, he said nothing, and the heavy-lidded eyes chose not to see.

Chapman was installed at Forbunds, a large and comfortable wood-built hotel in Oslo city centre, which had been commandeered by the Abwehr and the Luftwaffe. Von Gröning handed over 500 Kroner as spending money, and told him he could have more 'as and when he required it'. The reward would be paid when the report had been written up, taken to Berlin, and approved.

Chapman came face to face with the war of occupation for the first time. In France he had mixed with a handful of tarts, collaborators and black-marketeers, but had little contact with other French citizens. In London his conversations outside the security service had been few, and strictly supervised. Now, he observed Nazi rule at unpleasantly close proximity.

The invasion of Norway, in April 1940, had been swift and devastating. The nation was decapitated, and King Haakon fled into exile in London. The Norwegian Nazis, led by Vidkun Quisling, assumed office as a puppet government under German rule. Hitler had simple ambitions for Norway: to defend it against the expected British counter-invasion, to bleed the country white, and convert it to Nazism. The Norwegian people, however, declined to be bullied into fascism. Pressure and threats gave way to outright coercion. In spring 1942, Goebbels declared of the recalcitrant Norwegians: 'If they will not learn to love us, they shall at least learn to fear us.' Many had learned to fear the Nazis in the ensuing Gestapo-led terror, but more had learned to hate them. A few collaborated, as a few always will; the more extreme or ambitious joined the Norwegian Nazi party, or volunteered for the 'Viking Regiment' – the Norwegian legion deployed by Hitler on the Eastern Front. Quisling, vague, inefficient and fanatical, won the rare distinction of being so closely associated with a single characteristic – treachery – that a noun was created in his name. At the opposite moral pole an active Norwegian resistance movement organised protests, strikes, sabotage and even assassinations.

Between the extremes of collaboration and resistance, the majority of Norwegians maintained a sullen, insolent loathing for the German occupiers. As a mark of opposition many wore paperclips in their lapels. The paperclip is a Norwegian invention: the little twist of metal became a symbol of unity, a society binding together against oppression. Their anger blew cold in a series of small rebellions and acts of incivility. Waiters in restaurants would always serve their countrymen first; Norwegians would cross the street to avoid eye contact with a German and speak only in Norwegian; on buses no one would sit beside a German, even when the vehicle was jam-packed, a form of passive disobedience so infuriating to the Nazi occupiers that it became illegal to stand on a bus if a seat was available. Collaborators were shunned by former friends, neighbours and family, seldom openly rebuked, but socially ostracised. The resistance groups called this the 'Ice Front', Norwegian society's collective cold shoulder, intended to freeze out the enemy.

The Germans and their Norwegian collaborators sought refuge from the hostility in a handful of places where they could socialise, such as the Ritz Hotel and a large restaurant renamed

Löwenbräu, which admitted only Germans and collaborators. But even here, Chapman recalled, sealed off from the rest of Norway, 'It was an uneasy feeling.' Norwegians assumed Chapman was German and avoided him. They answered in monosyllables, or eyed him with ill-veiled contempt from behind what he called a 'wall of hatred'. He had experienced none of this antagonism in France. A naturally sociable man, Chapman was learning what it feels like to be loathed.

Chapman's discomfort was compounded by the sensation that his German handlers also regarded him with some distrust. The grinning Johnny Holst accompanied him everywhere, friendly but vigilant. The German officials who came and went at the Forbunds Hotel 'appeared somewhat suspicious and were not communicative'. His disingenuous questions about intelligence operations met with silence. Von Gröning had promised him 'complete freedom'. Both knew that Chapman's freedom was far from complete. The Abwehr officials he met never gave their names. Not once did he cross the threshold of Abwehr headquarters, a large block of flats at Klingenberggate. Von Gröning instructed him to relax and 'not to work'. He had assumed this was a reward, but gradually the realisation dawned that this enforced leisure was a security precaution, a way of keeping him at arm's length.

He was told to carry a pistol, to report if he felt he was being followed, and to ensure that he was never photographed. British agents were doubtless watching him, Von Gröning warned, and might even target him. But the Germans were also watching him. And so were the Norwegians.

Chapman had been in Oslo a few days when Praetorius, the man he knew as Walter Thomas, finally arrived, dirty, dishevelled after a three-day train journey via Sweden and more than usually grumpy. Praetorius, newly married to Friederike, his childhood sweetheart, had been undergoing training in Berlin for officers intended for the Eastern Front. He was furious at being ordered to babysit Chapman instead. Unlike Von Gröning, who had been only too delighted to escape the carnage, Praetorius saw himself as a knightly warrior in the old tradition: an ardent Nazi and anti-Communist, he was itching, he said, to do 'battle against the Reds' and was determined to win himself an Iron Cross. (Chapman concluded that Thomas had a 'hero complex'.) Alternately spouting Nazi propaganda and practising his English country dancing steps, Praetorius was once again a constant presence, eccentric, humourless and profoundly aggravating. After just a few days, Chapman begged Von Gröning to make him go away, but the spymaster, who found Praetorius no less annoying, said he had no choice: Berlin had specifically ordered that the young Nazi should be present at the debriefing and act as Chapman's 'companion'. Unbeknownst to either of them, Praetorius was compiling his own report.

After two solid weeks of interrogation, Von Gröning boarded the plane to Berlin with the final version of Chapman's story, neatly typed up by Molli Stirl, in his briefcase. Chapman could finally relax, unaware that his fate was being furiously debated at Abwehr headquarters in Berlin where one faction of the German secret service wanted him rewarded, and another wanted him eliminated. The argument can be partially reconstructed from post-war interrogations of Abwehr personnel. Von Gröning, naturally, led the supporters' club, pointing out that Chapman had performed 'the only successful sabotage ever carried out' by the sabotage branch of the Paris Abwehr. His most vigorous opponent was the officer newly appointed to head the Paris station, Von Eschwege, who insisted that Fritz was either 'controlled by the British' or a fraud who, so far from carrying out a successful mission, 'when he went to England did nothing, and lied about his activities'.

The argument was complicated by an internal turf war and a personality clash. According to an Abwehr officer present during the debate, Von Eschwege 'apparently had the idea, which is not unknown to any of us, that nothing which had been done before was any good'. Von Gröning, on the other hand, was described

Major Ronnie Reed, an unobtrusively brilliant BBC radio engineer who became Chapman's first case officer.

Rittmeister Stephan von Gröning (alias Doctor Graumann), Chapman's aristocratic German spymaster.

perating Chapman's German radio set.

Stephan von Gröning as a young officer in the White Dragoons, c.1914.

Oberleutnant Walter Praetorius (alias Thomas), Chapman's principal German minder – a Nazi fanatic with a taste for English folk-dancing.

Colonel Robin 'Tin Eye' Stephens, commander of Camp 020: interrog martinet and inspired amateur psychologist.

Franz Stoetzner (alias Franz Schmidt), the German agent with the cockney accent who spied in Britain before the war while working as a London waiter.

Karl Barton (alias Hermann Wojch), the principal sabotage instructor at La Bretonnière.

John Cecil Masterman: Oxford academic, thriller writer, sportsman spymaster; the intellectual behind tl Double Cross operation.

Reed

Iron Cross awarded to Eddie Chapman by a grateful Führer for his ['landing' success]. No other British citizen has ever received the medal.

[...]man in his pomp, posing with his Rolls-Royce. As honorary crime [corres]pondent for the *Sunday Telegraph*, Chapman specialised in warning readers to steer clear of people like himself.

Dagmar Lahlum, the Norwegian girlfriend unofficially recruited by Chapman into MI5.

Freda Stevenson, pictured here with baby Diane, her daughter fathered by Chapman. This was possibly the image sent to Chapman in Jersey prison.

Betty Farmer, the woman Chapman abandoned at the Hotel de la Plage in 1938. 'I shall leave, but I will always come back.'

Graffiti in the attic at La Bretonnière, the German spy school in Nantes, including what appears to be a likeness of Betty Farmer, Chapman's girlfriend, probably drawn by the apprentice spy himself.

Hitler caricatured as a carrot in the attics of La Bretonnière: evidence that Von Gröning may have actively encouraged a disrespectful attitude towards the Führer.

La Bretonnière. This photograph, taken by Stephan von Gröning in 1942, remained in his wallet for the rest of his life.

Chapman pictur[...] den with Billy H[...] styled 'King of S[...] Walker (*right*).

Chapman after his return to Britain in 1944.

Chapman protesting in 1953 after his attempts to serialise his memoirs in a newspaper were stymied under the Official Secrets Act.

Hammin[...] SS unifo[...] real life.

Ch[...]
cor[...]

as 'one of those "don't-tell-me-what-to-do-I-know"' types'. The dispute raged for five days until finally, judgment was passed, presumably by Canaris himself. The Abwehr needed a success story; there was nothing to prove that Chapman was double-dealing, and there was plenty of evidence, including English newspaper reports, to back up his account. He had shown exemplary bravery in the service of Germany and should be rewarded, congratulated, pampered, and closely watched.

Von Gröning returned to Oslo 'beaming with pleasure'. The Abwehr, he announced, had decided to award Chapman the sum of 110,000 Reichsmarks: 100,000 for his 'good work in England', and an additional 10,000 for the plot to sabotage the *City of Lancaster*. This was some 27 per cent less than the 150,000 Reichsmarks he had been promised in the original contract, but it was still a large sum, and an accurate reflection of circumstances: the Abwehr was only about 73 per cent sure Chapman was telling the truth. Like any experienced contract-criminal, Chapman asked to be paid 'in notes', but Von Gröning said that the money would be held for him 'in credit' at the Oslo Abwehr headquarters, where Chapman could 'draw on it when necessary'. He did not need to add that this way Chapman would be less tempted to abscond with the cash. He would also receive a monthly wage of 400 Kroner. Chapman signed a receipt, which was countersigned by Von Gröning – now not only his spymaster, but his private banker.

The scene that followed marked perhaps the oddest moment in the entire saga. According to Chapman, Von Gröning then rose 'solemnly' to his feet, and handed him a small leather case. Inside, on a red, white and black ribbon, was an Iron Cross – *das Eiserne Kreuz*, the highest symbol of bravery. First awarded in 1813 to Prussian troops during the Napoleonic wars, the Iron Cross was revived by the Kaiser in the First World War and by the Second World War had become a central element of Nazi iconography, the stark symbol of Aryan courage. Hitler himself proudly displayed the Iron Cross he was awarded as a corporal in

1914. Göring won two, one in each war. The mystique of the cross was such that postcards of the most famous recipients were printed and avidly collected by children and adults alike. The medal, Von Gröning said, was in recognition of Chapman's 'outstanding zeal and success'. No other British citizen has ever received the Iron Cross.

Chapman was astonished and privately amused by this extraordinary presentation. He reflected wryly to himself: 'If I stay with this mob long enough, I might end up a Reichsmarschall . . .'

As the Nazi occupation weighed ever more heavily on Norway, Chapman, under orders to enjoy himself, lived a lotus life: 'You are free to explore the countryside,' Von Gröning told him. 'Go yachting and bathing.' Chapman did what he was told. During the day he was left to explore his new home, always with Johnny Holst or Walter Praetorius in tow. At night they would go drinking at the Löwenbräu or the Ritz. It was hinted that his next mission might involve a sea crossing, and so Holst 'was put at his disposal to teach him yachting, whenever he needed him'. Holst was a wireless instructor, yet he was available to go sailing or drinking at a moment's notice, 'postponing classes whenever he felt so inclined'. Chapman's new companion was a strange man, cultured and refined in many ways, but a slob in others. He spoke Danish and Norwegian, loved music and the sea. When very drunk (which he was much of the time) he could be belligerent and morose; when merely tipsy (which he was the rest of the time) he was sentimental and lachrymose. He suffered from acute delirium tremens, and his hands shook violently. Holst was having an affair with another of the Abwehr secretaries, a German woman named Irene Merkl who had been a fifth columnist in Norway before the invasion. 'If the British ever come to Norway, she would be shot,' Holst would remark with pride.

Von Gröning, aware of Chapman's propensity for boredom, told him to 'brush up on his Morse', and so he was escorted one morning to the wireless training school, lodged in a large Oslo town house, the upstairs rooms of which had been divided into cubicles, each with a locked door. Trainee spies were brought in at different times, and locked in, to ensure they never spotted one another. Chapman's telegraphy was tested, and declared to be good, though 'rusty'. He was then 'hustled' out. Plainly, he could not be trusted to be left alone with a radio.

Life in Oslo drifted pleasantly by. Chapman, it seemed, was not expected to learn, or do, anything very much. A photographer named Rotkagel, the former manager of a Leica factory, was detailed to teach him photography, and he was issued with his own camera and film. Chapman found it strange to be 'regarded as an expert'; from time to time he was consulted on matters of sabotage, 'asked to give advice as a result of his exploits', and presented to visiting German dignitaries by a proud Von Gröning, as 'the man who has already been over there for us'.

One day, Chapman half-jokingly declared to Von Gröning that he wanted 'to buy a boat'. Instead of dismissing the idea, the German promptly produced a wad of cash. From Evanson's yard, with Holst's help and advice, he purchased a Swedish yawl, an elegant little sailing vessel with a small cabin, ideal for navigating through the fjords. As the days passed, the surveillance regime seemed to relax; Holst and Thomas no longer dogged his every step. He was even allowed to sail alone, with consequences that were almost disastrous when he put out into the Oslo fjord against Holst's advice and lost his sails in a storm. He was towed back to harbour, but instead of being mocked for his foolishness, this escape only seemed to 'enhance his stock' among the Germans.

Chapman was fêted, a free captive, rich and idle; he should have been happy. But the Ice Front had chilled him. The wintry stares of the Norwegians, the sense of unreality, compounded by his own double-dealing, had wrought a change. In Nantes, he had been content to take advantage of the situation but now, living a life of fake bonhomie and stolen luxury with his German companions, he found himself affected by the oppressive contempt of the Norwegians, a 'truly brave, patriotic people'.

The Ritz Hotel, a classical-fronted, cream-painted building with wrought iron balconies in the exclusive Skillebekk neighbourhood, had once been the preserve of Oslo's wealthy; now it was the chosen retreat of a different elite composed of occupiers and collaborators. Every evening, officers of the SS, the Gestapo and the Abwehr mingled with recruits to the Viking Regiment and members of the Quisling government.

One evening in late April, Chapman was drinking at the mahogany bar of the Ritz, when he spotted two young women at a corner table, laughing together. When one of them took out a cigarette, Chapman sauntered over and offered a light. '*Bitteschon*' – the girl shook her head, shot a glance of acid disdain, and lit her own cigarette. Chapman noticed that up close she was 'most attractive', with delicate features and large eyes with almost colourless pupils. Undaunted, Chapman drew up a chair. He was French, he lied, a journalist writing an article for a Paris newspaper. He bought more drinks; he made the girls laugh. Holst joined the group, and began chatting to the other girl in Norwegian, whose name was Mary Larsen, while Chapman set about charming her blonde friend, in French and English. Finally, she conceded that her name was Dagmar. Slowly, almost imperceptibly, the ice began to thaw. Chapman invited her to dinner. She refused point blank. Chapman persisted. Finally, she relented.

Only much later did Chapman pause to wonder why a beautiful girl who hated Germans should choose to drink in the city's most notorious Nazi hangout.

The Girl at the Ritz

Dagmar Mohne Hansen Lahlum was born in Eidsvoll, a small, rural town in south-east Norway where the Norwegian constitution was signed in 1814. The daughter of a shoemaker, Dagmar was anything but strait-laced and from an early age she was regarded by local gossips as altogether too pretty and opinionated for their respectable town. The neighbours muttered that she had fancy airs and would come to no good. Dagmar loathed living in Eidsvoll, claiming, with some justification, that nothing interesting had happened there since 1814. She would pore over magazines sent to her by an aunt in Oslo and try to reproduce the latest fashions with her needle and thread, while dreaming of escape: 'She was young, she wanted to explore the world, to learn English, and dance.'

Shortly before the war, at the age of seventeen, Dagmar packed up her few belongings, headed for the city and found work as a receptionist in a hotel in the capital. She enrolled in evening modelling classes and learned to sashay and swivel her hips. She had watched, appalled and a little excited, as the solid ranks of invading German troops marched down Karl Johanns Gate, but at first the occupation hardly touched her. At night, in her tiny flat at Frydenlundsgate, she read books about art and poetry, and painted elaborate clothing designs. 'She wanted to improve herself.' She, like Chapman, 'wanted adventure'.

Her first she quickly regretted. She met a much older man

named Johanssen who seemed worldly and sophisticated and married him with a 20,000 Kroner dowry from her father. Johanssen expected Dagmar to cook and clean like an obedient Hausfrau, which was not what Dagmar had in mind at all. She left him, and demanded her dowry back; Johanssen refused. On the night she met Chapman, Dagmar was celebrating her twenty-first birthday with her best friend Mary, and toasting the start of her divorce proceedings.

Dagmar would be the grand passion of Chapman's war, but few love affairs can have started more inauspiciously. She thought Chapman was an enemy invader, though conceded he was charming. With her Craven 'A' cigarettes, long ebony holder, high heels and fashionably risqué dresses he imagined she was just a good-time girl. Both were utterly mistaken. For Dagmar Lahlum, model and dressmaker, was also secretly working as an agent for Milorg, the spreading Norwegian resistance network. Though neither knew it, Eddie Chapman and his 'beautiful and adorable' new lover were fighting on the same side.

Chapman quickly became infatuated. He adjusted his lie, dropped the pretence of being a French journalist, and claimed to be German, born and raised in the US. He wined and dined Dagmar with every luxury that occupied Oslo could supply. No longer did she sew her own clothes, for he bought her anything she desired. He took her sailing on the fjords; they swam naked in the icy water, and made love in the woods. As always, Chapman's love and loyalty moved on the shifting tide of his moods. He was loyal to Britain, but happy to be courted by the Nazis; he was loyal to his MI5 spymasters, but considered his truest friend to be Von Gröning, the man he was betraying; he was still betrothed to Freda, but besotted with Dagmar. Von Gröning observed the blooming love affair with shrewd approval. A spy in love was a spy who might be manipulated, and Dagmar – of whom they had no suspicion – might be a most useful bargaining chip. It was precisely the same calculation MI5 had made over Freda.

Though Dagmar seemed to be in love, Chapman sensed tension and a little fear in her, something private and alert. She plainly disbelieved his claim to be German-American, and often asked how he had developed such a strange accent. She refused to accompany him to restaurants used by Norwegians. In the street, her fellow countrymen would stare at them, a Norwegian girl holding hands with a German, and she would blush deeply. The gossips noted sourly how Dagmar smoked black-market American cigarettes and sported an expensive new wardrobe. 'Because she had nice clothes everyone assumed she was Nazi. It was the rule: if you had money, you must be collaborating.' Chapman saw how her compatriots subtly slighted Dagmar; he sensed her hurt and embarrassment, and bristled on her behalf. One night, in the Löwenbräu, a legionnaire from the Viking Regiment made a barbed remark about Dagmar within earshot. The next moment the Norwegian was flat on his back, with Chapman beating the glue out of him for this 'fancied slight'. Johnny Holst had to drag him off. From her comments it was obvious that Dagmar was 'anti-Quisling', but he knew that behind her back the Norwegians called her a 'Nazi's tart'. Trapped in his tangle of lies, Chapman longed to tell her the truth, but held back, knowing the truth could kill them both.

The precariousness of the situation was underlined when Chapman was summoned to Von Gröning's flat one evening and presented to a tall, grey-haired man in an expensive-looking English suit. He introduced himself as 'Doktor König', in excellent English with an American accent, and he seemed to know Chapman's story alarmingly well. There was something about the intensity of his clinical manner and 'hawk-like' gaze that was deeply unnerving. Chapman concluded he must be 'some kind of psychologist'. Without preamble, König launched into a detailed interrogation that had clearly been prepared 'with a view to testing his reliability'. Chapman was being hunted.

König: 'Where could you leave a valuable package safely in London?'

Chapman: 'The Eagle Club, Soho.'

'Who would you leave it with?'

'Milly Blackwood,' said Chapman, thinking quickly. Milly had indeed been the owner of the Eagle, but she was now, he knew, safely dead.

'Where would you conceal a secret message for another agent?'

'In a telephone booth or a public lavatory.'

'Where did you leave your wireless?'

'I have the address of a house, in the garden of which, near a certain tree, I buried it.'

The interrogator paused, and gave Chapman a long look: 'I am in charge of an agent who will shortly be going to England on a mission. The agent might need the wireless.'

Suddenly, with a lurch, Chapman sensed the trap. The wireless, of course, was stashed away in a cupboard in Whitehall, and he had no way of contacting his British handlers to arrange for it to be buried. He could give an invented address for the hiding place, but if the Germans did send an agent to find it and turned up nothing, his entire story would unravel. No one in MI5 had spotted this flaw in his story. Even Von Gröning had missed it, or chosen to overlook it. Was it a bluff? Dare he counter-bluff? He was first vague, and then petulant, complaining it was 'unfair' to give his radio to another agent. 'I myself expect one day to be sent back to England,' he blustered. It was hardly a convincing argument. The Abwehr could easily find him another transmitter. The grey-haired interrogator eyed him coldly. It was, Chapman said with thumping understatement, an 'uncomfortable moment'.

That evening, the grey-haired man escorted Chapman to a quiet restaurant and began to ply him with cognac, while 'periodically asking awkward questions'. Chapman got drunk, but not nearly as drunk as he appeared. By the end of the evening, hawk-face was also slurring his words and seemed more 'benign', but as Chapman staggered to his feet, the man fixed him with an unblinking look. 'You are not absolutely sincere,' he said.

Chapman held the stare for a second, and then grinned: 'I know I am not.'

When Chapman returned to the flat in Grønnegate the next morning, the grey-haired visitor had vanished, and Von Gröning was in buoyant mood. 'The doctor was quite satisfied with your answers and information,' he said breezily. 'You passed the test.'

There were other tests. A few nights later, Chapman was sitting alone in the Löwenbräu, waiting for Dagmar, when a Norwegian woman aged about forty-five sat down beside him, and introduced herself as Anne. They began chatting in German. Anne remarked on his accent. Chapman replied that he had been raised in America. They switched to English, which she spoke perfectly. In an undertone, she began to complain about the occupation, the lack of food and the swaggering German soldiers. Chapman listened, but said nothing. She invited him to dinner. He politely declined. As soon as Dagmar arrived, Chapman rose swiftly and announced they were leaving. A few nights later he saw Anne again at the Löwenbräu. She was very drunk. Chapman looked away but she spotted him, weaved up, and hissed: 'I think you are a British spy.' The remark was loud enough to be heard at the next table. When Chapman related the incident to Von Gröning, the German remarked simply: 'Leave it to me.' Chapman told himself that this Anne must have been an *agent provocateur* for the Germans; but perhaps she had been a genuine member of the resistance, testing his loyalties, and he had exposed her. He never saw her again.

The underground war raged. One afternoon, as Chapman and Dagmar drank a cup of tea in his room, a shattering explosion rocked the hotel. Chapman stuffed his few belongings into a suitcase and he and Dagmar clattered down the staircase to join the throng in the street, staring in wonder as the top floor of the hotel blazed. The Norwegian fire brigade arrived and began putting out the fire, as slowly and inefficiently as possible, spraying water everywhere while the Norwegian crowd jeered and cheered. Chapman thought the scene worthy of a Marx Brothers script. By the time the firemen had completed their leisurely work, Forbunds Hotel was in ruins. Dagmar disappeared from Chapman's side and returned a few moments later: 'It is the work of the British,' she whispered.

Chapman and his minders moved in to new quarters, Kapelveien 15, a safe house in the northern suburb of Grafsin that would become the Oslo equivalent of Crespigny Road, with Holst and Praetorius playing the parts of Backwell and Tooth. In an echo of the domestic arrangements with Freda, Chapman urged Dagmar to live there too. At first she resisted. Her countrymen would spurn her even more as a 'kept woman', and who would pay the rent? Chapman laughed, explaining that there was 'sufficient money for them both'. Dagmar moved in.

The money was indeed plentiful, but not endless, and Chapman was burning through it at an astonishing rate. Von Gröning was only too happy to dole out cash on demand; indeed he encouraged Chapman to spend as much as possible, to host parties, buy Dagmar whatever she wanted and foot the bill for every occasion. There was a method to Von Gröning's profligacy by proxy. Once Chapman had spent his money, he would need to go back to work; an impecunious spy, like a spy in love, was easier to handle.

Chapman, typically, had no idea how much money was left, but he was not so careless that he failed to spot another aspect of Von Gröning's financial arrangements: the German was skimming his cut. If Chapman asked for, say, 10,000 Kroner, Von Gröning would agree, give him a chit to sign, but then hand over perhaps half that sum. However much he requested, Von Gröning always produced less, and 'pocketed the balance'. Von Gröning's speculations on the stock market had been disastrous, but in Chapman he had found an investment offering a substantial return, and not just in terms of career development. Hitherto, Chapman had regarded Von Gröning as his mentor, upright, aristocratic and unassailable. Now he had demonstrated that he was also an embezzler, but Chapman was happy to let his spymaster 'help himself'. Neither man alluded to what each knew was going on, their tacit understanding forming yet another strand in the web of complicity.

Kapelveien 15 could have been an illustratration from a Nordic book of fairy tales – a large wooden house set back off the road in a large garden dotted with fruit trees and currant bushes. Roses clambered over the roof. 'It was a delightful spot,' Chapman reflected. On the door was a nameplate: 'Feltman'. Like La Bretonnière, his new home had once had Jewish owners. Idly, Chapman wondered what had happened to them.

Joshua and Rachel Feltman had emigrated to Norway from Russia in the 1920s. They had opened a barber's shop, and then a clothes shop. They had done well. In 1927, Joshua bought the house at Grafsin. Rachel could have no children of her own, but she adopted a nephew, Herman, and raised him as her son. The neighbours welcomed them. Then came the horror.

Like everyone else, the Feltmans witnessed the invasion with mounting disbelief and deepening fear. Joshua was a big, placid man who believed the best of everyone. The Nazis were human too, he said. At first it seemed he might be right. But then, early in 1942, the Feltmans were summarily ordered to leave their home. They moved into a flat above the shop. Herman, now twenty-four years old, urged his parents to take refuge in neutral Sweden: the Germans were beginning to round up Jews and tales of frightful atrocities had begun to filter northwards from Europe. Joshua hesitated, and Herman decided to go alone, to prepare the way for his mother and father. With a Jewish friend he boarded a train for Stockholm. As the border approached, Nazi soldiers climbed aboard and began demanding documents. Herman's papers declared him to be Jewish. He jumped from the moving train, broke an arm and fractured his spine. He was still in hospital when the Germans arrested him, and shipped him to Poland.

Unaware of their son's fate, still Joshua and Rachel wavered, but then, when the Nazis began to corral the small community of Norwegian Jews, they ran. Milorg offered to help smuggle them to Sweden: a group of partisans would take them, on foot, to the border, and see them safely across. Joshua loaded their possessions onto his back, and they set off. No one knows exactly what happened next. Perhaps the partisans coveted the few chattels in Joshua's sack. Perhaps their guides were secret collaborators. Soon after Chapman and Dagmar moved into Kapelveien 15, the dead bodies of the Feltmans were found in woods near the Swedish border. A few weeks later, their only son Herman was gassed and cremated in Auschwitz.

Seventeen-year-old Leife Myhre, who lived at Number 13, watched the new neighbours move in. He had run errands on Saturday mornings for Joshua Feltman, and Rachel Feltman had given him biscuits. He liked the Feltmans, 'they were fair, hardworking, straightforward people', and he hated the Germans. At first some German officers had moved into Number 15, but now a new set of neighbours had taken their place. They wore civilian clothes, and over the fence he heard them speaking English. They had big parties, and afterwards they would line up the bottles and shoot them, one by one. Sometimes they shot rats in the garden. 'They were in extremely good physical condition. One day the telephone rang, and I saw one of them run all the way up the garden and then dive straight through an open widow to answer it.' Leife was impressed, in spite of himself. He never spoke to anyone in the house, except once, after the Norwegian woman moved in. 'She was very attractive, and not much older than me. Once, when I saw her on the street, I stopped her and said: "You shouldn't be mixing with these Germans you know." She looked around and blushed and then she whispered to me: "I am not working for them, you know".'

There was something in her expression – embarrassment, defiance, fear – that Leife never forgot.

Chapman, his lover, and his minders settled happily into the pretty house stolen from the murdered Feltmans. Chapman took photographs of the domesticated evening scene: Dagmar sewing a button on his jacket in the living room, her face shyly, or perhaps intentionally, averted; Holst, unconscious from drink on the sofa, his hand thrust down his trousers, wearing a smile of stupefaction. Chapman invariably won the shooting competitions in the back garden because Holst could not hold a gun straight on account of the DTs. Meanwhile, Praetorius would practise English country-dance steps on the back porch. Sometimes Von Gröning would come to dinner. Dagmar was told that the paunchy visitor was a Belgian journalist.

One morning Von Gröning appeared at the house and told Chapman they would be leaving for Berlin in a few hours, to see 'certain people, connected with sabotage organisation, [who] were interested in his story'. That evening they checked into the Hotel Alexandria in Mittelstrasse, and then drove on to a flat where three men were waiting: a Hauptmann in Wehrmacht uniform, a Luftwaffe lieutenant colonel and an SS officer in civilian clothes who was plainly drunk and 'applied himself freely to a bottle of cognac' throughout the meeting. They asked Chapman some vague questions about the De Havilland plant and other potential sabotage targets in Britain, in particular the location of 'vital machinery, requiring replacement from America'. Chapman pointed out, sensibly, that any such military factory would be heavily guarded. While the panel absorbed this sobering thought, another bottle of brandy was opened. When that was finished, the meeting broke up.

Von Gröning was livid, declaring he was 'disgusted with the whole affair'. The colonel was a fool, and the SS man was plastered, he said. Chapman was also somewhat baffled by the strange encounter, but the meeting had provided one useful piece of intelligence: the higher powers were evidently planning to send him on another mission to Britain. If that were the case, he would need something to present to MI5 on his return.

Chapman had not been entirely idle during those lazy days on the fjords, for as he cruised around Oslo he had been quietly filling out the questionnaire he had brought in his head. He noted down possible RAF targets – ammunition dumps, the huge tanks where the Luftwaffe stored petrol on the Eckberg isthmus, the harbours where the U-boats docked and refuelled. He memorised the faces of the officials he met, the names he picked up, the addresses of key German administration buildings and descriptions of the informers and collaborators who milled around the bars. 'It all depends on the opportunities that you see presented to you,' Rothschild had told him. Slowly, surreptitiously, Chapman drew a mental map of the German occupation of Oslo.

One afternoon after his return from Berlin, Chapman and Dagmar untied the little yawl from its mooring and set sail, slipping out under the shadow of Akershus castle and heading into the expanse of Oslo fjord. With Chapman at the tiller, they sailed past the Aker shipyards towards the Bygdøy peninsula, the finger of land that curls into Oslo bay like a question mark. A mile from the harbour, Chapman dropped anchor and they waded onto a small, pebble beach, empty except for some deserted fishing huts.

Bygdøy was Norway's most exclusive preserve, a gated, guarded enclave divided into a series of estates, including one of the royal properties. Now it was the home of Vidkun Quisling. The pair climbed through a patch of dense woodland, and found a path leading to the hilltop on which stood a huge stone mansion, once home to a Norwegian millionaire, and now Quisling's private fortress and administrative headquarters. He had named it Gimli, after the great hall in Norse mythology where righteous souls dwell for eternity. Leading Dagmar by the hand, Chapman kept to the woods skirting the estate until they came in sight of a machine-gun tower guarding a gated entrance.

Beyond it, an avenue of lime trees led to the villa; he measured the barbed-wire fences and counted the armed guards.

Back on board, Chapman opened a bottle of cognac, set sail, and as they scudded through the waves he gave the helm to Dagmar, while he sketched a map of the Quisling estate and its defences; Tar Robertson would be most interested. Chapman could never explain when, or even quite why, he decided to confess his true identity to Dagmar. Perhaps he simply could not bear to lie any more. He later denied that he had been 'under the influence of drink at the time', which suggests that he was at least a little tipsy. Undoubtedly, the Ice Front played a part. Dagmar had been ostracised by her own people as a 'Nazi whore': she, Chapman, and a handful of others within the Norwegian resistance knew otherwise, but he could see the effect it was having on her. Chapman knew that 'he risked losing her if he continued to impersonate a German', and holding on to Dagmar seemed more important than anything else.

Further down the coast, Chapman anchored the little yawl. At dusk, with Dagmar in his arms, he made his declaration: he told her he was a British spy, that the Germans believed him to be a German agent, and that he would shortly be returning to Britain on a mission. Dagmar was intrigued: she had always suspected that he was not German. Above all, she was relieved, for the discovery gave her a means to untangle her own motives and feelings. She had allowed herself to be picked up by a man she believed to be German because she thought he might have information useful to the resistance, but also because he was handsome, charming and generous. Now, having discovered his real identity, she could love him without shame. She was curious to learn the 'details of Chapman's work for the British', but Chapman insisted that she should know as little as possible. He swore her to silence. She agreed, and took his secret to the grave.

Thus was Dagmar Lahlum recruited, unofficially, into the British secret service. 'You could be of use,' Chapman told her. Von Gröning seemed to like her; she should take every opportunity to be 'alone with him' and get him to talk freely; she could also help to gather information on the other members of the Oslo Abwehr.

Chapman's declaration to Dagmar was an act of faith, but it was also a wild gamble. Her hatred of the Germans seemed as genuine as her feelings for him; he did not believe that she had been planted by the Germans at the Ritz as a honey-trap. But he could not be certain. He set her a small test: to locate the Oslo headquarters of the Abwehr, which Chapman already knew. If she found the Abwehr HQ, it would be proof of her commitment; and if she failed it, well, he would probably already be in a Gestapo prison, or dead. Dagmar accepted the challenge with gusto.

The next few days were anxious ones. Chapman deliberately left Dagmar alone in the company of Praetorius, Holst or Von Gröning, and then carefully studied their faces for any 'change of attitude' that might indicate a betrayal. He detected not a flicker of suspicion. Two days after his confession, Dagmar whispered that she had found the information he wanted: the Abwehr headquarters was at 8, Klingenberggate, and the head of station was a naval officer, with four rings on his sleeve. Chapman began to breathe easier. Not only was Dagmar apparently faithful; she might prove a first-class sub-agent, a formidable new branch of Agent Zigzag.

Dagmar seemed to be privy to all sort of interesting information; moreover, she was a vital prop. A man taking a photograph of a military installation would arouse suspicion, but what could be more natural than a young man taking snapshots of his Norwegian girlfriend? Von Gröning threw a party for Chapman's twenty-ninth birthday at his flat: Thomas gave him a radio, Holst an ivory ashtray, and Von Gröning, a Van Gogh print. Dagmar baked a cake, and took lots of photographs of the revellers, as souvenirs. That night, Chapman climbed into the attic of Kapelveien 15, peeled back the metal sheet that protected the wooden girder next to the chimney stack, and hid the film inside: here was a complete photographic record of the Oslo Abwehr team, 'obtained discreetly' by a vague, pretty Norwegian girl no one could ever suspect of spying.

The espionage partnership of Eddie Chapman and Dagmar Lahlum was also an alliance, at one remove, between the British secret services and the Norwegian underground. Dagmar had hinted at her links with the resistance movement, which subsequent events confirmed. One evening they found themselves near the university: a student demonstration was taking place, protesting against the latest attempt to Nazify the education system. Suddenly the police attacked, and began hauling off the student leaders. Dagmar pointed to a young man being led away, and whispered that he was a member of Jossings, an underground resistance group. Brandishing his SS pass, Chapman intervened and 'obtained the immediate release of Dagmar's young friend' but not before a loud 'argument with a German soldier and a German officer in the street'.

On 10 July 1943, as they were walking arm in arm through Oslo, Dagmar told Chapman to wait in the street, and then darted into a tobacconist. She returned a few minutes later, empty handed, looking flushed and excited, and whispered the news: 'The Allies have invaded Sicily.' The news of the invasion had not been broadcast on Norwegian radio, and Dagmar could only have obtained the information through the underground. Under Chapman's questioning, 'she intimated, without revealing the names of any of her contacts, that this information came through the patriotic Norwegian Jossings'.

Not for the last time, Chapman wondered who had caught whose eye at the Ritz bar.

Sabotage Consultant

At the end of summer, 1943, with the first chill settling on the fjords, Chapman was summoned to Von Gröning's flat and presented with a contract for 'new sabotage work' in Britain. Chapman should sign on the dotted line, the German blandly declared, shoving a piece of paper across the desk and unscrewing the lid of his silver fountain pen. The contract was similar to the first, and promised the same financial reward. Chapman read it carefully, and handed it back, politely observing that he 'did not consider the proposition of sufficient importance', and had plenty of money already.

Von Gröning was astonished, and then enraged. A furious row erupted, with the German bitterly pointing out that without his support Chapman would still be rotting in Romainville prison, or dead. Chapman declined to budge, saying the job was too imprecise, that mere sabotage was an unworthy task, and that the money was insufficient. His refusal was partly a ruse to buy time and delay the parting from Dagmar, but also a bid for a more explicit mission that he could take back to his British spymasters. Robertson's instructions had been clear: find out what the Germans desire, and we will know what they lack. Von Gröning's authority had been fatally compromised by his dependence on Chapman, and this was a defining moment in the relationship between patron and protégé. Von Gröning now needed his spy more than Chapman needed his spymaster. The older man raged and spluttered, threatening all manner of punishment, until his face had turned an alarming scarlet and the veins stood out on his neck. Finally, he dismissed Chapman, telling him that his allowance would be cut. Chapman shrugged: if his own income was reduced, then Von Gröning would also find himself out of pocket.

The 'deadlock' persisted for a week. One by one, the other members of the station, Praetorius, Holst, and even the secretaries, approached Chapman and told him of Von Gröning's fury, and the dire consequences of his refusal to sign the contract. Chapman held fast, insisting he was 'after some bigger and better job and would not accept anything so vague'. When Von Gröning cut off his funds altogether, Chapman responded with an angry letter, saying that if he persisted, then he was prepared to go back to Romainville and face his fate.

Von Gröning caved in, as Chapman knew he must. The German flew to Berlin, and returned the following day in 'good spirits'. The Abwehr chiefs had earmarked an important new espionage mission for Chapman, for which 'there would be a large reward'. Chapman would be sent back to Britain to find out why the enemy was winning the war under the sea.

For the first three years of the conflict, Germany's U-boats had ravaged Allied shipping with brutal success. Prowling in 'wolf packs', the submarines struck with terrifying efficiency, as Chapman knew from personal experience, before gliding away unseen and often unscathed. Recently however, the balance of the conflict had altered, and U-boats were being attacked and sunk at an alarming rate. The Germans remained ignorant that the Enigma code had been broken. Rather, Berlin decided that the British must have developed some sophisticated form of submarine-detection system that enabled them to track U-boats from the surface, and then take action, evasive or aggressive. Chapman's mission was to identify this submarine detector, find out how it worked, photograph it, steal it if possible, and then bring it back. For this he would be rewarded with 600,000

Reichsmarks, an additional 200,000 marks converted into the currency of his choice, and his own Abwehr command in occupied Europe.

Here was an almost unbelievable fortune, a prize for a virtually unattainable mission, and a ringing declaration of German faith in Chapman's abilities and loyalty. At first he hesitated, pointing out that he knew nothing of the technicalities involved and would 'need coaching in what he was to look for'. This would all be arranged, said Von Gröning, with the complaisance of a man whose investment might be about to produce a quite astonishing dividend.

To find this fabled weapon, Chapman would be exposed to the deepest secrets of Germany's underwater war. A document arrived from Berlin containing all the information, 'known or surmised', about this supposed submarine detector. A few days later he was escorted by Holst and Von Gröning to the Norwegian port of Trondheim, where three, intensely suspicious officers of the marine Abwehr reluctantly described what little they knew about Britain's submarine-tracking capability. The British, they explained, seemed to be using some sort of parabolic reflector with a 'rebounding ray' to pick up the submarines; the detonators used on British depth-charges also appeared to have an inbuilt device for measuring the distance from the target, and thus exploded with maximum devastation. Quite how the British asdic (later sonar) system worked was a mystery to them: perhaps, they speculated, it used an 'ultra-red ray device', or television, or a technique for detecting and measuring heat from the U-boat exhaust.

Chapman was left with the 'impression that these people knew very little about our U-boat detection devices', and were 'extremely worried' about this secret weapon able to track a submarine, night or day, from a distance of 'up to 200 miles'. One U-boat, they said, had been 'attacked in bad weather in thick fog', something hitherto thought impossible. U-boat casualties were 'extremely high', and mounting. The officers conceded they had no idea where the device came from, but offered 'the address of an engineering depot in Kensington that might be making it'. Throughout the interview, as Chapman took notes, the senior naval intelligence officer 'continually stared at him and remarked that he had seen him somewhere before'.

Back in Oslo, Chapman was summoned to see Kapitan-zur-See Reimar von Bonin, the chief of the Abwehr in occupied Norway. It was the first and only time that they would meet. Over lunch at Von Bonin's grand apartments in Munthesgate, the balding German officer, clad in full naval uniform with four gold bars on his sleeve, explained that the British anti-submarine device was so sensitive it could detect a U-boat lying on the seabed with its engines off, and surmised that the British must be using 'x–ray apparatus of some sort'.

The mission was scheduled for March 1944. As before, Chapman would be parachuted into a remote area of Britain with all the necessary equipment. When he had identified or, better still, obtained the device, he should steal a small fishing boat from the south coast of England, and sail ten miles out to sea, where he would be 'picked up by five seaplanes and escorted to the coast of Europe'. The Abwehr apparently believed that Chapman would be able simply to steal a boat, in the middle of a war, and set sail: this was either a measure of ignorance, or faith in Chapman's criminal talents, or both. He was taken to Bergen, and spent three days being trained by the harbour master in 'the use of a compass on a small fishing cutter'.

The preparations to pitch Chapman into the war at sea were interrupted, however, by a slightly different outbreak of hostilities: another turf war, this time within the German High Command. In December, a senior German air force officer arrived from Berlin declaring that 'Chapman was just the type of man the Luftwaffe was looking for to send on a mission'. The Luftwaffe had its own plans for the celebrated British spy, and its own paranoia. A second, rival mission was now unveiled: just as

Germany's U-boats were suffering from some new detection device, so British night-fighters seemed to be winning the war in the air with secret new technology. British aircraft had been downed containing a hitherto unknown radar system: not enough hardware had survived the crashes to reconstruct the equipment, but there was sufficient to alert the Luftwaffe that it was facing a dangerous new weapon. The technology in question was probably the American-designed radar system the AI 10 (Airborne Interceptor Mark 10), in use by British fighters and bombers, most notably the Mosquito, since late 1943. 'No reward would be too great if he could obtain a photograph or the plans of this device,' Chapman was told.

A few months earlier, Chapman had been the object of profound suspicion. Now, it seemed, with Nazi Germany on the defensive, he was the golden boy of the Abwehr, courted by both navy and air force, 'each wanting their part of the mission to have priority'. Von Gröning intervened in the internal tussle: the naval mission would take precedence (and the navy would pay for the operation); the night-fighter radar would be a subsidiary target.

Chapman found his skills being put to practical use: like some emeritus lecturer in espionage, he gave seminars as a 'kind of honorary consultant in sabotage methods' to a select audience of spooks, using the fictional attack on the De Havilland plant as a text-book case. Before he had been kept away from wireless operations, but now he was asked to teach telegraphy to two young Icelanders, Hjalti Bjornsson and Sigurdur Nordmann Juliusson. Germany believed Iceland might become the launchpad for an Allied invasion of the Continent, and so the Abwehr had begun to forge an Icelandic espionage network. Bjornsson and Juliusson had been recruited in Denmark by one Gubrandur Hlidar, a slightly peculiar Icelandic vet who was 'more interested in practising artificial insemination, in which he was a specialist, than espionage, in which he was not'. Hlidar's recruitment of Bjornsson and Juliusson suggests he should have stuck to his test tubes, for these two were not the stuff of spies: though thoroughly willing, they were also remarkably dense. Several weeks of intensive instruction was needed before they had mastered the most basic wireless techniques.

The last remants of the La Bretonnière gang began to break up. The relationship between Von Gröning and Praetorius, never friendly, was steadily deteriorating, with Praetorius, neurotic and touchy, accusing Von Gröning of plotting to keep him in Oslo to deny him the heroic military future he craved. Finally, after repeated lobbying to higher authorities to deploy him elsewhere, he got his wish. Praetorius was delighted with his new appointment, although his new position is not one normally associated with the fearsome Nazi war machine, let alone the Teutonic heroes of old: Praetorius had long been convinced of the therapeutic physical and cultural effects of English folk dancing. Somehow he had persuaded the German authorities of this, and was duly appointed dance instructor to the Wehrmacht.

When Chapman asked where the young Nazi had gone, Von Gröning said, with a look of disgust, that he was 'touring Germany instructing the German forces in sword-dancing, reels etc, which he had learned when in England'. Von Gröning was amused but amazed: the decision to deploy his deputy on the dance floor was yet further proof that the German High Command was in the hands of fools. A few weeks later, Praetorius sent a photograph of himself giving a dance lesson to the troops (sadly, this has not survived). The man Chapman knew as Thomas had been an irritating and pedantic companion, but a fund of entertaining eccentricities. Chapman felt a flicker of regret as the Nazi-dancer packed his white suit and dancing shoes, and twirled out of his life forever.

Alone in the evenings, Chapman and Von Gröning plotted the future; not the details of espionage but the sort of plans old friends make together to boost morale in bad times. They agreed to set up a club or a bar together in Paris: Chapman would act as

the manager, and Dagmar could be the hostess. Such an establishment, Von Gröning hinted, would make 'useful background
for carrying on his activities' after the war. They both knew it
was make-believe. With Praetorius out of the way, Von Gröning relaxed and became more outspoken. He no longer seemed
obliged to proclaim a jingoism he did not feel, nor to conceal his
feelings about Nazism: 'Hitler is by no means in charge of the
direction of military operations any longer,' he said. 'It is entirely
in the hands of the German general staff, and one no longer reads
"I, Hitler, command . . ." on army orders . . .'. He confided in
Chapman that he had always admired Churchill, and that he
secretly listened to the BBC every night in bed. When it was
reported that a number of British officers had been shot in Stalag
3, he openly 'expressed disgust'. He even 'aired his anti-Hitler
views in public', and told Chapman of his revulsion at the mass-
murder of European Jews. His sister Dorothea, he revealed, had
recently adopted a Jewish girl to save her from the gas chambers.

Von Gröning was an old-fashioned German patriot, committed to winning the war, but equally determined to oppose
the horrors of Nazism. Such views were not uncommon within
the Abwehr. Wilhelm Canaris had made sure to appoint men
who were loyal to him rather than to the Nazi party, and there is
evidence that from an early date he and others within the
Abwehr were actively conspiring against Hitler. Canaris had
employed Jews in the Abwehr, aided others to escape, and is
believed to have provided intelligence to the Allies revealing
German intentions. The intense rivalry between the Abwehr and
the SS had been steadily building, amid accusations that Canaris
was defeatist, if not actively treacherous. The Abwehr chief was
extracted from actual command, and would soon fall foul of
Nazi loyalists in dramatic fashion.

As the day of departure approached, Chapman and Dagmar
also made plans. From the moment he had confessed to her on
the boat, Dagmar 'knew he would one day leave her to return
to England'. They too built fantasies out of the future,

imagining the club they would run in Paris, the children they would have and the places they would go after the war. Dagmar should continue to act as his agent after he had gone, Chapman told her. She should maintain contact with the various members of the Abwehr, and generally 'keep her eyes and ears open for information that might later be of interest'. He would arrange for the British to make contact with her as soon as it was safe, but she should 'trust nobody unless she was approached by somebody who gave, as a password, her full name – Dagmar Mohne Hansen Lahlum'. Since she would be working as a British agent, Chapman grandly announced, Dagmar must be paid.

Just as he had left instructions for MI5 on looking after Freda, Chapman now set about making provision for Dagmar. Through Von Gröning, she should be paid a monthly allowance of 600 Kroner from his account until further notice. She should also be provided with somewhere to live. Von Gröning readily agreed: so long as Dagmar was under German protection, then Chapman's loyalty might be assured. Holst was sent to find suitable accommodation, and Dagmar was duly lodged in a comfortable little flat at 4a Tulensgate. Chapman now had two different women, under the protection of two different secret services, on opposing sides of the war.

On 8 March 1944, eleven months after coming to Norway, Chapman boarded a plane bound for Berlin, the first stop en route to Paris, and England. His parting from Dagmar was agonising. Chapman faced an uncertain future, but he left Dagmar in multiple jeopardy, employed and secretly paid as an unoffical British agent, but ostensibly 'kept' by the German Abwehr. If Chapman's betrayal was discovered then she, too, would fall under German suspicion. If Germany lost the war, her countrymen might seek reprisals against her for 'fraternising'. Dagmar wept, but insisted she was not afraid. If Norwegians mocked her, she would tell them to 'mind their own business'; if the 'Mrs Gossips' back in Eidsvoll wanted to cluck and mutter in their kitchens, then they could. They exchanged promises: she would keep her word, and he would come back for her, one day.

As they sped towards Berlin, Von Gröning and Chapman went over the details of the mission. His code, as before, would be the 'double transposition operation type', based on the code word ANTICHURCHDISESTABLISHMENTARIANISM (Chapman was never one to make life easy for the German receivers). The days and times of transmission would be worked out using a formula based on a fragment of a line from the First World War song *Take Me Back to Dear Old Blighty* – 'Liverpool, Leeds or Birmingham, I don't [care] . . .' All that remained was to establish a control signal, a word or phrase that would indicate he was operating freely. Chapman had already made his choice. Free messages would always contain the word DAGMAR, the equivalent of the FFFFF sign used on his first mission. Von Gröning duly informed Paris and Berlin: 'If the message does not include the word Dagmar, the agent is operating under control.'

Encoded in Chapman's control signal was a warning to his German handlers: if anything should happen to Dagmar, then all bets were off.

Lunch at the Lutétia

Zigzag had vanished, and was presumed dead. There had been a brief surge of hope when the Most Secret Sources reported that the Lisbon Abwehr station had been asked to 'provide a cover address for Fritzchen at Berlin's request'. But the request was never followed up, and there was no further mention of Fritzchen. The radio-listeners and codebreakers of Bletchley continued to scour the airwaves for any trace of the agent. Churchill himself demanded to be informed if and when he resurfaced. But there was nothing: nothing from Chapman himself, no indication from the Most Secret Sources that the German agent 'Fritz' was still operative, and no sightings reported by the network of SOE spies spread throughout occupied France. The Nantes station seemed to have closed down, and Von Gröning's name no longer appeared in Abwehr wireless traffic. Chapman had probably broken under interrogation. Perhaps the failure to blow up the *City of Lancaster* had brought him under suspicion, or perhaps he had been betrayed by a British mole. Men like Masterman and Robertson were not sentimental, yet the thought of what Chapman may have endured before execution gave them pause for thought.

One freezing spring morning on the rocky coast of Iceland, a seal hunter spotted three men 'whose appearance and activities seemed to him suspicious': they did not look like seal hunters, they were not hunting seals, and no other sane person would be trudging through the snowy dawn at ten degrees below zero. The hunter informed the local sheriff, who told the American commander stationed nearby, who sent out an expedition 'into the wastelands' to investigate. They found the three men quickly, which was just as well, for they had almost frozen to death. The leader of the luckless little band was German, and the other two were Icelanders who admitted, after some 'guttural protestations of innocence', that their names were Bjornsson and Juliusson.

The German, Ernst Christoph Fresnius, claimed to be gathering meteorological information for a German shipping institute, but it did not take long to persuade the bovine Bjornsson to confess that they had hidden a radio transmitter and a pedal-operated generator in a nearby cave. All three were shipped to Camp 020 in London, where Stephens swiftly extracted the truth, playing Fresnius off against his 'unsubtle retainers'. It was only a matter of hours before Stephens learned that the trio had been sent to monitor and report on troop movements, confirming that the Germans were 'worried still about the possible use of Iceland as a base for continental invasion'.

So far the case seemed predictable, but when Bjornsson and Juliusson began to describe their training at a spy school in Norway, Stephens suddenly sat up and paid attention. The wireless instructor in Oslo, they said, had been a 'mysterious figure, speaking bad German in a rather loud high-pitched voice, clad in a pepper-and-salt summer suit, displaying two gold teeth and enjoying the amenities of a private yacht'. There was only one person in the world with that combination of dentistry and sartorial taste. Photographs of Chapman were produced, and Bjornsson and Juliusson identified their Oslo radio instructor without hesitation. The Double Cross team was overjoyed. Even dry, hard John Masterman, from his monkish cell at the Reform Club, hailed the return of 'an old friend'. Zigzag had darted back onto MI5's radar. But what – with his sharp new suit and private yacht – was he up to?

Since Chapman's last trip to Berlin, the German capital had been thrashed and crushed by repeated and ferocious aerial bombardment. The city was barely recognisable as he and Von Gröning drove down shattered streets through 'mountains of rubble', rank with the stench of leaking gas, smoke and putrefaction. 'The whole city reeked of fire. It was like the ruins of Pompeii,' Chapman reflected. The faces of the Berliners were gouged with 'resignation and misery'.

Chapman and Von Gröning checked into the Metropol Hotel on Friedrichstrasse, and after a meagre meal of tinned meat, they were driven, past the bombed remnants of the Berlin Bank and the Kaiserhof Hotel, to the Luftwaffe headquarters – a huge concrete monolith of a building on Leipzigerstrasse. On the fifth floor a Luftwaffe captain displayed fragments of electrical instruments retrieved from British aircraft, including a dashboard-mounted screen with which, he explained, the enemy could apparently 'locate our night fighters and bombers with the greatest of ease'. The intelligence officer had only a vague notion of where these machines might be found, suggesting that Chapman might try 'Cossors of Hammersmith', the military manufacturer, or else locate a fighter base in England and obtain the device by theft or bribery.

Again Chapman was struck by the faith in his criminal talents: 'The Germans left it entirely to [my] sagacity to get through, with the aid of former pals.' Moreover, with every official he met, the scope of his mission to England expanded. He was introduced to another officer who explained that the Luftwaffe command believed bombers at certain British airfields were assigned to bomb specific German cities. As a subsidiary mission Chapman, or one of his gang, should spy on the airbases in Cambridgeshire and try to ascertain the bombing schedule. A civilian named Weiss then gave Chapman a four-hour lecture on 'radio-controlled rockets and flying bombs'. This was the first Chapman had heard of these terrifying pilotless bombs intended to blast Britain, finally, into submission. All countries were now racing to deploy these weapons, Weiss explained, in what would be the war's fiery finale. Chapman's task would be to find out if Britain had yet produced flying bombs, and when it intended to use them.

That night, in the hotel on Friedrichstrasse, Chapman and Von Gröning gazed out of the window of the Metropol Hotel, the only building in the neighbourhood still standing, 'an island in a sea of rubble'. From the exhaustion on the faces of Berliners, the appalling wreckage of the city, and the fantastical expectations pinned to Chapman's assignment, both men had reached the same conclusion: Germany was facing defeat and desperately attempting to turn the tide before the imminent continental invasion. Von Gröning now 'made no secret of the fact that he expected Germany to lose the war', and he confided that he had begun 'converting much of his money into articles of value' – assets that could be moved easily in the unpredictable aftermath of defeat – and stashing them in his mansion in Bremen. The flying bombs represented a last reckless gamble, Von Gröning said, but the Nazi propaganda machine was still predicting total victory. 'If their weapons are not successful,' he added soberly, 'the reaction will be enormous.'

Chapman and Von Gröning were ordered to proceed to Paris and await instructions: Chapman was lodged once more at the Grand Hotel, while Von Gröning stayed at the Lutétia, the SS headquarters on the Boulevard Raspail. Agonising suspense followed. The delay, Von Gröning explained with frustration, was 'due to the inability or reluctance of the Luftwaffe to find a plane'. Chapman wandered the streets of Paris, and beheld a city broken in morale and spirit. There was growing French resentment at the Allied bombing raids that killed Germans and ordinary civilians indiscriminately, and little enthusiasm for the expected invasion. In the cafés, people muttered: 'Life under the Germans is preferable to having no homes.'

In mid-April, word came through that Chapman would fly from Brussels. He and Von Gröning scrambled to Belgium by train, only to learn that the flight had been called off 'owing to the danger of interception by night-fighters'. They trailed disconsolately back to Paris. In May there was a fresh flurry, when Chapman was informed he would be dropped near Plymouth during a German bombing sortie, but again he was stood down. The Allied invasion could begin any day, Von Gröning told him, and 'if he landed in England before it started, his first and most important mission would be to discover the date and place [of the attack]'. Although Von Gröning expected Germany to lose the war eventually, he, along with most Germans in occupied France, remained airily confident that Germany's Channel defences could 'repel any attack'.

Adding to the tension, Chapman had been allocated a new 'shadow', in the shape of a young, slightly built man from the Lutétia known as Kraus, or Krausner. Von Gröning warned Chapman that Kraus, a homosexual who frequented the Paris underworld, had a reputation as a spycatcher and had trapped more enemy agents than anyone else in German counterespionage and was 'astute in posing off-hand questions'. Like every other German officer, he had a task for Chapman – the delivery of a camera and money to an agent already established in Britain.

One evening after dinner, Kraus asked nonchalantly if Chapman knew Dennis Wheatley, the British thriller writer. Chapman said he had met him. 'Is he working for British Intelligence?' asked Kraus.

Chapman pretended to be indignant: 'How the hell should I know?' Chapman did not know, as Kraus evidently did, that Wheatley had become a key member of the London Controlling Section, the top-secret nerve centre organising strategic deception under the direction of Lieutenant-Colonel John Bevan.

On Sunday morning in the Place Pigalle, Chapman recognised a fellow former hostage from Romainville, a young

Algerian named Amalou. That evening, in a café in the Latin Quarter called Le Refuge, Amalou explained that he had been released from the prison after Chapman; he didn't know why, nor why he had been arrested in the first place. When Chapman asked for news of Anthony Faramus, Amalou shrugged sadly: Faramus had been taken from the prison a few months after Chapman; no one knew if he was alive or dead.

Faramus was now in Mauthausen concentration camp. At Buchenwald, he had been starved, frozen in his ersatz tunic and wood-soled shoes, beaten, and worked in the slave gangs until he collapsed. 'If and when I come to my end,' he had reflected, 'the remains of my body will be dragged across the muck to the outside and dumped at a spot from which, later on, the crematorium wagon will come to fetch it.' Faramus had calculated that he might have 'approximately six months of natural life left' when, for no reason he could discern, he was loaded on to another train, and transferred to Mauthausen, the vast labour camp in upper Austria.

Here conditions were, if anything, worse than in Buchenwald, for this was truly, in the words of Faramus, 'an extermination camp, a boneyard'. The Mauthausen-Gusen complex of camps was intended to be the most hideous of all: here the 'Enemies of the Reich', the intelligentsia and others could be exterminated by lethal labour. Disease, violence, brutality and the gas chambers killed relentlessly. Over 56,000 people perished at Buchenwald; as many as 300,000 may have died at Mauthausen. Some workers sought death: skeleton-slaves working in the quarries at Mauthausen would wait for their guards to be distracted, find the heaviest boulder they could lift and hurl themselves off the cliff sides. Others, like Tony Faramus, his leg ulcerated and poisoned, his body riddled by disease, waited listlessly for the end. While Chapman wondered what had happened to his friend, Faramus was also racked by wonder: 'All the time, I wondered – why? Why such bestiality? What was the purpose of it all?'

A few days after the meeting with Amalou, Kraus casually remarked to Chapman that he would like to visit Le Refuge in the Latin Quarter. Chapman was stunned. He began 'to think furiously'. Had he been followed to the café? Had he said anything to Amalou that could expose him? Had he put himself, or Faramus, in deeper danger by inquiring after his friend? Was Amalou an informer? Chapman suggested they go to the Lido instead, and an unpleasantly 'knowing' smile darted across the face of Kraus.

Shortly afterwards, a letter from Dagmar arrived saying she was 'having a good time and had met a certain Sturmbann-führer', the agreed code that she was still being paid and was not under suspicion. Chapman noticed that the letter had already been opened.

On 6 June, the Allies invaded northern France in the largest seaborne invasion ever launched. Operation Overlord was supported by Operation Fortitude, the deception carried out by the Double Cross team. For months the double agents of B1A had been feeding disinformation to the Germans indicating that the invasion would be aimed at the Pas-de-Calais region. Allied troops poured into Normandy, wrong-footing the enemy in one of the most successful wartime deceptions ever achieved.

D-Day changed everything, including Chapman's mission. MI5 had come to believe Chapman could achieve 'the un-believable'; in parts of the Abwehr, there seems to have been a growing belief that he could work miracles. In the fervid days following the invasion, the German spy chiefs even discussed infiltrating Fritz into the Normandy beachhead to operate behind the lines, with 'any uniform he liked (that of a padre was suggested), any money he wanted and the assistance of other agents'. Berlin sent instructions that he should find the code used in transmissions between ships 'for the shelling of coastal towns by the navy in support of the land forces'. The plan foundered when it was pointed out that even a spy of Chapman's resource would find it hard to swim out to a ship in the middle of a bloody conflict disguised as a military chaplain, and then steal top-secret codes.

It was agreed that Chapman should instead train a team of fifth columnists to be left behind in Paris if the Germans retreated. He was set to work teaching Morse to two women volunteers who proved entirely unsuited to the task: one, an excitable Italian ballet dancer called Monica, the other a former typist named Gisella. Chapman noted with admiration Monica's 'dimples', but began to suspect that he was now marooned within the frantic German military bureaucracy.

Von Gröning was also depressed. He told Chapman he was convinced he would 'never leave', but had other reasons to worry: the Abwehr was no more. Following yet further evidence linking Abwehr officers to anti-Nazi activities, Hitler had pounced. He had summoned Canaris and accused him of allowing the secret service to 'fall to bits'. Canaris had shot back that this was hardly surprising as Germany was losing the war. Hitler fired Canaris immediately, shifting him to a meaningless position. The Abwehr was abolished, and its operations absorbed into the RSHA – or Reichssicherheitshauptamt 'Reich Security Main Office' – under Himmler's SS. Von Gröning found himself no longer working for the liberal Canaris but under the control of Walter Schellenberg, chief of the SS foreign intelligence service.

In his gloom, Von Gröning even contemplated his own spy mission, declaring he would volunteer to stay behind in the event of a retreat and pose as a French antiques salesman to coordinate the fifth column. Chapman put this plan down to an 'excess of brandy'. Chapman tried to cheer him up, and for his birthday bought him an engraved ivory statuette as a memento of their stay in Paris.

In June Germany produced its long-feared counterpunch, unleashing on London the first of its 'flying bombs' or V-1s (the 'V' standing for Vergeltungswaffe – 'reprisal weapon'). 'Terrible devastation will ensue,' Von Gröning predicted, 'since nothing could survive the explosion within a 4,000 metre radius.' The destruction would be such that if Chapman ever did reach Britain, he might be unable to use his radio since all power plants would be destroyed. On the 13th, the first day of the flying bomb barrage, the German and the Englishman tuned in to the BBC to hear the reports of the damage. Von Gröning's face fell: the bombing was the last item of news, the reference to Hitler's new weapon 'slight', even nonchalant. There had been 'few casualties'. The broadcaster was lying (more than 6,000 British civilians would die from V-1 attacks over the next nine months) but it was a fine piece of propaganda. Von Gröning dismissed it as such, but he admitted that the flying bombs would prove 'a flop' unless their effectiveness could be properly assessed.

Chapman had finally convinced himself that Germany would lose the war without his help when, once again, the spymasters sprang into unexpected action, and a message arrived from the new bosses in Berlin announcing that a plane was now 'at Chapman's disposal'; he would fly from Holland on 27 June. The reason for the sudden activity lay in the flying-bomb campaign. Uncertain of the effects of its mighty barrage due to the fog of British propaganda, Germany needed reliable eyes and ears on the ground: Chapman's new mission was to assess the destruction caused by the V-1s and send back details, along with weather reports and barometric readings. He would act as target spotter and damage assessor, to enable the gunners to aim their flying bombs from launch pads in northern France with greater precision.

In the panelled splendour of the Lutétia Hotel, Von Gröning ran through Chapman's mission. In order of priority, his tasks were: to obtain details of Britain's U-boat tracking apparatus; to locate and steal the device used in night fighter aircraft; to report on the effects of the V-1s, giving precise timings and the resulting damage; to provide weather reports; to locate the various US air bases in Britain; to identify which German cities were being targeted by each air base, and to employ another member of his gang to monitor them and report using a second radio.

The sheer complexity of Chapman's multiple mission reflected a mounting desperation on the part of German intelligence, a realisation that only a truly spectacular breakthrough could affect the momentum of the war. The Germans, unaware that their entire spy network had been turned against them, believed they had several active agents in Britain. Some of these were held in high regard. None had ever been asked to undertake a mission of such difficulty and danger. Fritz had attained near-mythical status, and somewhere in the upper echelons of German High Command it was believed, in a triumph of wishful thinking, that this lone British spy could yet help win the war for Germany.

For this exalted purpose, Chapman was issued with the best espionage kit Germany could provide, including a miniature Wetzlar camera, a Leica camera (to be passed on to the unnamed spy in Britain), a Leitz range-finder and exposure meter, and six rolls of film. No longer was there talk of Chapman unearthing his old radio in Britain: he now had two brand new sets complete with aerials, headphones, five crystals, and a bakelite Morse code key. For self-defence, and possible self-destruction, Chapman was handed a Colt revolver with seven rounds, and an aluminium phial containing a white liquid and several pills, poison with instant effects that 'might come in useful, should anything go wrong'. Finally, Chapman was presented with a bulky canvas bag containing £6,001 in used notes of various denominations (the equivalent of almost £200,000 today), separated into envelopes – the most money Chapman had seen since the smash-and-grab raids of the 1930s. As part of his cover, he carried two fake letters, one addressed to Mr James Hunt of St Luke's Mews, London; the other signed by 'Betty' and filled with 'harmless chatter'.

*   *   *

The Abwehr might have been disbanded, a failed organisation in many ways, but nobody could fault its officers' hospitality and sense of occasion. Von Gröning announced that a farewell luncheon would be held at the Lutétia Hotel for the departing Fritz, spy number V-6523. With every hour the Allies drew closer to Paris, but in Von Gröning's convivial universe, there was always time for a party.

And so, on 25 June 1944, a celebrated German spy and secret British double agent was guest of honour at a lunch party at the SS headquarters in occupied Paris. The guests were Von Gröning, the sinister Kraus, two attractive secretaries from the typing pool, and an intelligence officer from Bremen who was a friend of Von Gröning. In a panelled private dining room, around a table loaded with food and wine, the guests drank to Chapman's health and wished him good luck. Even Chapman found the occasion 'unreal'. Midway through the main course, the telephone rang and he was handed the receiver: it was a senior SS officer, conferring his personal best wishes and sending up 'two bottles of cognac and cigarettes for the party'. Von Gröning rose tipsily to his feet and gave a farewell speech, extolling Chapman's past exploits and predicting that his mission would have 'a profound effect on the war'. Was there, perhaps, just a glimmer of irony in Von Gröning's voice when he raised a glass to Chapman's future 'triumph'? Chapman noticed that Kraus wore his unnerving 'half-smile' throughout.

The bibulous farewell party spilled onto the pavement of the Boulevard Raspail, as Von Gröning, Chapman, and a large leather suitcase containing his equipment were loaded into a waiting car. 'The last glimpse I had of the chiefs of the Lutétia was the group of them standing waving from the front steps as we drove away.'

The Prodigal Crook

As a blustery dawn rose over Cambridgeshire on the morning of 29 June, three weeks after D-Day, a man in civilian clothes could be seen walking, unsteadily, down Six Mile Bottom Road, with a large leather suitcase balanced on his head, swearing to himself. Chapman was in a spectacularly bad mood. In the last twenty-four hours he had been wined and dined, shot at, and hurled out of a plane at nearly 4,000 feet; he had thrown up over his parachute overalls, and banged his head on a hard East Anglian road. And now he had been screamed at by a farmer's wife, who threatened to set the dogs on him.

A few hours earlier, after shaking hands with Von Gröning, Chapman had been strapped into a harness in the back of a German Junkers 88, at Soesterberg airfield, near Utrecht in Holland. The bomber pilot was a fresh-faced lad of about twenty-one. Schlichting, the pilot on his earlier flight, had, it seemed, been shot down in his 'invisible' Focke-Wulf. This was not news to inspire confidence. Shortly before midnight the bomber had climbed into the sky, crossed the North Sea at an altitude of just 50 feet, and then flew parallel to the coast, keeping 'out of the direct light of the rising moon'.

Once over the coast, the Junkers had come under attack from night fighters and anti-aircraft batteries. The engines screamed as the pilot took evasive action, spiralling up to 4,000 feet, and then plunging back down again – Chapman's stomach rolled with every twist. His guts lurched again as flak thudded into the plane's tail.

Over the drop zone, Chapman tumbled out of the hatch into the darkness, and drifted to earth for a dozen or so hideous minutes, buffeted by a strong wind and desperately trying to cling on to a large suitcase filled with radio and photographic equipment. Somewhere over Cambridge, clutching his cumbersome luggage, he had vomited the remains of the banquet from the Lutétia.

Chapman's second landing had been even worse than his first. Swinging wildly in the wind, he had narrowly avoided a hedge, and then landed hard on a country road between Cambridge and Newmarket, knocking himself out. For fifteen minutes he lay stunned, before staggering to his feet. Groggily, he cut loose his pack, wrapped his overalls, gloves, knee pads, belt and entrenching tool into the parachute, and hid the bundle under a hedge. Still dazed, he had knocked at the door of a nearby cottage and explained to the woman who answered it that he had just made a forced landing. The woman took one look at his civilian clothes, screeched in terror, and slammed the door in his face. Chapman had set off as fast as his jellied legs would carry him, fearful of a shotgun blast in the back. This was not the welcome he had been hoping for.

At a smallholding, Chapman steeled himself to try again. This time the reception was more cordial. He telephoned the nearest police station, and got through to the night-duty officer, who began, with plodding precision, to take down 'the details': name, place of birth, date of birth, married or single . . .

'Peeved,' Chapman brusquely instructed the man to contact his chief constable immediately and explain that a British double agent had landed. 'Don't be silly,' said the policeman on the other end. 'Go to bed.'

Enraged, Chapman shouted: 'That's exactly what they told me last time. Ring up your station in Wisbech. They'll remember me.'

Finally, a sleepy Ronnie Reed was roused from his bed by a ringing telephone. 'It's Eddie,'said a familiar, high-pitched voice. 'I'm back, with a new task.'

Two hours later, Chapman found himself back in Camp 020, staring at his own reflection in the glinting monocle of Tin Eye Stephens. Two weeks earlier, the Most Secret Sources had intercepted a message from Paris to Berlin, signed by Von Gröning, asking 'whether operation possible?'. B1A was alerted: if Von Gröning was back in business, then perhaps Zigzag was also about to resurface. An agent in Paris reported seeing a British man in the Lutétia Hotel answering to Chapman's description, 'a wiry type, a pure adventurer'.

And here, to Stephens's delight, was the rogue himself, 'expansive in his conceit', relating an almost impossible tale of survival, and describing the 'splendid time' he had had in occupied Norway. 'The courageous and ruthless Chapman has given satisfaction to his no less ruthless German employers,' wrote Stephens. 'He has survived who knows what tests. He was apparently able to match their best drinkers without giving the show away, and to lead a life as hard as any of them.'

After an hour of conversation, Chapman was 'tired beyond the point of useful investigation', but even a cursory interroga-tion suggested 'he will have a vast amount of intelligence of the highest order to impart'. Chapman was put to bed in a safe house in Hill Street in Mayfair, and fell into an exhausted sleep. Stephens, however, remained awake, writing and pondering. Tin Eye was possibly the least sentimental officer in the entire secret services, and Chapman scored highly in the three cate-gories of human being he most despised, as a spy, a spiv and a 'moral degenerate'. Yet he was impressed, even moved, by this strange young man: 'The outstanding feature of the case is the courage of Chapman. Yet there is something more to the story than that, for Chapman has faced the searching inquiries of the German secret service with infinite resource. He has rendered, and may still render his country great service. For that, in return,

Chapman deserves well of his country, and a pardon for his crimes.' A general instruction was circulated to all MI5 officers connected with the case stating that Zigzag should be 'greeted as a returned friend to whom we owe much and who is no way under suspicion or supervision of any kind'.

The next morning Chapman was driven to the Naval and Military Club, where he was reunited with Tar Robertson and Ronnie Reed over a substantial breakfast. The warmth of their welcome could not have been more heartfelt. Reed was particularly delighted to see his friend 'back safely, and roaring like a lion'. For the second time in two years, Chapman unburdened himself to his British spymasters. But this time his story was not the incoherent torrent of half-remembered facts he had brought from La Bretonnière, but the detailed, precise, minutely memorised dossier of a trained agent. He produced an undeveloped roll of film with photos of senior Abwehr officials, and a scrap of rice paper on which he had noted the codeword used by Oslo for radio traffic – PRESSEMOTTAGELSETRONDHEIMS-VEIEN – and the various crystal frequencies. He described in detail the people he had met, the places he had seen, and the various sensitive military sites he had identified as potential bombing targets. His observations were as meticulous and precise as his earlier reports had been vague and inchoate, offering a complete picture of the German occupying force: the location of the SS, Luftwaffe, and Abwehr headquarters in Oslo, tank depots, the U-Boat signals centre, air supply bases, naval yards, German divisional signs and flak defences. From memory, he sketched a map locating Vidkun Quisling's mansion in Bygdøy and described how he had 'purposely put ashore there whilst yachting to view the house'.

After breakfast, Chapman was given a medical examination by Dr Harold Dearden, the psychiatrist at Camp 020, who pronounced him 'mentally quite fit though physically tired'. At first his listeners were inclined to believe he was stretching the truth, but as the information poured out of Chapman, all scepticism evaporated. 'All the evidence appears to prove his complete innocence affirmatively and conclusively,' wrote Stephens. 'It is inconceivable [that], if he had revealed any part of the truth concerning his adventures in this country on the occasion of his previous visit, the Germans would have allowed him his freedom, still less have rewarded him with the very large sums of money which they paid him and even still less that they would now have sent him over once more.'

There was a simple way to check whether he was telling the whole truth. MI5 knew he had been involved in training Bjornsson and Juliusson, but Chapman himself had no idea that the two hopeless Icelandic spies had been caught. If he volunteered information about the Icelanders without prompting, wrote Stephens, 'it would be a first-rate check on his good faith'. Chapman did precisely that, offering a detailed account of the spies, their appearance and training, that tallied exactly with what his interrogators already knew. 'I think this goes far to indicate that Chapman is playing straight,' wrote Stephens. Chapman was genuine; even the suicide potions he brought were the real thing – pills of potassium cyanide made by Laroche of Paris, and also in liquid form: 'The only safe place for it is down the drain and well washed away,' concluded MI5's scientific department.

Another indication of Chapman's good faith lay in the revelation that the Leica camera and £1,000 from the fund he had brought were intended for another German spy in Britain, 'a man whom they undoubtedly believe to be one of the most valuable agents they have operating in this country'. Chapman's spymasters had taken pains to ensure that he did not discover the name of this other spy. But MI5 knew it: his name was Brutus.

Roman Garby-Czerniawski, alias Armand Walenty, was a Polish fighter pilot who had operated a secret anti-Nazi group in France until he was captured by the Germans in 1941. After eight months in prison, the Germans believed they had turned him, and allowed him to 'escape' in order to forge a Polish fifth column in Britain. Garby-Czerniawski had turned himself in, and was now being operated, very successfully, as Double Agent 'Brutus'.

For some time, Garby-Czerniawski's German handlers had been promising to supply him with more money and better photographic equipment. Shortly before Chapman landed, the Most Secret Sources had picked up an Abwehr message between Paris and Weisbaden saying that Fritz had been given 'money and a Leica' to pass to 'Hubert', the German codename for Brutus. When Chapman announced he was acting as a courier, he was merely confirming what MI5 already knew.

Here was fresh evidence that Chapman was 'safe'. But the supposed handover of the equipment from Zigzag to Brutus could pose a serious headache: it would require stage-managing and correlating not one, but two separate streams of false information, and the two agents would no longer be able to operate independently thereafter. 'Zigzag will be given, and will have to appear to carry out, instructions which would link Zigzag to Brutus. It does not suit us to have these two agents linked, but it is going to be very difficult to avoid.'

The extraordinary breadth of Chapman's mission offered much scope for deceiving the Germans once again, but MI5 was cautious. 'Although no one thinks for a moment that [Chapman] might be double crossing us, if he is to be used for any form of deception, this issue must, of course, be placed beyond all possible doubt.'

There were just two aspects of Chapman's story that troubled the meticulous Stephens: Chapman's loyalty to his German spymaster, Von Gröning, the man he called Dr Graumann, and Chapman's relationship with Dagmar Lahlum.

Chapman friendship with Von Gröning had intensified in the intervening months, and Chapman's loyalty to Britain might be tempered by his affection. 'It must always be borne in mind that he had a very close connection and high regard for Graumann,' wrote Stephens. 'He regards him as being anti-Nazi and liberal in his outlook.' Chapman was quick to defend Graumann, insisting he was 'a very able man, cautious and resourceful, but was handicapped by the poor material in the way of personnel that he had at his disposal'. He also pointed out that his spymaster's sister had adopted a Jewish child, although the more cynical heads in MI5 wondered whether, if true, this was simply 'a form of insurance for the future'.

Stephens had to consider the possibility that Von Gröning and Chapman might be in league together. There was always something unknowable and fickle in Chapman's makeup. The opportunist and the man of principle were one, for as Stephens observed: 'Chapman is a difficult subject and a certain percentage of his loyalties is still for Germany. One cannot escape the thought that, had Germany been winning the war, he could quite easily have stayed abroad. In England, he has no social standing; in Germany, among thugs, he is accepted. It is not easy to judge the workings of Chapman's mind: he is bound to make comparisons between his life of luxury among the Germans, where he is almost a law unto himself, and his treatment here, where he still has the law to fear.' Those doubts were echoed by Len Burt, the head of Special Branch and the senior police officer liaising with MI5 who, on the basis of Chapman's past record, remained 'quite convinced that Zigzag is a man without scruples who will blackmail anyone if he thinks it worth his while and will not stop even at selling out to the opposition if he thinks there is anything to be gained out of it'.

The riddle could not be solved immediately. Chapman must be watched, his relationship with Von Gröning probed: he should be handled with kid gloves. MI5 could not match the munificence of his Nazis handlers, but they could try: 'Although we do not propose to and cannot supply him with champagne for his meals, this is the sort of thing with which we have to compete.'

Of greater concern was Chapman's relationship with Dagmar Lahlum – 'the inevitable girlfriend', as one MI5 officer sighed.

By confiding in this untested woman, Zigzag had, in Stephens's view, 'blundered badly'. She could betray him at any moment with disastrous consequences: if Von Gröning realised he was being double-crossed, any information Chapman sent to Germany would then be interpreted, rightly, as the opposite of the truth. Zigzag would then be providing real, not false, intelligence to the enemy.

Chapman insisted, loudly and repeatedly, that Dagmar was not only loyal to him, but a skilled spy in her own right and vigorously anti-German. He described how he had wooed her, and how he had debated with himself for months before telling her the truth. 'She is not a "fast" girl,' he protested, 'and I am quite satisfied that she was not "planted" by the Germans in the café when I first met her.' If she had betrayed him to the Germans, 'he would have at once observed a change of attitude of the Germans towards him'. If the Germans had suspected Dagmar, or himself, they would not have agreed to provide her with a free apartment and a monthly stipend. Dagmar had his 'complete confidence'. But for Chapman's British handlers, 'the unofficial introduction of this girl into the service of the British government' added an unexpected and unwelcome complication.

Chapman's interrogators noted that he was 'anxious at every opportunity to talk about Dagmar Lahlum'. He returned to the subject again and again, insisting that he had made a promise to 'ensure her financial position', and clear her name after the war: 'One of his objects will be to reinstate her with her compatriots by asserting that she had double-crossed the Germans.' Chapman's passion seemed genuine enough, but then MI5 had not forgotten Freda Stevenson, who was still being supported by the British secret services. 'There was some sort of understanding, of which ZZ has by now doubtless repented, that if he ever came back he would marry Freda,' noted a sceptical interrogator.

As his trump card, Chapman described how Dagmar had

learned of the Sicily landings through the Norwegian underground, and how she was linked to the resistance movement. What better proof could there be of her bona fides? MI5 did not quite see it that way. British intelligence services were in contact with Milorg, the main Norwegian resistance group, but regarded the organisation as inefficient and unwieldy, and prone to leaks. That Dagmar was apparently part of Milorg and may have told them of Chapman's real identity only served to muddy the waters further. Dagmar was working for one secret organisation, in league with another, and being paid by a third: from the British point of view, the lady had too many suitors for comfort: 'Dagmar is in contact with the Norwegian underground movement, at the same time has the confidence of a British Secret Service Agent, and is at present being maintained by the German Secret Service.'

Stephens's faith in Chapman was undimmed, but he urged caution: 'I do not wish to be held wanting in admiration of a brave man [but] I must issue a warning about this strange character. In England, he is wanted for crime. In Germany he is admired and treated royally by the German Secret Service. It is not unnatural, therefore, in the years, that he has come to dislike the English in many respects and to admire the Germans. Indeed, there is more than admiration, there is a genuine affection for his spymaster Graumann. His present ambition is to settle down with Dagmar Lahlum in Paris at the end of the war. Where do the loyalties of Chapman lie? Personally, I think they are in fine balance.'

Chapman's supporters, including Tar Robertson, pointed out that he had thoroughly demonstrated his loyalty already. But set against this was his criminal past, his affection for Von Gröning, and now the problem of yet another romantic entanglement. After long debate, the spymasters agreed. There would be a final installment in 'one of the most fascinating chapters of contra-espionage history in the war'. Chapman would be given one more chance to prove his mettle.

On 30 June, two days after landing, Chapman sent his first radio message to Von Gröning, while Ronnie Reed looked on approvingly: 'HARD LANDING BUT ALL OK. FINDING BETTER PLACE. COMING AGAIN THURSDAY. DAGMAR.'

Doodlebugs

Britain, pummelled and pounded for so long, was braced for Hitler's flying bombs. Nazi propaganda had given early warning of a new weapon that would wreak vengeance for the bombing of the Fatherland and finally crush British resistance. Early in 1944, the Germans began instructing their agents that they should soon evacuate London for their own safety. The first robot bombs, powered by a jet engine, with a crude guidance system, had whined over the city on the night of 13 June. The bombs, each carrying 1,800 lbs of explosive, flew at around 400 mph with a buzzing drone like a venomous insect that would abruptly stop when the fuel ran out, leaving an eerie, empty silence as the bomb plummeted to earth, followed by the explosion.

At first the flying bombs came in ones and twos; then in swarms. On the night of 15 June, 217 missiles hammered into Britain, with forty-five dropping on central London. Unpredictable and hard to shoot down, the V-1s gave a horrible new twist of uncertainty to civilian life. People on the ground would stop to listen anxiously to the engine overhead, waiting for the sudden silence. Typically, the British found a comic nickname to blunt the fear of these atrocious weapons – 'doodlebugs'.

The bombs flew blind, and this was both a strength and a weakness. There was no-one to report where the payload had been dropped, and no way to aim them with confidence. A pattern emerged in London. The German gunners appeared to be targetting the heart of the city, but most of the bombs were dropping two or three miles short of Trafalgar Square. John Masterman made the obvious deduction: 'It was clear that the Germans could only correct their aim and secure results by adjustments based on experiment, and that their data must rest in the main upon reports from this country.' If those reports could be doctored, then the V-1s could be diverted to where they would do less damage.

By the time Chapman arrived in Britain with orders to report on the flying bombs, a rudimentary deception plan was in place. If the double agent's reports exaggerated the number of bombs in the north and west of London, but minimised those in the south and east, the Germans at the launchpads would logically assume that they were over-shooting, and reduce the range. The flying bombs were already falling short, and with a careful stream of false reports they might be lured even further south and east, away from the densely populated areas of central London and even into countryside where they would fall mainly in fields and woods. Clearly there were limits to this form of deception: 'If St Paul's was hit, it was useless and harmful to report that the bomb had descended upon a cinema in Islington,' since the Germans would swiftly discover the truth, and the credibility of the double agent would be compromised. Masterman ruled that the Twenty Committee must 'decide what measure of useful deception was possible without blowing the agents'.

To the hard-headed men of military intelligence, the plan was clear and logical, but persuading the British Cabinet that it should authorise a ruse that would spare some Londoners but might condemn others to death was far harder. The politicians argued, somewhat bizarrely, that public morale would be damaged if the flying bombs were diverted to new, hitherto un-scathed areas of the country since the bomb-scarred residents of central London had 'learned to live' (and die) with the devastation and they were best able to cope with a fresh bombardment.

The ministers baulked at the 'terrible responsibility . . . for directing the attack against any part of London'. Despite their qualms, the deception went ahead.

The barrage intensified. By the end of June some 660 V-1s had landed on London. The Germans seemed to be aiming for the Charing Cross area, but the mean point of impact was calculated to be Dulwich station in south London. Juan Pujol, the celebrated Spanish double agent codenamed 'Garbo' by the British, had volunteered to provide his German spymasters with accurate information about where the bombs were landing: 'I might take on the work of making daily observations . . . and let you have by radio an exact report on objectives hit so that you will be able to correct any possible errors of fire.' Garbo spiced up his reports with characteristic eruptions of Nazi fervour: 'I am certain you will be able to terrify this very pusillanimous people who will never admit that they are beaten.'

The Germans were hungry for more, and the arrival of Zigzag, with specific instructions to monitor bomb damage, was the clearest indication that the Germans were short of accurate intelligence, and thus vulnerable. Chapman also brought evidence of Berlin's faith in a weapon that 'his German masters confidently believe has reduced London and the South coast to a shambles'.

Chapman sent his first report, misrepresenting the location, timing and damage inflicted by the bombs, on 1 July. He continued to transmit disinformation in a steady stream for a month. The data had to be carefully coordinated so the double agents involved – most notably Zigzag and Garbo – 'should report actual incidents in North West London but give as the times of those incidents the actual times of incidents in South East London. If this is done skilfully it is hoped the enemy will identify the bomb which fell in South East London with the incident in North West London and plot it there.' The Germans must be persuaded that they were consistently overshooting. In the words of Dr Reginald Jones, the brilliant physicist assigned to

Air Intelligence: 'We could give correct points of impact for bombs that tended to have a longer range than usual, but couple these with the times of bombs that had actually fallen short.' When the enemy corrected their aim, they would therefore 'reduce the average range'. The resulting disinformation then had to be carefully vetted, before being sent over on Zigzag's wireless. All this took time. 'It is essential,' wrote Chapman's handler, 'that it should not be apparent to recipients that there is always a substantial time lag.' The gamble was huge. If Chapman was rumbled, then instead of taking his reports at face value the Germans would read them for what they were: the obverse of the truth, and instead of shortening their aim they would extend it. Rather than draw the flying bombs away from the target, Zigzag might inadvertently lead them to it.

To bolster Chapman's credibility, photographs were taken of the doodlebug damage at various points around London, so that he could send these on to the Germans via Lisbon. But Air Intelligence vetoed the move: 'I am afraid we cannot approve of their being sent over, since they would be of considerable value to the enemy, and naturally those that would be of no value to the enemy would stand Zigzag himself in very little stead.' Here was the essential dilemma of running a double agent: how to send information that appeared accurate, but could do no harm.

Chapman had been instructed to provide daily weather reports with barometric readings. MI5 asked the Twenty Committee whether he might send these without compromising security? Chapman had been provided with more than enough money to buy a barometer, after all, and therefore had little excuse not to send the readings to his German masters. Reluctantly, the authorities agreed. Chapman could send barometer readings but with 'slight errors introduced'.

Chapman's deception messages have survived only in fragments. MI5 was careful to destroy the traffic, aware of the potential repercussions if the inhabitants of south London realised they were being sacrificed to protect the centre of the city.

German intelligence in Oslo picked up Chapman's coded messages every morning, and Paris in the evening. At first reception was poor and patchy, but it improved after Chapman sent a volley of abuse. 'The outgoing traffic, apart from complaints of poor service, has consisted almost entirely of reports on the times and places of impact of flying bombs,' reported Chapman's case officer. There was no hint in the Most Secret Sources that Chapman's bomb reports were regarded with suspicion. His British handlers were delighted: 'The Zigzag channel was considered indispensable to the bomb damage deception scheme.'

The success of that scheme is still debated. At the very least, the Germans never corrected their range, and the bombs continued to fall short, in the suburbs and countryside, where they killed and destroyed, to be sure, but on a far lesser scale. Chapman has 'held his place in German confidence', wrote John Masterman. Masterman knew what it was like to be bombed. He had lain awake on the floor of the barber's shop at the Reform Club, listening to the doodlebugs overhead, and wondering, in the thudding silence, if the next one would destroy him. 'I was as frightened as the next man of the bombing,' he admitted. But the 'shambles' predicted by German propaganda had not materialised. St Paul's Cathedral, the Reform Club, and Masterman himself all survived the onslaught of the doodlebugs, and owed their survival, in some measure, to a double agent tapping out lies in Morse code on a German wireless.

Masterman was exultant: 'The deception was a very real triumph . . . saving many thousands of lives.'

On 25 July, the bomb deception scheme was suspended. Evening papers had begun to print maps showing where bombs had fallen, potentially threatening the deception. But in any case, radar-controlled anti-aircraft batteries from the US had begun to shoot down V-1s in large numbers, and a month later the threat had effectively been neutralised, though the bombs had killed

6,184 people. Chapman told his German handlers he was going in search of the 'secret equipment for which he was promised high reward'. Chapman's low boredom threshold was well known, as was his venality: the announcement that he was going in search of more lucrative espionage targets appears to have aroused no German suspicion.

Chapman had spent a month in his safe house, dutifully 'tapping out such messages as the Air Ministry want to put over', but he was becoming restive: 'If this state of affairs continues he will go bad on us,' wrote his case officer. 'He will turn his tortuous mind to working out schemes for making more money, which will almost certainly bring him to the notice of the Police. It would be extremely embarrassing for us if he should be arrested while still on our hands.' As ever, Chapman's libido was in constant need of exercise. One evening Reed accompanied him to a notorious pick-up bar in Cork Street and handed him a £20 note: 'Take your pick! But be back in half an hour.'

Chapman still could not walk the city's streets alone in case he was arrested, for Scotland Yard had a long memory. MI5 wondered whether that memory should now be erased. 'I do feel his exploits to date have amply earned him a pardon for the various outstanding crimes he is alleged to have committed,' wrote John Marriott, one of MI5's lawyers and Robertson's deputy. 'I agree,' wrote Tar. Under constitutional law no one may be pardoned for a crime unless already tried and convicted. Instead, police forces around the country with an interest in prosecuting Eddie Chapman were simply informed through Special Branch that the Home Secretary 'desired that no such proceedings should be brought'. This was a pardon in effect, if not in name. 'No action should be taken against him, at least not without prior consultation with us,' MI5 insisted. Chapman, however, was not informed that his slate had been wiped clean: the threat of prosecution remained a useful leash.

The spy chiefs now debated how best to employ Zigzag. Chapman himself volunteered to return to France, saying he could help 'comb out any German underground movement which may have been left behind'. That idea was vetoed: Chapman was too valuable as a double agent in Britain, feeding lies to the enemy. 'Any question of Zigzag's return to the Germans at this stage of the war is out of the question,' his handlers decided. Ronnie Reed took him to lunch at the RAC Club, and marvelled at his guiltless internal contradictions. In one breath Chapman would be describing his love for Dagmar, but in the next proclaiming he was 'anxious to write to Freda to tell her he was back in London'. Reed agreed to pass on the message, but advised Chapman to tell her he was 'very busy and would communicate with her in a few days time'. More worryingly, Chapman was talking about writing up his adventures as an 'autobiography', an idea that MI5 quashed immediately, pointing out that it would be 'impossible for him to disclose during the war, and in all probability for a long time thereafter, anything about his work for the Germans or for ourselves'. Chapman grumpily replied that he still wanted to write up an account 'while it was still fresh'. He promised to confine his reminiscences to 'his old criminal activities'. MI5 was not convinced.

Chapman had brought ample evidence of German anxieties over the vulnerability of its U-boat fleet. Tar concluded that the best way to 'stimulate Zigzag's interest', and baffle the enemy, would be to exploit those fears by sending over 'deceptive material about anti-submarine devices'. A new plan was formed: Chapman would dispatch a message to his handlers saying he had located the factory in the north of England where a new submarine detection device was being manufactured, but had been unable to obtain the device itself because the factory was 'in continual active operation'. He would then claim that he had managed to 'steal a document and photographs from an office in the building': the document could be transcribed and sent over by wireless, and the photographs sent via Lisbon. Both, needless to say, would be fake.

Through the Most Secret Sources and traditional espionage, the British knew that the German Navy was alarmed by the rising U-boat toll, and that they feared some new weapon must be in use. In fact, the Germans were wrong. As Ewen Montagu of Naval Intelligence observed, 'the increasing number of U-boat kills was due to other devices, most notably the Mark XXIV mine, and by intercepting and decoding U-boat signals using Ultra'. The single most important British weapon in the underwater war was the ability to pick up and read the U-boat radio traffic. However, if the Germans believed there was some other new and powerful underwater weapon in use, that fear should be encouraged, and expanded. As always when practising to deceive, MI5 stuck as close to the truth as possible while planting a deception.

British destroyers, frigates and corvettes had recently been fitted with a device called a 'hedgehog', a mortar bomb that exploded on contact with a submarine. The Most Secret Sources revealed that German intelligence had found out about the hedgehog through 'careless talk by merchant seamen'. Since they knew something about the weapons already, a great deal of misinformation could be loaded onto a little information: 'While we should not disclose details of their design and construction, we should notionally increase their range and explosive effect and, more important, try to convince [the Germans] that they were fitted with proximity fuses which would go off on a near miss without actual impact.' This 'proximity fuse' would supposedly trigger other depth charges once it had located the submarine. There was, of course, no such thing, but by making the humble hedgehog appear to be a beast of terrifying ferocity, Naval Intelligence hoped to further erode German morale, and make the U-boat fleet more wary of attacking convoys. Most importantly, if U-boat commanders feared that the Royal Navy had a rocket-propelled device that could hunt them at the bottom of the ocean, then they would be less likely to dive deep: nearer the surface, they were easier to kill.

Chapman duly sent out a message saying that he had heard about this 'proximity fuse', smaller than a normal depth charge and developed by Cossor's to attack deeply submerged U-boats. The response was encouraging: 'After passing the information on to the German navy, the Abwehr [*sic*] came back to Zigzag with much praise and an insistent demand that he should get more details.' Chapman reported (incorrectly) that 'all secret manufacture by Cossor's is now done in St Helens', and announced that he was heading north to try to gather more information. The stage was set for Operation Squid.

While the Admiralty worked out the details, Chapman was encouraged to enjoy himself. Agent Zigzag was still 'worth keeping sweet', yet a distinct sourness had begun to creep into the relationship between Chapman and the British secret services, for reasons that had little to do with the war and everything to do with personality – the warp and weft of espionage.

Ronnie Reed's role in the Zigzag case came to a sudden end when he was posted to the American forces as intelligence liaison officer in France. Reed's reputation (and, for that matter, his moustache) had grown over the previous two years, and he had eagerly embraced the 'wonderful experience' of seeing France for the first time. For Chapman, however, Reed's departure was a heavy blow. The two men had grown deeply fond of one another, sharing so many anxious moments hunched over the wireless. On the day of Reed's departure, Chapman presented his departing case officer with a small parcel, wrapped in tissue paper: inside, still in its leather case, was Chapman's Iron Cross. It was a typically spontaneous gesture of admiration and friendship. Reed was profoundly touched.

To replace Reed as the Zigzag case officer, in a rare but calamitous misjudgement, Tar Robertson appointed a man who could not have been more different, or less to Chapman's taste.

Major Michael Ryde was a crisp, by-the-book professional, with an overdeveloped sense of moral rectitude, an underdeveloped sense of humour, and a drink problem. The son and grandson of chartered surveyors, Ryde had married the only daughter of Sir Joseph Ball, a notorious political fixer and the head of MI5's investigative branch. Ball had steered his son-in-law into the security services just before the outbreak of war, and for three years Ryde had performed an exceptionally boring desk job as regional security liaison officer in Reading. Newly promoted to B1A, he was clever, fastidious and moralising; Ryde could be charming when sober, but was invariably unpleasant when drunk. He and Chapman loathed one another on sight. In the tangle of Chapman's loyalties, there was now an ironic symmetry. His closest friend, a German spymaster, must be betrayed out of a duty to his country; but the man who should have been his ally in that enterprise, would soon become his sworn enemy.

Ryde regarded his vulgar new ward as an encumbrance and an embarrassment, and within hours of taking on the case he had made it his personal goal to expel Chapman from the British secret services at the first opportunity.

Michael Ryde.

Going to the Dogs

As the war staggered towards its finale, the British secret services looked to the future and began to see their spy networks in a new light. Wartime espionage was a dirty business, and Chapman was by no means the only person of dubious character to find a home in MI5. But with victory in prospect, an element in the intelligence hierarchy now wondered whether there ever could – or rather should – be a place in it for a scoundrel like Eddie Chapman.

Chapman's new case officer, Major Ryde, was now his constant companion. It was torture for both, for few partnerships were more ill-matched than the roistering crook and his patrician shadow. Chapman insisted on going out on the town at every opportunity and MI5's expense. The £80 spending money and fifty clothing coupons he had been given on arrival evaporated in a few days. Chapman demanded more, pointing out that he had brought £6,001 in his suitcase when he parachuted into Britain the month before. Ryde tartly informed him that the £10 notes were out of date and unusable. Chapman was 'disagreeably surprised' but quite unabashed, and demanded that he should be allowed to keep the rest of the cash he had brought. MI5 watched the money pour into the hands of various Soho casino owners, and barmen 'with some apprehension'.

Ryde trailed after him resentfully. 'I have spent a good deal of time with Zigzag at the cost of a certain amount of boredom and a certain amount of money expended on entertaining him,' he complained. Ryde had nothing against strong drink; indeed, quite the reverse. He just did not want to drink in the company of men like Eddie Chapman.

Early in August, Ryde called a meeting with Tar Robertson to discuss the Zigzag case and, if possible, to end it. Ryde reported that Chapman seemed 'most discontented at the moment'; he was expensive, moody and entirely disreputable. 'He has been keeping the bad company of some professional pugilist with whom he has been hitting the high spots' and was 'always in the company of beautiful women' – a fact that seems to have vexed Ryde in a way that suggests envy more than disapproval. The case officer wrote a report, ending with the conclusion: 'The Zigzag case must be closed down at the earliest possible moment.' Ryde was immediately slapped into line by his superiors. John Masterman insisted that the word 'earliest' be replaced by 'latest', and Tar agreed: the case should be closed only when it was 'convenient' to do so. Stung, Ryde backed off: but he was now gunning for Chapman, and collecting all the ammunition he could.

Robertson took Chapman to lunch at his club, and found him in a state of seething resentment towards Ryde, complaining bitterly about 'the way his case was being run'. When asked about his future plans. Chapman 'did not seem to have any very clear ideas on the subject', Tar reported, though he spoke vaguely of setting up a club, or running a pub, or working for MI5 after the war. 'He is quite clearly restless and is likely to be so, as long as he is asked to perform the rather humdrum business of tapping a key at our instructions.'

Relations between Chapman and Ryde might be reaching crisis point, but in other respects the Zigzag case was ticking along most satisfactorily. The Germans seemed as devoutly trusting as ever. Early in August, Von Gröning had sent a message asking Chapman to suggest a method for delivering the camera and money to his fellow spy, and instructing him to find 'a suitable person' who could monitor bomber formations at airfields in East Anglia. The Air Ministry had vetoed any deception in this latter area, so Chapman stalled, saying he was still searching for a recruit since 'the friends he hoped to employ for this purpose are in prison or otherwise not available'.

Operation Squid, the plan to convince the Germans that Britain had some new and devastating weapon able to detect and destroy U-boats, moved into its next phase. The deception would take two forms. The first was a 'stolen' photograph purporting to show an underwater anti-submarine 'proximity fuse' which did not, of course, exist. This would have to be smuggled to the Germans via Lisbon. A real hedgehog depth charge was photographed alongside a ruler a foot and a half in length, which had been adapted to appear as if it was only six inches long, thus making the weapon appear one-third of its actual size. Chapman would tell the Germans he had bribed a merchant seaman bound for Lisbon to act as a 'mule', by hiding the photo 'in a French letter in a tin of Epsom Salts', and that he would convince the sailor he was smuggling drugs. In reality MI6 in Lisbon simply acted as 'postman', and arranged for the fake photograph in its tin to be delivered to the Germans by one of their agents disguised as a seaman. The German reaction was precisely as hoped: 'After they had received the photo the Abwehr were avid for full details of the fuse,' wrote Ewen Montagu.

Zigzag duly obliged. With the help of Professor Geoffrey J. Gollin, the brilliant scientific adviser to the Naval Intelligence Division, Montagu drew up a bogus letter from Professor A.B. Wood, an expert in underwater acoustics at the Admiralty Research Laboratory at Teddington, to a scientist at Cossor's munitions factory named Fleming. In it he extolled the virtues of a new, top-secret anti-submarine device. Chapman told his German handlers he had found the letter in the Manchester offices of Cossor's, and had copied it. He now sent the fake letter by radio, verbatim:

Dear Fleming,

I feel sure that you will be as pleased as I was to hear the results of the latest squid trials.

A standard deviation of plus or minus 15 feet is a wonderful improvement on the old method of depth-finding and my only regret is that our present target is incapable of greater speeds. Doubtless 13 knots is as much as the enemy is likely to reach in this war but we must always keep a 'jump' ahead, preferably two jumps!

I thought you might like the enclosed photos of the standard remote setting depth charge fuse for coupling direct to the squid Mk J indicator controller (as suggested by the late Captain Walker).

I hope to visit Manchester again soon and am looking forward to having another of our discussions which have proved so fruitful during the last three years.

Yours sincerely,

A.B. Wood

Professor

There was no Captain Walker, no 'Mk J indicator controller' and certainly no depth charge capable of detecting a submarine at a distance of 15 feet and then pursuing it at a speed of 13 knots. There was, however, a Fleming, Ian Fleming – the future creator of James Bond – who was then working in Naval Intelligence. Fleming may have been party to this subterfuge, designed to breed maximum anxiety among German U-boat commanders and keep them as close as possible to the surface. Ewen Montagu proclaimed the operation a triumph. 'We never found out what the assessment of this information by the German navy was, but the actions of the Abwehr made it seem that they must have been very favourable.'

Despite the success of Operation Squid, Ryde did his best to undermine the achievement. 'I do not myself believe there is any substantial chance of these photographs reaching Berlin,' he wrote. 'Unless the Admiralty press us to carry on the case, I am convinced that we ought to close it down and part company with Zigzag as soon as possible, giving him such financial bonus, if any, as he is thought to deserve . . .' Ryde seemed more determined than ever to expel Chapman, and the preparations for handing over the camera to Brutus offered an opportunity. It was decided that Zigzag would arrange to leave the money and camera in a marked package at a railway-station cloakroom, but while the handover was being organised, the Germans sent a radio message hinting at doubts over Chapman's loyalty. Brutus's German handler wrote that he did not wish his agent to make direct contact with Fritz, since the latter was, in his opinion, 'not quite reliable'. This may have reflected no more than internal rivalry, one spymaster questioning the dependability of another's agent, but it was enough for Ryde to declare that the Germans were 'dubious about Zigzag's integrity'.

German suspicions, Ryde wrote, may have been further stoked by widely reported statements made in Parliament about the V-1s by Duncan Sandys, the minister who chaired the War Cabinet committee on flying bombs. Sandys had let slip certain crucial details about bomb-damaged parts of London. 'The messages sent by Zigzag, if compared in detail with the recent speech made by Duncan Sandys in the House, show very serious discrepancies, and there is a possibility that the case will be blown on these grounds.' Then there was the question of Dagmar. 'Zigzag is liable to be compromised through the girlfriend he left behind in Oslo,' wrote Ryde, slowly but implacably chipping away at his own agent's credibility. When it was mooted that Chapman might continue to work for MI5 after the war, Ryde was scornful: 'It is unlikely that his private life will be such that he will remain suitable for employment.' He also pointed out that Chapman's value was dependent on his relationship with Von Gröning and that this link would become worthless with the end of the war.

Chapman, unaware of Ryde's machinations, had discovered a new and lucrative pastime. Through some of his old criminal contacts, he learned that dog races in south London were being 'fixed'. With the connivance of the owners, certain dogs were being fed meatballs laced with Luminal, an anti-epileptic drug. A mild hypnotic, the Luminal had no visible effect until the animal, usually the favourite, had run some distance, when it would slow down. For a consideration, Chapman arranged to receive a tip-off when a dog had been knobbled; he then bet heavily on the second favourite and usually collected a tidy profit, which he would split with his criminal informant.

One evening in August 1944, Chapman turned up at his safe house several hours late for an appointment to transmit to Germany, and explained casually that he had been at the dog track. 'Zigzag himself is going to the dogs,' his case officer puffed, gleeful to have been provided with such a convenient double entendre. Chapman, Ryde reported, was 'making quite large sums of money by backing the winners of races which have already been fixed'. When confronted, Chapman angrily insisted that he was merely profiting through information gathered from his contacts, a technique not so very far removed from espionage. Ryde, of course, did not see it that way. 'To take advantage of other people's dirty work to fleece the bookmakers cannot be regarded as a desirable occupation,' he sniffed.

Reluctantly, and under intense pressure, Masterman and Robertson accepted that Chapman might soon have 'served his purpose'. Yet they baulked at cutting him adrift. Tar insisted that Chapman had 'done an extremely good and brave job', and if the case was shut down then he should be properly looked after 'by giving him a fairly substantial sum of money'. With the avuncular concern he had always shown, Robertson wondered whether Chapman might be coaxed towards the straight and narrow by means of a legitimate job. Chapman was duly told that 'if he could put up some firm business proposition it might not be impossible for us to help him with the capital'. He had seemed enthusiastic, and talked of running a club in the West End or a hotel in Southend (The Ship Hope Hotel was for sale, he said), in order to be near Freda and Diane. Ryde declared that it would be a 'waste of money' for someone with such a long criminal record to open licensed premises, since the police would simply 'close them down as soon as they find out that he is in fact behind the business'. The only way to set up Chapman as an hotelier would be to alert the local chief constable, and explain the situation: 'If the latter, notwithstanding Zigzag's past record, appears willing to give his venture a fair chance so long as the hotel was properly conducted, then it might be worthwhile for Zigzag to go on with it.' Ryde doubted that any chief constable would agree to this proposition, or that Chapman would keep his nose clean: 'It is obvious that we cannot assist him financially if his idea of business is to work the dogs.'

Just as Ryde had predicted, Chapman was drifting back to his old haunts – the Shim-Sham club and the Nite Lite – and his old ways. The pull of the criminal brotherhood was growing stronger, yet his years as a secret agent had changed him: his primary allegiance was still to Britain, and the other secret fraternity of which he was now a part. When Ryde hinted that Chapman's days as an agent might be numbered, he had responded crossly, declaring that 'if we no longer require his services' he would 'get in touch with the Americans'.

Safe from prosecution thanks to the Home Secretary's un-official 'pardon', Chapman was allowed to move around London more freely, though Ryde followed at a distance, tutting, watching and gathering evidence. The spy manager was now actively spying on his spy: 'I have seen Zigzag walk up to a Norwegian and address him in Norwegian, I have seen him in the company of highly undesirable characters, speaking to a German Jewess in German, a Frenchman in French. I have heard him discussing with a man with a known criminal record conditions in Paris in such a way that it must have been apparent that he has been there within the last few months.' Chapman, Ryde reported to his superiors, was keen to write a memoir of his exploits: how soon before his natural swagger got the better of him, and he bragged to his nasty friends, he speculated? 'I am able to curb these indiscretions when I happen to be present,' he wrote, 'but there is no knowing what form these conversations take when I am not there.'

Ryde was overruled again. Whatever his personal behaviour, Chapman was still a trusted asset: 'The war may end at any moment and all contact with the Germans be lost and his case may die a natural death.' If this happened, Chapman should be let go with tact and generosity, and told that 'the necessity of closing the case was no reflection on him, but forced upon us by the war situation'.

Ryde grumbled and plotted: 'It is becoming increasingly clear to me that there are a number of serious security dangers which, in the case of a character like Zigzag, it is impossible to avoid.' Zigzag was proving harder to kill off than Ryde anticipated: every time he believed he had Chapman on the ropes, the man would bounce back with another demonstration of his worth. Von Gröning continued to send messages of support, demanding ever more intelligence: 'Try to get latest editions of monthly anti-submarine report issued by anti-submarine warfare division of Admiralty . . . Very important.' Von Gröning repeatedly congratulated Fritz on his performance: 'General report [is of] great interest.'

On 8 September, Germany launched its first V-2 attacks against Paris and London. The V-2 was a quite different creature from its predecessor: an early ballistic missile driven by liquid oxygen and alcohol, the rocket bomb had a range of 200 miles, flew at ten times the speed of the V-1 and carried a nose cone with a ton of high explosive. Chapman had learned of these weapons back in France, and warned British intelligence of a 'radio controlled rocket which will be bigger, very costly in fuel and not at all economical in construction'. Von Gröning instructed Chapman to act, once again, as a target locator for the new bombs: 'Continue giving data about place and time of explosions. Are they more frequent now?' The V-2 attacks were often devastating – 160 people were killed in a single explosion when a bomb fell on a Woolworth's department store in south London – but Chapman sent a reply down-playing the effects: 'Heard many rumours of explosions of gas works and mains but no information of the cause. Making inquiries.'

During his visit to the Luftwaffe headquarters in Berlin, Chapman had been shown fragments of British night-fighter radar equipment, and noticed that the pieces had serial numbers. He now asked Von Gröning to transmit a complete list of those serial numbers, notionally so that he could steal the correct device, but in fact to give the Air Ministry a clear idea of exactly what the Germans had salvaged. It was also decided that a display of petulance would keep Von Gröning keen. Chapman sent an angry message, complaining that he was not receiving sufficient backup and urgently needed more money. He also asked, pointedly, whether the German secret service intended to support him when the war was over.

Chapman could not have known it, but during his absence Hitler had destroyed the remains of the Abwehr. On 20 July, Claus von Stauffenberg, a German officer, tried and failed to assassinate Hitler by planting a bomb in an attaché case in the conference room at Hitler's 'Wolf's Lair' – his command post for the Eastern Front in Rastenburg, Prussia. The device exploded against the heavy leg of an oak table which probably shielded the Führer from the full force of the blast. Chapman would not have made such an elementary mistake. Five thousand members of the German military were arrested in the aftermath of the failed 20 July plot, including Canaris and his deputy, Hans Oster. They were tried, convicted of treason, and then hanged. Von Gröning does not appear to have been implicated in the plot, but as an Abwehr officer of the old school with anti-Nazi views, he was undoubtedly under suspicion.

Von Gröning's response to Chapman's complaint arrived after a gap of several days. It was an odd, and oddly moving message, the statement of a proud man whose world was falling apart:

WAR SITUATION NEED NOT AND WILL NOT
AFFECT YOUR RETURN YOU MUST MAKE
SUGGESTIONS IN GOOD TIME AND YOU WILL
HAVE EVERY SUPPORT WHATEVER HAPPENS.
WAS HOME, MY HOUSE DESTROYED BY BOMBS,
OTHERWISE   WOULD   HAVE   ANSWERED
SOONER. GRAUMANN.

The Von Gröning family home in Bremen, that great five-storey symbol of aristocratic eminence, had been flattened by Allied bombers. The house had been empty: the cook, chauffeur, valet, gardener, maids and other servants had been laid off long before. The gilded carriage had been stolen, the family cars commandeered. Von Gröning's pictures, antiques, china, silver, and other valuable *objets d'art* – the remains of his great inheritance – had been stored in the attic. All had been destroyed. The only item of value recovered from the rubble was a singed silver plate engraved with the names of his fallen comrades in the White Dragoons.

Case Dismissed

Chapman imagined his old friend, sitting in the bombed-out wreckage of a privileged life, drinking himself into amnesia. He was touched by Von Gröning's plight: 'SORRY YOUR BAD NEWS DON'T DRINK TOO MUCH. AM GOING TO MANCHESTER TO DO JOB. WHAT ABOUT PICKUP OFF NE COAST? CAN YOU LEAVE ME COVER AD-DRESS IN FRANCE ALSO RADIO POSSIBILITY FOR JIMMY OR MYSELF TO GO THERE. NEED FRENCH MONEY ALSO. DAGMAR.'

Von Gröning's message had hinted at a plan to continue espionage operations with Chapman, 'whatever happens'. The Allies were acutely conscious of the danger of Nazi resistance groups emerging in Germany to fight on after the war was over. Indeed, at Himmler's instigation diehard SS fanatics were already forming a partisan group, the so-called 'Werewolf' organisation, to continue a guerrilla campaign in Germany in the event of an occupation. Ryde grudgingly conceded that the message put the Zigzag case in a different light: it showed that the German spymaster 'has a post-war plan in mind and there is now a real purpose in keeping the case running' in order to find out 'whether Graumann intends to continue to work after the complete and final German collapse'. If Chapman could 'get the Germans to lay on an expedition to meet him somewhere in the North Sea,' Ryde reported, then an ambush might be staged.

As promised, the next day, Von Gröning sent over a complete list of all the serial numbers obtained from the equipment in downed British aircraft, 'a collection of words, figures, stops and dashes', that added up to another intelligence bonanza. The Air Ministry set about identifying the various bits of machinery. Montagu of Naval Intelligence was overjoyed: 'The Germans have told the Agent highly secret information about the state of their knowledge . . . there are also points in it of which we did not, in fact, know that the Germans were aware, even from our knowledge gained from Most Secret Sources.' A proposal to launch yet another deception plan based on the night-fighter intelligence was ruled out, however, on the grounds that 'German knowledge is too near the knuckle for us to try to tamper with it at this stage'.

Ryde fumed. Chapman had escaped again, and to make matters worse, Robertson had instructed him to discuss compensation with this unpleasant young man and decide whether 'we should out of our own funds supplement what ZZ has received from the Germans'. The money was disappearing fast. 'I still maintain that we are bound to give Zigzag a square deal,' wrote Tar, 'as he has done a very considerable service for this country.' The sum of £5,000 was suggested, as a 'settlement of our indebtedness to him [and] to impress upon Zigzag that we value the work which he has done for us at least as high as the Germans value that which he has done for them'.

One evening, in strained conversation with Ryde, Chapman remarked that he expected to be 'dealt with fairly' by the secret services.

'Could you give me some idea of what you have in mind?' Ryde asked, through gritted teeth.

'Well, the Germans gave me £6,000 when I came back here,' Chapman replied.

Ryde responded that 'of the £6,000 he had brought with him, £1,000 was for someone else and that being the case he had £5,000 from the Germans.'

Ryde could hardly believe that he was having to haggle with such an individual. He pointed out that Chapman had also kept the money from his first mission, and should be grateful. 'This argument did not seem to impress Zigzag,' who tersely pointed out that the entire case had so far 'only cost the British government about £200.'

'I think that is a matter about which you should feel gratified,' said Ryde, with all the considerable pomposity at his disposal. But Chapman was 'not at all impressed'. The discussion ended in deadlock, acrimony, and even deeper mutual antipathy.

The Germans, it seemed, were in a much more generous mood. Chapman had sent a message demanding 'at least £6,000 to be delivered to him by parachute'. In reply, the Germans had said that they would rather send the money through Lisbon, perhaps via the 'reliable sailor' who had delivered the photographs. But if that proved impossible, then they pledged to drop the money by air. 'Such promises are generally empty,' insisted Ryde, at the same time scenting another opportunity to put an end to his agent.

The Abwehr had often made a practice, in the past, of providing agents with forged British currency. This was an economy measure, but a foolish one, since several Nazi spies were uncovered trying to spend the fake cash. 'I think it would be important in closing the Zigzag case to destroy his faith in the Germans,' wrote Ryde. 'Zigzag's only interest in the case is the money he can make out of it, and if we were able to get the money and then prove to him that it was forged, we shall have gone a long way towards shattering the very high esteem which he undoubtedly has for Graumann and others . . . If the money is in fact counterfeit, Zigzag will probably send an unprintable message, closing the case himself.'

In the meantime Chapman sent a message to Von Gröning saying he was heading to the Liverpool docks to try to find a courier to bring the money back.

Ryde wanted to sack Chapman without a penny. He wanted

to see him off the premises in such a way that he could never come back, never demand anything else of the intelligence services, and never work as a spy again. For this he needed to demolish his credibility. Just one serious blunder would bring Chapman down. In the end, Ryde discovered two, furnished by Chapman's closest allies: Von Gröning, the newly homeless aristocrat, and Jimmy Hunt, a newly released convict.

Ryde was intrigued by the close relationship between Chapman and Von Gröning: 'Zigzag has always spoken of Graumann in the highest terms and has expressed something akin to affection for "the old man".' But there was something more to the mutual admiration in this case, something about Von Gröning he felt that Chapman was holding back. Ryde was a prig and a snob, but he was also a talented spy, with the intuitive ability to spot a lie.

One morning in the safe house, after Chapman had transmitted his morning message to Germany, Ryde deftly steered the conversation towards 'Dr Graumann', and wondered 'whether the Germans have any suspicion that he was being worked under control'. Before Chapman could answer, Ryde continued, as if thinking aloud: 'If Graumann did suspect this, it is unlikely that he would reveal his suspicions as it is in his own personal interests to keep the case going as long as possible.' Chapman agreed, 'without a moment's hesitation'.

'Graumann is my best security,' he added.

'What do you mean?' asked Ryde.

'He has made a great deal of money out of the case. For example when I ask for £6,000, Graumann probably draws £12,000 and pockets the change.'

Slowly it dawned on Ryde that Chapman was putting out enough rope to hang himself. If Chapman and Von Gröning were in league embezzling money from their German masters, then it was also probable that Chapman had confided that he was working for the British. If so, then Von Gröning, for reasons of greed and ambition, was betraying his own country with an agent he knew to be false. This evidence of financial collusion, wrote Ryde, 'increases my suspicion that he has at least told Graumann, his German spymaster, of his connection with us in this country'.

Seeing Ryde's expression, Chapman changed the subject. 'My impression was that Zigzag knew perfectly well what was in my mind but was not going to admit it, and my earlier suspicions were strengthened.'

Ryde conceded that the possible risks from a joint conspiracy involving Zigzag and his German boss might be limited, since Von Gröning's self-interest would probably ensure that he kept Chapman's secret. 'If it is true that Graumann is aware of Zigzag's position in this country it is very unlikely that anyone other than Graumann knows and there is probably little danger to us at present.' But more important to Ryde's campaign, if Chapman had revealed himself to his German spymaster but had kept the fact from the British, this was a major security breach, proof that he had lied. Ryde was elated: 'It may show that Zigzag has withheld from us this very important piece of information and it is against our principles to run a case with anyone who is found not to be absolutely open with us.'

If Chapman had told Von Gröning he was working for British intelligence, then who else had he let in on the secret? The question was soon answered.

Ryde was still debating how best to deploy this new evidence of Chapman's unreliability, when Jimmy Hunt accidentally administered the *coup de grâce*. One late October evening Ryde's deputy, an MI5 officer called Reisen, paid an unannounced visit to Chapman's flat, and found a debauched scene. Chapman was throwing a party. Characters from his seedy past and increasingly dubious present were ranged around the sitting room in various states of inebriation, including the boxer George Walker, a jobbing journalist named Frank Owens, and sundry other denizens of the Soho underworld. As Reisen entered the room, a large individual with the pallor of long-term imprisonment rose unsteadily to his feet. Here was Jimmy Hunt, the safe-cracker who had played such a crucial role in Chapman's early criminal life and then, as a figment of MI5's imagination, in his second career as a spy.

'I suppose you have come to take Eddie away on a job,' Hunt grinned knowingly. Reisen made a non-committal reply, determined not to betray his astonishment 'in the presence of so many others'. The implication of Hunt's remark was clear, and Reisen was 'quite certain that Hunt knew the nature of the job to which he referred'. Chapman had not merely spilled the beans: he had spilled them to a newly liberated, extremely drunk convict, and in so doing he had served up his own head, on a plate.

Ryde, delighted and vindictive, marshalled his evidence and moved in for the kill, as remorseless as if he had been terminating an enemy spy. Chapman had faced so many inquisitors in the past: Tin Eye Stevens, Praetorius, Von Gröning, Dernbach and a beautiful woman in a designer coat in Romainville jail; he had survived interrogations by the Gestapo, the Abwehr, and MI5; an *agent provocateur* in an Oslo bar, an inquisitive SS spy-catcher in Paris, and any number of agents posing as spies had all tried to trip him up. But it was the bean counter of Whitehall who trapped him in the end.

Ryde's denunciation was a masterpiece. 'I have long suspected that Zigzag has no regard whatever for the necessity of observing complete silence regarding his connection with us,' he wrote; by confiding in Hunt, Chapman had 'broken the most elementary security rules'. With malice aforethought, Ryde methodically laid out the case for the prosecution: Chapman had already confided in one unauthorised individual, Dagmar Lahlum, and was probably in league with his German spymaster; he had attempted to extract money from MI5, gambled in fixed dog races, and kept the company of professional criminals; he had threatened to work for a rival secret service, and he was costing a small fortune to maintain in a lifestyle of champagne and loose women. Leaving aside Von Gröning, who clearly had a vested interest in his success, the Germans were uncertain of their spy's loyalty, and the speech by Duncan Sandys had probably undermined his credibility anyway. Finally, and fatally, he had bragged to a known criminal about his work for the British secret services. 'This act of Zigzag's does of course provide a first-class excuse for closing the case with him in the wrong and for administering a very firm rebuke,' said Ryde, with relish. 'In view of the inflammable situation caused by Zigzag's indiscretions to his very doubtful friend . . . it seems to me that we should dismiss him, explaining that he has broken his side of the bargain and that from now on he need expect no assistance from us in any trouble he may find himself in the future.'

Nor should he be allowed to work as an intelligence agent for anyone else: 'We should impress upon Zigzag that we would take the strongest possible exception to any approach which he might feel inclined to make to the Americans or French or any other government.' In Ryde's view, Chapman should not receive another penny: 'I should be opposed to paying him any further money, for once we do this we lay ourselves open to further approaches . . . We can now say to Zigzag that he can expect no further assistance, either financial or legal, we have obtained for him from the police a clean sheet, and he has a large sum of money which he would never have obtained without assistance. He has now let us down badly.'

Ryde advised against continuing the Zigzag traffic with Germany without Chapman himself, arguing that any attempt to impersonate his radio technique would pose a 'considerable risk, because Zigzag has a distinctive style'. The case should simply be shut down in a clean break, leaving the Germans to believe that Chapman had been caught: 'As far as the Germans are concerned Zigzag is away contacting a courier. Should he never reappear on the air again the assumption will be that he has been arrested.'

Faced with Ryde's damning dossier, the MI5 chiefs had little choice but to agree. The Admiralty, with reluctance, acquiesced, although Operation Squid was still underway. 'My feeling,' wrote Masterman, 'is that his case should be closed now, that we should pay Zigzag nothing and that the Yard should be informed.' Tar Robertson did not object: 'We should close it now.' On 2 November 1944, Chapman was presented with a copy of the Official Secrets Act. Unaware of what was coming, he signed it, thereby stating: 'I understand that any disclosure by me, whether during or after the present war, of facts relating to the undertaking upon which I have been engaged . . . will be an offence punishable by imprisonment.' Having gagged Chapman, MI5 then sacked him.

Ryde was authorised to dismiss Chapman, which he did, 'as forcibly as possible', throwing him out of the Hill Street flat after a fierce lecture on the error of his ways and warning him that if he dared to reveal what he had done during the war he would be prosecuted. Ryde was exultant and ungenerous in victory and washed MI5's hands of Chapman with a flourish, and a threat: 'He must understand that he must now stand on his own feet, and should he make any approach we, the office, will consider whether he should not be interned or otherwise disposed of.'

Chapman had repeatedly risked his life for the British secret services; he had provided invaluable intelligence for the Allied war effort, he had penetrated the upper echelons of the German secret service, and helped disrupt V-weapon attacks on central London; even now, German intelligence officers were poring over documents, furnished by Zigzag, describing a non-existent anti-submarine weapon; he had extracted some £7,000 from the Nazi exchequer, £230,000 at modern prices, and cost the British government almost nothing. But he was also a criminal, expendable, and quite the wrong sort of person, in the eyes of many, to be hailed as a hero. This was the man MI5 would now 'dispose of', if he dared to bother them again.

The Zigzag case was closed, and at the age of thirty, Chapman's career as a secret agent came to an abrupt and permanent end. That evening, over dinner at his club with fellow officers, Major Ryde reviewed the fall of Eddie Chapman with placid self-satisfaction, concluding that: 'Zigzag should be thankful we are not going to lock him up.'

Tin Eye Stephens, however, saw Zigzag differently: Chapman was the worst of men, in whom war had brought out the best. Years later, Stephens wrote: 'Fiction has not, and probably never will, produce an espionage story to rival in fascination and improbability the true story of Edward Chapman, whom only war could invest with virtue, and that only for its duration.' In Germany, Stephan von Gröning waited in vain for a message from his agent and friend. When the Nazis retreated, he continued to listen and hope, and as Hitler's regime crumbled around him, he was listening still.

Chapman, by rights and inclination, might have been expected to react to his sacking with indignation. But in truth, MI5's ungrateful farewell had set him free at last. He was no longer in thrall to either the German or the British secret services. He had money and a medal from the former, and an informal pardon from the latter: no other secret agent could claim to have been rewarded in this way by *both* sides. MI5 had threatened dire reprisals if he revealed his story, but he knew that one day it would be told.

Chapman returned to what he knew best, for Britain at the end of the war was a criminal cornucopia. Through his old networks, he came into contact with Billy Hill, a nightclub owner and underworld boss who styled himself the 'King of Soho'. Hill had spent the war setting up some profitable black market and protection rackets. He was a 'hard character with considerable dash and more verve', in Chapman's view, and the ideal ally. Making money by drugging greyhounds was strictly a pastime. New money-making schemes beckoned. Chapman and Hill went into partnership.

Dismissal from his country's service also left Chapman free to pursue matters of the heart once more, for he had conceived yet another romantic quest. This time the focus was not Dagmar (who waited in Oslo), nor Freda (who continued to draw her stipend from MI5), nor his ex-wife Vera, nor Anita, the Portuguese prostitute from George's bar. Chapman was now determined to find Betty Farmer, the girl he had left behind at the Hotel de la Plage, six years earlier. Perhaps she was dead; perhaps she was married, or had moved away. But Chapman knew that if he could find Betty, and she would let him, he could make amends.

Chapman contacted Paul Backwell and Allan Tooth, the two former policemen who had served as his minders, and asked for their help. He also recruited a private detective, Doughy Baker. The search began to obsess Chapman, driving out every other thought, and every other woman: 'Uppermost in my mind was the desire to find Betty, my girl, whom I had last seen when I dived through a hotel window before my arrest.' Backwell and Tooth traced Betty only as far as a hotel on the Isle of Man in 1943. Her family thought she was working in a factory somewhere near London. A friend said Betty had been walking out with a Spitfire pilot, who was shot down in the sea off Margate.

Chapman arranged a summit meeting to discuss the search for Betty Farmer. Over lunch at the fashionable Berkeley Hotel (Chapman was as profligate and generous as ever), the ex-policemen explained that searching for a single woman in the chaos of wartime Britain was no easy task, particularly without a photograph: 'Is there anyone here who looks like her at all?' Chapman looked around the dining room, with its lunchtime clientele of debs and guardsmen, bankers and mobsters. He pointed to a slim woman with blonde hair, seated at a corner table, her back to the room. 'That girl,' he said, 'looks exactly like her from the back.' At that moment, the woman turned around.

'Jesus!' exclaimed Chapman. 'It *is* Betty. Excuse me gentlemen.'

Backwell and Tooth, discreet to the last, slipped away, as a waiter swept up the remains of a coffee cup that had dropped from Betty Farmer's astonished fingers when a man she had last seen in a Jersey courtroom tapped her on the shoulder. Chapman pulled up a chair.

'I shall go,' he had told her – in the distant days before the war – 'but I shall always come back.'

Aftermath

With the end of the war, the Double Cross team was quietly disbanded. It would be decades before anyone outside the Most Secret circle knew it had existed. A few eventually emerged from the shadows of British intelligence to tell their stories and reap some glory, but most did not.

Tommy 'Tar' Robertson gave up the spy game, and spent the rest of his life farming sheep in Worcestershire. The 'real genius' of the double-cross operation was awarded the US Legion of Merit by Harry Truman, the Royal Order of the Yugoslav Crown by King Peter in a bizarre ceremony at Claridge's, and an OBE from Britain for work too secret to be described. John Masterman, muscle-bound by duty, considered Tar's early retirement to be 'one of the greatest losses which MI5 ever suffered', but Robertson was entirely happy tending his sheep. He stopped wearing tartan trousers, but he continued to talk to strange characters in pubs. When Tar died in 1994, a small poem was offered as an epitaph to the spymaster who never lost the knack of listening:

> Blessed are they with cheery smile
> Who stop to chat for a little while.
> Blessed are they who never say:
> 'You've told me that story twice today.'

John Cecil Masterman, who liked lecturing more than listening, was knighted, feted and awarded the OBE. He returned to Oxford, his clubs, his cricket and his mystery novels. He became provost of Worcester College, and also Vice Chancellor of Oxford. In 1957 he published another detective novel *The Case of the Four Friends,* featuring a character called Chapman, which discussed the nature of the criminal mind: 'To work out the crime before it is committed, to foresee how it will be arranged, and then prevent it! That's a triumph indeed.' He sat on industrial boards and accepted governorships at the major public schools, a stalwart member of the great and good. 'Everything which is good in this curious world owes its origin to privileged persons,' he maintained.

But in 1970, for the first time in his life, Masterman broke ranks with the ruling classes by publishing a book about the Double Cross organisation. His account had been written immediately after the war, strictly for internal MI5 reading, but he had secretly kept a copy for himself. The spy scandals of the 1960s had shattered the morale of the British intelligence community, and Masterman was determined to restore some of its confidence by relating this story of unalloyed success. Roger Hollis, the head of MI5, and Alec Douglas-Home, the Prime Minister, refused to authorise publication, so Masterman published *The Double Cross System in the War of 1939-45* in the United States, where the Official Secrets Act could not stifle it. Many establishment figures, including some of Masterman's former colleagues in MI5, were scandalised; John Marriott never spoke to him again. In 1972, the British government bowed, and the book was published, subject to the removal of a number of contentious passages. 'How strange it was,' wrote Masterman, 'that I, who all my life, had been a supporter of the Establishment, should become, at eighty, a successful rebel.'

Others followed suit: Ewen Montagu published his account of Operation Mincemeat, the successful deception plan that had convinced the Germans the Allies intended to invade the

Balkans and Sardinia rather then Sicily. Montagu, by then Judge Advocate of the Fleet, even played a cameo role in the 1956 film *The Man Who Never Was*.

Paul Backwell, Chapman's wartime minder, became a captain in the Intelligence Corps, and Allan Tooth remained a senior NCO in the Field Security Service.

Ronnie Reed accepted a job with MI5 after the war as senior technical adviser to the security service. Between 1951 and 1957, he headed the counter-espionage section, responsible for investigating Soviet moles in Britain, including the Burgess, McLean and Philby cases. Reed officially retired in 1977, but was invited to stay on in MI5 as a senior advisor. He later wrote the definitive monograph on wartime radio work, which was published as an appendix to the official account of British Intelligence in the Second World War. Reed was much too self-effacing to put his name to it. He died in 1995, at the age of seventy-eight. The Iron Cross presented to Chapman by Von Gröning for services to the Third Reich and then passed on to Reed as a souvenir of their friendship, remains in the possession of the Reed family.

Victor, Lord Rothschild won the George Medal for his wartime work with explosives, joined the Zoology Department of Cambridge University, and went on to become security advisor to Margaret Thatcher. His student membership of the Cambridge Apostles, and his links with the KGB spies Guy Burgess and Anthony Blunt, led to allegations that he was the 'Fifth Man' in the Cambridge Spy Ring. He furiously denied the charges, and published an open letter to British newspapers in 1986 stating: 'I am not, and never have been, a Soviet agent.'

Michael Ryde, Chapman's last case officer, left MI5 soon after the war and rejoined the family firm of chartered accountants. He soon drank himself out of a job, however, and began a sad decent into alcoholism. One marriage disintegrated, and he walked out of the next, leaving two young children. In the pub, to general disbelief, Ryde would boast of his role in the case of Eddie Chapman, a man he had despised.

Terence Young survived the Battle of Arnhem to become a highly successful film-maker, and directed the first and second James Bond films, *Dr No* and *From Russia with Love* (in which a Russian spy develops a plan to kill Bond and steal a coding machine). The persona of the world's most famous secret agent was probably based on Young himself, with some cast members remarking that 'Sean Connery was simply doing a Terence Young impression'.

Jasper Maskelyne the conjuror virtually vanished after the war, to his intense irritation. He received no decoration, no formal recognition for his deception schemes, and official accounts of the North African campaign barely mentioned him. The audiences for his magic shows grew smaller, and the venues steadily less glamorous. Embittered, he gave up magic, emigrated to Kenya, set up a successful driving school, took part in the campaign against the Mau Mau rebels, and died in 1973.

Reginald Kearon, Captain of the *City of Lancaster*, went on to take command of five more merchant vessels in the course of the war. He was awarded the OBE for war service and the Lloyd's War Medal. The sea kept trying, and failing, to claim him: in 1948, unsinkable Reg Kearon went on a solo pleasure cruise in the Mediterranean and was later found 'drifting on a wreck in Haifa Bay'. He retired in 1954, the same year that the *City of Lancaster* (renamed *Lancastrian*) was broken up.

From 1945 Robin 'Tin Eye' Stephens ran Bad Nenndorf, the Combined Services Detailed Interrogation Centre (CSDIC) near Hanover, a secret prison set up following the British occupation of north-west Germany. This was the German version of Camp 020, where Tin Eye was charged with flushing the truth out of the numerous intelligence officers and spies picked up as the Allies pushed into Germany, including Himmler's assistant Walter Schellenburg, and Ernst Kaltenbrünner, Heydrich's successor as head of the RSHA, (a 'giant of evil' in

Stephens's view). Tin Eye was accused of using brutal methods to extract confessions, but he was acquitted of all charges, having damned his accusers as 'degenerates, most of them diseased by VD [and] pathological liars'.

Stephan von Gröning was arrested by American forces, and held in a prison camp outside Bremen. Homeless, he had been staying with his sister Dorothea and her adopted Jewish daughter when the soldiers arrived. The Americans got lost escorting him to the prison, so half-American Von Gröning showed them the way, in perfect English, with an upper-class accent. He was allowed to send one card a month to relatives. The man whose linen had always been ironed by servants, found himself pleading for handkerchiefs and toothpaste. He was released after six months and discovered, to his intense annoyance, that in order to obtain a ration book, and thus to eat, he had to get a job. Through family friends, he was found nominal employment at the Bremen Museum, but he rarely turned up for work.

The money may have all gone, but Von Gröning lived on his name, 'loyal to his own class' to the end. He married a much younger woman named Ingeborg, and though she worked, he did not. He would lie for long hours on the sofa, reading borrowed books. Von Gröning seldom spoke of the war. He believed Eddie Chapman had been captured, exposed as a spy and executed. He kept a photograph of La Bretonnière in his wallet.

Walter Praetorius, alias Thomas, the Nazi who loved folk dancing, was arrested, transferred to Bad Nenndorf and interrogated by Tin Eye Stephens. Stephens considered the camp inmates to be 'invariably foul', but Praetorius impressed him, perhaps because his Anglomania chimed with Tin-Eye's raw jingoism. Praetorius was released after several months of interrogation, with the verdict that he had 'had a long and possibly creditable record of service as a permanent official of the German Secret Service'. Praetorius settled in Goslar, West Germany, where he returned to teaching, and dancing.

On 5 May 1945, troops of the 41st US Cavalry liberated Mauthausen-Gusen concentration camp, and found a scene from Hell – human skeletons staggering through an abandoned factory of death. Among the emaciated ghosts was Anthony Faramus. He had lost a lung and seven ribs, his body had been racked by diphtheria, scarlet fever, gangrene and dysentery. But somehow the frail Jersey boy who blushed so easily had survived. Back in Britain, he was treated in an RAF hospital, and then discharged with £16 in cash, and a weekly allowance of £2. He arranged to meet up with Eddie Chapman through the journalist Frank Owens, who witnessed their 'awkward' meeting:

'I thought you were dead,' said Chapman.

'I thought so too, sometimes.'

'How did you make out?'

'Not so good.'

'I was always worried about how you got on.'

'I often felt the same way about you, Eddie, and wondered whether you'd make the grade. That was certainly a tricky game you were playing.'

There was an embarrassed silence.

'Where did you go?' asked Chapman.

'Many places so bad, Eddie, that I was sometimes even tempted to give your game away to the Jerries. Anyway, rather than do those swine a favour, I kept quiet.'

There was another long pause, before Chapman said: 'You know, Tony, if it hadn't been for me you wouldn't have had to go through all that.'

Faramus had never betrayed Chapman, and Chapman had maintained the confidence of the Germans, in part, he believed, to protect Faramus. They went to a nearby pub, and got very drunk. 'Millions died without being able to utter a single word,' Chapman reflected to his friend. 'We at least have lived to tell our stories.'

Faramus wrote a harrowing memoir, and obtained work as a film extra. In a painfully ironic piece of casting, he played the

part of a prisoner of war in the film *Colditz* – the inhabitants of
Colditz may have suffered, but never as he had done.

Faramus emigrated to Hollywood – and ended up as Clark
Gable's butler.

Dagmar Lahlum waited in vain for Chapman to come back,
while Norway carried out a grim accounting. Vidkun Quisling
was arrested at his mansion Gimli, tried for treason, and executed
by firing squad. Two members of the Norwegian resistance were
tried for the murder of the Feltmans, but acquitted. Dagmar's
neighbours back in Eidsvoll whispered behind her back, and
called her a 'German tart'; she heard them, but said nothing. She
never told her neighbours or family that she had assisted the
British secret services during the war. To get away from the 'Mrs
Gossips', she took a job as an assistant nurse aboard the cruise
ship, *Stvanger Fjord*, which sailed between Oslo, New York and
Nova Scotia. She and Chapman had both learned to love the sea
and, like him, 'she was always restless'. She worked in a book-
shop, then as a hairdresser and finally as an accountant. Dagmar
still wore the most fashionable clothes, and smoked Craven 'A'
cigarettes. She never married, never had children, and never lost
her looks. In old age she wore makeup and leopard skin hats, and
once her niece caught her dancing alone in front of the mirror.
When Dagmar died of Parkinson's disease in 1999, her niece
found a box of letters, carefully written out in English, on sheet
after sheet of airmail paper. They were addressed to Eddie
Chapman. None had ever been sent. Dagmar's niece burned
them all.

Freda Stevenson, rightly, saw no point in waiting. She became
a shorthand typist, and in 1949, she married a bank clerk five
years her junior. Four years later, she had become a newsagent's
clerk, divorced her first husband, and married a wealthy garage
proprietor called Abercrombie. Though the security service was
careful to destroy the agreement under which she was to be paid
£5 a month until further notice and removed all references from

the files, Freda may have continued to receive cheques from the London Co-operative Society, the fruits of Chapman's deal with MI5, until the day she died. Like Faramus, Freda was a survivor.

At the Berkeley Hotel, Eddie Chapman and Betty Farmer talked for hours, and got married shortly thereafter. It was a happy, enduring marriage, even though Chapman's eye wandered more or less continuously for the next fifty years. He left often, but he always came back. A daughter, Suzanne, was born in October 1954.

Zigzag never did go straight. After the war, he returned to the demimonde of London's West End, where the wastrels welcomed him home. During the 1950s, he smuggled gold across the Mediterranean. After buying a share in Billy Hill's motor yacht, *The Flamingo*, a former mine-sweeper, Chapman and a like-minded crew sailed to Morocco where they became involved in a ludicrous plot to smuggle 850,000 packets of cigarettes and kidnap the deposed sultan: the plan collapsed when the villainous crew got into a dockside brawl, and they were expelled from Tangiers, hotly pursued by a reporter from the *Sunday Chronicle* whom they invited on board, and then locked in his cabin. *The Flamingo* caught fire in Toulon harbour, possibly for insurance purposes, giving rise to suspicions that Chapman's sabotage skills had not deserted him. Soon after, the Hill gang knocked off a post-office van, escaping with £250,000. During the 1960s, Eddie and Betty Chapman moved to Africa's Gold Coast. Chapman became involved in a complicated building contract. There was a corruption inquiry, but by then he had come home.

Tin Eye Stephens had wondered 'what will happen when Chapman, embroiled again in crime, as he inevitably will be, stands up in court and pleads leniency on the grounds of highly secret wartime service?' He duly found out. Chapman would appear in court repeatedly over the next twenty years, but he never returned to prison. When he was charged with passing forged currency in 1948, he produced a character reference from an unnamed 'senior officer of the War office' stating that he was 'one of the bravest men who served in the last war'. The referee was almost certainly Ronnie Reed. MI5 had not entirely welched on its debt. Again, in 1974, he was found not guilty of hitting a man on the head with a glass during a dance party at the Watersplash Hotel in the New Forest. The fight was over a young woman named Theresa Chin. Chapman told the court: 'I was trained in unarmed combat for my wartime activities and I didn't need a glass to defend myself in a pub brawl. I could have killed him with my bare hands.' When he was acquitted, he offered to buy the jury a drink.

Chapman still mixed with blackmailers, high-rollers and low thieves. He drove a Rolls-Royce (though he never passed a driving test) and wore fur-collared coats. The newspapers loved him – 'Eddie Chapman, the gentleman crook'. He was even, for a time, the 'honorary crime correspondent' of the *Sunday Telegraph*, 'whose readers he proceeded to warn against the attentions of people like him'. In 1960, a reporter asked him if he missed the old days of crime. 'I do a bit,' he said wistfully. 'I've no regrets. No conscience about anything I've done. I like to think I was an honest villain.'

John Masterman once wrote: 'Sometimes in life you feel that there is something which you *must* do, and in which you must trust your own judgment and not that of any other person. Some call it conscience and some plain obstinacy. Well, you can take your choice.' War, briefly, brought out in Chapman an obstinate conscience. His vices were as extreme as his virtues, and to the end of his life, it was never clear whether he was on the side of the angels or the devils, whether he deceived the deceivers, or whether he had made a pact with his German spymaster. He died of heart failure in 1997, at the age of eighty-three: he may have ascended heavenwards; or perhaps he headed in the opposite direction. He is probably zigzagging still.

Chapman tried to publish an account of his wartime exploits, but like John Masterman he was blocked by MI5. He wrote a bowdlerised version of events which appeared in a French newspaper, *L'Etoile,* and then in the *News of the World* in 1953, but when Chapman strayed into official secrets the government lawyers stepped in. He was fined £50 and an entire edition of the newspaper had to be pulped. A second attempt at publication was thwarted by D-Notice. Eventually, a ghosted and semi-fictionalised memoir, *The Eddie Chapman Story,* which described his time in Germany but not his MI5 work, appeared in 1954. 'What is the truth about Eddie Chapman?' one paper demanded. 'Why, if these astounding claims are true, was he not arrested and convicted as a traitor to his country?'

Finally, in 1966, Chapman was allowed to publish another version, *The Real Eddie Chapman Story,* which referred, without giving details, to his work for MI5. This provided the basis for a rather poor film, *Triple Cross,* directed by Terence Young and starring Christopher Plummer as Chapman. The film bears only a superficial relation to the truth. Chapman was disappointed by it. He never received the recognition he thought he deserved; but then, Chapman could probably only have achieved *that* level of recognition by assassinating Hitler. Somehow, he became rather rich, and for a while owned a castle in Ireland and a health farm in Hertfordshire, not far from the De Havilland Mosquito plant.

In 1974, in a London bar, Chapman bumped into Leo Kreusch, the toothless German prizefighter who had taught him to shoot in La Bretonnière. Leo told Chapman the real name of the man he had always known as Graumann, revealing that he had survived the war and that he was now living in Bremen. Chapman wrote Von Gröning a letter, in which he recalled, with affection, the times they had spent together in Nantes, Paris and Oslo. He inquired whether his old friend knew what had happened to the Norwegian sailing yawl purchased with his reward money, and whether he remembered Dagmar Lahlum. 'I suppose she is married now,' he reflected nostalgically. Chapman described his properties, enclosing a photograph of the ancient Irish castle he had acquired, and invited Von Gröning to come and stay: 'What delightful memories we could exchange . . . I remember how much you used to like castles.'

This was not, perhaps, the most tactful approach, but Eddie could not know that Von Gröning was no longer a wealthy man.

Suzanne Chapman was married in 1979 at Shenley Lodge, the thirty-two room health spa owned by Eddie and Betty. Among the wedding guests that day was an elderly, short-sighted German gentleman who amused the children by reciting old-fashioned English nursery rhymes. When the party wound down, Eddie Chapman and Stephan von Gröning linked arms and wandered off together, deep in reminiscence. Betty was surprised and moved by the enduring bond between the spy and his spymaster: 'They were like brothers.' As the last wedding guests departed, laughter and singing could be heard drifting from the garden: the faint strains of *Lili Marlene*.

HI HU HA HA HA

Paperback Postscript

A few weeks after the publication of *Agent Zigzag*, I received a telephone call from the German Ambassador to London, Wolfgang Ischinger. 'I have just finished your book,' he said. 'You describe how Eddie Chapman was flown across the Channel by the Luftwaffe and then parachuted into Britain. I thought you might be interested to know that the man who commanded that flight was my father. Both he and the pilot, Fritz Schlichting, are still very much alive.'

Leutnant Fritz Schlichting, the young pilot
who flew Chapman to Britain in 1942.

Schlichting had been the tall, shy pilot with the Iron Cross at the controls of the Focke-Wulf reconnaissance plane in 1942, while Karl 'Charlie' Ischinger was his commanding officer and navigator, described by Chapman as a 'small, thickset young man of about twenty-eight, with steady blue eyes'. Chapman himself had believed these men were dead: 'The whole crew had been shot down and killed over England on their sixtieth sortie,' he wrote.

The discovery that the pilot and navigator had not only outlived the war, but survived still, led to a meeting with Fritz Schlichting at his home in Detmold, Germany. At the age of eighty-four, charming and hospitable, the former pilot recalled that day as if he had stepped off the runway at Le Bourget last week, rather than a long lifetime ago.

'We were the Luftwaffe Reconnaissance Squadron number 123 stationed in the Château du Buc, outside Versailles. We flew night flights over Britain, photographing the effects of bombing raids and helping to identify targets. It was dangerous work. I lost

Überleutnant Karl 'Charlie' Ischinger, commander of the Luftwaffe plane that flew Chapman to Britain in 1942, reporting to Major Armin Göbel, chief of Reconnaissance Squadron 123.

more than eighty comrades. The average number of flights before being shot down was about forty. I flew eighty-seven in all.

'One day my commanding officer, Major Gobin, told Charlie [Ischinger] and me that we had been chosen for a special mission. He told us to dress in civilian clothing, and go to Paris. We met the English spy and his handlers in a restaurant for dinner: we knew him only as "Fritz", like me. Much later I discovered his real name. He was delightful, excellent company. We all got on famously.

'We all met a few weeks later at Le Bourget airfield, and I showed him over the plane. Chapman seemed quite calm, although he asked lots of questions. On the way over the Channel we sang songs. There was a bad moment when Chapman was preparing to jump, and we realised that his parachute cord was not properly tied. If he had jumped like that, he would have fallen to his death. Charlie gave the signal, and Chapman opened the hatch. He had this huge pack on his back – heaven knows what was in it – and as he jumped it got wedged in the hole. He was struggling, but it wouldn't budge, so Charlie got out of his seat and gave him a big boot in the back.

'That was the last we saw of Chapman for about four months, but we heard that his mission had been successful. Everyone was very pleased with him. It never occurred to anyone that he might be working for the British. We met up with him again in Paris. It was a great reunion. Chapman handed Charlie and me two packages, containing a big box of chocolates and a pound of coffee which he had bought in Madrid on his way back. It was real coffee beans, not the fake stuff, so we were delighted.

'After the Chapman mission, as a reward, we were each presented with a special engraved silver goblet. I have always treasured it. Charlie is my still my best friend. He is ninety-seven now, and his health is not good, but we still have get-togethers when we remember the extraordinary night we dropped the English spy into Britain.'

★   ★   ★

The courtly Luftwaffe pilot was only one of several people to emerge from Chapman's past, adding fresh myths and memories, some affectionate, and some decidedly less so. An elderly, rather refined female voice came on the telephone at *The Times*, and without giving her name declared angrily: 'He was an absolute shit, you know. The handsomest man I ever met. But a prize shit.' Then she rang off. In Norway, another of Chapman's wronged women finally won recognition for her heroism. The Norwegian media picked up the Chapman story, and the national newspaper *Aftenposten* ran a front-page story with the headline: 'She died a German collaborator, but she was really a British spy.' It emerged that Dagmar had been brought before a war-crimes tribunal after the war, imprisoned for six months, and agreed to acknowledge her own guilt in lieu of a formal conviction. Reviled and ostracised by her countrymen, Dagmar had kept her promise to Chapman, and never revealed her wartime links with the British Secret Service.

John Williams, a friend of Chapman's, recalled the first time they had met, when Shenley Lodge was being run as a country club with bar and roulette table before its more respectable incarnation as a health farm: 'I arrived at the impressive front entrance of Shenley only to hear the most fearsome of noises from the roof of the mansion. It was on this roof I met Eddie, strapped into a Vickers machine gun firing at a sheet draped between two oak trees half a mile away!' Another acquaintance, the journalist Peter Kinsley, wrote a letter to *The Times* after *Agent Zigzag* was serialised: 'Eddie would have loved the publicity. His old friends said he should have worn a T-shirt emblazoned "I am a spy for MI5". The last time I met him he described how he had missed a fortune in ermine (to be used in Coronation robes) during a furs robbery, because he thought it was rabbit. He also said he successfully convinced a German au pair girl that he was a Post Office telephone engineer, and robbed the wall safe. He was also once visited by an income tax inspector, and produced a doctor's certificate that he had a weak heart and could not be "caused stress". Ten minutes later, he drove, in a Rolls-Royce, past the inspector waiting in the rain at a bus stop, and gave him a little wave.'

I received a mournful letter from Brian Simpson, a collector of wartime medals who had lived near Shenley Lodge in the 1980s. Simpson had heard of Chapman's adventures though a mutual friend, and asked if he could buy his Iron Cross. Sure enough, a few weeks later, Chapman duly produced the German medal; indeed, he produced two, saying that he had been given another one by Hitler himself. A deal was struck: Eddie Chapman took the money, and a delighted Simpson took the medals. Two decades later, on reading this book, the collector realised he had been conned. Chapman, of course, had given his own Iron Cross to Ronnie Reed many years earlier. Those in Simpson's possession were replicas. 'Your book came as quite a shock,' wrote Simpson. 'It now seems that Eddie had the last laugh. My wife was also offered a small jewelled dagger which Eddie said was

Tommy 'Tar' Robertson, head of Section B1A,
wearing the tartan trews of the Seaforth Highlanders
that earned him the nickname 'Passion Pants'.

given to him by Hermann Göring. She declined to take it.'
Chapman, needless to say, had never laid eyes on Göring.

One after another, Chapman's former associates, ex-lovers
and victims emerged from the past, to add their stories – some
true, some the legacy of Chapman's self-mythologizing. But
then, to my astonishment, there reappeared the only person who
really knew the truth about Eddie Chapman: Eddie Chapman
himself.

John Dixon, an independent film-maker, called me to say that he
had six hours of footage of Chapman talking about his life, not
one second of which had ever been broadcast. Dixon had shot
the film in 1996, the year before Chapman died, with a view to
making a documentary that never happened. He had kept the
film safe, thinking that one day Chapman's story would be told.
He now offered to show it to me.

Sitting in a small screening room in Soho, meeting Chapman for the first time from beyond the grave, was one of the
strangest experiences of my life. Chapman was old and
already ill when the film was made, but still vital. He exudes
a feral charm, as he lounges in an armchair, reminiscing,
smoking, chuckling, winking and flirting with the camera. He
describes parachuting into Britain, his relationship with Von
Gröning, the faked bombing of the de Havilland aircraft, and
his life in Jersey, France, Lisbon and Oslo. His criminal
exploits are remembered with airy pride.

But there is a valedictory tone to his words: this is the last
testament of a man talking to posterity, and setting the record
straight or, in some instances, bent. Because at the age of eighty-
two, Chapman is still a shameless liar. In one passage, for
example, he describes being taken to see Winston Churchill
in 1943 and sharing a bottle of brandy with the Prime Minister
while the latter sat in bed in his dressing gown. It is a splendid
story. It is also completely untrue.

Chapman could never have imagined that MI5 would decide

to release its records, and that the truth about his wartime service would one day be revealed. His own death is imminent, but here is Eddie Chapman still playing by his own rules: a grinning villain, spinning a yarn, looking you straight in the eye, and picking your pocket.

Ben Macintyre
April 2007

Eddie Chapman is reunited with his MI5 handlers at the Savoy, October 1980.
Chapman, back row, third from right; Tommy 'Tar' Robertson, back row, third from left;
Roman Garby-Czerniawski, double agent 'Brutus', front row, third from left.

APPENDIX

This is an exact copy of the explanation of Chapman's code, contained in the MI5 archives (KV2/455):

MULTIPLICATION CODE
Given to
An English Parachutist

This code is based on the word: 'CONSTANTINOPLE' which is agreed upon before the agent's departure. Constantinople is then given its numerical position in the alphabet in the following manner and multiplied by the date on which the transmission takes place. In this case the 8th has been chosen.

C	O	N	S	T	A	N	T	I	N	O	P	L	E
2	9	6	12	13	1	7	14	4	8	10	11	5	3
													8
23	6	8	97	05	3	7	15	8	4	80	92	2	4

The next procedure:
Write out the alphabet in full, giving each letter its numerical position.

a	b	c	d	e	f	g	h	i	j	k	m	n	o	p	q	r	s	t	u	v	w	x	y	z
1	2	3	4	5	6	7	8	9	10	11	12	13	14	15	16	17	18	19	20	21	22	23	24	25	26

The result of the multiplication is then written out and the message to be transmitted – in this case:

'I HAVE ARRIVED AND IN GOOD HEALTH'

is written below.

It will be noticed that the first five letters are 'f's. This is the agreed sign between the agent and his German Control that he is operating of his own free will. Should he be forced to transmit, the omission of the five 'f's would immediately disclose to the German Control that he had been apprehended.

The Method of Coding:
Add 'f'(which is the 6th letter) to the 2 above it, making 8, and selecting the 8th letter in the alphabet – 'h' –

In the second instance 'f' again (the 6th letter in the alphabet), added to 3, making 9 which is – 'i' –

This method is continued throughout the message including the signature 'FRITZ'.

```
2 3 6 8 9 7 0 5 3 7 1 5 8 4 8 0 9 2 2 4
f f f f f I H A  V E x A R R  I V E D A N
h i l n o p h f y f y f z v q v n f c r
D  I N G O O D H  E A L T H x F R  I T Z x
f l t o x v d m h h m y p b n r r v b b
```

The Groups of 5
are then read off horizontally instead of vertically as in other cases.

Thus:
HILNO PHFYL YFZVQ VNFCR FLTOX VDMHH MYPBN RRVBB

Note: It is always necessary to include the exact number of letters in the code before commencing the coded groups of five.

NOTES

The KV2 series is located at The National Archives, Kew.

Unless otherwise noted all interrogations are of Chapman by the MI5 officer named.

Newspapers extracts reproduced in the text have been edited.

Where three or more subsequent note entries refer to the same source only the first and last entries from the main text are shown as prompts.

1. The Hotel de la Plage

3 **with all the trimmings**   Interview with Leonard Maxie, former waiter at Hotel de la Plage, Jersey, July 2006.

3 **in the film business**   Interview with Betty Chapman, Amersham, 25.11.05.

3 **I shall go**   Ibid.

3 **How would you like**   Edward Chapman, *The Real Eddie Chapman Story*, (London, 1966), p. 32. Henceforth: *Chapman*.

4 **prince of the underworld**   Robin Stephens, 7.1.42, KV2 457.

5 **off the rails**   Interview with Betty Chapman, 25.11.05.

6 **jail-crop haircut**   *Chapman*, p. 27.

6 **three days**   Report by Laurie. C. Marshall, 15.1.43; MI5 ref. 133B. This file, newly released by MI5, has been allocated to KV2 457. Material in this file, henceforth: 'KV2 457 (additional)'.

6 **wire and whipcord body**   Frank Owens, introduction to ibid., p. 9.

6 **I mixed with all types**   Ibid., p. 27

7 **behaving in a manner**   Police record, KV2 455.

7 **with good looks**   Owens in *Chapman*, p. 9.

7 **women on the fringes**   R. Stephens, *Camp 020: MI5 and the Nazi Spies* (London, 2000), p. 218. Henceforth: *Camp 020*.

7 **infected a girl of 18**   Ibid.

7 **best cracksman**   KV2 457.

7 **cool, self-possessed**   *Chapman*, p. 28.

8 **shivering with fear** Interrogation by Ronald Reed, 7.1.43, KV2 457.
9 **He was able** Interview with Terence Young, 22.1.43, KV2 458.
9 **He is a crook** Ibid.
9 **I don't go along** *Sunday Telegraph*, 23 March 1963.
9 **went back to 'work'** Paul Backwell's report, KV2 456.
11 **Be prepared for trouble** *Jersey Evening Post*, 13.2.39.

2. Jersey Gaol

16 **done with deliberation** *Jersey Evening Post*, 14.2.39.
16 **dangerous criminal who** Ibid.
16 **dreary little cage** Anthony Faramus, *The Faramus Story* (London, no date stated, 1954?), p. 12. Henceforth: *Faramus*.
16 **dangerous criminal** Ibid.
16 **batman** Minutes of the Jersey prison board, Jersey Historical Archive.
16 **keep an eye on Chapman** Ibid.
17 **At that moment** Warder Packer's evidence to Jersey prison board, Jersey Historical Archive.
17 **Do you know** *Jersey Evening Post*, 6.7.39.
18 **interested in quarries** to **Your name is Chapman** Ibid.
20 **free-for-all** *Daily Express*, 8.7.39.
20 **This appeared to** *Jersey Evening Post*, 6.7.39.
21 **gross misconduct** Minutes of the Jersey prison board, Jersey Historical Archive.
21 **You have never** Ibid.

3. Island at War

24 **Nationalism as a God** H.G. Wells, *Outline of History* (London, 1920), p. 209.
26 **sort of dispossessed** *Faramus*, p. 10.
27 **Look we've reason** Interrogation, 1.1.43, KV2 456.
28 **If I could work a bluff** Interrogation, 17.12.42, KV2 455.
28 **It all sounds fine talk** *Chapman*, p. 48–9.
28 **His whole theme** *Faramus*, p. 29.
29 **tale of loathing** Ibid., p. 30.
30 **The British police** Interrogation, 17.12.42, KV2 455.

4. Romainville

32 **stank of drink** *Faramus*, p. 39.
32 **How would you** Ibid., p. 36.
32 **Alles verboten** *The Trial of German Major War Criminals*, vol. 6 (London, 1946), p. 141.
33 **Madame prisonniers** *Faramus*, p. 40.
34 **professional denouncer** Interrogation by E. Goodacre, 18.12.42, KV2 455.
34 **It wasn't safe to talk** Interrogation by Goodacre, 17.12.42, KV2 455.

34 **were real love affairs** *Faramus*, p. 43.
35 **the scholarly, staid** Interrogation by Victor Rothschild, 28.1.43, KV2 458.
36 **What happened?** *Faramus*, p. 48.
36 **All right for you** Ibid., p. 37.
37 **Supposing you didn't** *Faramus*, p. 49.
37 **You'd have to trust** Ibid.
37 **They'll probably send** Ibid.,p. 37.
38 **simply a trained brute** *Chapman*, p. 62.
38 **a man of understanding** Ibid., p. 62.
38 **no use** Interrogation by Stephens, 7.1.42, KV2 457.
38 **In times of war** Interrogation by Stephens, 17.12.42, KV2 455.
39 **half-threat** Ibid.
39 **Supposing you slip** *Faramus*, p. 37.
39 **Goodbye and good luck** Ibid., p. 49.
39 **You are among friends** *Chapman*, p. 64.
49 **Welcome to the Villa** Ibid., p. 66.

5. Villa de la Bretonnière

42 **one of the most important** Interrogation by Stephens, 17.12.42, KV2 455.
43 **respectable business man** Ibid.
43 **surprisingly soft** Ibid.
43 **Look, you will see** Interrogation by Rothschild, 2.1.43, KV2 456.
43 **absolutely first class** T.A. Robertson (attrib), report of SOE training course, KV4 172.
44 **by the time of the fall** John Curry, *The Security Service 1908–1945: The Official History* (London, 1999), KV4 1–3.
46 **There is a well-defined** Cited in Emily Jane Wilson, *The War in the Dark: The Security Service and the Abwehr 1940–1944*, PhD thesis (Cambridge, 2003)
46 **typically Prussian neck** Ibid.
46 **Suspect everyone** Evelyn Waugh, cited in ibid.
47 **was left with the** Curry, op. cit.
48 **Chiefly line of Clan** Letter by Walter Praetorius, 1979, on Thomas Family website.
49 **kind, gentle type** Walter Praetorius file, KV 2 524.
49 **rabid Nazi** Ibid.
49 **superiority of the German** Ibid.
50 **might be trained** ISOS intercept, 2.2.42, KV2 456.

6. Dr Graumann

52 **He just got hold** Interrogation, 1.1.43, KV2 456.
53 **pocket money** Ibid.
53 **He liked life** Interrogation by Rothschild, 2.1.43, KV2 456.
54 **Had a good trip?** Interrogation, 1.1.43, KV2 456.
54 **What do you want** Interrogation by Rothschild, 2.1.43, KV2 456.
54 **take it out and light** Interrogation by Goodacre, 17.12.42, KV2 455.
54 **Good God!** Interrogation by Stephens, 17.12.42, KV2 455.

54 **Look here, if you** Ibid.
55 **more or less reckless** Interrogation by Rothschild 28.1.43, KV2 458.
55 **Mary had a little** Interrogation by Rothschild, 2.1.43, KV2 456.
55 **which I thought** Ibid.
55 **terribly English accent** Interrogation by Stephens, 3.1.43, KV2 456.
55 **very good private tutor** Interrogation by Reed, 21.12.43, KV2 456.
55 **I'll show you a photograph** Interrogation by Stephens, 3.1.43, KV2 456.
56 **really good brandy** *Chapman*, p. 66.
57 **uncomfortable** Interview with Ingeborg von Gröning, Bremen, 22.05.06.
57 **He was delightful** Ibid.
58 **illicit association** Gladys von Gröning, immigration file, HO 405/16169.
59 **He could mix in** Interview with Ingeborg von Gröning, Bremen, 22.05.06.
59 **Home corner** *Chapman*, p. 73.
60 **German spirit** Ibid., p. 71.
60 **Heil Hitler** Ibid., p. 69.
60 **the hopes of every** Ibid., p. 72.
61 **of every kind** Interrogation by Stephens, 17.12.42, KV2 455.
61 **a fairly high bug** Interrogation by Stephens, 19.12.42, KV2 455.
62 **one of our best** Ibid.
62 **like a gigolo** Report by Reed, 1.1.43, KV2 457.
62 **an old Gestapo man** Interrogation by Goodacre, 17 12 42, KV2 455.
62 **black senders** Ibid.
63 **unbreakable** Reed report, 15.3.43, KV2 459.
63 **my little mottoes** Interrogation, 1.1.43, KV2 456.
63 **It is very cold** ISOS intercept, 20.10.42, KV2 460.
63 **A man went** Ibid., 23.10.42.
64 **What silly business** Ibid., 14.10.42.
64 **I had everything** Interrogation by Stephens, 17.12.42, KV2 455.

7. Codebreakers

65 **Dear France . . .** ISOS intercept, 13.10.42, KV2 460.
66 **brilliant guesswork** Peter Twinn, in F.H. Hinsley and Alan Stripp (eds.), *Codebreakers: The Inside Story of Bletchley Park* (Oxford, 2001).
66 **It's amazing how** Cited in Penelope Fitzgerald, *The Knox Brothers*, (London, 2001), p. 98.
66 **My Golden Eggs** Cited in Wilson, op cit
68 **By means of the** J.C. Masterman, *The Double Cross System in the War 1939–1945* (London, 1972), p. 3.
68 **Immensely personable** Address by Christopher Harmer at memorial service for T.A. Robertson, 1909–94, at Pershore Abbey, in papers of Lieutenant Colonel T.A. Robertson, courtesy of the Trustees of the Liddell Hart Centre for Military Archives, King's College, London.
68 **Tar was in no sense** J. C. Masterman, *On the Chariot Wheel: An Autobiography* (Oxford, 1975), p. 219.
69 **involved a great** Harmer, op. cit.
69 **Passion Pants** Ibid.
70 **almost obsessively anxious** Masterman, *On the Chariot Wheel*, p. 108.
70 **My predominant feeling** Ibid., p. 114.
70 **real genius** Cited in Wilson, op. cit.

71 **At 58 St James's Street** Masterman, *On the Chariot Wheel*, p. 377.
71 **Some had to perish** Masterman, *The Double Cross System*, p. 54.
71 **certain persons who** Ibid., p. 1.
71 **see with the eyes** Ibid., p. 22.
72 **is prone to be** Ibid., p. 24.
72 **principle of generosity** Ibid., p. 25.
73 **of high intelligence** Masterman, *On the Chariot Wheel*, p. 219.
74 **We were obsessed** Ibid.
74 **Could any intelligence** Ewen Montagu, *Beyond Top Secret Ultra* (London, 1977), p. 134.
75 **now prepare sabotage** Reed notes of ISOS intercepts, 30.6.42, KV2 456.
75 **any connection with the** Ibid., 28.7.42.
75 **he merely succeeded** Reed report, 20.8.41, KV2 455.
75 **When he arrives** RSS report, 19.9.41, KV2 455.
75 **practically every day** Memo, KV2 455.
75 **learned to recognise** Ibid.
75 **Is my message** Reed report, 20.8.41, KV2 455.

8. The Mosquito

76 **to shoot his** Reed report, 8.2.42, KV2 458.
77 **I was suffering more** Interrogation by Rothschild, 2.1.43, KV2 456.
77 **made all the right** Interrogation by Goodacre, 17.12.42, KV2 455.
77 **Monsieur Ferdinand** Ibid.
77 **a tremendous bloodbath** Interrogation by Major D.B. 'Stimmy' Stimson,17.12.42, KV2 455.
78 **very cleverly planned** Ibid.
78 **courage and daring** KV2 457.
78 **full-scale attack** Backwell report, 30.12.42, KV2 456.
78 **terrific Blitz** Interrogation by Stephens, 17.12.42, KV2 455.
78 **You can imagine** Ibid.
78 **It is rather awkward** Interrogation by Rothschild, 2.1.43, KV2 456.
81 **He insisted on exact** Ibid.
81 **like bloody monks** Interrogation, 1.1.43, KV2 456.
82 **There was a hell** Ibid.
82 **undesirable emotional** ISOS intercept, 2.10.42, KV2 460.
82 **nihilistic** Backwell notes, KV2 456.
82 **Could something be** Interrogation by Goodacre, 18.12.42, KV2 455.
82 **impossible** Ibid.
82 **if he could return** Backwell notes, KV2 456.
83 **I don't suppose there** Memo, KV2 456.
84 **It makes me furious** See *A Short History of the DH98 Mosquito*, bbc.co.uk
85 **preliminary detailed** ISOS intercepts, 12.10.42, KV2 460.
85 **Things seem at last** Memo, 24.9.42, KV2 456.

9. Under Unseen Eyes

86 **terrific Chrysler** Interrogation by Goodacre, 17.12.42, KV2 455.
86 **the chief wanted** Interrogation by Stephens, 17.12.42, KV2 455.

87 **Let Fritz go first** to **Each time I looked**   Ibid.
87 **Americans?**   Interrogation by Rothschild, 2.1.43, KV2 456.
87 **No, it's just two**   Ibid.
87 **Well, we would**   Ibid.
87 **a big mission**   Interrogation by Stephens, 17.12.42, KV2 455.
88 **in all probability**   Memo, KV2 456.
88 **West End**   Ibid.
88 **You have remembered**   Interrogation by Stephens, 3.1.43, KV2 456.
88 **I am highly**   Ibid.
88 **exploding in all directions**   Interrogation by Rothschild, 2.1.43, KV2 456.
88 **in a rotary motion**   Interrogation by R. Short, 18.12.42, KV2 455.
89 **a faint greeny colour**   Ibid.
89 **like a mosaic**   Interrogation by Stephens, 3.1.43, KV2 456.
90 **Look, don't think**   Interrogation by Rothschild, 2.1.43, KV2 456.
90 **If you feel you're** to **I don't think**   Ibid.
90 **Fritz is spiritually**   ISOS intercepts, 26.9.42, KV2 460.
91 **Show Fritz photos**   Memo, KV2 456.
91 **safer than anywhere else**   Ibid.
91 **new operational objective**   Reed note, ISOS Intercept, 7.12.42, KV2 456.
91 **made familiar in every**   ISOS intercepts, 7.12.42, KV2 460.
92 **apathetic**   Interrogation, 1.1.43, KV2 456.
92 **There were no scenes**   Interrogation by Stephens, 17.12 42, KV2 455.
93 **Why should I send**   *Chapman,* p. 103.
93 **Rendez-vous with**   Interrogation by Goodacre, 18.12.42, KV2 455.
93 **very small fry**   Ibid.
94 **I think it was**   Interrogation by Stephens, 17.12 42, KV2 455.

10. The Drop

95 **visibly relieved**   Reed's note, ISOS Intercept, 10.12.42, KV2 456.
95 **some place further**   Interrogation by Goodacre, 17 12 42, KV2 455.
95 **British red tape**   Chapman statement, 18.12.42, KV2 455.
96 **Young couple require**   Memo, KV2 455.
97 **nuisance work**   Interrogation by Rothschild, 2.1.43, KV2 456.
97 **Take your time**   Interrogation by Stephens, 17.12.42, KV2 455.
97 **Of course our agents**   Ibid.
97 **Walter is ready to go**   Interrogation by Stephens, 7.1.42, KV2 457.
98 **give as little information**   Interrogation by Goodacre, 18.12.42, KV2 455.
98 **a number of small**   Ibid.
98 **various people who**   Interrogation by Stephens, 17.12.42, KV2 455.
98 **Joli Albert**   Ibid.
98 **holiday**   Camp 020 report, 11.7.44, KV2 459.
98 **in the first or second**   Reed report, 1.1.43, KV2 456.
99 **Don't you worry**   Interrogation by Goodacre, 18.12.42, KV2 455.
99 **it was hard to tell**   *Faramus,* p. 74.
99 **It was hard**   Ibid., p. 78.
99 **If you do this**   Interrogation by Stephens, 17.12.42, KV2 455.
100 **I have rather**   Ibid.
100 **anything which could**   Interrogation by Rothschild, 2.1.43, KV2 456.
100 **You don't mind**   Ibid.
101 **if there was any**   Interrogation by Stephens, 7.1.42, KV2 457.

101 **home** *Chapman*, p. 107.
101 **genuine comradeship** Ibid.
102 **Reichsbank, Berlin** Interrogation by Stephens, 7.1.42, KV2 457.
102 **England** Ibid.
102 **You have beautiful** Interrogation by Stephens, 17.12.42, KV2 455.
102 **of the larynx type** Interrogation by Stimson, 17.12.42, KV2 455.
103 **evade attack** Ibid.
103 **We shall be waiting** Interrogation by Stephens, 17.12.42, KV2 455.
104 **Far from being nervous** Interrogation by Stimson, 17.12.42, KV2 455.

11. Martha's Exciting Night

105 **Keep a close watch** Memo, KV2 455.
105 **very soon be going** Reed notes on ISOS intercepts, KV2 456.
105 **Agent X is probably** Memo, KV2 455.
106 **It may be of intelligence** RSS memo, 8.10.42, KV2 455.
106 **too many possibilities** Memo, KV2 455.
107 **flying column** to **pretend to be looking** Ibid.
107 **fully fledged saboteur** Memo, 1.10.42, KV2 455.
107 **We quite realise** Memo, 4.10.42, KV2 455.
108 **Who is it** Police report, KV2 455.
108 **A British airman** to **Yes** Ibid.
109 **just arrived from** Report of Sgt J. Vail, KV2 455.
109 **He shook hands** to **very polite** Ibid.
110 **George Clarke will** Report of Deputy Chief Constable Ely, KV2 455.
112 **mentally and physically** Stephens report, 17.12.42, KV2 455.

12. Camp 020

113 **A breaker is born** *Camp 020*, p. 107.
113 **There must be certain** Ibid.
113 **Italy is a country** Ibid., p. KV4 14, p. 306.
113 **weeping and romantic** *Camp 020*, p. 54.
114 **shifty Polish Jews** Ibid., p. 73.
114 **unintelligent** Ibid., p 295.
114 **lunatic cells ready** Ibid., p. 40.
115 **No chivalry** Ibid.,p 19.
115 **It is a question** Ibid., p. 71.
115 **Your name is Chapman** Interrogation by Stephens, 17.12.42, KV2 455.
116 **That was plain** Stephens report, 18.12.42, KV2 544.
116 **with some bitterness** Ibid.
117 **blow hot-blow cold** *Camp 020*, p. 109.
117 **They treated you** See interrogation by Stephens, 17.12.42, KV2 455.
117 **I don't know what** Cited in Montagu, op. cit., p. 108.
117 **No spy, however astute** *Camp 020*, p. 105.
117 **Physically and mentally** Ibid., p. 58.
118 **It is quite clear** Reed memo, 21.12.42, KV2 456.
118 **He is a hostage** Interrogation by Goodacre, 18.12.42, KV2 455.
119 **That was a private** Interrogation by Stephens, 17.12.42, KV2 455.

119 **natural inexactitudes** Stephens memo, KV2 455.
119 **confessed to an** *Camp 020*, p. 218.
119 **Today there is no** Stephens report, 7.1.42, KV2 457.
120 **one the principal** Reed notes on ISOS intercepts, 28.7.42, KV2 456.
120 **On no occasion** Robertson memo, 24.12.42, KV2 456.
120 **today was the supposed** Chapman statement, 18.12.42, KV2 455.
120 **It is important** Ibid.
121 **Dr Graumann especially** Ibid.
121 **in sharper focus** Reed report, 15.3.43, KV2 459.
121 **Mon Commandant** Chapman to Stephens, 18.12.42, KV2 455.
122 **If Chapman is** Stephens report, 7.1.42, KV2 457.
123 **hatred for the Hun** Ibid.
123 **As I figure it** Stephens report, 18.12.42, KV2 455.
123 **he will go sour** to **My opinion** Ibid.
123 **In our opinion** Joint statement by interrogators, 18.12.42, KV2 455.
124 **We have chosen** Robertson memo, 18.12.42, KV2 455.

13. 35, Crespigny Road

126 **Ah, Mr Reed** to **I'm going** Transcript of videotaped interview with Ronnie Reed, 1994, courtesy of Nicholas Reed.
126 **humble genius** Interview with Charles Chilton, 5.10.06.
127 **lurid past** Reed memo, 19.12.42, KV2 455.
127 **he would have** Ibid.
127 **Mon Commandant** Chapman to Stephens, 19.12.42, KV2 455.
128 **rather weakly** Reed report, 20.12.42, KV2 455.
128 **FFFFF HAVE ARRIVED** Ibid.
128 **definitely Fritz** ISOS intercepts, 20.9.42, KV2 460.
128 **recognised his style** Reed notes on ISOS intercepts, KV2 456.
128 **GET MORRIS** Reed notes, KV2 456, and ISOS intercepts, 21.12.42, KV2 460.
129 **THANKS FOR** Reed notes, KV2 456.
129 **Zigzag's powers of** Reed report, KV2 458.
129 **the Germans had** Memo, KV2 456.
129 **gratuitous** Memo Masterman to Robertson, 17.12.42, KV2 455.
130 **a very good** Report, 19.12.42, KV2 455.
130 **It does seem** Robertson memo, 30.1.43., KV2 458.
130 **something queer was** Air ministry report, 7.2.43, KV2 458.
130 **They pandered to** Stephens report, 7.1.42, KV2 457.
131 **a dangerous criminal** Robertson briefing, 21.12.42, KV2 456.
131 **The success of this** to **stand his round** Ibid.
132 **who had looked** Note, KV2 456.
132 **permanent companions** Ibid.
132 **Conversation was strained** Backwell notes, KV2 458.
132 **settle in** to **a mine of information** Ibid.
133 **often speaks of** Backwell notes, KV2 456.
133 **what it was that** Tooth notes, KV2 456.
134 **In Germany he** to **I can only glean** Ibid.
134 **I think we should** Reed memo, 26.12.42, KV2 456.
135 **Running a team** Masterman, *The Double Cross System,* p. 90.
135 **I had, with my memories** Masterman, *On the Chariot Wheel,* p. 212.

136 **made defeat seem**   Ibid.
136 **the rabble of the universe**   Stephens report, 7.1.42, KV2 457.
136 **most fascinating case**   Ibid.
136 **what manner of man**   *Camp 020*, p. 105.
136 **PLEASE COME AT**   Reed report, KV2 456.
137 **We should know**   Reed report, 1.1.43, KV2 456.
137 **Eddie had moods**   Backwell notes, KV2 458.
138 **a method not calculated**   Reed memo 23.12.42, KV2 456.
138 **CALL AT 1000**   Reed report, 10.2.42, KV2 458.
138 **My God, I believe**   Reed report, 28.12.42, KV2 456.

14. What a Way Out

139 **He was non-judgemental**   Harmer, op. cit.
140 **From the fact**   Reed report, 28.12.42, KV2 456.
140 **undoubtedly have** to **They may forget**   Ibid.
140 **Message of 14 letters**   ISOS intercepts, 27.12.42, KV2 460.
140 **annoying**   Reed report, 28.12.42, KV2 456.
141 **Preparations should now**   Undated note, KV2 456.
141 **silly joking messages**   Marshall interrogation, 24.12.42, KV2 456.
141–2 **The men must** to **a little sinister**   Ibid.
142 **We should do all**   Masterman memo, 26.12.42, KV2 456.
142 **the principle of**   Masterman, *The Double Cross System*, p. 19.
142 **also conveyed**   Frank Ruskell, cited in *Short History of the DH98 Mosquito*, op. cit.
143 **He seemed more**   Backwell report, 30.12.42, KV2 456.
143 **would completely ruin**   Cover story narrative, KV2 459.
144 **FFFFF WENT DOWN**   Memo, KV2 456.
144 **PLEASE SEND SPECIFIC**   Reed report, 10.2.42, KV2 458.
144 **PLEASE GIVE NAME**   Memo 5.1.43, KV2 456.
144 **LANDED TWO MILES**   Ibid.
145 **well known and accepted**   Backwell notes, KV2 458.
145 **Eddie soon began** to **terribly restless**   Ibid.
145 **feelings of nihilism**   Tooth notes, KV2 456.
146 **His inherent boisterousness**   Reed report 15.3.43, KV2 459.
146 **quite impossible**   Minutes of meeting, 31.12.42, KV2 456.
146 **cloistered life**   Robertson report, 11.1.43, KV2 457.
146 **very pale**   Tooth notes, KV2 456.
146 **reference to secret**   Ibid.
146 **I have another**   Reed report, 1.1.43, KV2 456.
146–8 **Any individual enterprise** to **I believe he has**   Ibid.

15. Freda and Diane

149 **He wants to provide**   Backwell report, KV2 456.
149 **impossible**   Ibid.
149 **know of his existence**   Marshall report, 15.1.43, MI5 ref. 133B, KV2 457 (additional).
149 **Personal matters**   Backwell report, KV2 456.

149 **My sources of information** Handwritten note, accompanying Backwell note of 12.1.43, KV2 457 (additional).

149 **He feels his present** Backwell note, 12.1.43, KV2 457 (additional).

150 **The question of Freda** Ibid.

150 **if she bore any** Reed Report, 15.3.43, KV2 459. Document 254 B.

150–1 **truculent and moody** to **feminine relaxation** Ibid.

152 **Luckily there was** Backwell report, KV2 458.

152 **just back from abroad** Ibid.

152 **There was one** Ibid.

152 **cat-burglar** Marshall report, 7.1.43, KV2 457 (additional).

152 **slightly drunk** Tooth notes, 7.1.43, KV2 457 (additional).

152 **Hullo, stranger** to **some jocular remark** Ibid.

153 **The man apologised** Backwell report, KV2 458.

153 **I suppose it is natural** Reed report, 7.1.43, KV2 457 (additional).

153 **so far our inquiries** Reed memo, 13.1.43, KV2 457 (additional).

153 **it was not in the interests** Marshall report, 15.1.43, MI5 ref. 133B, KV2 457 (additional).

154 **talk to him about** Marshall report, 23.1.43, KV2 458.

154 **build up his morale** to **folly of expressing** Ibid.

155 **FFFFF DISGUSTED** Reed report, 15.3.43, KV2 459. Document 254 B.

155 **not to reap** Ibid.

155 **new arrangements** Ibid.

156 **Kalium** Interrogation by Rothschild, 2.1.43, KV2 456.

156 **This kept Eddie busy** Backwell notes, KV2 458.

156 **In this frame of mind** Reed report, 15.3.43, KV2 459. Document 254 B.

156 **tends to break down** Marshall report, 15.1.43., MI5 ref. 133B, KV2 457 (additional).

157 **serious and intimate** to **Do you consider** Ibid.

158 **a most valuable character** Reed handwritten note on ibid.

159 **He would now** Reed report, 1.1.43, KV2 456.

159 **part of the household** Backwell notes, KV2 458.

159 **quite content to limit** to **to get Freda up** Ibid.

159–60 **Eddie, we're on** to **Oh no, not just** Interview with Ronnie Reed, 1994, Nicholas Reed

160 **Freda must have** Backwell notes, KV2 458.

160 **Although she knew** Ibid.

160 **Since he has** Tooth notes, 26.1.43, KV2 458.

161 **his capacity to live** Tooth notes, KV2 456.

161 **would fulfil his** Ibid.

161 **Previously, he had** Tooth notes, 26.1.43, KV2 458.

161 **What a man!** Reed handwritten note on ibid.

161 **It is extraordinary** Reed report, 15.3.43, KV2 459. Document 254 B.

161 **this resolution provides** Ibid.

16. Abracadabra

164 **look, from the air** Charles Fraser-Smith, *The Secret War of Charles Fraser-Smith* (London, 1981), p. 121.

164 **danger that the** Masterman handwritten note on Reed memo, 7.1.43, KV2 457.

165 **vast hole** Fraser-Smith, op. cit.

165 **FFFFF WALTER READY** Reed report, 15.3.43, KV2 459.
166 **extremely difficult** Masterman memo, 27.1.43, KV2 458.
166 **publish a small paragraph** to **not having taken place** Ibid.
166 **meant him deliberately** Masterman memo, 27.1.43, KV2 458.
167 **the censors** Ibid.
167 **FFFFF ARRANGEMENTS** Reed report, KV2 458.
167 **to see if high** Colonel Sir John Turner memo, KV2 458.
167 **something had occurred** Reed memo, KV2 458.
168 **inky blackness** Reed report, 31.1.43, KV2 458.
168 **in a state of great** to **scene of destruction** Ibid
168 **masterpiece** *Fraser-Smith*, op. cit.
168 **FFFFF WALTER BLOWN** Reed report, 15.3.43, KV2 459. Document 254 B.
168 **champagne all round** Stephen report, 7.1.42, KV2 457.
168 **CONGRATULATIONS** Reed report, 15.3.43, KV2 459. Document 254 B.
169 **The Security Service** Robertson memo, 11.1.43, KV2 457.
170 **to depart in** Reed Report, 15.3.43, KV2 459. Document 254 B.
170 **vague** Ibid.
170 **to be immortalised** Ibid.
171 **declined to encourage** Masterman, *The Double Cross System*, p. 132.
171 **Perhaps we missed** Ibid.
171 **frank and straightforward** Reed report, 13.3.43, KV2 459.
171 **a man whose** Shanks report. 6.1.43, KV2 457.
171 **a spark of decency** to **whether a patriot or** Ibid.
172 **a refined manner** Marshall report, 15.1.43, MI5 ref. 133B, KV2 457 (additional).
172 **His natural and instinctive** Ibid.
172 **the bogus certainties** Malcolm Muggeridge, *Chronicles of Wasted Time*, vol. II, (London, 1979), p. 222.
172 **When one takes** Cited in Kenneth Rose, *Elusive Rothschild: The Life of Victor, Third Baron* (London, 2003), p. 67.
173 **I think it's terrific (ff)** Interrogation by Rothschild, 2.1.43, KV2 456.

17. The Greater the Adventure

175 **I consider you** Robertson report, 2.2.43, KV2 458.
175 **few, a very few** *Camp 020*, p. 176.
175 **far too valuable** Reed note, KV2 456.
176 **I am not at all** Robertson report, 2.2.43, KV2 458.
176 **people for whom** to **We are preparing** Ibid.
176 **Always speak slowly** Robertson (attrib.), report of SOE training course, KV4 172.
176 **procuring** *mental* Ibid.
176–7 **one with a brutal** Ibid.
177 **FFFFF PICK UP BY** Reed notes on ISOS intercepts, KV2 456.
177 **IMPOSSIBLE PICK** Reed report, 13.3.43., KV2 459.
177 **NORMAL** Ibid.
177 **The suggestion was** Reed report, 15.3.43, KV2 459. Document 254 B.
177 **any attempt to return** Ibid.
177 **not over-anxious** Reed report, 13.3.43, KV2 459.

177 **not prepared to offer**   Robertson memo, KV2 457.
177 **unenviable and practically**   Reed report, 13.3.43, KV2 459.
178 **provided the man**   Memo, KV2 457.
178 **Points I would**   Chapman undated note, KV2 458.
178 **in a position**   Marshall report, 2.2.43, KV2 456.
178 **Zigzag is fully**   Ibid.
179 **to get as much**   Ibid.
179 **paying for his stay**   Tooth notes, KV2 456.
179 **principle of generosity**   Masterman, *The Double Cross System*, p. 18.
179 **the risk to his**   Marshall report, 2.2.43, KV2 456.
179 **If Zigzag successfully** to **Substantial payment**   Ibid.
180 **It was almost**   Reed report, 15.3.43, KV2 459. Document 254 B.
180 **going rather too**   Reed memo, 10.2.43, KV2 458.
180 **After making such**   Reed report, 15.3.43, KV2 459. Document 254 B.
180 **FFFFF DANGEROUS TO**   Reed memo, 10.2.43, KV2 458.
181 **awkwardness** to **seen a chance**   Ibid.
181 **Gelignite Inquiries**   *Evening Standard*, 12.2.43.
181 **A man was questioned**   Ibid.
181 **185 names have**   *News Chronicle*, 10.2.43.
181 **FFFFF JIMMY**   Reed memo, 10.2.43, KV2 458.
181 **No further transmissions**   Ibid.
182 **absolutely inexcusable**   Reed report, 15.3.43, KV2 459. Document 254 B.
182 **to live as man**   Reed report, 8.2.43, KV2 458.
182 **Victor, do you**   Interrogation by Rothschild, 28.1.43, KV2 458.
182 **Freda returned home**   Backwell notes, KV2 458.
182 **unhesitatingly**   Ibid.
183 **What shoes**   Reed notes, 10.2.43, KV2 458.
183 **not shaken in**   Reed memo, 10.2.43, KV2 458.
183 **Poor Freddy Sampson**   Backwell notes, KV2 458.
183 **We can rely**   Reed report, 8.2.43, KV2 458.
184 **Blue starfish**   Reed report, 15.3.43, KV2 459. Document 254 B.
184 **AA guns camouflaged**   Ibid.
184 **picked up the**   Stephens notes, KV2 456.
184 **There is no information**   Robertson, 11.1.43, KV2 457.
184 **It is imperative**   Reed memo, 10.2.43, KV2 458.
185 **gloomy picture**   Reed report, 15.3.43, KV2 459. Document 254 B.
185 **a vast number** to **that the code in**   Ibid.
185 **instructions which**   Robertson note, KV2 457.
186 **In spite of the**   Backwell report, KV2 456.
186 **deep-seated liking**   Robertson memo, 11.1.43, KV2 457.
186 **You may see lots**   Interrogation by Rothschild, 28.1.43, KV2 458.
186 **Obviously if he were**   Reed report, 13.3.43, KV2 459.
186 **It all depends on**   Interrogation by Rothschild, 28.1.43, KV2 458.
186 **You will see that**   Reed report, 15.3.43, KV2 459. Document 254 B.
187 **genuinely inspired**   Robertson memo, 11.1.43, KV2 457.
187 **the excellent personal**   Ibid.
187 **He will be greeted**   Reed report, 8.2.43., KV2 458.
187 **Zigzag is confident** to **might possibly**   Ibid.
188 **Except in special**   Robertson memo, 11.1.43, KV2 457.
188 **The story of many**   Stephens report, 7.1.42, KV2 457.

18 Stowaway Spy

191 **a man who had** Reed report, 3.3.43, KV2 458.
191 **From now on this** ibid.
192 **impressed me as** ibid.
192 **lie low** Reed memo, 10.2.43, KV2 458.
192 **complete set of forged** Reed report, 3.3.43, KV2 458.
192 **vast and complicated** Reed report, 15.3.43, KV2 459. Document 254 B.
193 **This course** Reed report, 3.3.43, KV2 458.
193 **ham chat** Reed notes, KV2 458.
193 **please send with** to **suspicious** Ibid.
193 **The 'laughing out'** Reed report, 15.3.43, KV2 459. Document 254 B.
194 **We shall not have** Reed notes, KV2 458.
194 **Mrs West thanks** Reed report, 15.3.43, KV2 459. Document 254 B.
194 **that if any other** Ibid.
194 **It is Lew Leibich** Ibid.
195 **Goodbye for the present** Handwritten note to Marshall, 3.3.43, KV2 458.
195 **did not know what** Reed report, 3.3.43, KV2 458.
195–6 **in the approved** to **which he had coveted** Ibid.
196 **Zigzag is himself** Reed report, 15.3.43, KV2 459. Document 254 B.
197 **The case of Zigzag** Ibid.

19. Joli Albert

198 **fearing prying fingers** Reed report, 26.3.43, KV2 459.
198 **bad lad** Ibid.
198 **Nervous expectancy** *Chapman*, p. 137.
199 **Anson was seasick** Reed report, 18.4.43, KV2 461.
199 **no harm would** Reed report, 26.3.43, KV2 459.
199 **a high-class burglar** Major R.L. Brown report, 26.4.43, KV2 461.
200 **for pleasure** Ibid.
200 **Several members** Reed report, 26.3.43, KV2 459.
200 **The gunlayer summed** Ibid.
200 **Happy go lucky** Brown report, 26.4.43, KV2 461.
200 **He said he did** Extracts from ship's log, *City of Lancaster*, KV2 459.
201 **sort of international** Masterman, *The Case of the Four Friends*, (London, 1961), p. 19.
201 **Pay no attention** Major R.L. Brown report, 26.4.43, KV2 461.
201 **If I find this** Ibid.
201 **No names** Ibid.
201 **'brûlé'** Reed report, 15.3.43, KV2 459. Document 254 B.
202 ***Joli Albert*** Camp 020 report, 11.7.44, KV2 459.
202 **blank faces** Stephens report, 29.6.44, KV2 459.
202 **'telephone'** Camp 020 report, 11.7.44, KV2 459.
202 **did not know** Ibid.
202 **forget the whole** Ibid.
203 **mind his own** Extracts from ship's log, *City of Lancaster*, KV2 459.
203 **any future offence** Ibid.
203 **He instructed me** Reed report, 26.3.43, KV2 459.
204 **apologised for the** Camp 020 report, 11.7.44, KV2 459.

204 'connected with Johnny' Stephens report, 29.6.44, KV2 459.
205 contravened the ISOS intercept, 27.5.45, KV2 459.
205 told the Germans Memo, 23.3.43, KV2 459.
205 not to interrupt Report of meeting, 22.3.43, KV2 459.
205 Whatever view we Ibid.
206 acquainted with the Ibid.
206 brought back in irons Ibid.
206 It would be quite Ibid.
206 a small aperture Memo, undated, KV2 459.
207 could not possibly Ibid.
208 the Queensberry rules Extracts from ship's log, *City of Lancaster*, KV2 459.
208 Have you met Ibid.
208 trying to get a Reed report, 26.3.43, KV2 459.
268-9 he had put to to in order to send Ibid.
210 Convinced Z playing Telegram, KV2 459.
210 This is typical of Stephens report, 27.6.43, KV2 460.
210 with possibly fatal Ibid.
210 He thought that Ibid.
210 politically complicated Reed report, 26.3.43, KV2 459.
210 It would be most Ibid.
211 I come from Ronnie Rothschild memo, 28.3.43, KV2 461.
211 if possible intact Ibid.

20. Damp Squib

212 Are you Fritz? Camp 020 report, 11.7.44, KV2 459.
212 other articles difficult Ibid.
213 in disgrace Ibid.
213 old friend Major Michael Ryde report, 24.10.44, KV2 460.
213 about 50 Camp 020 report, 11.7.44, KV2 459.
213-14 vague replies to advance Ibid.
214 Timing is the essential Robertson (attrib.), report of SOE training course, KV4 172.
214 I landed at about Reed report, 15.3.43, KV2 459. Document 254 B.
218 The life of a secret Masterman, *The Double Cross System*, p. 32.
218 would bring him Camp 020 report, 11.7.44, KV2 459.
218 reserve the more Ibid.
219 I had two suitcases *Chapman*, p. 158.
220 certainly raised his Camp 020 report, 11.7.44, KV2 459.
220 The Germans have shown Masterman memo, 18.4.43, KV2 461.
220 There must either Montagu memo, 18.4.43, KV2 461.
220 perfectly good Rothschild memo, 25.4.43, KV2 461.
220 as big a bang Ibid.
220 A good decent bang Ibid.
220 who will previously Rothschild, 'Plan Damp Squib', KV2 461.
220-1 fall down and pretend to The story of the sabotage Ibid.
221 sharp explosion Letter, Colonel Leslie Wood to Rothschild, KV2 461.
221 Herewith your three toys Ibid.
221 binding up a notional Masterman, handwritten note attached to Rothschild, 'Plan Damp Squib', KV2 461.

221 **When the** *City of Lancaster* Masterman memo, KV2 461.
222 **as each piece** Brown report, 26.4.43, KV2 461.
222 **who was very dirty** Reed report, 26.4.43, KV2 461.
222 **holding in his hand** Ibid.
222 **swanking** Brown report, 26.4.43, KV2 461.
222 **beyond his station** Ibid.
222 **The standard of** Reed report, 26.4.43, KV2 461
222 **infernal machine** Ibid.
222 **a spur to rumour** Rothschild, 'Plan Damp Squib', KV2 461.
222 **Approximately 50 people** Memo, 26.4.43, KV2 461.
222 **He has no objection** Reed report, 26.4.43, KV2 461.
223 **discussed Zigzag at** Duff Cooper to Dick White, 5.5.43, KV2 459.
223 **if and when contact** Ibid.
223 **comprehensive memoranda** Rothschild memo, 6.12.43, KV2 461.
223 **I promised Mr Hoover** Ibid.

21. The Ice Front

224 **deeply affected** Interview with Ingeborg von Gröning, Bremen, 22.05.06.
224 **Thank God you** *Chapman,* p. 161.
224 **the old man** Ryde report 24.10.44, KV2 460.
225 **enjoy a well-earned** Camp 020 report, 11.7.44, KV2 459.
225 **bachelor flat** to **companion** Ibid.
226 **pathetically grateful** *Chapman,* p.164.
226 **proud of his protégé** Camp 020 report, 11.7.44, KV2 459.
226 **best security** Ryde report, 24.10.44, KV2 460.
226 **man who had** Camp 020 report, 11.7.44, KV2 459.
226 **Absolute personal** Masterman, *The Double Cross System,* p. 187.
227 **better for selfish** Ibid., p. 72.
227 **watchful** Interview with Ingeborg von Gröning, Bremen, 22.05.06.
227 **Stephan made up** Ibid.
227 **as and when he** Camp 020 report, 11.7.44, KV2 459.
228 **If they will not** Olav Riste and Berit Nökleby, *Norway 1940–45: The Resistance Movement* (Oslo, 2004), p. 51.
229 **It was an uneasy** *Chapman,* p. 171.
229 **wall of hatred** Ibid.
229 **appeared somewhat** Camp 020 report, 11.7.44, KV2 459.
229 **complete freedom** Stephens report, 29.6.44, KV2 459.
230 **not to work** Camp 020 report, 11.7.44, KV2 459.
230 **battle against the** *Chapman,* p. 172.
230 **hero complex** Ibid.
230 **companion** Camp 020 report, 11.7.44, KV2 459.
230 **the only successful** Rothschild interview with Agent JIGGER (Von Schoenich), Paris, 8.11.44, KV2 460.
230–1 **controlled by the** to **one of those** Ibid.
231 **beaming with pleasure** *Chapman,* p. 174.
231 **good work in England** Camp 020 report 11.7.44, KV2 459.
231 **in notes** to **draw on it when** Ibid.
231–2 **solemnly** to **If I stay with** *Chapman,* p. 175.
232 **You are free** Camp 020 report, 11.7.44, KV2 459.

232–2 **Go yachting** to **to buy a boat**   Ibid.
  233 **enhance his stock**   Camp 020 report, 11.7.44, KV2 459.
  234 **truly brave**   *Chapman*, p. 171.
  234 *Bitte schön*   Ibid., p. 176.
  234 **most attractive**   Ibid.

22. The Girl at the Ritz

  235 **She was young**   Interview with Bibbi Røset, Oslo, 15.6.06.
  235 **She wanted to**   Ibid.
  235 **wanted adventure**   Ibid.
  236 **beautiful and adorable**   Camp 020 report, 11.7.44, KV2 459.
  237 **Because she had**   Interview with Bibbi Røset, Oslo, 15.6.06.
  237 **fancied slight**   Camp 020 report, 11.7.44, KV2 459.
  237 **anti-Quisling**   *Chapman*, p. 177.
  237 **Nazi's tart**   Interview with Bibbi Røset, Oslo, 15.6.06.
  237 **hawk-like**   *Chapman*, p. 178.
  237 **some kind of psychologist**   Stephens report, 29.6.44, KV2 459.
  237 **with a view to**   Camp 020 report, 11.7.44, KV2 459.
  237 **Where could you (ff)**   Ibid.
  238 **I myself expect**   Ibid.
  238 **uncomfortable moment**   Stephens report, 29.6.44, KV2 459.
  238 **periodically asking**   Ibid.
  238 **benign**   *Chapman*, p. 179.
  239 **You are not**   Camp 020 report 11.7.44, KV2 459.
  239 **I know I am not**   Ibid.
  239 **The doctor was**   Ibid.
  239 **I think you are**   *Chapman*, p. 180.
  239 **Leave it to**   Ibid.
  240 **It is the work**   Camp 020 report, 11.7.44, KV2 459.
  240 **kept woman**   Ibid.
  240 **sufficient money**   Ibid.
  240 **pocketed the balance**   Ryde report, 24.10.44, KV2 460.
  241 **help himself**   Ibid.
  241 **It was a delightful**   *Chapman*, p. 196.
  242 **they were fair**   Interview with Leife Myhre, Oslo, 16.6.06.
  242 **They were in** to **I am not working**   Ibid.
  243 **certain people**   Camp 020 report, 11.7.44, KV2 459.
  243 **applied himself** to **disgusted with the**   Ibid.
  244 **It all depends**   Interrogation by Rothschild, 28.1.43, KV2 458.
  245 **under the influence**   Camp 020 report, 11.7.44, KV2 459.
  245 **Nazi whore**   Interview with Bibbi Røset, Oslo, 15.6.06.
  245 **he risked losing**   Camp 020 report, 11.7.44, KV2 459.
245–7 **details of Chapman's** to **she intimated**   Ibid.

23. Sabotage Consultant

  248 **new sabotage work**   Camp 020 report, 11.7.44, KV2 459.
248–50 **did not consider** to **extremely high**   Ibid.

251 **the address of an** Stephens report, 29.6.44, KV2 459.
251 **continually stared at him** Camp 020 report, 11.7.44, KV2 459.
251 **x–ray apparatus** Ibid.
251 **picked up by five seaplanes** Stephens report, 29.6.44, KV2 459.
251 **the use of a compass** Camp 020 report, 11.7.44, KV2 459.
251–2 **Chapman was just to each wanting their part** Ibid.
252 **kind of honorary** Masterman, *The Double Cross System*, p. 171.
252 **more interested in** *Camp 020*, p. 350.
253 **touring Germany** Camp 020 report, 11.7.44, KV2 459.
254 **useful background for** Ryde report, 27.7.44, KV2 460.
254 **Hitler is by no means** Stephens report, 29.6.44, KV2 459.
254 **It is entirely to aired his anti-Hitler** Ibid.
254 **knew he would one** Camp 020 report, 11.7.44, KV2 459.
255 **keep her eyes and** Ibid.
255 **trust nobody unless** Ibid.
255 **mind their own** Interview with Bibbi Røset, Oslo, 15.6.06.
255 **Mrs Gossips** Ibid.
256 **double transposition** Camp 020 report, 11.7.44, KV2 459.
256 **Liverpool, Leeds or** Reed memo, 7.7.44, KV2 459.
256 **If the message does** Ibid.

24. Lunch at the Lutétia

257 **provide a cover address** ISOS intercept, 15.12.44., KV2 459
257 **whose appearance and** *Camp 020*, p. 298.
258 **into the wastelands** Ibid.
258 **guttural protestations** Ibid.
258 **unsubtle retainers** Ibid., p. 299.
258 **worried still about** Ibid.
258 **mysterious figure** Masterman, *The Double Cross System*, p. 171.
258 **an old friend** Ibid.
259 **The whole city** Camp 020 report, 11.7.44, KV2 459.
259 **resignation and misery** Ibid.
259 **locate our night** Camp 020 report, 11.7.44, KV2 459.
259–60 **Cossors of Hammersmith to made no secret of** Ibid.
260 **converting much of** Stephens report, 29.6.44, KV2 459.
260 **If their weapons are to Life under the Germans** Ibid.
261 **owing to the danger** Camp 020 report, 11.7.44, KV2 459.
261 **if he landed in England to astute in posing** Ibid.
261 **Is he working** *News of the World*, 25.10.53.
261 **How the hell** Ibid.
262 **If and when I come** *Faramus*, p. 93.
262 **approximately six months** Ibid., p. 100.
262 **an extermination camp** Ibid., p.136.
262 **All the time** Ibid., p.82.
263 **to think furiously** Camp 020 report, 11.7.44, KV2 459.
263 **knowing** *Chapman*, p. 241.
263 **having a good time** Camp 020 report, 11.7.44, KV2 459.
263 **any uniform he liked** Stephens report, 29.6.44, KV2 459.
263 **for the shelling of** Camp 020 report, 11.7.44, KV2 459.

264 dimples Stephens report, 29.6.44, KV2 459.
264 never leave Ibid.
264 fall to bits Cited in obituary of Erich Vermehren de Saventhem by Richard Bassett, *Independent*, 3.5.05.
264 excess of brandy *Chapman*, p. 237.
264 Terrible devastation will Camp 020 report, 11.7.44, KV2 459.
265 slight Ibid.
265 few casualties Ibid
265 a flop Report, 13.7.44, KV2 460.
265 at Chapman's disposal Camp 020 report, 11.7.44, KV2 459.
266 harmless chatter Ibid.
267 unreal *News of the World*, 1.11.53.
267 two bottles of cognac Camp 020 report, 11.7.44, KV2 459.
267 a profound effect *News of the World*, 1.11.53.
267 triumph Ibid.
267 half-smile *News of the World*, 25.10.53.
267 The last glimpse *Chapman*, p. 244.

25. The Prodigal Crook

268 out of the direct *News of the World*, 1.11.54.
269 Peeved Camp 020 report, 11.7.44, KV2 459.
269 Don't be silly Ibid.
269 That's exactly what *News of the World*, 1.11.53.
270 It's Eddie Interview with Ronnie Reed, 1994, Nicholas Reed.
270 whether operation possible ISOS intercept, 10.6.44, KV2 459.
270 a wiry type Memo, 25.9.44, KV2 460.
270 expansive in his conceit *Camp 020*, p. 224.
270 splendid time Memo, 28.6.44, KV2 459.
270 The courageous and Stephens in Camp 020 report, 11.7.44, KV2 459.
270 tired beyond the point Camp 020 report, 11.7.44, KV2 459.
270 moral degenerate *Camp 020*, p. 218.
270 The outstanding feature Stephens in Camp 020 report, 11.7.44, KV2 459.
271 greeted as a returned Milmo memo, 29.6.44, KV2 459.
271 back safely, and Interview with Ronnie Reed, 1994, Nicholas Reed
271 purposely put ashore Camp 020 report, 11.7.44, KV2 459.
271 mentally quite fit Dearden, cited in Stephens report, 29.6.44, KV2 459.
272 All the evidence appears Reed memo, 28.6.44, KV2 459.
272 it would be a first-rate Stephens in Camp 020 report, 11.7.44, KV2 459.
272 I think this goes far Ibid.
272 The only safe place Memo, 10.7.44, KV2 459.
272 a man whom they Reed memo, 28.6.44, KV2 459.
273 escape Thaddeus Holt, *The Deceivers: Allied Military Deception in the Second World War* (London, 2004), p. 853.
273 money and a Leica Reed report, 28.6.43, KV2 459.
273 Zigzag will be given Milmo memo, 1.8.44, KV2 460.
273 Although no one thinks Milmo memo, 28.6.44, KV2 459.
273 It must always be Memo, 29.6.44, KV2 459.
274 a very able man Camp 020 Report, 11.7.44, KV2 459.
274 a form of insurance Stephens Report, 29.6.44, KV2 459.
274 Chapman is a difficult Camp 020 Report, 11.7.44, KV2 459.

274 **quite convinced that** Ryde, memo of meeting, 14. 8. 44, KV2 460.
274 **Although we do not** Milmo memo, 28.6.44, KV2 459.
274 **the inevitable girlfriend** Camp 020 report, 11.7.44, KV2 459.
275 **blundered badly** Stephens report, 29.6.44, KV2 459.
275 **She is not a** Camp 020 report, 11.7.44, KV2 459.
275 **he would have at to One of his objects** Ibid.
275 **There was some sort** Marriott memo, 29.7.43, KV2 459.
276 **Dagmar is in contact** Camp 020 report, 11.7.44, KV2 459.
276 **I do not wish to be held** Stephens in Camp 020 report, 11.7.44, KV2 459.
276 **one of the most** Stephens report, 29.6.44, KV2 459.
277 **HARD LANDING BUT** Ibid.

26. Doodlebugs

279 **It was clear that** Masterman, *The Double Cross System*, p. 179.
279 **If St Paul's was hit** Ibid.
279 **decide what measure** Ibid.
279 **learned to live** Michael Howard, *Strategic Deception in the Second World War* (London, 1995), p. 178.
280 **terrible responsibility** to **I am certain you** Ibid.
280 **his German masters** Reed memo, 28.6.44, KV2 459.
280 **should report actual** Masterman, *The Double Cross System*, p. 181.
281 **We could give correct** Ibid.
281 **reduce the average range** Ibid.
281 **It is essential** Memo, KV2 460.
281 **I am afraid we** Note from Air Ministry, 29.8.44, KV2 460.
281 **slight errors introduced** J.A. Drew memo, 11.7.44, KV2 459.
282 **The outgoing traffic** Ryde report, 26.7.44, KV2 460.
282 **The Zigzag channel** Ryde to Robertson, 13.9.44, KV2 460.
282 **held his place** Masterman, *The Double Cross System*, p. 172.
282 **I was as frightened** Masterman, *Chariot Wheel* p. 212.
283 **secret equipment for** Memo, 1.8.44, KV2 460.
283 **tapping out such** Ryde, memo of meeting, 14.8.44, KV2 460.
283 **If this state of affairs** Ibid.
283 **Take your pick!** Interview with Ronnie Reed, 1994, Nicholas Reed.
283 **I do feel his exploits** Marriott memo, 29.7.43, KV2 459.
283 **I agree** Ibid.
283 **desired that no such** Sir Alexander Maxwell memo, 15.7.44, KV2 460.
283 **No action should** D.I. Wilson note, with ibid.
284 **comb out any German** Ryde, memo of meeting, 14.8.44, KV2 460.
284 **Any question of Zigzag's** Ibid.
284 **anxious to write to Freda** Stephens report, 29.6.44, KV2 459.
284 **very busy and would** Ibid.
284 **autobiography** Ryde memo, 26.7.44, KV2 460.
284 **impossible for him** Ryde memo 6.8.44, KV2 460.
284 **while it was still fresh** Ryde memo, 26.7.44, KV2 460.
284 **his old criminal activities** Ibid.
284 **stimulate Zigzag's interest** Ryde, memo of meeting, 14.8.44, KV2 460.
284 **deceptive material about** Memo, 1.8.44, KV2 460.
284 **in continual active** Ibid.

284 **steal a document** Ibid.
285 **the increasing number** Montagu, op. cit., p. 114.
285 **careless talk by** Ibid.
285 **While we should not** Ibid., p. 124.
286 **After passing the** Ibid., p. 125.
286 **all secret manufacture** Memo, 1.8.44, KV2 460.
286 **worth keeping sweet** Ryde memo, 6.8.44, KV2 460.
286 **wonderful experience** Interview with Ronnie Reed, 1994, Nicholas Reed

27. Going to the Dogs

288 **disagreeably surprised** Camp 020 report, 11.7.44, KV2 459.
288 **with some apprehension** Ibid.
288 **I have spent a good** Ryde report, 24.8.44, KV2 460.
289 **most discontented at** Ryde memo, 8.8.44, KV2 460.
289 **He has been keeping** *Camp 020*, p. 225.
289 **always in the company** Ibid.
289 **The Zigzag case must** Ryde, memo of meeting, 14.8.44, KV2 460.
289 **the way his case** Robertson memo, 15.8.44, KV2 460.
289 **did not seem** Ibid.
289 **He is quite clearly** Ibid.
290 **a suitable person** Memo, 1.8.44, KV2 460.
290 **the friends he hoped** Ibid.
290 **in a French letter** Montagu, op. cit., p. 126
290 **After they had received** Ibid.
291 **Dear Fleming** Fake letter from A.B. Wood, KV2 460.
291 **We never found out** Montagu, op. cit., p. 126.
291 **I do not myself** Ryde to Robertson, 13.9.44, KV2 460.
292 **not quite reliable** ISOS intercept, 25.9.44, KV2 460.
292 **dubious about Zigzag's integrity** Ryde to Robertson, 13.9.44, KV2 460.
292 **The messages sent** Ibid.
292 **Zigzag is liable** Memo, 1.8.44, KV2 460.
292 **It is unlikely that his** Ibid.
293 **Zigzag himself is** Ryde memo, 6.8.44, KV2 460.
293 **making quite large** Ibid.
293 **To take advantage** Ibid.
293 **served his purpose** Robertson memo, 15.8.44, KV2 460.
293 **done an extremely good** Ibid.
293 **by giving him** Ibid.
293 **if he could put up** Ryde memo, 6.8.44, KV2 460.
294 **waste of money** to **It is obvious that we** Ibid.
294 **if we no longer require** Ryde, memo of meeting, 14.8.44, KV2 460.
294 **I have seen Zigzag** Ryde to Robertson, 13.9.44, KV2 460.
295 **I am able to curb these** Ibid.
295 **The war may end** Ryde report, 24.8.44, KV2 460.
295 **the necessity of closing** Ryde, memo of meeting, 14.8.44, KV2 460.
295 **It is becoming increasingly** Ryde to Robertson, 13.9.44, KV2 460.
292 **Try to get latest editions** ISOS intercept, 4.9.44, KV2 460.
292 **General report great** Ibid.
292 **radio controlled rocket** Stephens Report, 29.6.44, KV2 459.

295 **Continue giving data** ISOS intercept, 4.9.44, KV2 460.
296 **Heard many rumours** Message sent 14.9.44, KV2 460.
297 **WAR SITUATION NEED NOT** ISOS intercept, 28.8.44, KV2 460.

28. Case Dismissed

298 **SORRY YOUR BAD** Ryde report, 24.8.44, KV2 460.
298 **has a post-war plan** to **get the Germans to lay** Ibid.
299 **a collection of words** Montagu memo, 29.8.44, KV2 460.
299 **The Germans have told** Ibid.
299 **German knowledge is** Ibid.
299 **we should out of our** Ryde memo, 6.8.44, KV2 460.
299 **I still maintain that we are** Ryde, memo of meeting, 14.8.44, KV2 460.
299 **settlement of our** Ibid.
299 **dealt with fairly (ff)** Ryde report, 24.8.44, KV2 460.
300 **at least £6,300** Ryde to Robertson, 13.9.44, KV2 460.
300 **reliable sailor** Ryde report, 19.9.44, KV2 460.
300 **Such promises are** Ryde to Robertson, 13.9.44, KV2 460.
300 **I think it would be** Ryde report, 19.9.44, KV2 460.
301 **Zigzag has always** Ryde report, 24.10.44, KV2 460.
301–4 **whether the Germans** to **As far as the Germans** Ibid.
305 **My feeling** Masterman, handwritten note on ibid.
305 **We should close it now** Ibid.
305 **I understand that** Signed copy of Official Secrets Act, 2.11.44, KV2 461.
305 **as forcibly as possible** Ryde report, 24.10.44, KV2 460.
305 **He must understand** Ibid.
306 **Zigzag should be thankful** Ibid.
306 **Fiction has not** *Camp 020*, p. 217.
306 **hard character with** *Sunday Chronicle*, 24.7.54.
307 **Uppermost in my mind** Eddie Chapman, *Free Agent*, p. 11.
307 **Is there anyone** Interview with Betty Chapman, 25.11.05
307 **That girl** Eddie Chapman, *Free Agent*, p. 12
307 **Jesus!** Ibid.
308 **I shall go** Interview with Betty Chapman, 25.11.05.

Aftermath

309 **real genius** Cited in Wilson, op. cit.
309 **one of the greatest** Masterman, *On the Chariot Wheel*, p. 219.
309 **Blessed are they** Address by Christopher Harmer at memorial service for T.A. Robertson at Pershore Abbey.
310 **To work out the crime** Masterman, *The Case of the Four Friends*, p. 14.
310 **Everything which is good** Masterman, *On the Chariot Wheel*, p. 371.
310 **How strange it was** Ibid., p. 361.
311 **I am not, and never** *Daily Telegraph*, 4.12.86.
312 **Sean Connery was simply** Lois Maxwell (Miss Moneypenny), cited in Wikipedia.
312 **drifting on a wreck** Lloyd's Register of Captains, National Maritime Museum.

312 **giant of evil** *Camp 020*, p. 22.

313 **degenerates, most of them** FO 371/70830 paper CG 2290/G, cited by Hoare in *Camp 020*, p. 8.

313 **loyal to his own class** Interview with Ingeborg von Gröning, Bremen, 22.05.06.

313 **invariably foul** FO 371/70830 paper CG 2290/G.

313 **had a long and possibly** *Camp 020*, p. 72.

314 **awkward** *Faramus*, p. 177.

314 **I thought you were dead (ff)** Ibid.

314 **Millions died without** Eddie Chapman's foreword to Ibid., p. 7.

315 **German tart** Interview with Bibbi Røset, Oslo, 15.6.06.

315 **Mrs Gossips** Ibid.

315 **she was always** Ibid.

316 **what will happen when** *Camp 020*, p. 226.

317 **senior officer of the** *Evening Standard*, 13.10.48.

317 **one of the bravest men** Ibid.

317 **I was trained in** *Daily Telegraph*, 10.10.74.

317 **honorary crime** *The Times*, obituary of Eddie Chapman, 26.12.97.

317 **I do a bit** *Daily Express*, 'The Sentimenal Screwsman', 21.10.60.

317 **Sometimes in life** Masterman, *Chariot Wheel*, p. 361.

318 **What is the truth** *News of the World*, 'A Traitor or a Hero?', 10.1.54.

318 **A lot of water** Chapman to Von Gröning, 1.11.74, courtesy of Ingeborg von Gröning.

319 **They were like** Interview with Betty Chapman, 25.11.05.

ACKNOWLEDGEMENTS

Dozens of people in five countries have generously contributed to the writing of this book, with research help, interviews, advice, and access to photographs, documents and memories. In Britain, I am indebted to Betty Chapman, Tony Faramus, Howard Davies and Hugh Alexander at the National Archives, Mary Teviot for her splendid genealogical sleuthing; Professor M.R.D Foot and Calder Walton for their invaluable historical expertise; Major A.J. Edwards and the late Colonel Tony Williams at the Military Intelligence Museum archive; Caroline Lamb at the Liddell Hart Centre for military archives; Dunia Garcia-Ontiveros at the National Maritime Museum; George Malcolmson, Royal Navy Submarine Museum; David Capus, Metropolitan Police Service Records Management Branch. Andrea and Edward Ryde, Sophia and Charles Kitson, Margery Barrie, Carolyn Elton, Nicholas Reed and Charles Chilton all helped me to build up a more complete picture of the various case officers. In Jersey, I am grateful to Steven Guy-Gibbens, Governor HM Prison La Moye, and Paul Matthews, Deputy Judicial Greffier, for granting me access to closed prison, police and judicial records; to Linda Romeril and Stuart Nicolle at the Jersey Historical Archives, and Jan Hadley and John Guegan of the Jersey *Evening Post*. In Norway, Alf Magnussen of *Aftenposten* was supremely helpful in tracking down memories of Dagmar through Bibbi Røset, Leife Myhre and Harald Næss (who kindly allowed me to destroy part of his roof with a crowbar in the search for

Chapman's concealed film). In America, Anne Cameron Berlin carried out useful preliminary research in the US National Archives. In Germany, I am grateful to Peter Steinkamp for his work at the Bundesarchiv-Militärarchiv in Freiburg, and to Petra and Ingeborg von Gröning for their hospitality and help. I am also grateful to Georges and Caroline Paruit, the owners of La Bretonnière in Nantes.

For a secretive organisation, MI5 has been a model of openness: not only providing access to hitherto classified files, but assisting in the search for additional material. To the other individuals who prefer not to be named: you know who you are, and how grateful I am.

Robert Thomson, Keith Blackmore, Anne Spackman, Bob Kirwin, Daniel Finkelstein and all my colleagues on *The Times* have been supportive and tolerant, and occasionally both; Michael Evans was typically generous with his expertise. Denise Reeves performed several miracles of picture research.

Michael Fishwick and Trâm-Anh Doan of Bloomsbury have been the most delightful and expert collaborators, and Kate Johnson's work on the manuscript was, as usual, superb, saving me from a multitude of embarrassments. All remaining errors are entirely the result of my own intransigence.

Finally my thanks and love to Kate Muir, as always, for her support, patience, and fine editorial judgement. This book is dedicated to her.

SELECT BIBLIOGRAPHY

Archives:
National Archives, Kew
National Martime Museum, Greenwich
undesarchiv-Militärarchiv, Freiburg
National Archives, Washington DC
British Library Newspaper Archive, Colindale
Jersey Historical Archives
Jersey Newspaper Archives, St Helier
Jersey Judicial Archives

Printed Sources:

Andrew, C., Secret *Service: The Making of the British Intelligence Community* (London, 1985)

Bennett, R., *Behind the Battle: Intelligence in the War with Germany 1939-45* (London, 1999)

Carter, M., *Anthony Blunt: His Lives* (London, 2001)

Chapman, Edward, *The Eddie Chapman Story;* foreword by Frank Owens (London, 1953)

———*Free Agent: The Further Adventures of Eddie Chapman* (London, 1955)

———*The Real Eddie Chapman Story* (London, 1966)

Curry, J., *The Security Service 1908-1945: The Official History* (London, 1999)

Farago, Ladislas, *The Game of the Foxes: The Untold Story of German Espionage in the US and Great Britain During World War Two* (New York, London, 1972)

Faramus, Anthony Charles, *The Faramus Story* (London, no edition or year stated)

――――*Journey into Darkness: A True Story of Human Endurance* (London, 1990)

Foot, M.R.D., SOE: *The Special Operations Executive 1940–1946* (London, 1999)

Harris, Tomas, *Garbo: The Spy Who Saved D-Day;* Introduction by Mark Seaman (London, 2004)

Haufler, Hervie, *The Spies Who Never Were: The True Stories of the Nazi Spies Who Were Actually Double Agents* (New York, 2006)

Hesketh, R., *Fortitude: The D-Day Deception Campaign* (London, 1999)

Hinsley, F.H., *British Intelligence in the Second World War: Its Influence on Strategy and Operations* (London, 1979), Vol I.

Hinsley, F.H. and Simkins, C.A.G., *British Intelligence in the Second World War: Security and Counter-Intelligence* (London, 1990), Vol. IV.

Holt, Thaddeus, *The Deceivers: Allied Military Deception in the Second World War* (London, 2004)

Michael Howard, *Strategic Deception in the Second World War* (London, 1995)

Kahn, David, *Hitler's Spies: German Military Intelligence in World War II* (New York, 2000)

Knightley, Philip, *The Second Oldest Profession* (London 1986)

Liddell, G., *The Guy Liddell Diaries, 1939-1945,* Volumes I and II (ed. Nigel West) (London, 2005)

Macksey, Kenneth, *The Searchers: Radio Intercept in Two World Wars* (London, 2003)

Masterman, J.C., *The Double Cross System in the War 1939–1945* (London, 1972)

――――*On the Chariot Wheel: An Autobiography* (Oxford, 1975)

Miller, Russell, *Codename Tricycle: The True Story of the Second World War's Most Extraordinary Double Agent* (London, 2005)

Montagu, Ewen, *Beyond Top Secret Ultra* (London 1977)

――――*The Man Who Never Was* (Oxford, 1996)

Paine, Lauran, *The Abwehr: German Military Intelligence in World War II* (London, 1984)

Popov, Dusko, *Spy/Counterspy* (New York, 1974)

Rose, Kenneth, *Elusive Rothschild: The Life of Victor, Third Baron* (London, 2003)

Sebag-Montefiore, Hugh, *Enigma: The Battle for the Code* (London, 2000)

Schenk, P., *Invasion of England 1940: The Planning of Operation Sealion* (London, 1990)

Stephens, R. 'Tin Eye', *Camp 020: MI5 and the Nazi Spies;* Introduction by Oliver Hoare (London, 2000)

Stevenson, William, *A Man Called Intrepid: the Secret War of 1939–45* (London, 1976)

Waller, John H., *The Unseen War in Europe: Espionage and Conspiracy in the Second World War* (New York, London, 1996)

West, Nigel, *MI5: British Security Service Operations 1909-45* (London, 1981)

Wilson, Emily Jane, *The War in the Dark: The Security Service and the Abwehr 1940–1944*, PhD thesis (Cambridge, 2003)

Winterbotham, F.W., *The Ultra Secret* (London, 1974)

PICTURE CREDITS

Plate sections

Eddie Chapman, 16 December 1942. (*KV2 462*, © *the National Archives*)

Chapman at Camp 020. (*KV2 462*, © *the National Archives*)

Chapman eating Christmas dinner, 1942. (*KV2 462*, © *the National Archives*)

Chapman during Christmas dinner, 1942. (*KV2 462*, © *the National Archives*)

An Irish identity pass for Chapman created by Nazi forgers. (*KV2 462*, © *the National Archives*)

Jersey under Occupation. (© *Popperfoto*)

Norway under Occupation. (© *Fox photos/Getty Images*)

The entrance to Fort de Romainville. (*From the collection of Anthony Faramus, in* Journey into Darkness, *Grafton Books, 1990*)

Faramus at Mauthausen–Gusen death camp. (*From the collection of Anthony Faramus, in* Journey into Darkness, *Grafton Books, 1990*)

Faramus as a POW in *The Colditz Story*. (*From the collection of Anthony Faramus, in* Journey into Darkness, *Grafton Books, 1990*)

The Mosquito bomber under construction at the De Havilland aircraft factory. (© The Times)

A Mosquito being prepared for a bombing run over Germany. (© The Times)

The De Havilland aircraft factory. (*KV2 457*, © *the National Archives*)

The faked sabotage of the De Havilland plant. (*KV2 458*, © *the National Archives*)

The *City of Lancaster*. (© *National Maritime Museum*)

The coal bomb constructed by Nazi engineers. (*KV461*, © *the National Archives*)

An X-ray of the coal bomb. (*KV2 461*, © *the National Archives*)

The doctored photograph for the Operation Squid deception. (*KV2 460*, © *the National Archives*)

Rittmeister Stephan von Gröning (alias Doctor Graumann). (*Courtesy of Ingeborg von Gröning*)

Stephan von Gröning as a young officer. (*Courtesy of Ingeborg von Gröning*)

Oberleutnant Walter Praetorius. (© *the National Archives*)

Franz Stoetzner (alias Franz Schmidt). (*Courtesy of MI5*)

Karl Barton (alias Hermann Wojch). (*Courtesy of MI5*)

Colonel Robin 'Tin Eye' Stephens. (© *BBC*)

Victor, Lord Rothschild. (© *Topfoto*)

John Cecil Masterman. (*National Portrait Gallery, London*)

Jasper Maskelyne. (© *British Library, London*)

Major Ronnie Reed. (*Courtesy of Nicholas Reed*)

Reed operating Chapman's German radio set. (*Courtesy of Nicholas Reed*)

Dagmar Lahlum. (*Courtesy of Bibbi Røset*)

Freda Stevenson with baby Diane. (*KV2 462*, © *the National Archives*)

Betty Farmer. (© *News International Syndication*)

Graffiti in the attic at La Bretonnière. (*Author's collection*)

Hitler caricatured as a carrot in the attic at La Bretonnière. (*Author's collection*)

La Bretonnière, 1942. (*Courtesy of Ingeborg von Gröning*)

Chapman after his return to Britain in 1944. (© *News International Syndication*)

Chapman in a West End drinking den. (© *News International Syndication*)

Chapman protesting in 1953 after his attempts to serialise his memoirs in a newspaper were stymied under the Official Secrets Act. (© *Topham/AP*)

Chapman in full SS uniform. (© *Popperfoto.com*)

The Iron Cross. (*Courtesy of Nicholas Reed, photo by Richard Pohle*)

Chapman posing with his Rolls-Royce. (© Daily Telegraph)

Images in the text

INDEX

DOUBLE CROSS
THE TRUE STORY OF THE D-DAY SPIES

D-Day, 6 June 1944, the turning point of the Second World War, was a victory of arms. But it was also a triumph for a different kind of operation: one of deceit . . .

At the heart of the deception was the 'Double Cross System', a team of double agents whose bravery, treachery, greed and inspiration succeeded in convincing the Nazis that Calais and Norway, not Normandy, were the targets of the 150,000-strong Allied invasion force. These were not conventional warriors, but their masterpiece of deceit saved thousands of lives. Their codenames were Bronx, Brutus, Treasure, Tricycle and Garbo. This is their story.

'I have seldom enjoyed a spy story more than this one, and fiction will make dreary reading hereafter'
Max Hastings, *Sunday Times*

'Addictive and deeply moving'
Independent

'Utterly gripping'
Antony Beevor

BLOOMSBURY

Rittmeister Stephan von Gröning (alias Doctor Graumann), Chapman's aristocratic German spymaster.

Stephan von Gröning as a young officer in the White Dragoons, c.1914.

Oberleutnant Walter Praetorius (alias Thomas), Chapman's principal German minder – a Nazi fanatic with a taste for English folk-dancing.

Franz Stoetzner (alias Franz Schmidt), the German agent with the cockney accent who spied in Britain before the war while working as a London waiter.

Karl Barton (alias Hermann Wojch), the principal sabotage instructor at La Bretonnière.

Colonel Robin 'Tin Eye' Stephens, commander of Camp 020: interrogator, martinet and inspired amateur psychologist.

Victor, Lord Rothschild: peer, millionaire, scientist, and head of MI5's wartime explosives and sabotage section. Rothschild and Chapman discovered a shared passion for blowing things up.

John Cecil Masterman: Oxford academic, thriller writer, sportsman and spymaster; the intellectual behind the Double Cross operation.

Jasper Maskelyne, the professional conjuror employed by the War Office to baffle and deceive the Germans.

Major Ronnie Reed, an unobtrusively brilliant BBC radio engineer who became Chapman's first case officer.

Reed operating Chapman's German radio set.

Dagmar Lahlum, the Norwegian girlfriend unofficially recruited by Chapman into MI5.

Freda Stevenson, pictured here with baby Diane, her daughter fathered by Chapman. This was possibly the image sent to Chapman in Jersey prison.

Betty Farmer, the woman Chapman abandoned at the Hotel de la Plage in 1938. 'I shall leave, but I will always come back.'

Graffiti in the attic at La Bretonnière, the German spy school in Nantes, including what appears to be a likeness of Betty Farmer, Chapman's girlfriend, probably drawn by the apprentice spy himself.

Hitler caricatured as a carrot in the attics of La Bretonnière: evidence that Von Gröning may have actively encouraged a disrespectful attitude towards the Führer.

La Bretonnière. This photograph, taken by Stephan von Gröning in 1942, remained in his wallet for the rest of his life.

Chapman pictured in a West End drinking den with Billy Hill, crime baron and self-styled 'King of Soho', and the boxer George Walker (*right*).

Chapman after his return to Britain in 1944.

Chapman protesting in 1953 after his attempts to serialise his memoirs in a newspaper were stymied under the Official Secrets Act.

Hamming it up for the camera in full SS uniform, an outfit he never wore in real life.

The Iron Cross awarded to Eddie Chapman by a grateful Führer for his 'outstanding success'. No other British citizen has ever received the medal.

Chapman in his pomp, posing with his Rolls-Royce. As honorary crime correspondent for the *Sunday Telegraph*, Chapman specialised in warning readers to steer clear of people like himself.

'Of course, he's Kristal's curator. And Art's childhood friend. I knew him when he was a boy.'

'Saul suggested that you and Callum were very close.'

'Ms Joyce,' Marlene teased, 'whatever are you insinuating?'

'I'm sorry, but I have to ask these things. I just wondered if you and Callum had a relationship?'

'As you know, Callum Oak was the most talented student I ever had. I thought I recognised a direct line from Cézanne to Bomberg to Auerbach to Oak. And yes, I'd gladly have rogered him senseless.'

Shanti winced.

'Don't go all Miss Jean Brodie on me, DI Joyce. We're talking about art school in the nineties. What do you think we got up too? Macramé?'

Shanti re-tackled the question. 'So you had a sexual relationship?'

Marlene paused. 'Regretfully not. Callum is a man of old-fashioned values. No matter how poorly his partner treated him, he believed in the sanctity of marriage and suchlike oppressive nonsense. And of course once he discovered she was pregnant, he felt honour bound to marry her and be a steady father. He wanted her to take his name, but Kristal was having none of that.'

'How did that feel, that he'd chosen Kristal?' asked Shanti.

'Over me? Is that what you're trying to say? I do wish you'd spit it out, Ms Joyce.'

'Were you in love with Callum?'

'It's all a long time ago, but I dare say I was. He was so terribly good-looking, and more than anything, I loved him as an artist. On the other hand, I wasn't a fool. I was a good deal older than him, in addition to which, over the years I began to notice another side to him that was less appealing.'

'Meaning?'

'Meaning he was weak, Inspector Joyce. Like most men, he was cowardly inside, and that's why he let Kristal walk all over him. Maybe that's why I've been a singleton most of my life, because I've never found a strong enough man. A lucky escape, perhaps, but on the other hand, I managed to retain my friendship with Callum, which was – is – hugely important to me. I just wish I could put him in a time machine and take him back to *that*.' She stabbed a twig of a finger at the shimmering seascape.

Shanti glanced at the clock on the mantelpiece. They'd been there more than an hour, and Marlene appeared as grey and burnt out as cigarette ash. Shanti gave Caine a nudge and they rose to leave.

'Well, thank you once again, Marlene. We'll let ourselves out.'

'Before you go, I want you to promise that you won't give Art a hard time over those plants.'

'Plants?' said Caine. 'I didn't notice any plants. Did you, Shanti?'

'Must have escaped my attention, Caine.' And to her own astonishment, she found herself stooping to peck the old lady gently on her powdery cheek.

They walked slowly back to the car, and Shanti navigated the narrow streets towards Swanpool Beach.

'So what have we learned, Caine?'

'Marlene cared for Art as a child and was deeply in love with Callum although she never rogered him . . .'

'. . . and Art has a kinder side to him. But did you notice how flustered Marlene got when I asked if her godson helped anyone else with their recreational needs?'

'Yes, and I know what you're thinking, Shanti. You're planning to pay Art a surprise visit, aren't you?'

'Maybe you really are telepathic. Yes, that's exactly what I'm planning. I'd say we've got more than enough to obtain a warrant. Listen, Caine, between you and me, I couldn't give a damn what Art sticks up his nose. I'm on the hunt for a murderer here. What I want to know is why he was so cagey about his activities in the hours before the murder. And I think the threat of a stiff sentence for dealing might focus his mind.'

Once they had parked, Shanti and Caine removed their socks and shoes. Then they wandered amongst the happy families on the beach – a dad building elaborate sandcastles with his baby daughter; a noisy family playing beach cricket; a row of pensioners slumped in deckchairs, one with a large pink belly, another with a magazine over her face – until they spotted Amma and Paul close to the water's edge.

'Caine, Caine, come and swim with me!' shouted Paul with a dripping ice cream in his hand.

'Try and stop me,' said Caine, wrapping a towel around his waist and wriggling into swimming trunks.

Feeling more than a little self-conscious, Shanti changed into a white costume that she hadn't worn since she took Paul to Turtle Tots at Parliament Hill Lido. While Amma laid out the picnic, she made a call to Benno, asking him to organise a search warrant for Art's weekend place in Charmouth.

'That shouldn't be a problem, boss. How many do you want in the team? Will you need dogs?'

'Let's keep it simple, Benno. Just you and me and Caine. I'm not expecting much aggro from Art. Could you sort it for first light on Wednesday? I'm looking forward to giving him a wake-up call.'

After they had eaten, Shanti lay on the hot sand and closed her eyes. Above the lazy rush of waves, she could hear the muffled shouts of Paul and Caine playing football, and her mind returned to the riddle of the floating artist.

Her primary suspect was still Art Havfruen, because of the festering resentment towards his mother and his irrefutable link with ketamine. If he turned out to be a dealer, that wouldn't prove he was a killer, but it might force him to answer the questions he'd been so deftly avoiding up until now. Then there was Art's old school buddy, spider man Spencer, whose kudos in the art world, not to mention his personal wealth, had expanded like a web since Kristal's death. She thought too about Oliver Sweetman, the round-headed ginger colossus who had given most of his life to serve his idol. He had the practical skills and certainly the physical strength required, but he seemed too gentle to carry out such a complex and dastardly deed. Then of course there was Callum Oak, the tragic widower, who had been undermined and emasculated by Kristal throughout his life. And last on her list was Marlene Moss, as frail as a fledgling, but thwarted in love by Kristal, who had diverted her protégé from his artistic path.

These were the suspects in the front line, but behind them stood an army of possibilities: the nearly two hundred guests who had been present at the fatal private view; numerous employees at the Meat Hook Gallery; the couriers from MasterMoves; not to mention the scattered Havfruen and Rasmussen family from Denmark. Fortunately Shanti could be sure that Benno and his team were painstakingly following up each of these possibilities.

But at the heart of it all was the mystery of the CCTV footage, which clearly put Kristal and Art together in the very room where she was later found dead. And yet the tank had remained sealed from the moment it arrived to the moment her body was discovered.

Before her head burst with the pressure of the puzzle, Shanti hauled herself to her feet and wandered down to the sea, where Caine was now patiently teaching Paul to swim.

'Look at me, Mum!'

'Wow! That's proper front crawl. Don't go too deep now.'

At first the water felt shockingly cold around her ankles. Then surprisingly cool and refreshing around her waist. Then ecstatically warm and delightful as she submerged herself in the waves.

She kicked onto her back and remembered how as a child she had been a semi-aquatic creature. Diving down through the looking-glass surface, she entered a secret world – an amniotic realm of spangled beauty in which she floated with the weightlessness and solitude of an unborn child.

And when, twenty minutes later, she lay drying out on the powdery sand, she found that her bloodstream was cascading with endorphins, as if her whole being had been restored to factory settings.

The sun, the sea and the exercise had had the same therapeutic effect on Paul, she could tell. He seemed happier and more invigorated than he had been since ... since when? Since forever.

Amma was watching her grandson too.

'Look at those two, Shanti, just like—'

'Do not say "like father and son"!'

'No, but I like your Vincent Caine. He's lovely with Paul, and oh my goodness, what a body! He reminds me of your father when we first met, God rest his soul.'

'Mum, I beg you not to keep on about this. You know better than anyone how my marriage ended. I am off men for a long time. Possibly forever. Besides, I don't know anything about Caine. He's very secretive, you know. Maybe he has a partner. Maybe he's gay. And you know what? I don't care either way. Life is simpler without men.'

'It's only because I love you, Shanti. I want to see you happy.'

'And I love you too, Mum. Now please, help me pack everything away. It's a long drive home, and look at the sky – I think there's a storm brewing.'

Chapter 17

The Naked Fugitive

Vincent Caine floated upside down in his black raincoat, high above the moon. Somewhere in the darkness below his inverted head, the illuminated face of the clock tower stood at 4.55 a.m.

This was the sight that met Benno as he rolled his battered Ford Focus through the sodium-lit streets towards the sea. The peculiar image was a reflection in a gigantic puddle in the Cobb Gate car park, the result of a biblical quantity of rain in the night.

Benno steered the car gently through the floodwaters around the clock tower in an effort to avoid drenching the waiting cop, whose damp hair hung in rat's tails around his shoulders.

'Rough night,' said Benno, pushing open the passenger door. 'You haven't just walked through the Undercliff, have you?'

Caine climbed inside the steamy interior and the two men clasped hands.

'No. I stayed in town with Zeb. He always has a spare room.'

Benno accelerated gently out of the sleeping town, past the

Marine Theatre and up Church Street, the engine groaning and grumbling with the ascent.

'You look tired, Vince.'

'I haven't been sleeping well. It's not like me.'

'To be honest, I'm amazed you agreed to get involved with this case.'

'Shanti is very persuasive. How is she settling in at the nick, by the way?'

'Well, she's acquiring what you might call grudging respect. A bit like you, mate. You know how hard it is to impress that lot. I actually think some of them would like to see her take a nose-dive on the Havfruen case. But they recognise she's running a tight investigation, and she's almost obsessive about record-keeping.'

At the crown of the A3052, by Timber Hill, the insipid prospect of morning seeped through the melancholy air.

'I've brought the bosher,' said Benno, waving his thumb towards the back seat. 'Does it make me a bad person that I'm itching to use it? It's that arrogance I can't stand. To be honest, I can't wait to give young Art his early alarm call.'

Caine glanced over his shoulder. The bosher, also known as a battering ram or the big red key, was lying across the seat like a pet dog.

He nodded without enthusiasm, but his mind was elsewhere. The day after the Falmouth trip, something had happened that had thrown him off centre, so that the benefits of the retreat seemed a distant memory. It was nothing dramatic. A rare letter from his father, which Zeb had delivered to the cabin. But even the sight of the familiar lettering on the envelope was enough to stir a viper's nest of anxiety in Caine's stomach.

He had propped the unopened letter on the table, yet its very presence in the cabin disturbed his morning routine to such an extent that he rose from the meditation cushion and ripped open the envelope. He skimmed the contents briefly, then stuffed the page into the stove.

It was nothing really. Just brief news of his younger half-sister, always on her travels; and something about a new office block being built opposite the terraced house where Caine and his brother had spent their childhood, and where the old man now lived alone. There wasn't anything remotely disconcerting in the letter, and yet ever since it arrived, he had been restless and unable to clear his mind. Every time he closed his eyes, foul memories disgorged themselves like effluent from a broken pipe.

He had thought back to his time in Thailand – that whole venture a bid to distance himself from his father. A younger version of Caine had sought counsel from his first Buddhist teacher, and the old man had reminded him of the allegory 'Holding on to anger is like grasping a hot coal with the intention of throwing it at another. You are the one who gets burned.'

How true that was. And in that precious time at the forest monastery, Caine had been taught the most valuable practice of all – to simply let go. *Let it go. Let it go. Let it go.*

Yet here he was all those years later, and all it took was the sight of his father's handwriting to remind him of the hot coal that still seared his hand.

It was easy to blame his father, but there were other compli-cated emotions that had destabilised him and diverted him from his spiritual practice. An image of a woman in a white swimming costume, moving like a dolphin through the sea. When she turned to wave at him and the boy, her face had been radiant. As if the sea had carried away her worries and cares.

Let it go. Let it go. Let it go.

At the A35 roundabout, Benno swung off towards Charmouth, and soon they were rolling along the village's main street, between large comfortable houses with curtains closed like timorous eyelids. A grey streak in the headlamps caused Benno to brake rapidly as a cat scuttled over a wall.

At the bottom of the hill, he turned right and followed a rutted lane past a spectral school playground. At the end of the lane was a gravelled car park by the beach, and here Shanti was waiting in her Saab, studying documents by the light of her phone as dogged wipers dismissed the rain.

Caine stepped outside and took a punch from a gust of unseasonably cold air. The dawn was as damp as a dishcloth.

Benno lifted the bosher from the back of the car and they climbed into the Saab for a briefing.

'Morning, Benno. What's up, Caine? You seem a bit distracted. Are you up for this?'

'Of course. I'm fine. I'm on it.'

'Good. That's Art's property up there.' She pointed to a bungalow on the edge of the village near the shore. A street light illuminated the building, which, in contrast to its neighbours, appeared to have been given a stylish makeover. Instead of dreary pebble-dash, an architect had cladded the facade with cool grey timbers, while poky UPVC window frames had been replaced by expanses of tinted glass.

'I'm assuming our boy is fast asleep right now, so it may take a while to rouse him. But equally I don't want to give him time to flush away his gear. So from the first knock, I'm giving him exactly two minutes, then we go in.'

Benno caressed the bosher.

'Caine, you come in with me. Benno, outside the front door until we've apprehended Art. Then a detailed interior search, please.'

The two men nodded.

'Right. It's 5.21. Let's do this . . .'

The car park was littered with driftwood, plastic bottles and tangled fishing nets, thrown up by the careless fingers of the sea. In the half-light, the village came into focus: gleaming rooftops on a gentle hillside, where a sad donkey grazed. To their left, the huge slabs of grey blue lias cliffs slid like melting chocolate towards the sea.

Outside Art's bungalow, a bright red Alfa Romeo Spider sat haughtily. There was no gate, but at the top of a driveway, a set of steps constructed of railway sleepers ascended a sloping low-maintenance garden of white shingle, pampas grass and spiky palms. Creeping steadily forward, Shanti nudged Caine and pointed out a curtained French window, which opened onto a balcony above the garden at the side of the property.

'Maybe the bedroom,' she whispered.

The front door was a smooth grey slab. Benno rolled his shoulders, as if limbering up for a forced entry. But Caine raised a finger as a signal to pause. Then he bent down and began lifting pots and stones around the door.

'What the fuck are you doing?' hissed Shanti.

'Give me a moment,' said Caine.

Eventually he rose, with a smile on his face and a Yale key between his fingers.

'How the hell ...?'

'You wanted my local knowledge,' he whispered. 'Well, most Dorset folk keep a spare key in a wellie boot or under a garden ornament. Sorry, Benno, I know you were looking forward to that.'

Benno gave him a good-natured smile.

'Ready?' said Shanti.

Nods all round. She stepped forward and raised the hooded skull doorknocker. Then she rapped loudly several times.

They waited in the cold rain as Benno examined his watch.

'That's two minutes, boss. Not a murmur.'

'Probably fast asleep, but possibly up to no good,' said Shanti. 'Want to try that key, Caine?'

The lock was new and the door eased open soundlessly. Benno took up his position outside, while Shanti and Caine slipped into the silent building.

They found themselves in an entrance hall with a musty odour of bodies, and a distant whiff of cannabis and stale takeaways.

'Art Havfruen! This is DI Shanti Joyce!' called Shanti. Her voice sounded shockingly loud. 'I have a warrant to search your property. I'd like to do this with your full cooperation.'

No response. They moved into a room on the right, a large lounge dotted with Mies van der Rohe furniture, slender tubes of metal fused with rectangular slabs of black leather. A glass coffee table was cluttered with magazines, beer bottles, a TV remote, an untidy pile of banknotes and coins, a well-used glass bong and a clutter of head shop paraphernalia. Resting against one wall was a large framed poster – the distinctive tilted bowler and smirking wink from *A Clockwork Orange*.

They returned to the hallway and crept past a sleek but messy bathroom. At the end of the corridor, they came to a closed door. Shanti paused and placed her ear against it, then she turned the handle and pushed it gently open.

Amongst the shadows they made out a large bed where two figures lay beneath a black duvet. One was a girl, although all that could be seen was a mass of golden hair spilling onto the black satin pillow. The other was Art Havfruen, who sat up quickly, exposing his startlingly white chest and a ruffled confusion of fair hair.

'What the fuck . . .?'

'Art Havfruen, we have a warrant to—'

But Art was up and out of bed, a pale streak of bare limbs. In one bound he dived through the curtains, turned a handle and disappeared through the French windows.

The girl sat up too, and Shanti immediately moved to stop her following her lover. She was about to call out to Benno to alert him to the full-frontal fugitive, but Caine was already gone.

Caine chased Art onto the balcony just in time to see the naked young man clambering awkwardly over the side and landing with a groan on the shingle below.

In one elegant movement, he vaulted after him, his coat open wide like the spread wings of a raven. He landed neatly on the pebbles with knees bent, but Art was well ahead of him, tearing down the garden towards the lane to the beach.

Out of the corner of his eye, Caine saw Benno moving to join the chase.

'I've got him, Benno! You stay with Shanti!'

Then he was off on the trail of the desperate ivory man.

'Art!' he bellowed. 'There's no point in running!'

For someone who'd only woken moments before and whose diet was mainly chemical, Art moved like a bullet from a gun – a ghost sprinter cutting through the stormy morning. Was it the reawakening of a schoolboy athlete, or a core of fear that drove him on?

Near a closed fossil shop and café by the seafront, Caine thought he had him. He dived forward to grab a skinny arm, but at that moment Art jerked suddenly sideways and Caine's hands found nothing but air. His heart was hammering in his chest. He had a sickening feeling that Art meant to harm himself – to run into the sea and obliterate the despair that he chose to bury beneath blankets of cocaine and ketamine.

By the time Caine rounded the corner, his boots skidding on the wet surface, Art had already bounded over the sea wall, his pale form half limping, half sprinting across the stony beach. A wave crashed against the concrete seafront, sending a plume of froth over Caine's head. Down below, Art leapt from rock to rock like an albino rat, his snowy skin slick with spume.

Through the mizzle, Caine could tell that the tide was rising fast, so that Art's escape route narrowed to a dead end, the beach tapering to a point from which there were only two escape routes: the deadly blue lias cliffs to his right, or the churning vortex of waves to his left.

But Art was a man possessed, all flailing arms and slithering legs. Several times he fell and hauled himself upright, with Caine bounding behind. As Caine drew close, he noticed with horror that Art's bare feet were gashed and slashed by the jagged rocks.

Why was he so determined to escape? Caine wondered if the best tactic was simply to stop and wait. Surely there was nowhere for the runaway to go? He watched Art lurch from side to side as if choosing between the killer cliffs and the suicide of the sea. Eventually he ran towards the crashing waves, then changed his mind, wheeled about and began clambering over heaps of flotsam and jetsam at the base of the cliffs.

Caine knew only too well that these were not ordinary cliffs that might be scaled by an experienced climber. These cliffs were nature's slag heaps. A vast blue-black edifice of oozing clay, crammed with flints and fossils from two hundred million years before man.

Glancing back to see where Caine was standing, Art chose a place where the cliff was less steep – a messy spillage of flaky rock created by a recent fall – and began to scramble on all fours like a pale crab up the gluey landslip.

'Stop! Stop, Art!' shouted Caine. 'It's too dangerous. You could trigger another slip, or get trapped!' But his words were stolen by the wind and hurled into the sea.

Oblivious to the danger, Art clambered onto the mud mountain, which had been further softened and destabilised by a night of torrential rain. As Caine watched helplessly, he scrambled up the incline, hands and feet plunging deep into the foul substance, even as the rain and wind buffeted his already ungainly progress. Caine could see that Art's bloodied legs were sinking to their knees into the clay, and now the pale man reached out frantically, but there was nothing solid to cling to. As Caine reached the foot of the landslip, Art appeared to be swallowed up by the earth itself, disappearing into a void between two huge mounds of clay, ton upon ton of oozing blue lias pressing against him.

Above the crashing waves, Caine heard a low rumble – or rather, he felt the sensation in his feet. It was as if a vast Jurassic creature had awoken. High above his head, small pieces of flint began to leap and fall, and he realised with a surge of terror that the landslip that Art had stumbled into was only a prelude to the main event, and the whole section of cliff was about to give way.

With lumps of mud raining from above, he struggled towards the sinking boy. At last he lay flat on the clay, but not too close to the hole into which Art had fallen. He could see the whiteness of Art's body below, almost submerged in the cloying compound. In the grey soup of mud and salt water, what Caine fixed on was a pair of blazing eyes – the desperate, terrified eyes of A Boy Named Art.

And what he felt more powerfully than fear, more powerfully even than self-protection, was an overwhelming sense of pity for another human being. He leaned into the dark fissure as far as he could and reached towards the flailing hands. Art's arms were slippery with mud, and he was fighting so frantically, it seemed impossible to get a grip. For a brief moment, Caine had a vision of the young man being swallowed forever by the hungry earth.

'Calm yourself, Art!' he shouted powerlessly. 'Stop fighting. Just give me your hands and push slowly against the clay!'

A huge missile of earth tumbled from the sky and slammed painfully against Caine's shoulder. He feared that they were caught in a perfect storm – if they weren't crushed by the impending rock fall, they would be drowned by the incoming tide.

But with head down, he managed at last to get a firm grip around Art's bloodied wrists. At first, it was like wrenching a stubborn cork from a bottle. But slowly Art began to rise from the mire. First came the pale chest, then the stomach, then his mud-caked genitals. Now, as Caine tumbled backwards, Art's writhing legs emerged, and finally – like a baby being pulled from its mother – the clay released him from its hold.

The cliff gave out another vast groan, and as Caine and his broken captive stumbled and tumbled onto the beach, an avalanche of rock and clay spewed from land to ocean, missing them by half a body's length.

Caine hauled the young man a few metres away and laid him on his back. As he fought to regain his breath, he looked back and saw the astonishing spectacle of a full-grown hawthorn tree, with a length of barbed-wire fence trailing from it, drifting absolutely upright down the cliff towards the sea.

When the rumbling had ceased, Caine examined Art for serious injuries. The boy resembled an ancient bog man, but he was alive, and although his feet were badly lacerated, no bones seemed to be broken.

Caine knew there was no time to rest. The incoming tide was fast cutting off their escape route. He peeled off his own coat and wrapped it around Art's shivering shoulders, then, with considerable difficulty, he hauled the exhausted boy up onto his back and waded through the rising surf towards the concrete steps.

The young man was a dead weight – all the fight had left him – and it was a relief to finally set him down. When he had recovered his breath, Caine helped Art to his feet and, supporting his limping, wilting body, hauled him towards the car park, where the first dog walkers of the day were pulling on wellingtons and clipping leads to collars. They stared wide-eyed at the half-drowned barefoot boy, swathed in a filthy coat, leaning heavily against the bedraggled black-haired man.

'Morning,' said Caine. 'I think it's blowing over now.'

Chapter 18

The Ghostly Girl

'Haven't I seen you before?' said Shanti.

The girl sat up in the black sheets and pushed the mass of golden hair from her thin shoulders.

'Don't think so.'

'Well I think I have. What's your name, sweetheart?'

'Do I have to say?'

'I'm afraid you do.'

'Tess.'

'Tess what?'

'Tess Strawbridge.'

'Right, Tess, do you want to put on some clothes? Then we can have a nice cup of tea and a chat.'

Shanti looked around the room. A bundle of Art's things had been dumped on the floor – a tangled suit wrapped around some pointy boots. The girl's clothes were folded neatly on a chair.

'How old are you, Tess?' asked Shanti, tossing some underwear across.

'Eighteen.'

'No you're not.'

'I am. How do you know?'

'Because this is a school uniform, darling.'

'Yeah, well I'm in the sixth form.'

'You know what? At my local comp, the sixth-formers don't wear a uniform.'

'Are you going to arrest me?'

'I don't think so, love,' said Shanti in a soothing voice. 'Not if you're helpful, anyway.'

As they passed the living room, the girl said, 'Why's he poking about in there? Art will go apeshit.'

'This is Sergeant Bennett. It's his job to gather evidence and it looks like it's his lucky day.'

'I'll have one if you're making one,' called Benno. 'Two sugars, please.'

They sat on tall stools in the halogen-lit kitchen. In her navy blazer, skirt and white cotton shirt, Tess Strawbridge appeared exactly what she was – a nervy schoolgirl. Shanti placed her phone on the counter top.

'Tess, I'd like to record our chat, if that's OK?'

'No, it's not OK. How would you like it if I recorded you?'

'You can do that if you want, but I have to tell you that if you won't answer my questions on record, we'll have to take a drive to the police station and do it there.'

The girl gave the faintest nod of acceptance and Shanti tapped the red button on the screen.

'So, you're Art's girlfriend.'

The girl shrugged.

'Where do you live, Tess?'

'Charmouth. Sort of.'

'And I'm going to ask again how old you are . . . ?'

Tears streamed down her pretty face like pearls. She raised her hand to her mouth and mumbled something.

'I can't hear you, Tess.'

Her face reappeared, looking suddenly defiant. 'All right, I'm fifteen. Get over it.'

'Does your mum know that you stay here?'

'My mum doesn't give a shit.'

'What about your dad? Does he know?'

'Never met him.'

'OK, darling. You're doing really well. Listen, I shouldn't do this, but I'll tell you a secret – I'm not blaming you for anything. It's Art we're interested in. Can you tell me how you first met?'

Tess wiped her eyes with the back of her hand. 'I go to school in Lyme and get the bus back to Charmouth. I was walking home one day when he came out of a shop – dead cool – and we literally bumped into each other. He said I was the spit of someone he knew. Then he asked where I lived. I told him up Stonebarrow way. He offered me a lift, 'cos it's a long walk. I wasn't going to accept – stranger danger and that – but then I saw his car! I felt like a movie star and all my mates were well jel. I gave him my number and, you know, things went on from there.'

'Does he give you drugs?'

'No. I don't take that shit . . . well, a bit of green sometimes.'

'Does he give you money?'

'Art is loaded. He doesn't care. He leaves like stashes of cash all over the place. If I need something, he just says help yourself.'

'Tess, I want to ask you some personal questions now – is

that OK? Does Art like you to wear your school uniform? Some men get a kick from that, don't they?'

'Nah, he's not into that. He likes me to wear the stuff in the wardrobe.'

'Right, I'm pausing the interview for a moment . . .'

Shanti went out of the kitchen into the living room, where Benno, in latex gloves, was bagging and tagging. A quick nod towards the kitchen meant *Keep an eye on her, we don't want another runner.*

She went back into the bedroom and switched on the light. There was a small fitted wardrobe on one wall. Although she half knew what she might find, it was still a shock when she opened the door. Several loose threads of the investigation began to knot neatly together.

Tess hadn't moved from the tall stool in the kitchen, but she looked paler and more vulnerable than ever.

'Right, I'm recording again. Interview with Tess Strawbridge, part two. So, Tess, you told me that Art liked you to wear the clothes I've just seen in the wardrobe in his bedroom – that is, a short white lacy dress and a pair of red Doc Marten boots. Is that correct?'

'It turned him on.'

'So he asked you to wear these clothes around the flat?'

'Yeah. With loads of smeary lipstick.'

'And where else? In bed?'

'Not the boots, obvs.'

'And how about outside the house – did you ever wear the outfit in public?'

'A couple of times, but it always caused a hassle. I wore it at his mum's show – she was, like, a famous artist. Art didn't invite me, he said it was going to be boring. But I wanted to go especially when I heard there would be TV people and that. He went on his own but I got fed up sitting here, so I thought I'd give him a nice surprise. I called Matt Scabs—'

'Hang on. Who is Matt Scabs?'

'Soz. He's a cab driver. Him and his brother Bob Scars.'

'Matt Scabs and Bob Scars? You're making this up!'

'It's like a joke – Matt's Cabs and Bob's Cars. Everyone knows that.'

'OK, so you called Matt Scabs and he drove you to the Meat Hook Gallery. That's quite a journey; how did you pay for it? You know I will follow up everything you tell me.'

The girl hesitated.

'Tell me the truth, Tess.'

'Like I say, Art leaves cash all over the place. He lets me take what I need.'

'So you arrived at the gallery. Did the cab wait for you?'

'Yeah, Matt went for coffee in Bruton and I said I'd call him when I was ready. I saw a big swanky crowd heading out of the car park and up through the gardens towards this weird building like a massive bollock on stilts. I texted Art and he came rushing back. I thought he would be happy to see me with all his fave clothes and everything. But he went mental. He was horrible. He shoved me in this huge dark room and said I was a fucking embarrassment. He made me cry, so I ran outside and called Matt. Then I nipped onto the lane through a hole in the hedge. There were lots of cars passing with posh guests inside, so I hid out of sight until Matt arrived. Then I went home.'

Shanti felt exhilaration coursing through her veins. This was what a breakthrough felt like. At last she had cracked that piece of the puzzle – the CCTV footage that had foxed them all. How could Kristal Havfruen have been arguing with her son and yet be found hours later in a tank in the same room? A tank that had not once been tampered with? The answer was that the woman arguing with Art was not Kristal at all. It was Tess.

'You said you wore the clothes in public a couple of times. Can you tell me about the second occasion?'

'It was at her funeral . . . his mum. She died in a mental way. You probably heard about it.'

'Yes, I heard about it.'

'After she died, Art and me started arguing like 24/7. He was no fun any more – doing loads of gear and getting really psycho. He said there was no way I could come to the funeral. The actual words he said were, "It wouldn't be appropriate." I'm, like, "Appropriate never stopped you shagging me, did it?" Anyhow, he stormed off and left me and then I decided to really fuck him off and turn up at the church in the dress and boots and the make-up and everything.'

Thank you, God! thought Shanti. I'm not insane.

'Did Matt Scabs take you to the funeral, Tess? Remember, I will be checking all of this.'

'It was Bob Scars that time.'

'And what did Art do when he saw you?'

'Oh, he spotted me hiding in the churchyard and lost it big time. Dragged me by my hair and said I was insane to come there. Accused me of trying to ruin the saddest day of his life.'

'What did you do?'

Tess sniffed. 'Backed off, didn't I? I'm not a total bitch. I could see he was upset. I feel like that about my dad sometimes. But Art wasn't making it any easier by snorting like a ton of nose candy.'

She glanced furtively at Shanti, as if she knew she was saying too much.

'It's OK, Tess. We know about Art's habits.'

'Yeah, he doesn't exactly hide it, does he?'

'I saw you sitting in the churchyard, didn't I?'

Tess's eyes widened. 'That was never you! Christ! You were well gorge in that black dress. But you scared the shit out of me. I thought you were a fucking ghost or something. Ended up hiding in these spooky woods crapping myself.'

Shanti found herself actually laughing with relief. 'I think we scared each other good and proper. OK, Tess. You're being more helpful than you know. Listen, I want you to go back to the day of the private view at the art gallery. Think about this very carefully before you answer. Were you with Art all afternoon before the show?'

Tess nodded. 'Yeah. It was Saturday, wasn't it? I stayed over Friday night. We slept really late and spent the day together here. Art watched the footie, then he left for the gallery around four thirty.'

'But you thought you'd surprise him.'

'Honest, I thought he'd like it, but it went down like a cup of cold vom.'

So there it is, thought Shanti. The alibi Art had been so reluctant to provide. And now she knew why. Art Havfruen was having a relationship with an underage girl. And if that wasn't bad enough, he persuaded that girl to dress as his mother. Perhaps that revelation was even more awkward than being accused of her murder.

As Shanti finished the interview, she heard Caine's voice outside. The front door opened and a pair of outlandish figures appeared, like extras from an apocalyptic horror movie.

'Jesus, Caine!' said Shanti. 'What the hell happened to you?'

'Let's just say the cliffs around here are a reminder of impermanence.'

They were both coated from head to foot in cracking grey clay, and where they emerged from the mud-caked coat, Art's face and spindly legs were smeared with blood.

'Oh, Art! Are you all right, babes?' said Tess, rushing to his side.

As Benno steered Art towards the shower, Shanti led Tess back to the kitchen and sat her down in front of a bowl of cereal.

'Now what am I supposed to do?' wailed Tess. 'I know Art's a bit mental, but I love him. He can be dead kind and funny. I wish I hadn't told you all that stuff now. Art always says you can never trust the feds.'

'Listen, Tess,' said Shanti. 'A good friend of mine is a child welfare officer, OK? She's a lovely person. She's on her way now, and if you agree, she'll have a chat with you and maybe with your mum too. She can help sort things out at school. I want to make sure you're getting all the support you need.'

When Art emerged in his crumpled suit, looking alarmingly pale, Benno clipped on the handcuffs and read him his rights: 'Art Havfruen, I'm arresting you for possession of Class A substances, and on suspicion of indecent activity with a minor as defined in Section 9 of the Sexual Offences Act 2003. You do not have to say anything, but it may harm your defence . . .'

For the first time since Shanti had met him, the Boy Named Art was silent. As Benno led him from the bungalow, he glanced back sadly at Tess Strawbridge, the under-parented child in her school uniform, eating Coco Pops and watching cartoons on the sofa.

In the kitchen, Caine replayed the interview with Tess, which Shanti had shown him on her phone. As he listened, he slowly scrubbed his hands with a nailbrush at the sink – that blue lias stuck to the skin as if it was mixed with glue. Even after he had dried himself, his hands were coated in a film of grey silt.

Out in the living room, the welfare officer had arrived and Caine heard the muffled sound of soothing voices below the whoops and whistles of the TV. He discovered a kettle behind the Italian coffee machine and began to make tea, even borrowing a teaspoon of Art's honey in return for his exertions.

At last someone switched off the TV, and he heard voices receding and a car leaving the bungalow. Then Shanti entered the kitchen with a wry smile on her face.

'Jesus, Caine. Have you seen yourself? You look a fright!'

Caine glanced at a tinted glass cupboard door. A man stared back at him – an ancient, haggard man with a grey mane and parchment skin. It was a horrible apparition of his future self.

He slumped onto a stool and stirred his tea.

'You look absolutely done in, Caine. But listen, you did well today. No way would I have caught Art on my own. And I think Benno's sprinting days are over.'

'But there's so much fallout, Shanti! Not just Art, but that poor girl too.'

'Maybe she'll get the care she needs now. Benno took a preliminary tongue swab, and thank God it seems there's nothing in her system except a trace of cannabis. Which means Art didn't coerce her with anything stronger. That's the good news; the bad news is that she refuses to press charges against him. She says she really loved him and everything was consensual.'

'But she's underage ...'

'Unfortunately, if she refuses to testify, Art will probably get away with nothing more than a fine for possession, or more likely just a caution. I hate the law sometimes.'

She fumbled in a cupboard and found a jar of instant coffee. 'But listen, Caine, I have to admit that you were right and I was wrong. Art has a cast-iron alibi for the day of the murder. He was innocent all along.'

'Innocent?' Caine shook his grey head. 'I wonder if humans are capable of innocence.'

'Well, the lad needs some therapy ... and a course of multi-vitamins.'

Caine exhaled deeply. 'It's the same story every time – it all comes back to early parenting. Children are like plants, Shanti ... or seedlings, rather. I've been thinking about this a lot lately. If they are watered with love and encouragement, then they blossom. But if they are disparaged, or denied that love ... it's like weedkiller.'

'And you were doing so well ... we've had a whole morning without philosophy. You know, Action Caine is so much more impressive than Philosopher Caine. I loved the way you dived through that window.'

Caine sipped his tea in gloomy silence, reflecting on the teaching that all actions had consequences – the way that weed-killer parenting had wilted Art. And Tess. And Paul ... And maybe himself as well.

And then, in the empty bungalow, something glorious

happened. It was as if Shanti was responding to the sadness in his heart. She looked at him kindly and said:

'You know what, Caine? We should get you cleaned up and back on your feet. I need you on this case.'

She sat him on a stool by the sink and began patiently to sponge his face and hair with warm water.

It took a long time, and Caine gave himself up to the experience. It was as if Shanti was washing away his worries, and the silt spiralling down the plughole was the pain rinsing from his heart . . .

Let it go. Let it go. Let it go.

And although Shanti kept talking relentlessly about the case, it didn't diminish the tenderness he felt in her fingertips.

'You know what's creepy, Caine? The way Tess resembles a young Kristal – did you notice that? Just lean over a bit more, we don't want to mess up Art's expensive kitchen . . . I guess that's what attracted him in the first place – talk about Freudian. OK, close your eyes, you've got that damned clay in every pore . . . Anyway, you can see why I was fooled by the CCTV footage and the apparition in the graveyard, too . . . Just wait there a moment . . .'

She ran out of the kitchen and returned with a small glass bottle. 'Strictly against regs to borrow shampoo from a suspect, but it's Art who got you into this state. Mmm, nice – Tea Tree Oil for Men.'

Caine barely heard a word. As Shanti massaged the shampoo into his hair, he was transported into a mindful world of bliss, in which every nerve of his scalp was being caressed.

'Anyway, this changes everything. I'm going to officially eliminate Art as a murder suspect, and I'm shifting to the theory that Kristal was murdered at Mangrove House, where the tank and formaldehyde were delivered earlier in the day. We can be pretty certain that she was transported – already dead – inside that tank to the gallery. Art failed to notice that the figure in the tank was an actual body because he was off his face as usual, and also distracted by a guest appearance from Tess. In any case, the lights in the master gallery were dimmed, which is presumably why the guys from MasterMoves didn't notice anything either ... I suppose the same goes for Ollie Sweetman when he polished the tank and placed the boots on top.'

Shanti reached for a towel and sighed. 'Trouble is, it feels like one step forward and five steps back. That damned eternal question remains – who killed Kristal? I don't know about you, but I'm coming full circle to Callum Oak. I've never trusted the guy. He had plenty of motive, as well as the brawn and brain to do it. What do you think, Caine? Don't tell me to embrace uncertainty, or I will throttle you with this towel.'

As she dried his hair, Caine felt like a warm cat lying sleepily on his mistress's lap. It was all he could do not to purr.

'Caine. I asked you a question ...'

Shanti stood up and began to clean the sink, and Caine emerged from his blissful stupor.

'I know this is a little outside your radar, Shanti, but there are moments in every case when the best thing to do is pause and reflect on the situation. I think we need to spend time in the forest.'

'Oh, that's very helpful, Caine. Why didn't I think of that? We should go and have a chat with a tree. In fact, let's ask all your favourite trees to take a vote on who killed Kristal.'

'I'm being serious. I feel that we have all the clues and information in our hands. It's amazing how often answers come to me in nature. In fact I've just remembered something . . .'

'Jesus, Caine. Make sure it's a helpful thing.'

'It's a line from a poem . . . Wordsworth, I think . . . "One impulse from a vernal wood may teach you more of man, of moral evil and of good, than all the sages can."'

Chapter 19

A Sinister Symbiosis

Everything was going nicely until the call from Paul's school.

Shanti and Caine had locked the bungalow and replaced the key beneath the pot where Caine had found it, and as they walked towards the car park, the sun lit up the sea like a bright future.

Then Shanti's phone vibrated and there seemed to be an urgency in its tone.

'Hello? Is that Shantala?'

'Who is this?'

'Yvonne Khan, Paul's head teacher. Is this a convenient moment?'

'Oh, Yvonne . . . Yes, of course. Paul's not in trouble again, is he? I thought he seemed more settled lately . . .'

'I don't want to blow this out of proportion, Shantala, but I've decided to exclude Paul for a short time. I'm really sorry.'

'Exclude him from school? But he's only eight years old.'

'I know that, but I have to put the well-being of my staff first.

I hope you understand. Is there someone who can collect him right away?'

With trembling hands, Shanti called Amma. She told her to collect Paul as soon as she could and that she would be home in less than an hour.

Caine listened quietly as Shanti explained what had happened. Then, without hesitation, he reassured her that he was there for her and Paul, and he would gladly accompany her to Yeovil.

On the drive, with concern etched across her face, Shanti described the ways in which Paul's behaviour had deteriorated since the divorce, to the point where he sometimes raged at her and Amma. And lately she had noted something in her son's eyes that terrified her. It was a glint of pleasure at the effect his behaviour had on others. A first understanding that he had power. The reason it terrified Shanti was because it was the exact same look – in embryonic form – that she had witnessed on the face of her ex-husband, who was an unreconstructed emotional bully.

And now Paul had unleashed that aggression in the classroom, and when the teachers had intervened, it was they who had received a torrent of expletives and abuse.

'Listen, Shantala, we all love Paul to bits,' Ms Khan had reassured her. 'This exclusion is only for a few days. I just want to give him a chance to reflect. All the staff appreciate the pressures of your job – especially this Havfruen case. But I think you and I need to have a proper conversation as soon as possible. I want to know if everything is OK. Perhaps I can help in some way . . .'

So Shanti drove – a little too fast – across the Marshwood Vale, through Crewkerne and West Coker towards Yeovil, and when they arrived in her quiet cul-de-sac, the thing that swayed her towards Caine's invitation to come to the cabin with Paul was the almost mesmeric effect her colleague had on the boy. To Shanti's astonishment, Paul stepped calmly out of the house and took the tall man's hand. It was as if the confusion and anger evaporated when he saw Caine.

On the drive to Lyme and on the long, slow walk through the woods, Shanti realised that for once, the best thing was to step back and let Caine and Paul sort things out in their own mysterious, masculine way.

The way Caine did it was to take the boy outside himself. He showed him nests hidden in coppices. A green and red wood-pecker drilling for bugs. With a sharp penknife, they made a spear from a length of hazel.

And at one point she heard Paul say, 'Look at the bees, Caine!'

'Yes, they're busy this year. It's a good sign because it means the meadow is healthy. You know the way it works, Paul? Bees and flowers are friends. They work together. It's called a symbi-otic relationship.'

'Is that like you and Mum? Are you sinbotic?'

'Symbiotic? Ha, you'd better ask her! But everything works better with cooperation. Teachers and pupils can be symbiotic too.'

When they finally reached the Lost Chimney and climbed the steep track to the cabin, Shanti watched as Paul pulled off his shoes and placed them neatly alongside Caine's. He parked the spear next to Caine's surfboards. Then he wandered around the unfamiliar environment in an almost reverential way.

Shanti had to give it to him – Caine was a natural with the boy. He didn't try too hard, or pester the lad with questions;

instead he busied himself with tasks that would intrigue any eight-year-old, and soon the two of them were outside gathering firewood.

Caine told Shanti to make herself at home – there were books inside, or she was welcome to rest on his bed, or on the chair on the deck. She roamed around the cabin, which still felt foreign to her: the domain of a man, and an unusual man at that. There was that shrine, with sticks of incense, a candle, a small vase of wild flowers and a tiny animal skull. Beside the bronze Buddha she noticed something unusual – a small framed photograph placed face down. Glancing over her shoulder to make sure Caine and Paul were out of sight, she lifted it and studied the faded photo of an elderly man. His hair was almost white, but there was something familiar about the unusually high cheekbones. And when she looked at the oil-well eyes, she had no doubt that this was Caine's father. So why was the image here on the shrine? And why was it face down?

She replaced the photo exactly where she had found it, walked to the bookshelf, grabbed the slimmest novel she could find and stepped outside, where Caine was teaching Paul to split kindling with a hatchet.

There was something about this place that was out of time – out of everything. Now Caine and the boy nursed the fire into life within a ring of stones. Such simple, primal activities, but she realised that her ex had never been a hands-on dad, and besides, he hated the countryside.

When the meal was ready, she even restrained herself from fussing about Paul's filthy hands. And although the food was vegetarian, Paul tucked in as if he hadn't eaten for a month, chewing a corn on the cob, dripping with butter, straight off a blade. When they had finished, Caine slung a hammock across the porch and showed Paul how to climb inside. Within five minutes, the boy was asleep.

'He hasn't done that for years,' said Shanti. 'I mean, fallen asleep in the day. Thanks, Caine. You really seem to get him, and he's so angry with me these days.'

'Oh, I get him all right,' said Caine, pouring tea into two mugs and settling at her feet on the deck. 'I've had a little experience with random fathers.'

The slogan on Shanti's mug said: *Keep Calm and Meditate.*

The slogan on Caine's mug said: *This too shall pass. (It might pass like a kidney stone, but it will pass.)*

'I guess I was lucky,' said Shanti. 'You've met my mum – she drives me nuts, but she was always behind me. Dad, too. I was in my early teens when he died, and I never thought I'd get over it. The grief didn't go away, but it changed, and now the sadness has turned to love.'

'That's beautiful, Shanti. Although Paul may forget it sometimes, you are a wonderful mother to him. In the meantime, how nice is this? To sit here and watch the sun set over the sea.'

The sunset? With a surge of anxiety, Shanti realised that she hadn't even thought about the investigation for hours. What had happened to the day? And there was no phone signal out here! Supposing someone needed to contact her urgently?

Sod it. Let Benno take the reins for a while.

'So, tell me about this Buddhist thing, Caine. I mean what's it all about? I don't want a six-hour lecture … tell me in three words.'

'Compassion. Equanimity. Love.'

'A little more … though not too much.'

'Buddhism is about treading lightly. Living life to the full without hurting others. Accepting the dappled quality of life. Being the master of your own mind. Letting go. Being free.'

'OK, I'd like some of that. But I mean, there are lots of different sects, no? What kind of Buddhist are you?'

'I don't know. I guess I'm a free-range Buddhist.'

'Is that like being a free-range cop?'

'Maybe. I take whatever works for me. The Buddha says we shouldn't believe anything we read or hear – even what he says – unless it concurs with our common sense and is conducive to the good of all.'

'Like pick and mix.'

'If you want to know what I really think, I believe there's something like a golden thread that runs through all great religions, and all great art, and all great literature, and through nature too – especially through nature. It doesn't really matter where you grab a hold of it.'

'Hmm ... that is either unbelievably profound or the most pretentious bullshit I've ever heard in my life. I'll think about it and let you know.'

They sat for a long time watching the trees slow-waltzing in the breeze.

'Shanti, would you excuse me for a while? I usually wander down to the sea at this time of day. Just to sit, you know.'

'Sure,' said Shanti. 'Look, I've got a book.'

'*Siddhartha* by Hermann Hesse. That's a great choice. It's a magical story. You'll love it.'

As he wandered down the track towards the little bay, Caine felt a complex brew of emotions. Something like tenderness towards this little family, the unexpected visitors in the guest house of his life, but hanging over it an anxiety that he thought he had laid to rest long ago, but that was now resurfacing. Would he ever be free of what had happened? And the turbulence of the police work didn't help. So much agitation.

There was a flat patch of grass on a clifftop where he liked to sit gazing over the sea. The graceful arm of an oak shaded his head. As he settled cross-legged between the mossy roots, a memory came to him of his old teacher, whose name was Tu, addressing the young monks. He had held up a glass of water in his skinny brown hand. 'The water is our mind,' he had told them, with merriment twinkling in his eyes. 'Watch when I shake the glass ...' The water trembled. 'This is the agitated mind. The water becomes cloudy and obscure. So how can I make it clear again?' 'Stop agitating!' they had called. So Tu ceased shaking, and like magic, the water fell calm. 'When worry and desire cease, the mind becomes clear. Equilibrium is the natural state. And when there is clarity, we are able to see into the depths. This is insight.'

And Caine had a powerful feeling that if he could still his mind, the solution to the Havfruen case would fall upon him as naturally as autumn fell over the forest.

When he opened his eyes an hour or so later, Paul was standing barefoot at his side holding the spear. Just watching his meditation. Caine smiled and rose slowly to his feet. He took the boy's hand and they turned towards the cabin.

'What's that, Caine?' said Paul, pointing with his spear towards the base of the ancient tree.

'Oh, that's a fungus called chanterelle. You can eat it when it's cooked.'

'It looks like disgusting custard.'

'You know what, Paul? This is another example of symbiosis ... like the bees working with the flowers, the chanterelle and the oak work together like friends.'

'How can a tree and a fungus be friends?'

'Well, if I remember, the fungus has little threads that twist around the roots. The threads help the tree get good things from the soil, like nutrients and water, and protect the tree from nasty diseases. In return, the tree gives the chanterelle sugars, which make it tasty to eat.'

'That's cool. Disgusting but cool.'

As they climbed the track, Caine became aware of an unusual tingling at the bottom of his spine. The feeling ran slowly upwards, vertebra by vertebra, until it tickled the base of his neck. Then it exploded in his head.

Of course! This was the insight he had been waiting for! Like Wordsworth's impulse from a vernal wood.

'Paul, you are something of a genius, boy!'

'Am I?'

'You don't know it, but you are. I think you've just hit the symbiotic nail on its symbiotic head.'

'I don't get it.'

'It doesn't matter. Your mum will. Just run up to the cabin and say "symbiotic"! Tell her you've solved the case.'

Shanti was relaxing in the old chair on the deck, trying to make sense of Caine's novel.

'Hello. Did you find Caine?'

'Symbiotic!' said Paul.

'You what?'

'Symbiotic, Mum. Caine says I solved the case.'

'Oh, there you are, Caine. Do you have any idea what my son is talking about?'

'I think he may be right. Paul and I were talking about symbiosis – you know, the way two things in nature help each other out?'

'Like the birds that clean the crocodile's teeth?'

'Exactly. Well, listen. Whoever killed Kristal needed two qualities, right?'

'Caine, I never thought I would say this, but could you slow down a little?'

'I think we've been approaching this investigation from the wrong angle.'

'We should be interviewing crocodiles?'

'No. I mean maybe we should be looking at partnerships.'

'OK ...'

'Specifically partnerships in which two people have complementary skills they could bring to the crime.'

Shanti closed the book and sat forward. 'So you're saying the crime might have been committed by two people?'

'Exactly. Brawn and brain.'

'One person with the intellect to plan it, and another with the physical strength to place Kristal in the tank.'

Shanti was on her feet in seconds, stuffing various items into her shoulder bag. 'Paul, I need you to stay here with Caine. I have a job to do.'

'Yay! What shall we do, Caine?'

'Shanti, you shouldn't go alone!' cautioned Caine.

'Look after Paul, please. I can handle this.'

And with that, she set off, sprinting down the narrow track

from the cabin towards the coast path. As she ran, she noted with some satisfaction that she was infinitely fitter than the first time she had struggled this way.

'Did I crack the case?' asked Paul when she had gone.

'I think you did, Paul,' said Caine, with an anxious hand on the boy's shoulder. 'Or maybe we did it together.'

'Symbiotic?' said Paul.

'Symbiotic,' said Caine.

Chapter 20

Tea for the Killerman

The daylight was fading as she arrived at Paradise Park. In the log cabin reception room, Colin Leggit was rearranging a display of leaflets advertising local attractions.

'Be with you in a minute,' he told her over his shoulder. 'Just putting these in order. Otherwise you're looking for Monkey World and you end up in Wookey Hole.'

'I need to speak to you immediately, Mr Leggit.'

The neatly bearded man turned round.

'Oh, it's you again. Haven't you caught that killer yet?'

'Is Oliver here?'

'He is. But he won't want to be disturbed at this time of day. I told you before, he's very particular about his timetable.'

'Frankly, Mr Leggit, I couldn't care less about timetables.'

'No need to be rude, young lady. Now if you'll give me a minute, I'll point out his chalet—'

'Shangri-La, I know. Near the dovecote.'

'I was going to tell you that he's got company, just so you

know. Everyone's talking about it. He's got a girlfriend. I've seen her myself through the curtains. And that's all the more reason why he won't want to be disturbed. It's teatime for Ollie . . .'

Shanti left Leggit with his hands full of Cheddar Gorge leaflets. She made her way along the immaculate drive between the pastel-coloured static homes, from which cooking smells wafted and TVs flickered. The presence of a guest in Sweetman's chalet might complicate things. She'd have to send the woman packing.

Shanti knew perfectly well that she should call Benno, but she burned to do this alone.

Shangri-La was set in an isolated spot on the western side of the park, near a stream. In front of her, an elaborate dovecote sat on top of a post. Within numerous doorways the beautiful creatures crooned and groomed each other like bridesmaids. As Shanti approached, she realised that Leggit had been correct. Sweetman was not alone.

She jumped up and down a few times in order to get a better view. There was definite movement behind the lace curtains – the unmistakable hulk of Oliver Sweetman carrying plates and cutlery. And a second figure: the outline of a woman seated at the table. Was Sweetman serving tea for his guest?

Shanti crept forward and crouched below a slightly opened window. She could hear Oliver's gentle Cornish tones, as soothing as a child at a dolls' tea party.

'Now we won't have our cake till we've had our soup. I made tomato 'cos that's your favourite, and look, I grated cheese on top for a treat . . .'

Shanti slipped around to the front, where plastic steps led to the entrance. She took a deep breath and rapped firmly on the flimsy door.

'Now then, whoever can that be?' said Sweetman from inside. 'We don't usually get visitors, do we? Perhaps Mr Leggit has come to pay a call. Let's hope there's nothing wrong with the doves.'

The static home swayed and creaked as he lumbered towards the door.

Shanti heard the lock being turned, and the door swung outwards, almost knocking her off the step. Above her head, framed by the interior lights, stood the mountainous hulk of Oliver Sweetman.

'Oh, it's Shanti Joyce,' he said. 'But it's not golf time now.' And he began to close the door.

'This won't take a moment, Oliver,' she said, grabbing the edge and pulling firmly. 'I'm not here to play mini golf. Just a little chat, if that's OK?'

His freckled face peered around the door. 'Well, see, I've got company, and we're having tea if you don't mind . . .'

Shanti hauled against him. The man was as strong as a bison.

'Oliver, you may have forgotten that I'm a police detective. I'd like to ask you a few questions.'

'You come back tomorrow, Shanti Joyce. I'll call Mr Leggit.'

'Mr Leggit said it was all right. He said you wouldn't mind, because this is important.'

She could feel him hesitating and considering the irregular request.

'Well, I can't pretend I like it, but I suppose you'd better come in if that's what Mr Leggit says. But I'm telling you now, Shanti Joyce, there's not enough soup for three.'

The smell was the first thing Shanti noticed. Tomato soup, yes; but another smell, like pickled onions. As she followed his huge back, it occurred to her that she'd smelt that stench before.

With that realisation came a stab of fear in her chest. She reached into her shoulder bag and her fingers found the canister of pepper spray.

There was a small doorway that opened into the living and dining area. In order to squeeze through, Sweetman had to constrict his massive arms and bunch up his shoulders. Shanti followed into a long, narrow room where a table stood in front of an L-shaped settee. It was covered with a red and white checked tablecloth and set with an elaborate meal.

Sitting on the settee, with her back to the window, was Kristal Havfruen.

As Sweetman returned to his place beside her, Shanti's heart belted like a traction engine.

'Better budge up, Kristal,' he said. 'Seems we've got a visitor.'

Kristal's impassive face was smeared with red lipstick and her green eyes stared coldly into the steaming bowl of soup.

Shanti blinked, unable to process what she was seeing. Then the whole thing came together – the whiff of formaldehyde, the frozen posture. This was the unspeakably lifelike effigy that Kristal had created for her happening.

'Well, don't stand on ceremony,' said Sweetman. 'There's not enough soup, but I suppose you can have some tea and cake if you behave nicely.'

His voice betrayed his annoyance. As far as Oliver was concerned, Shanti had disturbed a cosy evening with his lover.

'Hello, Kristal,' she stammered. Whatever reality Sweetman lived in, it was best to play along.

'That smell, Oliver – isn't that formaldehyde?'

'It is! We took lots of showers, didn't we, Kristal? But it won't wash away.'

Shanti nodded as if it all made perfect sense.

'In any case,' continued Sweetman, leaning across to nuzzle the side of the effigy's neck, 'the smell grows on you after a while, doesn't it, dear?'

Kristal said nothing in return.

Oliver tucked a napkin into his collar and adjusted Kristal's napkin too.

'She barely eats a thing. That's why she's so skinny.'

With a faint air of desperation, he began spooning the red gunk into Kristal's unsmiling mouth. It splattered down her lacy dress and onto the table.

'Hurry up and sit down, Shanti Joyce. You're making her uncomfortable.'

Almost in a trance, Shanti took a seat on the orange and purple settee beside Kristal.

'Oh please, Kristal,' said Sweetman. 'Just a few mouthfuls for me. Here . . . you watch Ollie . . .'

And he began ladling spoonfuls of soup between his own slurping lips.

Shanti felt as paralysed as her blonde-headed neighbour.

Eventually she managed, 'Oliver? Can I ask you something?'

'S'pose so.'

'Ollie. This isn't really Kristal, is it?'

He stared at her with horror and disbelief.

'Don't know what you're talking about.'

'Sorry. I shouldn't have said that. I mean that this is quiet Kristal, isn't it? The one who's nice to you. Not the one who used to tell you off and slap your hand.'

Sweetman scrunched his eyes tightly, as if trying to shut out the world. 'I don't know. I don't know nothing.'

'You were at the funeral, remember? You saw the other Kristal in the glass coffin. I'm wondering whether you helped to swap them over. Did you help to give Kristal an injection in her studio that sent her to sleep?'

The twitching eyelids remained closed. The shaky spoon hovered.

'Did you lift this nice, quiet Kristal out of the tank and put sleepy Kristal inside?'

'It's a secret,' he whispered.

'And who asked you to keep that secret?'

'If I tell, it won't be a secret, silly.'

'Was it Callum, Ollie? Was it Callum Oak?'

'Not listening. Can't hear . . .'

'Did Callum ask you to keep it secret?'

'Tra-la-la . . . I got my pointy things in my heary holes.'

'Oliver, please. I need to know the truth.'

He pushed himself upright and raised the humanoid from her seat. Then he tenderly wiped her smeared lips with a napkin.

'It's past bedtime, as a matter of fact. Pyjamas on, Kristal. Pyjamas on, Shanti Joyce. It's time to lock the door.'

He bumbled across the room and through the narrow doorway. Alone with Kristal, Shanti heard the lock turn, and a moment later Oliver returned, pushing a key into his shirt pocket.

'It's too late to leave now, Shanti Joyce. You'll have to sleep with Kristal and me. Although we don't sleep all the time, do we, dear?'

Shanti's fingers tightened around the pepper spray.

'Oliver Sweetman. Did you murder Kristal Havfruen at

Mangrove House on the afternoon of the twenty-second of July?'

His flame-coloured head twitched with confusion.

'Now you've done it, Shanti Joyce . . . Now you made me kill you too.'

'Ollie, if you do that, you will go to prison, and then who will look after Kristal?'

His face was puffy and red. His eyes blinked rapidly as he approached her, arms outstretched, fingers opening and closing in the air.

Shanti retreated to the back of the room and grabbed the mannequin by the arm. It was heavier than she'd expected – not hollow like a shop dummy, but a dense mass of resin and silicone. She managed to yank it from its seat and drag it towards her, carrying the tablecloth with it and sending Kristal's bowl tumbling to the carpet, where soup splattered like a massacre.

Oliver was shaking. 'Don't you touch her, Shanti Joyce! She ain't done nothing to you.'

'She's not real, Oliver! She's made of plastic! Look!' She pinched Kristal's cold cheeks. Poked her in the ribs. 'She doesn't make a sound, does she? That's *because she's not real!*'

Suddenly Sweetman towered over her. 'You're frightening her. She doesn't like that. Ollie don't like it neither. Put her down now. Otherwise you know what I'll do . . .'

Shanti snatched the canister from her bag and pointed it at him. 'Stop right there, Oliver, or I'll spray this in your eyes. It will hurt.'

'Don't care! Want Kristal.'

He drew closer. Shanti aimed the canister at his spherical

face and pressed hard with her forefinger. Nothing except a weedy hiss. The damned thing was empty!

As Sweetman circled the chaotic table, she scanned the surface for a weapon. In desperation, she seized a small knife beside the sponge cake.

'That little knife won't hurt me,' sniggered Oliver. 'I'm not a cake.'

'It's not for you, Ollie.' And in one swift movement she brought the knife to the mannequin's neck. With her other hand, she pulled at Kristal's hair so the polymer neck was exposed. 'Stay right where you are, Oliver Sweetman, or I will cut her throat.'

Sweetman froze.

'I'm going to go now and you are not going to follow me. If I hear you behind me, I swear I will kill her.'

Sweetman slumped onto the settee and buried his face in his hands. 'Don't! Don't! She didn't do nothing to you!'

'Hand me the keys from your pocket, Oliver.'

He dumped them sulkily on the table like a schoolboy relinquishing contraband. With the cake knife held tightly to the mannequin's throat, Shanti backed out of the lounge and along the corridor towards the door. Sweetman sat motionless, his lower lip trembling. Fumbling behind her, Shanti unlocked the door and kicked it open with her heel. Then she stepped backwards down the steps.

As she retreated from the chalet, she dropped the cake knife and let the dummy swing by its arm at her side. Using her free hand, she pulled her phone from her pocket. She was about to call for backup when she heard an inhuman howl, and pivoted to see Sweetman lunging at her, arms outstretched, face crimson, like a hysterical child. 'Give her back to me!' he bawled, tugging at Kristal's legs.

Shanti hauled in the other direction, and to her dismay, Kristal's right arm came away in her hand. Sweetman stared aghast, then carefully laid the dismembered body on the ground and lunged at her.

Rotating the resin arm above her head, Shanti swung it hard and made contact with Sweetman's head with a thud. The big man emitted a groan and then tumbled backwards, cracking his skull against the base of the dovecote, from which a cooing flock exploded into the night.

In seconds, she was upon him. By the time she had hand-cuffed his wrists behind his back, many curtains were twitching along the avenues of Paradise Park.

As Sweetman groaned and stirred, Shanti heard the sound of a fast-approaching vehicle, the throaty roar of an engine from somewhere behind the chalets, and suddenly a red Vauxhall Astra came hurtling towards her.

It whirled around the dovecote and skidded to a halt in a burst of squealing tyres and scorching brakes.

Chapter 21

The Arm of the Law

As Caine leapt from the driving seat, the glare of his headlamps illuminated Shanti in the act of hauling a dazed and handcuffed Oliver Sweetman into a sitting position against the column of the dovecote. At her side was a disembodied arm.

A little further away, near the steps of the static home, lay a one-armed corpse, its white mini dress splattered with red.

'Shanti! Shanti! Are you OK?'

She rose to her feet and stared at him intently.

'OK, I'm going to ask you one question, Vincent Caine, and I want an answer right away.'

'All right,' said Caine. 'I'll try.'

'Where is Paul? If you tell me that you have left my son on his own in the middle of a forest, I will have you prosecuted for neglect.'

'Hold on, Shanti. Of course I didn't.'

'So where—'

'Paul is with Zeb.'

'Zeb? Who the actual fuck is Zeb? He's a voice on the phone. I've never met him. And neither has Paul. Does he even exist?'

'Relax, Shanti. Paul is one hundred per cent safe, I guarantee it. Zeb is the local youth leader and has four kids of his own. I left Paul playing snooker.'

'You had so better be right.'

'Trust me, Shanti. I would put my life in Zeb's hands. I couldn't just let you handle this on your own.'

'I handled it, Caine.' She pointed a foot in the direction of Sweetman, who was groaning softly.

'I can see that. But why didn't you call for backup?'

'I did. Eventually. Benno's on his way now.'

'Was he violent, Shanti? Did he attack you?'

'Wait a minute, Caine. I haven't finished *my* questions yet. How did you do that? The squealie car thing? You don't own a car. You can't even drive a car.'

'I never said that. I said I don't *like* to drive. This is Zeb's car.'

'I need to speak to Paul.'

'Of course. You've got Zeb's number.'

'Keep an eye on him,' she said, nodding towards Sweetman. 'He's a bloody maniac.'

As Shanti wandered off to make her call, the doves hovered and descended like migrants returning to their homeland.

In the distance, Caine heard the faint wail of sirens. And from all around, in the glow of Victorian street lamps, the bemused residents of Paradise began to emerge nervously from their static homes, in dressing gowns and nightwear and string vests and underwear.

'Can you keep back, please?' he called to the gawping crowd. 'This is a murder inquiry.'

There was an audible intake of breath.

'Not our Ollie.'

'Like a big dove, he is.'

'Soft as a feather.'

A bald gentleman wearing nothing but a bath towel and round spectacles stepped forward and tugged Caine's sleeve. 'I don't want to teach you your job, young fellow, but that body over there with the missing arm? I don't think it's real. That's tomato soup, not blood. Ollie wouldn't kill a real person.'

'Thanks,' said Caine. 'It's a bit complicated . . .'

The night was split with sirens and pulsing lights as Benno's Ford Focus led a patrol car and an ambulance rapidly along the drive towards them.

Shanti returned looking happier.

'Everything OK, Shanti?' asked a blinking blue Caine.

'He potted the black. And there's a nice girl looking after him.'

'One of Zeb's daughters. She's a sweetheart.'

'I'm sorry, Caine.'

'No problem. You have good reason to be protective.'

'I was in such a hurry. It felt like everything rested on this. My life, my career, my reputation.'

'Hey. It's OK. You did well.' He rubbed her shoulder gently.

She smiled at him. 'I like that you broke your holy oath of non-driving to rescue me.'

'Shanti, I've never known anyone in less need of rescuing.'

'Sweetman killed Kristal. He more or less admitted it. In any case, the mannequin puts him at the scene. It still reeks of formaldehyde. He's been living with her, Caine – as man and wife.'

'Poor Ollie.'

'Poor Shanti. He was all set for a *ménage à trois*.'

When the paramedics who had been examining Sweetman were satisfied, Benno hauled the big man to his feet.

'Do you want to do this, boss?' he asked.

'Oliver Sweetman, I am arresting you for the murder of Kristal Havfruen, at Mangrove House, Devon, on the twenty-second of July. You do not have to say anything. But it may harm your defence if you do not mention when questioned something which you later rely on in court. Anything you do say may be given in evidence.'

'No, you killed her . . . you killed my Kristal!' sobbed Sweetman.

'Shall we take him to the station, boss?' asked Benno.

'I don't want to go on no train,' Sweetman wailed.

'He's very confused,' said Shanti. 'I don't think we'll get much out of him here, poor man. But there is one person I'd like to talk to.'

She pointed towards the diminutive figure of the park's proprietor amongst the crowd. He was immaculately dressed in striped pyjamas, dressing gown and slippers.

'Mr Leggit, we'd like a word, please.'

As the neon convoy retreated, Shanti, Caine and Leggit sat on a bench beneath an ornate lamp post, looking across at Shangri-La, which had been sealed off in preparation for the crime scene investigation team. The bench appeared to be another Sweetman creation, artfully constructed from interwoven driftwood, with a cat on one arm.

'I can't believe Ollie would be involved in this,' said Leggit, shaking his head in disbelief. 'Paradise will never be the same again.'

'Mr Leggit,' said Shanti, 'I'm going to ask you to cast your mind back to Saturday the twenty-second of July.'

'I'm sorry, but I can't remember back that far.'

'It was the day of Kristal Havfruen's murder ... Mr Leggit, please, I need you to concentrate.'

'I didn't know anything about that murder until the following day, when my wife saw it on the news. Saturday is changeover day, you see. It's the busiest day of the week in Paradise.'

'How about we approach it another way, Mr Leggit?' suggested Caine. 'Have you ever noticed any unusual visitors on those Saturdays? People who don't arrive with luggage, perhaps, or who don't check in with you?'

'Now you've put me in a tizzy. You see, my wife and I have to clean the short-let chalets on Saturdays. Most people don't realise how much work is involved in running a place like this, but there are folk coming and going all day long. As for unusual ... well, I remember a naturist family who turned up one Saturday, and that needed some careful handling. We sometimes have a clown from Chard for a children's tea party. He was unusual too – blue and yellow hair. But he made the children cry so we sent him away. People don't like clowns any more and I'm not sure why.'

'Anyone else? We're thinking of people who might have visited Oliver.'

'Ah! Well you said unusual. Mr Oak often comes on a Saturday to collect Ollie. He drives a silver estate ... a Volvo, I think.'

'Busted!' muttered Shanti.

'But there's nothing unusual about that. Ollie sometimes worked over there at the weekend, so I would certainly have seen him in July, quite possibly on the day you mention.'

'Back of the net!' whispered Shanti.

'That's helpful,' said Caine. 'How about anyone else? Did Ollie have other visitors?'

'Ollie has lived here for years and years. I know him extremely well and he's the kindest gentleman you could ever meet. I simply can't believe he would hurt anyone. You should see him with his doves. They're more like homing pigeons – they follow him wherever he goes and literally eat out of his hands. I always think that you can tell a lot about people by the way animals respond to them.'

'That's very true,' said Caine. 'But you see, we think someone might have made Oliver do something terrible without him realising it. That's why our questions are important. What other friends did he have?'

'Everyone! Everyone was Oliver's friend.'

'Visitors from outside the park?'

'A little old lady in a small car like a Golf. She came several times over the years. I remember because she was a heavy smoker, and we don't allow smoking in Paradise.'

'Ah! Can you tell us more?'

'I encourage people to leave their cars at the top car park and walk. Safer for children and animals, you see. But she was partially disabled so she used to drive down to Shangri-La, then Ollie would help her into a wheelchair and push her around, showing off his handiwork. I remember this clearly because it seemed odd to see a lady in a wheelchair with a cigarette in her hand. I pointed out the No Smoking sign, but she responded with such a sweet smile that I let it go.'

'And why did she visit Oliver?' asked Shanti.

'I think they were old friends. She would sometimes take him out for the day in her car.'

'Could you put a date on any of these visits? That Saturday in July?'

'Oh dear . . . possibly. I don't monitor Ollie's movements, you know.'

'Hang on,' said Shanti. 'I saw a security camera in the reception lodge . . .'

'Yes, we have several on site.'

'That's wonderful. So you can retrieve footage?'

'I'll trust you to keep this to yourself, but they are all dummy cameras. As I said, we never had crime in Paradise until you lot came along.'

'Thank you, Mr Leggit,' said Caine. 'That's been most helpful. Will you promise to call if you think of any other details? No matter how trivial.'

'I will. And will you promise that Ollie will be well looked after? In many ways he's a genius, but in other ways he's a child. He'll be terribly disorientated and anxious about his birds.'

'You have my word,' said Caine. 'I'll keep an eye on him myself.'

Shanti's Saab and Zeb's Astra drove in tandem back to Lyme, where Shanti had to prise Paul away from the older girls who were making a fuss of him.

'It's late, darling,' she said. 'Amma will be worried. Say thank you to Zeb and goodbye to Caine.'

Paul hugged Caine and climbed peacefully into the passenger seat of Shanti's car, where he promptly fell asleep.

'He's exhausted, poor lamb.'

'That was a long walk he did earlier.'

'Oh yes, I'd forgotten. And then he must have walked all the way back to Lyme with you.'

'Well, he rode on my shoulders most of the way.'

'You're very good with him, Caine.'

They stood beside the Saab, high above the twinkling lights of Lyme.

'So,' said Caine. 'What are you thinking?'

'It pains me to say it, but you were bang on. It's exactly what you said – a symbiotic crime. It's too late tonight, but tomorrow morning I'm going to arrest the person who planned Kristal's murder and coerced Oliver into killing her.'

'And that person is . . . ?'

'Caine, you know who it is.'

'Marlene.'

'Oak.'

'Did you say Marlene, Caine?'

'Did you say Oak, Shanti?'

'Jesus, and I thought you were a professional. Let me spell this out for you. Oliver is on the payroll, right? He is completely malleable and does exactly what Oak tells him. On top of that, Oak has a big, *big* motive – Kristal humiliated him for decades: deprived him of sex, mocked his painting, et cetera et cetera. He was also skint. By murdering Kristal, he gets rid of the woman he hates and solves his financial difficulties by inheriting a fat stack of Danish krone . . . Wait a minute, I haven't finished. Oak also had the perfect opportunity. He had keys to Kristal's studio and not a single soul saw his movements. His alibi doesn't stack up, Caine. On the afternoon of the twenty-second, when he claims he was walking the dogs on the beach, he could have been anywhere. I reckon those stinky dogs pooed in the garden while their master bullied poor old Ollie into stuffing his wife in a glass tank.'

'Woo!' said Caine. 'That is a very impressive list. And it would be completely convincing except for one thing . . .'

'Which is?'

'Which is that you're wrong. I think you're forgetting how symbiosis works. Listen, Oak and Sweetman aren't complementary. Oak is a strong man too. He could have carried this out on his own, so why would he enlist Sweetman to help?'

'I don't know . . . Maybe he didn't have the guts to do it himself. Maybe he wanted to finger Sweetman. Balls to symbiosis, Caine. Tomorrow morning we are heading to Mangrove House, where I will take the greatest pleasure in bringing that pious bugger to justice. I bet you a jar of honey I'm right.'

'Organic?'

'Organic.'

Chapter 22

Doughnuts at the Deathbed

On the way to Mangrove House the following morning, the discussion resumed as if it had never ceased.

'So I was talking to Paul about your symbiosis theory,' said Shanti at the wheel.

'You're coming round to it?' asked Caine, drawing cryptic symbols in his notebook.

'Jesus, Caine, you really haven't thought this through.'

'How so?'

'OK, think about this – Paul said you came up with all this superstitious jiggery-pokery when you noticed some kind of fungus growing against a tree.'

'That's true.'

'And what kind of tree was it?'

'An oak tree.'

'Exactly. An oak tree. Get it? Oak! The universe is speaking to you and you're not listening. Now, if you remember, I supplied you with a long and credible list of motives that make Oak the killer. Can you give me even one decent reason why you think he's innocent?'

'I looked into his eyes.'

'You looked into his eyes! And tell me, what did you see in there?'

'Shanti, Callum is a deeply moral man and a sensitive artist. That's why Kristal was able to walk all over him.'

'And what about Sweetman? Everyone described him as gentle too. He keeps doves and plays mini golf and has cake for tea. But he is a twisted killer, as I nearly experienced myself. He also has sex with dummies.'

'It's not the same.'

'Detective work is about motive. What was Marlene's motive?'

'She was in love with Callum.'

'But that was years ago. She fell out of love with him, remember? Trust me, Oak is our man.'

'I do trust you, Shanti. But my intuition tells me that you're making a mistake.'

'And what is that based on? Your third eye? This is a murder investigation, DI Caine. Not a men's workshop in the sweat lodge.'

'Ah, maybe you're right. This is why I'll never make a good cop. To be honest, I find the whole thing deeply upsetting.'

'What are you upset about? Tissues in the glove compartment, by the way.'

'I'm upset about all of it – Ollie, Art, Tess … Police work destabilises me. It knocks me off centre.'

'Listen, I don't give out compliments easily, but you *are* a good cop. But you need to leave feelings out of it. Feelings are great in families and, you know . . . relationships. But solving a crime requires cold, hard logic. Cops are scientists, Caine. Ask me about my emotions.'

'OK, what are your emotions?'

'Right now, I am pumped for action. Like an Amazon warrior. I think today is going to be massive. Right . . . We're here now, so leave your notebook and your feelings in the car.'

They climbed out and walked towards the high sunbeam gates of Mangrove House. They were closed and locked, with weeds growing around the stone gateposts. Even from here, they could see that there were no vehicles near the house.

'It doesn't look like Mr Oak is home,' Shanti muttered. 'How very convenient.'

'He's probably shopping. Or in church.'

'Church, my arse. He's done a runner. He'll have heard about Sweetman by now and he's shitting his corduroy breeches.'

Caine pulled off his coat and bundled it through the car window. 'I'll take a look around,' he said.

Shanti watched as he swiftly scaled the gates and dropped to the other side, as fluid as a jaguar, then jogged briskly up the drive. He circled the house; checked a shed or two; nipped up the spiral staircase by the garage, from where he scanned the gardens and peered into Oak's studio.

In five minutes, he was back at her side. 'You're right, there's no one home. The dogs are indoors, but Callum has laid newspaper on the floor and piled their bowls with food. It's as if he's away overnight.'

What Shanti thought was: You agile bastard. You're not even out breath!

What she said was, 'Benno, get me an ANPR on Oak's

vehicle. Got the details? Silver Volvo estate: Golf One Five Sierra Alpha Juliette Yankee. Super-fast. Over.'

Then she paced restlessly about the Saab, waiting for a response. 'Are you ready for this, Caine? I'm Shanti Schwarzenegger today. I'm on an Oak hunt.'

Caine seemed more relaxed. 'How's Paul?' he asked.

'He's better. He's with my mum. But he's calmer. He wants to learn how to meditate.'

The phone buzzed in her pocket.

'Benno, that was quick ... He what? ... Is he now? OK, great work ... No, we won't need backup. We've got this covered. You know what Caine's like when he's after a scalp – a bloody animal.'

She fired up the engine and the vehicle was moving before Caine was fully inside. As he fastened his seat belt, Shanti gunned up the lane, gravel spitting from beneath the tyres.

'The ANPR cameras picked him up on the A30, heading west towards Bodmin. Benno will get back to us with more up-to-date sightings.'

'What are you thinking?'

'I'm thinking that Callous Callum the Killer is a desperate man. I'm thinking that he's heading straight for Falmouth. That's the place he knows best ... It's where all the anger began.'

'Shanti, can I make a suggestion? Why don't you simply call Callum and ask him where he's going?'

'Oh, Caine, you really are the sweetest cop in the force. I bet villains feel warm all over when DI Caine nabs them.'

They hurtled past the outskirts of Exeter, pushing 110 mph over the long flank of Dartmoor. Shanti adjusted a dial until she found Radio Devon.

'Ooh, I used to love this one!' she said, cranking up the volume. '*You gotta search for the hero inside yourself*... What kind of music do you like, Caine ...? Pink Floyd? Björk? Manfred Mann?'

'All kinds of stuff. I'm a big Philip Glass fan. I like Brian Eno, too, especially the early stuff like *Music for Airports*.'

'Don't know that one. I'm a soul girl really – anything you can dance to ...'

'You're really enjoying this, aren't you?' said Caine with a wry smile.

'Don't tell me you didn't get a kick out of that drive last night. All the squealie-wheelie stuff.'

'To be honest, I prefer a spiritual journey.'

'Guess where he is now?' called Benno from inside the dashboard. Shanti dipped the music.

'Um ... heading towards Falmouth?' she suggested.

'How did you know that, boss? Yes, he's an hour ahead of you. Let me intercept him before someone gets hurt. We've got three units within twenty miles. Over.'

'Do you ever watch cricket, Benno? You know what happens when too many players run for the same ball? This is my catch. Over and out.'

To Caine she said, 'Learn from me, Caine. You have to get inside the killer's head. Like an actor, you know? Best scenario: Oak's wandering tearfully around the art school looking for his lost virginity. Worst scenario: Marlene knows that Oak has murdered his wife and he's terrified that she'll squeal. He's killed once. How much trouble is an old lady? It would take two minutes with a pillow.'

'Shanti, I really don't think Oak is a serial killer. But if he does do something silly – to himself or someone else – and you refused backup, that could terminate your career. You know that. Why take the risk?'

She said nothing. Just gritted her teeth, pushed her foot down, and stared down the asphalt towards Land's End.

As the old gold hands on the marketplace clock pointed to 10.25, they touched down in Falmouth. By 10.27, Shanti was reversing into a tiny space on Vernon Place behind Oak's silver Volvo, thirty yards from Marlene's door.

'Gotcha!' she breathed as her heels hit the pavement.

With hands cupped over eyes, she peered into the depths of Oak's car, then legged it along the row of terraced houses, built for a smaller, more peaceful age.

Thrusting her thumb against the doorbell, all she heard was the wind, and the distant wail of gulls.

Marlene's bell was deceased.

She rapped and pounded on the door. Gave it twenty seconds, then ran around the back. Caine chased after her, along a narrow cobbled alleyway where washing fluttered like families dancing upside down.

'This is the one,' said Caine, opening the latch of a knee-high gate. They stepped into an unloved yard where a brown bra hung stiffly on a line. In an ashtray beside a white plastic chair, cardboard roaches and cigarette stubs spumed like lava. The door of the small conservatory was open, and they slid into the tropical interior, as hot and heady as a hemp rainforest.

Shanti tested the handle into the house and nodded. They entered the kitchen.

'Marlene!' she called. 'Marlene!'

No answer.

Caine followed her into the art-filled sitting room. The house felt cold. No one had sat here for a while. Something about the place felt wrong.

Like a gunslinger in a Western, he pirouetted around the banister and crept up the carpeted stairs beside the Stannah stairlift. Shanti followed, treads creaking under her boots. The atmosphere was thick with nicotine and dust, like a pyramid inhabited by chain-smoking mummies.

Caine skulked along the sloping corridor, checking out an olive bathroom fitted with grab bars and hoists like a geriatric gymnasium. Another door opened into a spare room, filled with a spare bed and a lifetime's spare things. At the far end of the landing, a low pink door bore an enamelled Monet name plaque: *Marlene*.

Slow as a sloth, Shanti turned the handle and they stepped cautiously into the claustrophobic interior, where a dozen candles burned.

Marlene was laid out on the bed. Eyelids closed deep within their sockets. Cheekbones protruding like hips. Her parchment hands encircled a ceramic bowl filled with dog ends as though it was a holy icon. The room reeked of tobacco and warm urine.

Callum Oak was kneeling with his back towards them, hands raised in supplication. He wore coffee-coloured corduroys and a white grandad shirt with vermilion braces. The back of his curly head showed the first signs of balding.

In his raised hands he held aloft a stubby bible and a silver cross, which sparkled in the light of the flickering flames.

'Step away from the body,' ordered Shanti. 'Move slowly, Mr Oak, so I can see your hands.'

Callum Oak turned to face her. His palms still raised. A never-ending prayer tumbling from his lips.

'Callum Oak, I am charging you with the murder of your wife, Kristal Havfruen, and also the lady beside you, your friend Marlene Moss.'

Oak stopped praying, dropped his arms and stared at her in disbelief.

'Will this be a weekly occurrence? Accusing me of murder, I mean.'

'What did Marlene ever do to you, Callum?'

'But I never touched Marlene!'

On the bed, Marlene's thin eyelids sprang open, and she smiled. 'Someone's using my name in vain,' she said.

'Jesus! Marlene! You're alive!' said Shanti.

'Another excellent observation from the West Country constabulary.'

'But then ... then what is *he* doing here?' said Shanti, pointing at Oak.

'I've been leading us in prayer,' he said.

'Leading us into sleep more like,' said Marlene. 'It's the bible readings that send me off. We should tape it, Ms Joyce, and sell it to insomniacs. We'd make a fortune.'

'I'm sorry. I'm rather confused.'

As he rose to his full height, Oak's curls grazed the ceiling. 'Look, I don't see that this is any of your business, but Marlene phoned me to say that the illness had reached a critical stage, so I drove down to share her vigil.'

'It's true!' wailed Marlene theatrically. 'The Grim Reaper has me in his cold embrace.'

'I'm sorry, Marlene. How long have they given you, if you don't mind me asking?'

'A week. A month. The worst thing is, I just paid my car

insurance. Someone give me a drink, for Christ's sake. I'm absolutely parched.'

Callum took a glass of water from the bedside table and gently raised her fragile head. She pecked at the liquid like a pigeon in a puddle, then irritably brushed him aside.

'Do the fun bit again, dear. You were arresting Callum . . .'

'Yes, um . . . Callum Oak, I have reason to believe that you coerced Oliver Sweetman into murdering your wife. What do you have to say?'

'Don't just stand there, Callum,' snapped Marlene. 'Speak up for yourself for once in your life.'

'Look, I've had enough of your insinuations, Inspector Joyce. I hear you arrested poor Ollie last night, but unless you have some actual evidence against me, I'd ask you to leave the house immediately.'

'Hooray!' said Marlene, whose voice had been restored by the water. 'You tell her!'

Caine stepped forward and gently took hold of the old woman's hand. 'Marlene, perhaps the best thing would be if you told us the whole story from beginning to end. I'd like to know exactly what happened on the day of the private view. Here, let me sit you up a little.'

He plumped the pillows against the bedstead and raised her feather-light body.

'Ooh, such strong hands!' sighed Marlene. 'Now there's a real man! Razor-sharp detective skills, too. I spotted that intellect the moment I saw him. Get out the cuffs, DI Caine, and bear me away.'

'We've been through this, Marlene,' said Shanti. 'I'm trying to arrest a murderer, not someone who's been growing wacky baccy in the conservatory.'

Marlene fixed Shanti with her beady eyes. A wicked smile flickered across her emaciated face. 'You underestimate me, Inspector Joyce. If you will allow me to misquote Elizabeth I, "I may have the body of a weak and feeble woman, but I have the heart and stomach of a cold-blooded serial killer."'

Every eye in the room was fixed on the weeny woman half submerged in a cumulus of pillows.

'Ah ha! Just look at you all! You don't know whether to believe me or not. Well, if I was handing out the gongs at the police ball, I'd give a big shiny one to handsome Mr Caine. I'd make him wear a uniform, though.'

'Is this for real?' gasped Shanti.

'I don't know why you're all so shocked. That bitch had it coming for years.'

A hand shot to Oak's mouth, and he backed away from the bed as if the old woman had the plague.

'So tell me, Marlene,' said Shanti suspiciously. 'How did you carry out this offence?'

'Shall I tell her, or shall I take it to my grave? That's the question ... I know, let's make a deal – if Callum pops downstairs and makes us all a nice cup of tea, then Marlene will reveal all. Does that sound fair?'

'I ... I will do no such thing!' gasped Callum Oak. 'Marlene ... I always thought of you as my dearest friend. Now you tell me that you killed my wife. Am I to believe you? Someone tell me – what am I supposed to do?'

Marlene sighed and lit a cigarette. 'Callum, I honestly don't care what you do. All I ask is that you run along and make the tea. I wouldn't swear to it, but I think there may be a bag of jam doughnuts in the larder. I'm sure Mr Caine would enjoy a doughnut.'

Oak backed towards the door with an expression of utter bewilderment plastered across his boyish face.

'You'd better hurry, Callum,' called Marlene. 'Otherwise I might be dead.'

Chapter 23

All the Deadly Details

Callum Oak's footsteps thundered down the stairs. They heard him gasping and puffing in dismay as he leapt four steps at a time.

Almost submerged in the bed, the emaciated old lady pulled deeply on her cigarette, a mischievous grin on her elfin face.

'Such a weak man,' she sighed. 'Handsome, but spineless. But look at me! I'm so spoiled. It's such a treat to have all these lovely visitors in my bedroom. Now it is rather a long story, so we may as well get comfy. There are folding chairs in the spare room, Mr Caine. And Ms Joyce, would you be so kind as to empty the potty? It's a bit whiffy, isn't it?'

When Oak returned with a tray, he was gasping with emotion. There were no clear surfaces amongst the numerous candles in the tiny bedroom, so he placed everything on the floor – plates, doughnuts, a teapot, four cups, teaspoons, milk and sugar. Caine thought of honey.

'Now gather round, children,' began the aged raconteur, smoke streaming from each nostril. 'It's story time!'

Shanti found her phone and furtively hit Record.

'To be honest, I would have gladly murdered Kristal the moment I laid eyes on her. I'm sorry, Callum, but that girl was so full of herself, with her little tits poking out like this and her little arse poking out like that. But it wasn't until years later, when I was diagnosed with this death thing, that the plot began to fully form into its magnificent shape. What did I have to lose, Inspector Joyce? Bugger all is the answer to that. All those hours I spent waiting in hospital corridors, reading my Agatha Christies, until eventually I thought: if not now, then it will never happen. By a stroke of fortune, I had already begun to squirrel away the odd bit of ketamine each time I visited Mangrove House. Art was always careless with his powders, and the original plan was to give myself a happy exit to the hereafter if life became a bore. But with the help of Milly, Molly and Mandy, I was able to control the pain ... and by the way, Inspector Caine, I was quite wrong – all the plants *are* girls. Isn't that marvellous! Milly was just a slow developer, but she has a lovely head of bud now ...'

Oak, who had been uncomfortably perched on the end of the bed, rose to his feet. 'Sorry, would anyone mind if I opened the window? I feel rather queasy.'

He jiggled the sash until it burst open. A smoky weather front departed the room and a blast of salty ozone burst in.

'On the day Art delivered the flowerpots, he told me about the ghastly show that his mother was planning with that silly man Spencer at the Meat Hook Gallery. All that pretentious nonsense and the absolutely puerile "happening" in the final gallery with the melodramatic music and spotlights and the ridiculous pretend Kristal floating in the glass tank ... as if Damien Hirst hadn't done the same thing thirty years ago. Pah! I know Hirst and even he would have laughed. And as for the masters ... Turner would have spat in her eye! Frida would have smacked her silly bottom. After Art had gone, I sat in my living room smoking my little spliffs, ruminating on your painting, Callum Oak. Suddenly, it was as if the Muse herself had waltzed into the living room. A moment of pure artistic genius! It came to me that there was a far more creative application for my ketamine collection.'

Oak groaned and shook his head in disbelief.

'Now for a sturdy young body like Mr Caine's here, or Ms Joyce's, there would be no difficulty in carrying out my little scheme, but look ...' She raised the sleeve of her nightie and flexed a bicep like a sparrow's. 'Nothing wrong up here.' She tapped her thin hairline. 'But the old bod has seen better days. It came to me that I needed an accomplice – someone with a bit of brawn.'

'Ollie!' mumbled Oak like a terrified child.

'Do stop whimpering, Callum. And eat your doughnut or give it to DI Caine. If you'd had the balls to deal with her years ago, I would never have had to do this.'

She brushed ash from the quilt and sipped her tea.

'Yes, poor dear Ollie. Such an easily manipulated man.' She sighed deeply. 'Of course, I didn't bother him with the details until the day. He would only have got muddled. Now, as I said, Art had told me all about this monstrous artwork Kristal had planned, and that it would be collected from her studio on the day of the private view. I realised there would be a window of opportunity.

'You know how close I've been to the family, Callum, and in all those years I've never seen you miss a holy day of obligation. As luck would have it, the twenty-second of July is the feast day of St Mary Magdalene, which is rather fitting, since she was a fallen woman like me – I bet she liked a little wacky baccy too. So I telephoned the very helpful vicar of Branscombe and asked what time the service was due to begin, and how long it was likely to go on for. We humans are creatures of habit, Ms Joyce, so I also guessed that Callum would stop at the Fountain Head for half a pint of Branoc and a crab sandwich . . . Was I correct, Callum? I also calculated that Ollie would not be at Mangrove House, given that Callum was at church. So I left Falmouth bright and early and whizzed up to Paradise Park.

'How did I feel? Elated! Delirious with excitement! It was the first time I had used my little car for ages – and the last, as it turned out. It was a golden day. The sun was shining, and I had a *mission*, Ms Joyce! I'm sure you know how that feels. In my handbag, I carried a hypodermic syringe, which I had pilfered from the nice nurse who visits me. It was pre-filled with enough ketamine to take down a mammoth. I stopped only once, at Trago Mills, to buy a large polythene sheet. As I expected, I found dear Ollie feeding his doves. At first he was reluctant to break his routine, but after a little persuasion, he warmed to the idea of a day out with Auntie Marlene.'

Oak, looking decidedly nauseous, clutched his bible and stared with increasing horror.

'On the way, he told me that Kristal had been particularly horrid lately – all spiky and agitated. On several occasions she had told him that he was stupid and useless. So I put an idea to

247

him: "Shall we help her relax, Ollie?" Oliver thought it was a splendid suggestion.

'I was delighted to find that no one was at home at Mangrove House except Kristal, tearing about in her studio like an insane poodle, barking into her phone and generally being the puffed-up prima donna we all loved to despise. "What are you doing here?" she shrieked at me. She was wearing the usual ridiculous pre-teen clothing. "You know I cannot be disturbed when I am preparing for a show." Ollie smiled that lovely innocent smile of his and, just as I had instructed, moved behind Kristal to grab her, enveloping her entire torso and arms. She started screaming. I popped open my handbag, and then—'

Callum had turned a bilious shade of green. He rushed from the room and vomited copiously into the avocado toilet bowl.

'A weak constitution,' sighed Marlene, lighting another cigarette from the stub of the old one. 'It's all that religion that does it. Where was I now . . . ah, yes. Ollie had a good grip on her, but she made such a song and dance that he began to get distressed. That's when I moved in as fast as the old pins would allow. I *plunged* the syringe deep into her jugular – decades of studying anatomy classes really paid off – and pressed it home. I must admit that my hands are rather shaky these days, so it wasn't the neatest job, but it did the trick. Within seconds, that abominable screeching subsided and Kristal went all flippety-flop in Ollie's arms. "You see," I said to him. "She's all relaxed and happy now, Ollie. She's having a lovely, lovely sleep. Night night, Kristal!"'

Oak staggered back into the room, wiping his mouth with a handkerchief. His bloodshot eyes fixed on Marlene and his mouth opened as if he was about to speak. But no words were forthcoming.

Marlene smiled triumphantly as she continued. 'My main concern was the disposal of the body, preferably with a degree of elegance and drama. Getting away with my crime . . . well, that was just a bonus. But I've never been afraid of doing bird . . . Is that the expression, Ms Joyce?'

'Not since the 1970s,' said Shanti.

'I'd love to pretend I had every detail planned in advance, but to be honest, it wasn't until I was standing in Kristal's studio that the Muse really came up trumps. As Ollie laid her out on a couch, I noticed a boxed object sitting on a pallet by the French doors, ready for collection. It was plastered with FRAGILE stickers and I guessed that this must be the centrepiece of Kristal's self-indulgent pageant. It was all in such poor taste, Ms Joyce, that was the thing I really objected to! Poor aesthetics would be an imprisonable offence if I had my way.

'I asked Ollie to remove the plywood packing, and inside was the glass tank with an astonishingly lifelike replica of Madame Havfruen floating within. Bingo! Bingo, Mr Caine! Bingo, Ms Joyce! Ollie is so good with his hands, it took him only moments to unscrew the lid, and oh, the stench of that formaldehyde! How it aggravates the breathing. Nonetheless, needs must. I instructed him to don rubber gloves and a mask and apron, which were readily available in the studio. Then I told him to carefully remove the effigy from the tank. He appeared a little distressed and doubtful at this stage of the proceedings, so I promised that he could keep synthetic Kristal as a reward for his labours. He cheered up quite a bit at that, and laid the vile mannequin on the polythene sheet as instructed. Then as gently as a parent bathing a newborn, he lowered the real sleeping Kristal inside the tank. It took a bit of poking about to create that nice foetal position, but he managed it in the end.

'It was perfect! I knew that Kristal would be drowning peacefully, avoiding all that disagreeable thrashing about, so she would look beautiful for her big night, just as she would have wanted . . . Oh, Callum, you're not going to vomit again . . . ?'

The bathroom door banged.

Marlene winked confidentially. 'Frankly, it was a merciful end for a woman who deserved none. Then it was plain sailing. Ollie re-boxed the tank and we sped away in my little car, giggling like infants, with synthetic Kristal tucked up in the boot. This was his prize: to keep a kind, gentle Kristal forever – a new, improved version of the woman he'd always adored. One who would never utter an unkind word. He was absolutely thrilled. And he promised, promised, promised to keep our little secret.

'Back at Shangri-La, we had tea and took it in turns to shower and dress for the private view. Although I did my best to dissuade him, I just couldn't prevent him from taking Kristal into the shower with him. Distasteful as it was, at least it washed away some of that formaldehyde.

'We arrived at the gallery in plenty of time, and it was the crowning moment of a perfect day to witness the awe with which my masterpiece was received. Huge fun! And of course I pretended to be as shocked as everyone else. Ollie was as good as gold, but to be honest, I dread to think what became of that poor mannequin when I dropped him off back at Shangri-La that night . . . All those pent-up emotions.'

There was a stunned silence. Even Caine, who had been convinced of Marlene's guilt, was slow to speak. Eventually he managed a question that had been troubling him. 'The gloves, plastic sheet and syringe. Where did you dispose of them?'

Marlene dismissed the question with a flick of her hand. 'I'm no master criminal, Mr Caine, but I've never understood why murderers dump incriminating evidence so close to the scene for the boys in blue to find in minutes. I flung the syringe over a bridge outside Axminster, where it must have plopped into the river. The sheet we discarded on a farm close to Paradise Park, one of those places covered in pools of slurry and cast-off farm equipment – the kind of spot where bad smells are par for the course. As for the gloves, Ollie shoved them in a bin outside Sainsbury's in Chard.'

'So you killed Kristal because she was a prima donna and a bully?' asked Shanti, with a note of hostility in her voice. 'Or was it because she thwarted you in love so many years ago?'

'Oh no, dear. I mean, all of those reasons are perfectly valid. But my motive was infinitely grander. I killed Kristal to save Art.'

'Art, your godson?'

'No, silly girl, not A Boy Named Art – I'm talking about *Art*, the lifeblood of humanity! When Kristal came to Falmouth as a student with that horrible, licentious sex show, she turned my beloved school upside down. Many people claimed that she was good for the place – look at the Havfruen Building and all the money that flowed in. But over the years, I had lovingly, *painstakingly* created a hothouse of creativity, where the heirs to Velázquez, Rembrandt, Ingres, Delacroix and Cézanne bloomed. Where did all that "performance art" and "conceptualism" leave my painting school? I'll tell you where! Unloved! Underfunded! Dying, Ms Joyce ... as I am now. Kristal had the audacity to claim that she gave birth to Art, but as far as I was concerned, she murdered Art itself. And for that . . . I killed her.'

The wind had left Marlene's sails. She slumped into the pillows like a deflating balloon.

'Can I say it now?' asked Shanti.

'All right by me,' said Caine.

'Marlene Moss, I am arresting you for the murder of Kristal Havfruen. You do not have to say anything, but it may harm your defence if you do not mention when questioned something which you later rely on in court. Anything you do say may be given in evidence.'

Marlene rallied a little and her cloudy eyes sparkled. 'Oh, how utterly marvellous! You've no idea how long I've waited to hear those words. Will I get the flashing lights? And the big burly constables? And the sirens? Don't forget the sirens, I beg you.'

'First we'll need to verify everything you've told us,' said Shanti. 'But if it turns out to be true, I'm afraid you'll be in no position to demand anything.'

'But I will go to prison? Surely I will. I demand a life sentence.'

'I hate to disappoint you, Marlene,' said Caine, 'but given your health, it's more likely that you will be cared for in a secure hospital.'

'Oh really! That doesn't seem fair at all. This was premeditated murder, Mr Caine.'

'Marlene, I honestly don't think prison is the place for you.'

'Well, look, supposing we add a few more offences?'

'What sort of offences?'

'Oh, all kinds of things. For example, do you remember Ratty, the painting tutor I mentioned who committed suicide by flinging himself off a cliff? He took me out to paint the hills and sky, but it turned out the only hills Ratty had in mind were these.' She lifted her breasts like empty paper bags.

Shanti and Caine stared in disbelief.

'We were working side by side on the clifftop and he kept coming over and pawing me, so I used my easel to give him a little shove. I didn't mean to send him to his doom, but it was rather satisfying. I spread a rumour that he had been driven insane by Kristal's happening – you know, *Preconception*. I couldn't believe how easily I got away with it. Then murder became a habit, Mr Caine, and I've always had a problem with habits.'

The tiny bedroom fell silent. All eyes were on the old lady sucking the last breath of nicotine from the stub of her cigarette.

'Murder is like smoking,' explained Marlene Moss. 'It's just so moreish!'

Chapter 24

The Motel on the Moor

The final departure from Vernon Place was not what Marlene had hoped for – horizontal in an ambulance rather than hand-cuffed in a wailing patrol car.

By the time Shanti had released Callum Oak, debriefed the SOCO squad and overseen a full search of Marlene's house, it was after 9 p.m. She called home and spoke to Paul.

'Sweetheart, I'm sorry. I thought I'd be back hours ago . . . but guess what?'

'What?'

'You were right about symbiosis. We cracked the case. I'll tell you all about it when I see you.'

'Tonight?'

'No. Not tonight. I'm still in Cornwall. I won't be home until very late, or tomorrow. But Amma will look after you, and listen, Paul . . . I've got some holiday coming up. We're going to spend lots of time together. What would you like to do?'

'Go to Caine's place. Sleep in a hammock.'

***

Plump raindrops tumbled onto the windscreen, and following an hour stuck in roadworks outside Truro, it was after 11 p.m. by the time they reached the lonesome wilderness of Bodmin Moor.

The satisfaction of concluding the case had crumpled into sheer exhaustion. Shanti realised they wouldn't arrive in Lyme Regis until the small hours, and then Caine would have an hour and a half's walk through the Undercliff, and she would have another hour's drive to Yeovil.

The man was annoyingly telepathic. 'There's a motel up here on the moor. It's a bit of a dive, but we can get a meal and a shower and a bed.'

'Two beds.'

'Of course that's what I mean. Pull in over there and we'll see what it's like.'

The Blisland Motel was quite possibly the most depressing place Shanti had ever seen – a drab single-storey building within rumbling distance of the A30, fronted by a potholed car park full of heavy goods vehicles. But she was freezing now and it was an effort to keep her eyes open.

In the motel reception, a bowl of ancient potpourri on the untidy desk battled with the odour of overcooked vegetables. Above a filing cabinet, a faded picture of a wild Bodmin pony was draped with a lonely strand of tinsel from a long-forgotten Christmas. The pony looked as weary as Shanti felt. She pinged a bell on the desk. It was a full ten minutes before a large woman in a nightie appeared.

'We're closed.'

'We were hoping to get two rooms.'

'Fell out with your chap, did you?'

'He's not my chap. We're work colleagues.'

'None of my business, I'm sure. But there's only one twin room and I haven't made the beds.'

'Is there another hotel around here? Or a B and B?'

'Ha! Not for miles. It's a nice room. Views across the moor. We've got a star, you know.'

'What do you mean, you've got a star?'

'Some places don't have no stars. We got a star and we do a nice breakfast.' She leaned across and whispered, 'I wouldn't mind getting cosy if he was *my* colleague.'

'For God's sake. Can you get us some sheets? And I want a discount too, or you won't have that star for much longer.'

The room was large, with two single beds. Shanti had brought no nightclothes and not even a toothbrush. But that wasn't the worst thing. To her utter dismay, she noticed that the bathroom had been constructed behind nothing more than a glass screen at the end of the room. With a cautious finger she slid back the door and took in an array of hideous details: algae around the shower, stray pubic hairs, crescent nail clippings by a half-full bin, a mottled mirror, and a commune of watching spiders.

'Caine, I need a shower. And I need to get to bed. So bugger off and meditate or walk on the moor or something and don't come back till I'm in the land of the fairies. Is that OK?'

He grinned at her. 'Do you want me to sleep in the car? That would be fine.'

'Yes. No. Shit. Just give me half an hour, OK. And here . . . make your sodding bed.'

She hurled a set of nylon sheets and pillowcases in his direction.

Despite the rumbling traffic, Shanti plunged into a bottomless sleep. She dreamed that she was still driving while the incessant rain hammered on the windscreen. In the passenger seat beside her sat the skeletal form of Marlene Moss. 'Marlene?' Shanti asked. 'Was it really you? How could you do that? How could you kill Kristal?' The old lady turned to tell her something of great significance, but when she opened her mouth, her face was that of Munch's *Scream*.

She struggled to wake, and when she did, she found that a sickly dawn was breaking outside the worn curtains, and the relentless sound was not the rain on the windscreen but water pounding on the glass screen, behind which her work colleague, Vincent Caine, was soaping his athletic body.

Shanti lay motionless beneath the viscous sheets and found she could do nothing but feign sleep and watch. Well, she could have closed her eyes or turned to face the other way, but that would have been sort of ... wasteful. Still in her dreamy stupor, the sight of Vincent Caine appeared to her as a bronzed vision, his toned torso formed an elongated triangle from wide shoulders to lean waist. For a full ten minutes she was obliged to spy through her fingers as Caine raised his face in ecstasy to the streaming water. She contemplated the sparkling rivulets cascading down the furrow of his spine, the chiselled dimples of his buttocks and it was without doubt the most unsettling thing she had ever seen.

How much easier it would be if Caine had some obvious defect – a sagging beer paunch; a dense coat of ape-like hair; a tiny gerbil's penis. She would never mention his shortcoming, but she would always know that her colleague was not quite as perfect as he pretended to be. But as he worked shampoo through his long tresses, and she took advantage of his tightly closed eyes to fully scrutinise his anatomy, it became evident that none of these things were true. Caine was as faultless a physical specimen as ever walked the earth. His abdomen was as honed as a peppermill; his golden skin was smooth but for a silky black trail connecting navel to pubic hair. And his penis was shockingly long and sleepily beautiful.

Supposing they teamed up on another case? How could she work with him now? How could she delete this data from her hard drive? She lay rigidly unmoving as Caine dried himself carefully, dressed and slipped from the room. And later, as they sat opposite each other in the Blisland Breakfast Bar, cautiously prodding their one-star breakfast – tinned pineapple and a soft-boiled egg for him, the Full Cornish for her – her mind returned again and again to the steaming spectacle of Caine's muscular waterfall body, which had nothing – absolutely nothing – to do with the case in hand and the pressing business of the day.

They drove silently through the morning, lost in their own thoughts. Near the clock tower in Lyme Regis, Caine climbed out of the car. He slung his bag over his shoulder, waved once and began to walk away.

Shanti wound down her window and called to him.

'Caine . . . come here a moment.'

He returned to her window and smiled. For the first time, she acknowledged that maybe Dawn Knightly had been right. There was something strangely attractive about the man.

'Listen . . . I should say thanks and everything.'

'You're welcome.' Jesus, his teeth were white.

'And I was wondering . . . maybe this is a bit much to ask, but

Paul has developed a bit of a thing about sleeping in a hammock. I'll have to wind things down at the station, which could take a week or two, but if you're free and it's not too much trouble, I guess we'll need a debrief, if you know what I mean. There are still a few loose threads that need tying up . . .'

'Let's do that, Shanti. Let's tie up those loose threads.'

Caine stood watching the Saab heading up Broad Street. When she had gone, he turned up the collar of his coat and set off in the direction of the Undercliff.

The silence of the forest was like a tonic. How he longed for the solitude of his cabin. Life was so much simpler on your own.

And yet she talked about threads. Against all his instincts, a slender thread seemed to run from his heart back towards the town, up Broad Street and all the way along the winding West Country roads and lanes to the strong, brown-eyed woman in the retreating Saab.

She had called it a debrief, but Caine sensed something beyond the call of duty from this unexpected visitor in his life.

As she neared Yeovil, the brown-eyed woman was experiencing something that she hadn't felt for a long time. It was such an unfamiliar sensation that she had trouble naming it . . . Happiness, that was what it was. She cranked up the dial on the radio, singing loudly all the way.

On the industrial outskirts of town, she ran into heavy traffic, and as she accelerated in slow fits and starts, her eyes wandered to a huge billboard advertising, of all things, meat-free soya sausages. Below the words *TENDER AND SATISFYING*, a vast glistening sausage was impaled on a fork.

She found herself blushing, and then laughing out loud. What the hell was wrong with her? Too much time on her own.

She drove into the silent cul-de-sac that was her new home, and when she saw the apple-faced boy with the football, her own face lit up with joy.

Chapter 25

The Wings of a Dove

Caine showed his ID to the guard at the barrier. He was pleased to notice that beyond the high mesh fences, the many windows of the secure hospital overlooked fields and woodland.

He was directed towards a reception desk in the main building, where a male nurse and a female doctor assured him that patient C193 Oliver Sweetman had settled in nicely and was in good spirits – his ready smile and obliging ways had already made him friends on the ward.

'So long as he can get into the gardens, he seems perfectly happy,' said the doctor. 'I'll take you to find him if you want.'

Caine followed her along a maze of magnolia corridors and through a TV lounge where the troubled souls of society sat out their days. Along the way she talked about the many challenges of balancing care with custody.

'The public have a right to feel safe, and our service users, as we call them, need to have their mental health issues treated humanely and effectively.'

'And none of that comes cheap,' said Caine.

'Everyone here is considered a danger to themselves or to others,' said the doctor, as she tapped a code into an airlock security door. 'I know about Oliver's culpability in the Havfruen case, but a man like that wouldn't last a week in a mainstream prison.'

'I agree,' said Caine. 'Thankfully his lawyer did a good job. He successfully argued that Ollie couldn't be charged because he didn't have the capacity to form a criminal intent.'

They stepped into the gardens, where men of various ages wandered around the gravelled paths with visitors or nurses.

Caine spotted Oliver on a bench, his orange hair in shocking contrast to the green rhododendron leaves.

'Hello, Ollie. Remember me?'

'Hello, Vincent Caine. You want to see what I made?'

'I certainly do.'

Caine and the doctor followed the big man along a neatly edged path towards a tidy grassed area surrounded by trees and brick buildings bristling with security cameras.

In the centre of the lawn stood an extraordinarily elaborate structure on a thick wooden post. It was a dovecote, but infinitely more elaborate than the one at Paradise Park. This was a veritable palace for doves, with dozens of arched doorways, staircases, delicate crenellations, spires and turrets.

'It's astonishing, Ollie!' said Caine. 'I'd love to know where it all comes from.'

'From the workshop over there,' Oliver said.

'We heard that Ollie liked making things,' explained the doctor. 'So we gave him access to the workshops. Then he built this incredible thing, and one of the gardeners helped him to instal it.'

Oliver seemed to be in a dream, a distant smile on his face. He was staring through the high fence at the countryside and the pale sky beyond.

'I think he's a kind of a genius really,' said Caine. 'It's a shame he doesn't have his birds any more.'

'That's what I was going to tell you,' said the doctor. 'It was like magic. One day we saw him standing here, staring up at the sky, just as he is now. We couldn't work out what he was doing, and then . . . well, you'll see for yourself.'

Oliver's hands were raised in front of him like Francis of Assisi, and from out of the heavens, first one, then two and then three white birds descended.

As Caine and the doctor looked on, an entire flock of doves appeared like angels. They settled all over the dovecote palace and on Oliver's arms and shoulders and the top of his flaming head.

'They must have followed him from Paradise Park,' said Caine. 'Just like homing pigeons.'

'There's my girls,' said Ollie happily. 'There's my beauties. Fly free, my lovelies . . . fly free . . .'

Chapter 26

I Cannot Put You Down

'I know what you're thinking, Caine.'

'I wasn't thinking anything.'

'Jesus, Caine, it's not even possible not to think.'

'That's what you think, Shanti.'

There was a long pause. But out here at Caine's cove, those silences felt as easy as the lull between waves.

Behind them, at the edge of the forest, Paul slept soundly in a hammock cocoon slung between two trees.

Caine watched the smoke from the campfire. Eventually he said:

'So what do you think I was thinking?'

'That you were right and I was wrong.'

'See, Shanti, this was always my problem as a cop. I actually don't believe in right and wrong, or good and bad. The Buddha didn't either. He reckoned that there is skilful action and unskilful action. Skilful action is what benefits you and other beings. And unskilful action is what impedes the journey.'

'Well I don't know how that would work in a court of law. Anyway, look, I've got something for you ...'

She rummaged in her bag, and passed him a jar in a paper bag.

'Organic honey, like I promised. Now we're square. You did good. I did good. I don't want to hear another word about it.'

Caine smiled and thanked her. He shoved another piece of driftwood onto the flames, sending a surge of sparks towards the stars. The summer was at an end. A sprinkle of gold had tumbled over the Undercliff.

'So I guess that's it, Caine. The Havfruen case is closed. Marlene will go to trial in a few months – if she lasts that long. Then the press will go crazy for a few days and the whole thing will settle down.'

The kettle began to boil and Caine wrapped a towel around one hand and removed it carefully from the fire. Slowly and methodically, he made tea.

The slogan on Caine's mug said: *Born-again Buddhist (and again and again and again . . .)*. The slogan on Shanti's mug said: *I can't believe it's not Buddha.*

'You deserve some time out, Shanti. Relax. Do stuff with Paul. You are always welcome here, you know that.'

'Thanks, Caine, that's exactly what I'm going to do. I feel I've proved something to the Yeovil crew, and I've proved something to myself as well. But you know what else this case has proved, don't you?'

'What's that?'

'It proves that you are no longer sick. The Super is most impressed with your efforts. He says he can't wait to welcome you back to the team.'

'I can't go back into that station, Shanti.'

'Not even to work with me?'

Maybe he imagined it, but it seemed that Shanti had shifted a fraction closer on the sand. He unfolded a blanket and wrapped it around her shoulders.

'The thing is, DI Caine, although you're a bit of a freak, we're almost like mates, aren't we?'

'Almost. Now, you said there were some loose threads?'

'There are a couple of things. I wondered if you ever heard from the Danes?'

'Of course. I meant to tell you. This is unbelievably bizarre! You're not going to believe it . . .'

'You know what, Caine? My credulity has been stretched so far since I met you . . . It's like giving birth – you think you can't stretch any further, but somehow you do.'

'I got a message from Aksel. Remember him?'

'Rasmussen's nephew.'

'Right. Him and brother Carl are setting up an art museum in Copenhagen. It seems there's been a huge resurgence of interest in Kristal's work since her death, so the Rasmussen family have invested a small fortune in a permanent Havfruen collection, taking up an entire floor.'

'I won't be visiting.'

'They already have the body casts. And Spencer persuaded Callum to sell them *Preconception2*, the steel sculpture in his garden. I expect he was glad to see the back of it. But here's the thing . . . it seems that Spencer finally pulled off a deal on that unique and priceless Havfruen artwork he was talking about.'

'Do I want to know this?'

'The church authorities wouldn't allow Kristal's glass coffin to be buried at Branscombe, so . . .'

'Oh no!'

'That's right. Kristal's coffin was filled with formaldehyde and resealed. She will be gazed upon forever.'

'That's obscene! Is it even legal?'

'It's what she would have wanted.'

High above Shanti's head, the indigo sky was pricked with inestimable pinholes, a reminder of how tiny and insignificant her troubles were.

'Is that everything, Shanti? Is that all the loose threads?'

'You know it isn't.'

'I'm sorry, I don't understand.'

'Listen, Caine. I've been honest with you, haven't I? You know everything about me. You've met my mum. I've talked about my dad. Paul thinks you're his best mate. And I've even told you about my divorce.'

'It's true. You are incredibly open.'

'But this is it. I don't know anything about you. Not one thing. You are an enigma. A man of mystery.'

'There's nothing to tell.'

'You're such a liar, Caine. You call yourself a Buddhist . . .'

'A Buddhist is just someone walking a path. I never claimed to be enlightened.'

She glared fiercely with those big brown eyes.

'Let me know when that happens, Vincent Caine! In the meantime, maybe this is a bad idea – you know, you and me and Paul on the beach.'

'Mum! Be quiet!' called a voice from the cocoon.

'Oh, I'm sorry, Paul. It's just that Caine is—'

'I mean, why don't you be quiet and listen to Caine?'

'Jesus. OK. Right, go back to sleep, sweetheart. I won't shout any more.'

She lowered her voice. 'OK, I'll be straight with you, Caine. I probably shouldn't have done this, but last time I visited the cabin, I noticed a photograph face down on the . . . what do you call it?'

'The shrine.'

'Right. On the shrine. That's Papa Caine, isn't it?'

There was another pause. But this one was awkward. Uneasy. Tense.

'Thing is, Caine, in a normal house – my house, for example – there are photos everywhere. I mean, we literally have an entire wall in the kitchen covered with pictures of the family. There are even a few of my ex, you know, for Paul's sake. But as far as I can tell, that weird little photo, face down on the . . .'

'On the shrine.'

'Yeah, the shrine. Well, that's the only image you have of your family . . . So it does kinda make a girl wonder . . .'

Caine said nothing. He sipped his tea and stared into the embers.

A long time passed. And then Shanti said, 'You know what? Forget it. I was beginning to think that you were different from other men. I thought you were all about honesty and openness and being in touch with your feelings.'

'I'm sorry, Shanti. It's hard. Can I just say that some stuff happened? A long time ago. It's like a shadow in my life. I am trying to deal with it, but it's something I have to do alone.'

'What are you saying? Are you telling me that you were a bent cop or something?'

'No, of course not! Nothing like that. All of this happened when I was practically a kid. I was a victim – just like Ollie and Tess and even Art. It's the reason I left home and went travelling. That's how I ended up in the forest monastery in Thailand, and it was the best thing that ever happened to me. One thing they taught us is that actions have consequences, and the consequences of what happened in my family were huge. That's all I can say right now. I know you want to tie up all the loose threads, but life isn't always that simple. One day I will tell you everything. I promise I will.'

'You know these mugs, Caine?'

'What mugs?'

'Your mug collection.'

'OK.'

'Did you take them into work when you were based in Yeovil?'

'I don't know. Maybe.'

'You see, this is why people laugh at you. It's time someone told you the truth – these mugs are just terrible. In fact, Vincent Caine, your mug collection is the shittiest mug collection in the West Country. Maybe the whole world.'

'That seems a bit harsh. You haven't seen them all.'

'*Seen them all?* You're trying to tell me that you have a mug that will change my mind?'

'I'm sorry, Shanti. I'm sorry about the mugs and I'm sorry I can't be more open with you. I hope you will forgive me some day. But I will tell you something . . .'

'Go on.'

A flame danced in each eye.

'Remember that first morning, when you walked into the cabin?'

'How can I forget?'

'It was like a ray of sunshine entering my life.'

She felt herself melting. It was hard to be angry with a soft man on the soft sand.

'OK. Maybe I was a bit unfair about the shitty mugs. They're *your* shitty mugs after all. You know what? Let's forget all about it. Let's forget about Kristal Havfruen. Let's forget about your dark and sordid past. It's very beautiful out here. It's good for Paul, too. Tell me one of your stories, Vincent Caine. A nice story.'

She shuffled a little closer, and the heat of their bodies was warmer than fire.

'A story, eh? Well, after I left home, I went wandering. I visited many places and eventually I was drawn to the monastery in Thailand. You know the saying? "When the student is ready, the teacher shall appear."'

'I think I read that on a shitty mug.'

'That's possible. Anyway, I stayed in the forest for nearly three years. We meditated for hours each day and studied the Dharma, which is the fundamental teaching of Buddhism—'

'Hold on – did you shave your head and wear robes?'

'The whole thing. At night, I slept in a dormitory with ten other students from all over the world. We became close friends, and every evening our old teacher, Tu, would tell us stories – you know, Buddhist tales thousands of years old. Some of them were really funny, and some were very wise.'

'Go on. Tell me one.' She lay on her back at his side.

'Let me think . . . OK, well an old Zen master and a young monk are walking in the mountains. After many miles, they come to a river and meet a young woman trying to cross to the other side. She's a guest at a wedding and she doesn't want to spoil her beautiful clothes. Without a thought, the old master bows, lifts her in his arms, carries her across the river and sets her gently on the other side. When she is gone, the master and the student walk on in silence.

'After a few hours, the old man realises that the young monk is kind of seething. "What's the matter, son?" he says. "You seem troubled." The young one replies, "Master, I can't believe what you did back there!" The old man isn't aware that he's done anything lately except sort of *be*. "What did I do?" he asks. "What? You know perfectly well what you did! Remember that young woman – the outrageously beautiful young woman by the river with the golden nose ring and the long fingernails . . . Well, you literally picked her up and you literally carried her across that river. And we are *so* banned from touching women!" The old monk smiles, and then he says, "Listen, my son, I literally left her on the riverbank. But you, it seems, are still carrying her."'

'Is this another of your sexist folk tales, Caine? About the predatory powers of women?'

'It's thousands of years old and it's kind of a sweet story.'

'But what's it got to do with you? Or with me?'

'This is the problem, Shanti. I'm that young monk. And I literally cannot put you down.'

'Jesus, Caine!'

'Would you do one thing for me?'

'Possibly.'

'We've known each other a little while, and I wonder if there's any chance you could call me Vincent? You know, instead of Jesus Caine.'

She laughed and said she'd think about it.

They watched the smoke rise to the stars, and for the first

time in her life, Shanti truly heard the silence. So deep, it was like noise. Without realising it, she found she was resting her head in his lap, and she felt peace settle in every cell of her body.

'Sometimes ... not very often ... I'd quite like to kiss you, Vincent Caine.'

'That's OK. I could live with that.'

'But then I remember I'm a professional and you are my work colleague.'

'There's no harm in a kiss.'

'But the trouble with kissing is it's a gateway drug.'

'What does that mean?'

'You start with kissing, and before you know it, you've moved onto the hard stuff.'

'And the soft stuff, Shanti ... Don't forget the soft stuff ...'

Chapter 27

Six Months Later

The swarm of journalists around the main doors of Yeovil police HQ buzzed like an agitated wasps' nest.

From her elevated position on the top step, Shanti looked down at a churning sea of TV crews, flashing cameras, waggling woolly microphones and numerous vehicles bristling with aerials and antennae and satellite dishes.

'DI Joyce? DI Joyce! Can you give us a statement?'

'One at a time, please,' said Benno at her side.

Shanti waited for calm. Then she began to speak.

'Now that the trial has concluded, I am able to make a final statement about this unusual and distressing case. In August of last year, we made two significant arrests. One of the accused, Oliver Sweetman, was deemed unfit to stand trial and is now receiving psychiatric care. We have reason to believe that Mr Sweetman, an otherwise gentle and talented man, was coerced into this brutal act by a devious and manipulative woman who had killed on previous occasions.'

'Was that Marlene Moss, Inspector?'

'Yes, the person I am referring to is an eighty-four-year-old retired art teacher from Falmouth named Marlene Moss. However . . .'

She paused for the buzzing to abate.

'However, I am sorry to say that earlier this week, as a result of a long-term illness, Ms Moss passed away before the judge was able to pronounce sentence, thereby evading justice. There are no winners in a case like this – simply a number of victims who have lost a great deal. I want to pass on my sincere condolences to the families concerned, and in particular, I'd like to take the opportunity to offer my apologies to the victim's husband, Callum Oak, who suffered a double misfortune. Not only did he have to cope with the sudden loss of his wife; in addition, he had to put up with the media . . . and with me and my team, who were in a hurry to solve this case as rapidly as possible. Thanks for bearing with us, sir, and I would like to convey my warmest wishes to you and your family.'

It was as if a stick had been poked in the nest. 'Inspector . . . Inspector Joyce, did you have a partner on this case?'

'Thank you. I'd like to acknowledge the dedicated work of the whole team, led by Sergeant Bennett to my left. But yes, there were two detectives leading this inquiry. I worked hand in glove with DI Vincent Caine.'

'Is that the man they call Veggie Cop?'

'Hasn't Caine retired from police work?'

'What was the nature of your working relationship?'

'Inspector Caine has previously taken time out on leave, but he was fully invested in this case and it is doubtful it would have been solved so smoothly and effectively without his contribution. It was a pleasure to work with someone of his calibre. In fact, it has been noted that DI Caine and I have complementary skills – you could almost call it a symbiotic relationship.'

'DI Joyce, people are describing you and Vincent Caine as the West Country's new crime-fighting duo. Can you say something about that?'

'Will you be working together on future cases?'

'Ha, well I don't know about that. You'll have to ask DI Caine himself. DI Caine? Is he here? He was here earlier ...'

In a light rain shower at Swanvale cemetery in Falmouth, a modest burial ceremony was drawing to an end.

Apart from the impassive undertaker and his entourage, there were only two mourners at the funeral of Marlene Moss. In the damp shadows at the back of the graveyard, a tall, long-haired man in a black coat brushed a tear from his eye. Some distance away, a younger man in a rumpled suit and pointy boots stood silently in the mizzle that drifted in from the sea.

When the perfunctory ceremony had reached a conclusion and the coffin had been lowered into the grave, Caine walked over and shook Art's hand.

'It was good of you to come.'

'She was my godmother. I knew her all my life. At least I thought I knew her.'

'Perhaps we never fully know anyone. Least of all ourselves. I thought perhaps your father would come ...'

'Don't go there. Dad practically had a meltdown trying to choose between doing his Christian duty by coming to the funeral, and the fact that Marlene turned out to be the devil incarnate. In the end, he decided to battle it out on canvas.'

'Good decision.'

'Yeah. I'm trying to persuade him to take over Mum's studio and sleep in the big bedroom, but he says he's happy where he is.'

'These things take time, Art. But I'm glad to hear he's painting. Callum has a huge talent, as you know.'

'Yeah, his work is changing. Like he's beginning to find himself again. Saul went over to Mangrove to take a look and he was well impressed. Don't say anything, mate, but there's a chance of a Callum Oak show at the Meat Hook next year.'

'And what about you, Art?'

'I'm OK. I'm getting my shit together. Maybe I'll go travelling or something. I haven't touched so much as a spliff in weeks.'

'Not even a little snifter this morning?'

'Christ . . . yeah, all right, I had a toot before the burial, but after today . . .'

'It's your choice, Art. In the end, everything is our own choice. A teacher once said that drugs are spiritual baby food.'

'Fuck, that's deep! I'll have to think about that one.'

'You squeaked through this by the skin of your teeth. But now you're free. If you make wise choices, you will have an amazing life.'

'Yeah, thanks, Caine. All cops are bastards, but you're better than most. You saved my life, you know that?'

'It's good of you to see it that way. I suppose you wouldn't have been halfway up a cliff if we hadn't visited so early in the morning. Listen, I won't pretend I approved of that relationship with Tess. You know it's only because she refused to cooperate that you didn't go before a judge.'

'That's because she loves me.'

They had been strolling along a narrow pathway between the

graves. Now they paused at an intersection where the path divided. Caine could see the red Alfa Romeo below.

'That's my car down there. You want a ride back to Lyme?'

'Thanks, but I have a return ticket to Axminster and a book to read. But come and see me any time if you need support.'

'Yeah. I might do that. That's decent of you.'

'Have you noticed? We're standing at a crossroads. From here, the path divides. Make a choice, Art. Walk towards the light.'

'For a cop, you talk in weird riddles.'

'I don't think I am a cop.'

'Well if you're not a cop, what the fuck are you?'

'I'm a human being, just like you. So while I'm at it, I'd like to pass on one more piece of advice. The fun stuff is just that. It's fun. Then it's gone. But it's actually the hard times that teach us. Times like this – times of adversity – are an opportunity to awaken and grow. Sit with the suffering, don't try to dull the pain. Here, borrow this. I've read it anyway . . . Catch!'

'What's this?'

'Poems by Rumi. My favourite is called "The Guest House".'

'Cheers. I'll check it out. Like I say, you're a weird one, Vincent Caine – cop or no cop. But I'm kind of glad I met you.'

They shook hands and went their separate ways.

The man in the black coat. And the boy named Art.

The Guest House

This being human is a guest house.
Every morning a new arrival.

A joy, a depression, a meanness,
some momentary awareness comes
as an unexpected visitor.

Welcome and entertain them all!
Even if they're a crowd of sorrows,
who violently sweep your house
empty of its furniture,
still, treat each guest honourably.
He may be clearing you out
for some new delight.

The dark thought, the shame, the malice,
meet them at the door laughing,
and invite them in.

Be grateful for whoever comes,
because each has been sent
as a guide from beyond.

>   Jalal ad-Din Rumi, reproduced with the kind
>   permission of the translator, Coleman Barks

Acknowledgements

I am beyond fortunate to be represented by British Book Award Agent of the Year Madeleine Milburn, and her dynamic team, who provided rock solid support in the creation of this series.

Huge thanks to Publishing Director Krystyna Green, and her creative crew, for welcoming Shanti and Caine to the illustrious Constable family of crime.

Blessings and all good things to my talented friend, author and psychologist, Paddy Magrane, who inspired, supported and contributed so much to this book. May your path shine.

Thanks to serving police officer Mike Harper and bestselling author and former police officer Rebecca Bradley for insights into investigative procedure.

Alayasri and Suddhacitta for precious Buddhist teachings.

Coleman Barks, renowned interpreter of Rumi's works, for kind permission to reproduce 'The Guest House'.

Hugs to my shockingly brilliant friend Paul Blow, who created the stunning original cover art.